Household Welfare

and Vietnam's

Transition

WORLD BANK

REGIONAL AND

SECTORAL STUDIES

Household Welfare and Vietnam's Transition

EDITED BY

DAVID DOLLAR

PAUL GLEWWE

JENNIE LITVACK

The World Bank
Washington, D.C.

The World Bank Regional and Sectoral Studies series provides an outlet for work that
is relatively focused in its subject matter or geographic coverage and that contributes
to the intellec
tual foundations of development operations and policy formulation. Some sources
cited in this publication may be informal documents that are not readily available.

All of the editors work at the World Bank. David Dollar is research manager in the
Development Research Group, Development Economics Department. Paul Glewwe
is a senior economist in the Development Research Group. Jennie Litvack is an
economist in the Public Sector Management Division of the Poverty Reduction and
Economic Management Network.

Cover design by Sam Ferro and Sherry Holmberg. Cover photo by Jennie Litvack.

Library of Congress Cataloging-in-Publication Data

Household welfare and Vietnam's transition /
edited by David Dollar, Paul Glewwe, Jennie Litvack.
       p. cm. — (World Bank regional and sectoral studies)
   Includes bibliographical references (p.).
   ISBN 0-8213-4162-6
   1. Households—Economic aspects—Vietnam. 2. Vietnam—Economic
policy. 3. Vietnam—Economic conditions. 4. Poverty—Vietnam.
I. Dollar, David. II. Glewwe, Paul, 1958– . III. Litvack, Jennie I. (Jennie, Ilene),
1963– . IV. Series.
HC444.H68   1998
338.9597—dc21

                                                97-46963
                                                     CIP

Contents

Foreword   xv

Contributors   xvii

Map   xviii

1. Macroeconomic Reform and Poverty Reduction in Vietnam   **1**
  David Dollar and Jennie Litvack
  Economic Reform and Macroeconomic Performance, 1985–95   3
    A Weak Macroeconomy   3
    Reform of Agriculture and the Private Sector   5
    Reform of the Macroeconomy   6
    A Successful Structural Adjustment   8
    Widespread Benefits   10
    Lurking Challenges   11
  The Impact of Economic Growth on Poverty Reduction   13
    Income Distribution in Other Transition Economies   13
    Estimates of Poverty Incidence   14
    Projections of Future Poverty Incidence   16
  A Poverty Alleviation Strategy for Vietnam   19
    The Role of Government in a Market Economy   20
    Lessons Learned   21
  Notes   25
  References   26

2. Poverty and Inequality in the Early Reform Period   **29**
  David Dollar and Paul Glewwe
  Data Available for Examining Poverty and Inequality in Vietnam   29
  Household Characteristics and Household Welfare in Vietnam   30
    Characteristics of Vietnamese Households   31

Measuring Household Welfare Using per Capita
  Consumption Expenditures   33
Welfare Levels among Different Vietnamese Households   34
Inequality in Vietnam   38
  Measurement of Inequality   39
  Factors Associated with Inequality in Vietnam   40
Poverty in Vietnam   43
  Measuring Poverty   44
  Choosing a Poverty Line   45
  Analysis of Poverty in Vietnam   46
A Closer Examination of Regional Variation   50
Appendix: Calculation of Total Household Expenditures   54
  Food Expenditures   54
  Nonfood Expenditures   55
Notes   58
References   60

3. Agriculture and Rural Poverty in Vietnam   **61**
  Thomas B. Wiens
Reforming Institutions in Rural Vietnam   61
Characterizing Rural Poverty   63
  Location and Economic Environment   64
  Land Quality and Tenure   66
  Labor and Dependents   68
  Infrastructure   69
  Farm Production   71
  Net Rural Income   75
  Credit and Poverty   76
Promoting Crop Production   78
  The Paddy Rice Supply Function   79
  Labor   81
  Land and Irrigation   81
  Fertilizer and Agrochemicals   83
  Capital Services   84
  Prices of Competing Crops   85
  Nonfarm Employment   85
  Infrastructure   86
  Health and Education   86
  Extension   87
  Farm Size   87
  Regional Differences   88
  Net Value of Crop Output   88
  The Cash Farm Economy   91
Conclusion   93

Notes   96
References   98

4. Infrastructure and Poverty in Vietnam   **99**
   Dominique van de Walle
Poverty and Infrastructure in Vietnam, 1992–93   101
Availability of Physical Infrastructure in Rural Vietnam   101
   Drinking Water   104
   Sewerage and Sanitation   107
   Access to Irrigation   109
   Sources of Energy   112
   Transportation   115
   Summary   116
Explaining Crop Income   117
   Determinants of Crop Income   117
   The Benefits from Irrigation: Policy Simulations   119
   Household Labor Costs   128
   The Cost of Expanding Irrigation   129
Conclusion   130
Notes   131
References   133

5. Nonfarm Household Enterprises in Vietnam   **137**
   Wim P. M. Vijverberg
The Current Business Environment   139
Nonfarm Self-employment in the Context of Labor Market Activities 141
   Descriptive Analysis   142
   Multivariate Probit Model   148
   Nonfarm Self-employment and the Incidence of Poverty   151
Characteristics of Nonfarm Enterprises   151
   Labor Force   153
   Capital Stocks   159
   Taxation   159
   Profitability   160
   Enterprise Performance and Household Poverty   161
Determinants of Nonfarm Enterprise Income   165
   Defining the Model   166
   Estimating the Model   167
Considerations for Public Policy   172
Notes   175
References   176

6. Private Transfers in Vietnam   **175**
   Donald Cox, James Fetzer, and Emmanuel Jimenez
Description of the Data Set   181

Descriptive Evidence   183
    Scope and Magnitude of Transfers   183
    Transfer Patterns   187
Multivariate Analysis   188
    Specification of Transfer Functions   189
    Multivariate Results   191
Private Transfer Effects of Employment Loss   195
Conclusion   196
Appendix: Sample Selection Criteria   197
Notes   198
References   199

7. School Enrollment and Completion in Vietnam:
    An Investigation of Recent Trends   **201**
    Paul Glewwe and Hanan Jacoby
An Overview of the Current Education System   202
Recent Trends in Education   204
Descriptive Analysis   206
    Changes over Time in School Enrollment
        and Labor Force Participation   206
    Regional Variation in School Enrollment, Fees, and Quality   213
    Summary   217
Regression Analysis   217
    An Empirical Model of School Continuation Decisions   218
    Results   221
Conclusion   226
Appendix   228
Notes   232
References   234

8. Access to Health Care during Transition: The Role
    of the Private Sector in Vietnam   **235**
    Paul Gertler and Jennie Litvack
Structure and Performance of the Health Sector   236
Access to Health Care   240
Policy Reform   242
    Targeting Public Expenditure to the Poor   244
    Reforming Drug Policy   245
Summary and Conclusion   249
Appendix   252
Notes   254
References   254

9. Will Vietnam Grow Out of Malnutrition?   **257**
    Ninez Ponce, Paul Gertler, and Paul Glewwe
Institutional Changes in Vietnam   258

Nutritional Status in Vietnam   260
  Measuring Nutritional Status   260
  Malnutrition in Vietnam, 1992–93   261
The Relationship between Income and Nutritional Status in Vietnam   264
  Descriptive Analysis   264
  Multivariate Analysis   266
Economic Growth and Child Growth: Future Prospects   273
Conclusion   274
Notes   275
References   275

10. Poverty and Fertility in Vietnam   **277**
  Jaikishan Desai
Data and Descriptive Information   278
  Sample Bias   279
  Fertility Patterns and Trends   281
  Sample Selection and Socioeconomic Differences
    in Marital Fertility   287
Do the Poor Have More Children?   291
  Theoretical Background   291
  Selection of Variables   293
  Regression Results   298
Conclusion and Policy Directions   307
Appendix   313
Notes   316
References   318

**Appendix Description of the Vietnam Living
Standards Survey (VNLSS)**   **321**

Figures
1.1 Annual per Capita Foodgrain Production, Vietnam, 1979–95   4
1.2 Growth in Domestic Credit and Its Components, Vietnam, 1987–95 7
1.3 Government Revenue, Expenditure, and Fiscal
    Balance, Vietnam, 1985–95   8
1.4 Savings and Investment, Vietnam, 1985–95   11

3.1 Irrigated Area and Fertilizer Use in Vietnam   72
3.2 Crop Revenues and Input Costs in Vietnam, by Income Quintile   74
3.3 Crop Production in Vietnam by Use, by Region   75
3.4 Sources of Income for Farm Households in Vietnam, by Income
    Quintile   76

4.1 Sources of Drinking Water in Rural Vietnam, 1992–93   105
4.2 Sources of Drinking Water in Vietnam, 1992–93   106
4.3 Sanitation Facilities Used in Rural Vietnam, 1992–93   110
4.4 Sanitation Facilities Used in Urban Vietnam, 1992–93   111

4.5   Distribution of Total Land and Irrigated Annual Cropland
      in Vietnam, 1992–93   113

5.1   Frequency Distribution of Family Enterprise Start-up Dates,
      Vietnam, 1992–93   141
5.2   Distribution of Hours of Family Labor, Total Capital Resources,
      and Annual Enterprise Income, Vietnam, 1992–93   158

6.1   Vietnamese Households Receiving Private Transfers, by Region   186
6.2   Vietnamese Households Giving Private Transfers, by Region   186
6.3   Sources of Private Transfers in Urban Vietnamese Households   188
6.4   Sources of Private Transfers in Rural Vietnamese Households   189
6.5   Probability of Receiving Net Transfers, as a Function of
      Household Head's Age   194

7.1   School Enrollment and Labor Force Participation among
      Children Aged 6–11 and 12–17 in Vietnam, 1980–92   207
7.2   School Enrollment and Labor Force Participation among
      Children Aged 12–17 in Urban and Rural Vietnam, 1980–92   208
7.3   School Enrollment Rate among Children Aged 12–17 in
      Northern Regions of Vietnam, 1980–92   210
7.4   School Enrollment Rate among Children Aged 12–17 in
      Southern Regions of Vietnam, 1980–92   210
7.5   Labor Force Participation among Children Aged 12–17 in
      Vietnam, by Region, 1980–92   211
7.6   School Leavers by Last Grade Attained, Vietnam, 1985–92   212
7.7   School Enrollment Rate among Children Aged 12–17 in
      Vietnam, by Income Quintile, 1980–92   212

8.1   Utilization of Public Sector Health Services in Vietnam, 1987–93   238
8.2   Contact Rate with the Health Care System in Vietnam, 1993   240
8.3   Utilization Rates of the Public Sector Health Care System in
      Vietnam, 1993   241
8.4   Health Facilities and Personnel in Rural Communes in
      Vietnam, 1993   243

9.1   Incidence of Child Malnutrition In Vietnam, Based on
      Three Indicators, 1992–93   262
9.2   Median Child Height in the U.S. National Center for Health
      Statistics and Vietnam Living Standards Survey Samples   263
9.3   Income, Child Malnutrition, and Public Health Investments
      in 12 Developing Countries, 1989–92   264
9.4   GDP per Capita and Child Malnutrition in Vietnam, 1982–93   265
9.5   Mean per Capita Household Expenditure and Child Malnutrition
      in Vietnam, by Region, 1992–93   266
9.6   Change in Prevalence of Child Malnutrition and Economic
      Growth in Vietnam, by Region   267

9.7 Projected Child Malnutrition Rates in Vietnam Based on
     Three Economic Growth Rates, 1993–2013   274

10.1 Age Distribution of All Women Aged 15–49 in the
     Sampled Households and in the Fertility Sample   280
10.2 Age-specific Fertility Rates of Women Aged 15–49,
     1986–87 and 1991–92   288
10.3 Life-cycle Variation in Different Household
     Expenditure Measures   294

Tables

1.1 National Poverty Incidence in Vietnam under Different
     Distributional Scenarios, Selected Years   15
1.2 Poverty Incidence (Headcount Index) and Growth Rate
     in Vietnam, by Region, 1993–94   17
1.3 Effect on Poverty Incidence (Headcount Index) of
     Different Growth Scenarios in Vietnam, 1993–94   18

2.1 Characteristics of Vietnamese Households, by Region   32
2.2 Characteristics of Vietnamese Households, by
     Expenditure Quintile   35
2.3 Nonincome Indicators of Living Standards in Vietnam   38
2.4 Expenditure Inequality in Vietnam and Other Developing
     Countries   40
2.5 Inequality in Vietnam, 1992–93   41
2.6 Urban and Rural Poverty Lines in Vietnam, by Region   47
2.7 Poverty Indexes in Vietnam, 1992–93   48
2.8 Expenditure Levels and Poverty in Rural Areas of Vietnam,
     by Region   50
2.9 Determinants of Log per Capita Expenditure in Rural
     Areas of Vietnam   51
2.10 Selected Characteristics of Rural Areas in Vietnam, by Region,
     1992–93   52

3.1 Rural Poverty's Link to Geography in Vietnam, 1992–93   64
3.2 Paddy Rice Supply Function Estimates   82
3.3 Supply Function for Net Value of Crop Output   89

4.1 Rural Poor and Nonpoor with Access to Infrastructure
     in Vietnam, 1992–93   102
4.2 Rural Poor and Nonpoor with Access to Infrastructure
     in North and South Vietnam, 1992–93   103
4.3 Sources of Drinking Water in Rural and Urban Vietnam, 1992–93   104
4.4 Sources of Drinking Water in Rural and Urban Vietnam,
     by Region, 1992–93   107
4.5 Toilet Facilities in Rural and Urban Vietnam, 1992–93   109

4.6   Toilet Facilities in Rural and Urban Vietnam, by Region,
      1992–93   109
4.7   Average Area of Land per Capita in Rural Vietnam, 1992–93   110
4.8   Average Area of Land per Capita in Rural Vietnam,
      by Region, 1992–93   112
4.9   Sources of Lighting in Rural and Urban Vietnam, 1992–93   115
4.10 Cooking Fuel in Rural and Urban Vietnam, 1992–93   115
4.11 Marginal Effect on Net Crop Income, Allowing for
      Interaction Effects   120
4.12 National Distribution of Impacts of Irrigation Expansion
      under Four Scenarios   122
4.13 Distribution of per Capita Impacts under Simulation 1,
      by Expenditure Group and Region   124
4.14 Distribution of per Capita Impacts under Simulation 2,
      by Expenditure Group and Region   124
4.15 Distribution of per Capita Impacts under Simulation 3,
      by Expenditure Group and Region   126
4.16 Distribution of per Capita Impacts under Simulation 4,
      by Expenditure Group and Region   126

5.1a Labor Market Participation in Vietnam, by Rural or Urban
      Residence and by Gender, 1992–93   143
5.1b Labor Market Participation in Vietnam, by Region, 1992–93   144
5.1c Labor Market Participation in Vietnam, by Ethnic Group,
      1992–93   144
5.1d Labor Market Participation in Vietnam, by Age and Gender,
      1992–93   146
5.1e Labor Market Participation in Vietnam, by Years of
      Schooling, 1992–93   147
5.2   Probit Estimates of Whether a Household Operates a
      Nonfarm Enterprise   149
5.3   Labor Market Activity and the Standard of Living in Vietnam,
      by per Capita Expenditure Quintile, 1992–93   152
5.4   Characteristics of Nonfarm Family Enterprises in Vietnam,
      1992–93   154
5.5   Family Enterprise Characteristics in Vietnam, by Quintile,
      1992–93   162
5.6   Income from Nonfarm Family Enterprises as a Share of
      Household Expenditure   163
5.7   Income from Nonfarm Enterprises and Household Well-being
      in Vietnam, 1992–93   164
5.8   Determinants of Hourly Enterprise Income, Vietnam, 1992–93   168
5.9   Determinants of Monthly Enterprise Income in Vietnam,
      1992–93   170

6.1 Characteristics of Households in Vietnam, by Private
    Transfer Status   184
6.2 Effects of Public and Private Transfers on the Distribution
    of Income in Vietnam   187
6.3 Transfers over the Life Cycle in Vietnam   187
6.4 Transfers among Rural and Urban Households in Vietnam   189
6.5 Probit and Ordinary Least Squares Estimates: Transfers Received 192
6A.1 Selection Criteria   198

7.1 School Quality Indicators for Rural Areas of Vietnam, 1992–93   203
7.2 School Enrollment in Vietnam in Selected Years, 1980–94   204
7.3 Effect of Years of Schooling on Wages in Vietnam, 1992–93   209
7.4 School Enrollment Rates in Vietnam, by Quintile
    and Region, 1992–93   213
7.5 Share of Schools for Which Quality Problems Cited
    in Rural Vietnam, by Region, 1992–93   214
7.6 Expenses and School Fees at Public Schools in Vietnam,
    by Region, 1992–93   215
7.7 Descriptive Statistics of Explanatory Variables   220
7.8 Determinants of Enrollment in and Completion
    of Primary School   222
7.9 Determinants of Enrollment in and Completion
    of Lower Secondary School   224
7A.1 First-Stage Estimates for Primary Enrollment Regression   228
7A.2 First-Stage Estimates for Primary Completion and
    for Secondary Enrollment and Completion Regressions   230

8.1 Health Status Indicators in Selected Asian Countries,
    1960 and 1990   236
8.2 Health Care Infrastructure in Selected Asian Countries, 1991   238
8.3 Annual Health Care Expenditures in Selected Asian
    Countries, 1991   239
8.4 Uses and Sources of Health Sector Funds in Vietnam, 1993   239
8.5 Estimated Income Elasticities of the Demand for Medical Care   246
8A.1 Two-Part Models of the Demand for Public Hospital Care   252
8A.2 Two-Part Models of the Demand for Commune Health
    Center Care   252
8A.3 Two-Part Models of the Demand for Private Provider Care   253
8A.4 Two-Part Models of the Demand for Private Drugs   253

9.1 Multivariate Regression Results   270
9.2 Description of Variables   272

10.1 Age Distribution of All Women Aged 15–49 in the
    Sampled Households and in the Fertility Sample   280

10.2 Demographic Characteristics of Women Selected for the
Fertility Section of the 1992–93 Vietnam Living Standards
Survey, by Age Cohort 282
10.3 Statistics for the Fertility Process, by Age Cohort 284
10.4 Age-specific Fertility Rates and Total Fertility Rate 286
10.5 Mean Number of Children Ever Born to Married Women
Aged 20–39 in Rural Vietnam, by Women's Age Cohort
and Socioeconomic Characteristics 290
10.6 Means and Standard Deviations of Dependent and
Independent Variables for Fertility Regression Models for
Married Women Aged 25–39 in Rural Vietnam 299
10.7 Regression Results for Children Ever Born to Ever-married
Women Aged 25–39 in Rural Vietnam 300
10.8 Regression Results for Children Ever Born to Ever-married
Women Aged 25–39 in Rural Vietnam, Taking into Account
Effects of Commune Characteristics 304
10.9 Regression Results for Children Ever Born to Ever-married
Women Aged 25–39 Who Have Begun Childbearing
in Rural Vietnam: Commune Fixed Effects Specification 306
10.10 Regression Results for Children Ever Born to Married
Women Aged 25–39 in Urban Vietnam 307
10A.1 Instrumenting Regressions for Log of Real Household
Expenditure per Adult in Rural Areas 313
10A.2 Instrumenting Regressions for Log of Real Household
Expenditure per Adult in Urban Areas 315

Foreword

Vietnam's development since 1985 provides important lessons for economic and social policy. Among the world's 40 poorest countries in 1985, Vietnam has since had—by far—the fastest growth rate. This rapid growth has transformed the country, reducing poverty from about 75 percent of the population to about 50 percent. At the same time, the transition from a planned to a market economy has created new challenges for public policy in a wide range of areas.

This volume examines various aspects of Vietnam's transition. Which macroeconomic and structural reforms led to growth? What effect has reform had on the household economy—both small businesses in urban areas and farm households in rural areas? How has the transition affected education, health, fertility, and child nutrition—crucial factors for the emergence of a healthy and highly skilled population? These are some of the questions addressed by a group of researchers from inside and outside the World Bank.

The research presented in the volume developed from a collaborative effort of the Vietnamese government, the World Bank, the United Nations Development Programme, and the Swedish International Development Agency. In 1992–93 these agencies collaborated on the design and implementation of Vietnam's first nationally representative household survey. The wealth of information generated by this Living Standards Survey has been used by the government and scholars to analyze poverty and inequality in Vietnam. This kind of effort—producing high-quality information that can be used to inform policymaking—is one of the most important contributions of the World Bank and development cooperation more broadly.

Following up on this initial success, the same agencies are now collaborating on a new survey that will come about five years after the first one.

This second Living Standards Survey will return to most of the original 4,800 households (creating a unique panel data set) and add 2,000 more, producing a data set that will be representative of Vietnam in 1998.

This volume provides a wealth of information on Vietnam in 1992–93 and an analysis of economic and social policy. It shows how micro-level data can be used to analyze the likely effect of different government expenditures and activities. It focuses in particular on the effect different policies have on the poor, and in so doing it challenges stereotypes about poverty-focused expenditures. Some social services, for example, hardly reach the poor, while others are highly pro-poor. Given that Vietnam has good human capital but many other deficiencies, certain investments in infrastructure—such as rural roads or irrigation—may have a dramatic effect on the incomes of poor households. These findings have already influenced policies in Vietnam and the World Bank's assistance strategy for the country.

The studies in this volume should be of interest to anyone interested in Vietnam and anyone who wants to learn how this low-income country has managed to make impressive strides since 1985.

Joseph E. Stiglitz
Chief Economist and Senior Vice President
The World Bank

Contributors

Donald Cox is professor of economics at Boston College.

Jaikishan R. Desai is a consultant in Macroeconomics 1 of the Africa Economic Management and Social Policy Unit at the World Bank.

David Dollar is research manager in the Development Research Group at the World Bank.

James Fetzer is assistant professor of economics at Suffolk University.

Paul J. Gertler is professor of economics, finance, and public policy at the University of California at Berkeley, where he holds joint appointments in the Haas School of Business and School of Public Health.

Paul Glewwe is senior economist in the Development Research Group at the World Bank.

Hanan G. Jacoby is a consultant in the Development Research Group at the World Bank.

Emmanuel Jimenez is research manager in the Development Research Group at the World Bank.

Jennie I. Litvack is economist in the Poverty Reduction and Economic Management Network at the World Bank.

Ninez A. Ponce is health services research fellow in the Department of Health Services at the University of California at Los Angeles.

Dominique van de Walle is senior economist in the Development Research Group at the World Bank.

Wim P. M. Vijverberg is professor of economics and political science at the University of Texas at Dallas.

Thomas Wiens is lead rural specialist in the Environmentally and Socially Sustainable Development Department of the Latin America and Caribbean Region at the World Bank.

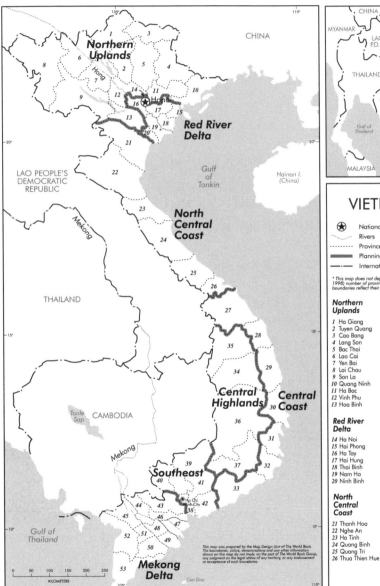

Macroeconomic Reform and Poverty Reduction in Vietnam

David Dollar and Jennie Litvack

Vietnam's development over the past decade represents one of the more dramatic turnarounds in economic history. In the mid-1980s the country was experiencing hyperinflation and economic stagnation, hunger was widespread, and hundreds of thousands of people were fleeing the country in unsafe boats. Ten years later the government had restored macroeconomic stability, GDP growth had accelerated to 9–10 percent, exports had increased tenfold, and overseas Vietnamese were returning with their capital to take advantage of burgeoning investment opportunities. Despite this turnaround, Vietnam remains a very poor country. In 1993 the incidence of poverty was 55 percent and per capita GNP was $200. A decade of rapid growth has produced higher living standards for most of the population, but it has not been sufficient to erase the legacy of a long period of war, isolation, and economic mismanagement.

This book focuses on household welfare during Vietnam's structural adjustment and transition to a market economy. Because half of Vietnam's population lives below the poverty line, the effect of reform on the poor is an especially important issue. The questions addressed here are large and complicated. Vietnam contains about 75 million people and 15 million households, each of which has been affected differently. Furthermore, there are many different dimensions to economic welfare. Even with vast amounts of data, analyzing the impact of reform on household welfare is a difficult task. In the case of Vietnam the task is compounded by the lack of useful data. This book draws heavily on a nationally representative household survey, the Vietnam Living Standards Survey, carried out during 1992–93—the first such survey ever conducted in Vietnam. These data provide a thorough assessment of the situation at that time. We cannot draw firm conclusions about the impact of Vietnam's transition on household welfare using only the 1992–93 Living Standards Survey because the data are from only one point in time. Thus we will draw on other data, both macroeconomic and microeconomic, so that we will be able to make some tentative judgments about the changes in household welfare between 1985 and 1993.

Despite the remarkable changes that have occurred in Vietnam, the country is still at an early stage in its transition to a market economy. That transition will continue for at least another decade. As additional representative household surveys are conducted during that time, it will be possible to monitor progress in poverty alleviation and, more broadly, changes in household welfare. Thus in this book we lay the foundation for future work on household welfare in Vietnam.

Finally, the book is intended to aid policymaking. The effect of growth on poverty reduction in Vietnam over the next decade will be influenced by household behavior and by a host of government policies and expenditures. In addition, the book estimates the possible effects of different interventions and makes recommendations concerning an efficient poverty alleviation strategy.

This first chapter sets the stage for the remaining chapters. It reviews the main features of Vietnam's reform program and the country's macroeconomic performance from 1985 to 1995. The second section of the chapter then estimates the impact of growth on poverty for 1985–94 under a variety of assumptions about the distribution of the benefits from growth. The estimated decline in poverty since the mid-1980s has been remarkable: from about 75 percent of the population in 1984 to 55 percent in 1993. This reduction is comparable to that achieved by other high-growth East Asian economies in the early stages of their stunning economic performance. Critics of structural adjustment often contend that it hurts the poor.[1] The outcome in Vietnam was exactly the opposite: structural adjustment ushered in an era of rapid growth that led to a sharp decline in poverty.

The second section also examines the likely impact of continued rapid growth on poverty between 1994 and 2000, again using a variety of assumptions about changes in the distribution of income. If rapid growth is sustained, poverty incidence could fall to 35 percent—or even lower—by 2000. The extent of this reduction will depend not only on the rate of growth but also on how broadly based growth is, in particular on how well it reaches households at the lower end of the income distribution.

The third section of this chapter considers the most important factors—including government policy and expenditures—that will influence the extent to which the benefits of growth are widely diffused. We discuss the principal reasons for government intervention: efficiency (correcting discrepancies between social and private costs and benefits) and equity (changing the distribution of household welfare that is set by purely market activities). The discussion highlights the need to select policies that can achieve distributional objectives as efficiently as possible. The last section previews the issues that will be taken up in later chapters and highlights some of the key findings. It also addresses some general methodological issues concerning the use of cross-sectional data to estimate the impact of different policy options.

While the focus of the book is Vietnam, the findings will be relevant to anyone interested in growth and poverty reduction in the least developed countries. The World Bank (1996) reports that there were 40 countries, totaling 1.7 billion people, with per capita GNP below $520 in 1994. Vietnam is part of this least developed group and in fact is near the bottom in terms of per capita GNP. Of these countries, one-half had average per capita GNP growth rates that were negative in 1985–94, and the highest growth rate, excluding that of Vietnam, was about 3 percent. Vietnam's growth rate of nearly 5 percent per capita over 1986–95 makes it highly unusual among very poor countries. Which key factors have enabled Vietnam to stand out among the least developed countries? How have structural adjustment and reform affected poverty and household welfare? Which policies and public expenditures will sustain a high rate of poverty reduction? The answers to these questions will be pertinent to people interested in economic development.

Economic Reform and Macroeconomic Performance, 1985–95

During 1986–95 Vietnam's economic system went through a remarkable transformation. The impetus for this reform can be found in the economy's poor performance in the mid-1980s, a period of high inflation and slow growth. The government's attempt to develop the economy on the basis of collectivized agriculture and subsidized state industries yielded very poor results. This disappointing performance led to an era of stabilization and structural reforms that were aimed at transforming the centrally planned system into a market economy.

A Weak Macroeconomy

The macroeconomic problems of the mid-1980s were particularly acute in the agricultural sector. Agriculture went through a difficult period following the country's reunification in 1976.[2] By 1982, however, annual food-grain production had returned to the pre-reunification level of about 300 kilograms per capita (the same level as in colonial Vietnam of the 1930s). But production stagnated there throughout the mid-1980s (figure 1.1).[3]

Three hundred kilograms of grain per capita is roughly a subsistence level, given traditional distribution patterns. Years in which production fell below this threshold caused severe hardship and, often, large-scale emigration. The slow growth of agriculture in the mid-1980s, just keeping pace with population growth, kept the country at subsistence level. When

Figure 1.1 Annual per Capita Foodgrain Production, Vietnam, 1979–95

Kilograms per capita

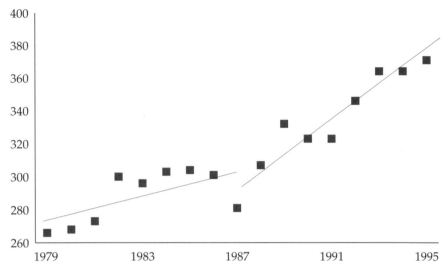

Source: For 1979–87, Fforde and de Vylder 1988; for 1988–95, World Bank 1993b and 1994 (see note 3 at the end of the chapter).

bad harvests reduced food production in 1987, famine became widespread, and the country appealed for international food aid. The weak performance in agriculture—and the related concern that there would not be enough food for a growing population—was one of the important factors pushing the government to change its development strategy.

Weak performance was visible in other sectors of the economy as well. Overall GDP growth was 2.3 percent in 1986, about the same as population growth, and fell to 0.7 percent in 1987.[4] Vietnam was receiving significant aid from the Soviet Union at the time, but this assistance was not effectively channeled into investment. National accounts data from this period are of doubtful quality, but still provide a broad picture of macroeconomic trends. The investment rate in the mid-1980s was very low—5–8 percent of GDP. The current account deficit, which measures the net inflow of foreign savings, was greater, around 10 percent of GDP. Thus domestic savings were negative throughout this period. The large external deficit was financed by Soviet aid. Much of this aid came in the form of intermediate goods—petroleum, fertilizer, and steel—that were passed on to producers, and ultimately consumers, at subsidized prices. Thus Soviet aid financed consumption rather than investment.

Government revenue was also used to subsidize both producers and consumers, resulting in a fiscal deficit that could not be easily financed. The fiscal deficit fluctuated between 5 percent and 10 percent of GDP in the mid-1980s. In principle, a deficit of this magnitude could have been financed by Soviet aid. In practice, however, the commodities imported from the Soviet Union were passed on to enterprises and agricultural collectives at low prices and did not generate sufficient revenue to finance the budget deficit. The government instead relied on credit from the state bank. The ensuing credit growth was a primary source of high inflation. In 1987 credit to the government increased by about 300 percent, to state enterprises by about 200 percent, and overall by about 250 percent. This expansion generated inflation of nearly 400 percent a year in 1986–87. The economy was allegedly a planned system with fixed prices at that time, but "fixed" prices were being revised several times per month.

It is difficult to exaggerate the disastrous condition of the economy in this period. It may seem inconsistent to report that Vietnam has grown well for about a decade but that its per capita GNP was still only $200 in 1994. There is no inconsistency, however, because in the mid-1980s Vietnam was one of the world's poorest countries. Per capita growth was negative, famine was widespread, people were leaving the country in large numbers, hyperinflation had set in, domestic savings were negative, investment was low, and the country was dependent on Soviet aid equal to about 10 percent of GDP. Furthermore, by 1987 it was clear that Soviet aid would begin to wane, given the country's economic problems. The Communist Party had already decided at an important party congress in December 1986 to initiate some fundamental economic changes. Little changed during 1987, but the worsening economic crisis that year spurred the government to introduce some radical reforms beginning in 1988.

Reform of Agriculture and the Private Sector

Vietnam's program of *doi moi* (renovation) began in the agricultural sector.[5] Collectives were dismantled in 1988 and land was distributed among peasant households. Initially, the property rights to land were left vague. But in 1993 a new land law clarified that peasants had the right to use the land distributed to them for 20 years and that this right could be renewed. Further, peasants could sell or mortgage the right to use their land (see World Bank 1993b, chapter 2). Just as important as the reform of property rights was the reform of prices introduced early in 1989. Controlled prices for most goods and services were abolished. For several years the country had been functioning with a system of dual pricing, in which most output (both agricultural and industrial) had to be sold to the state at official prices, and the balance could be sold at market prices. The abolition of these controlled prices and the system of state procurement in 1989 strengthened the incentive to produce.

In the case of rice, for example, the official price in 1988 was about one-tenth the free market price. Paddy production responded quickly to the improved incentives, with large increases in per capita output in 1988 and

1989 (see figure 1.1). Production stagnated in 1990 and 1991 because of problems with weather and with the supply of fertilizer, owing to the collapse of trade and aid relations with the Soviet Union. By 1992 a commercial market for imported fertilizer had replaced the previous system of state distribution. In 1992, 1993, and 1995 paddy production reached new historical highs. Per capita production in 1995 (nearly 375 kilograms) was about 25 percent higher than the subsistence level that characterized the mid-1980s.

Reforms in agriculture were particularly important because it was the largest sector of the economy, accounting in 1989 for 40 percent of GDP at market prices. But there were analogous reforms in other sectors as well. For years, private production of goods and services had been tightly restricted. Official policy changed in the late 1980s to increasingly tolerate and even encourage the private sector. Price liberalization in 1989 gave major impetus to this trend. In 1989 overall GDP growth accelerated to 8 percent. There was rapid growth in agriculture, services, and construction, all areas in which the private sector was able to respond quickly to strengthened incentives. On the other hand, industry—which remained largely under state control—showed negative growth for the year.

Reform of the Macroeconomy

At the same time that the government was introducing these structural reforms, it was trying to cope with serious macroeconomic problems, including high inflation and the impending cutoff of Soviet aid. The fundamental problem was that the government and state enterprises were spending too much and this excess was being financed by Soviet aid and central bank credit. Strong measures to deal with this situation were introduced in 1989. Production and consumption subsidies were eliminated from the budget. At the same time, interest rates on loans to state firms were raised above the level of inflation (that is, to 9 percent per month in the spring of 1989, when inflation was about 7 percent per month). The state bank made a serious effort to control the growth of credit during the first half of 1989. This policy, combined with the strong output response in the agricultural sector, sharply reduced inflation by mid-1989. The policy, however, also created severe hardships for state enterprises. Thus there was strong pressure on the state bank to ease up on its credit and interest rate policies, once some initial success with disinflation had been achieved. Interest rates were lowered and credit growth expanded in the second half of 1989. Inflation resumed at a moderate rate. Overall, 1989 was a year of modest restraint. Domestic credit grew by about 150 percent, down from 400 percent in 1988 (figure 1.2).

In 1990–92 the government took additional steps to control the growth of credit and hence inflation.[6] Credit was no longer used to finance the budget by 1991. Loans to state enterprises were also controlled more carefully and priced appropriately. This hardening of the budget constraint led

Figure 1.2 Growth in Domestic Credit and Its Components, Vietnam, 1987–95

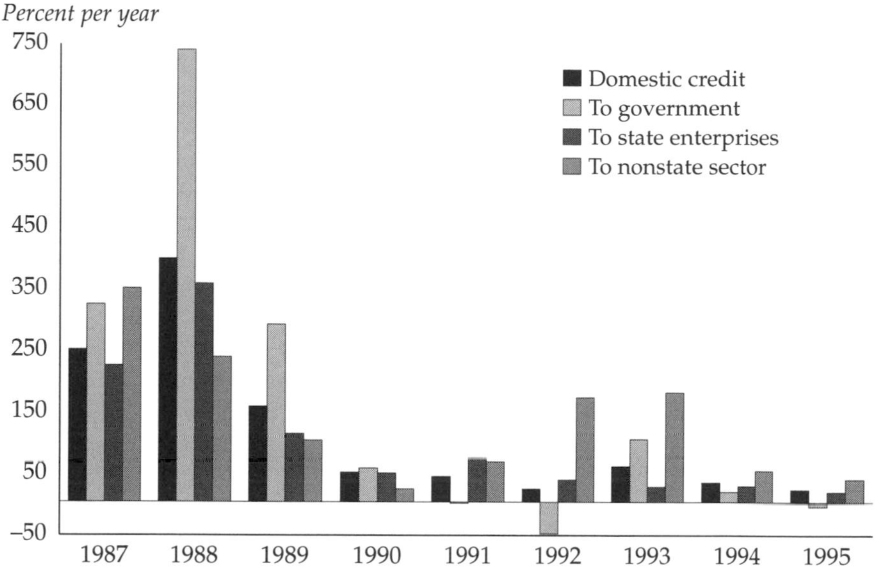

Percent per year

Source: State Bank of Vietnam.

to a major restructuring of the sector. Between 1988 and 1992 about 800,000 workers—one-third of the 1988 state-enterprise labor force—left the sector, and the number of firms declined from 12,000 to 7,000. These policies gradually brought the expansion of credit under control. In 1995 domestic credit increased 20.3 percent, none of which went toward the budget, credit to state firms increased 16.7 percent, and credit to the private sector increased 37.2 percent. The restrained monetary policy succeeded in bringing inflation down to about 10 percent per year during 1993–95.

The disinflation program required imposing discipline on state enterprises and on the budget. During 1985–89 the fiscal deficit ranged between 5 percent and 10 percent of GDP and had been financed largely by bank credit. The tight credit policies in 1990–92 necessitated a large fiscal adjustment. Revenue as a share of GDP was fairly stable during this period, so that the brunt of adjustment fell on the expenditure side of the budget. Total government spending was reduced by 6 percentage points of GDP between 1989 and 1991 (figure 1.3). Part of the savings came from a military demobilization that returned about half a million soldiers to the civilian labor force. In addition, the government cut back sharply on its investment program. Furthermore, wage increases for civil servants lagged behind the ongoing, moderate inflation. Salaries for teachers and health workers had fallen so low by 1991 that it was difficult for communities to get them to perform their duties without additional stipends (World Bank 1993b, chapter 7).

Figure 1.3 Government Revenue, Expenditure, and Fiscal Balance, Vietnam, 1985–95

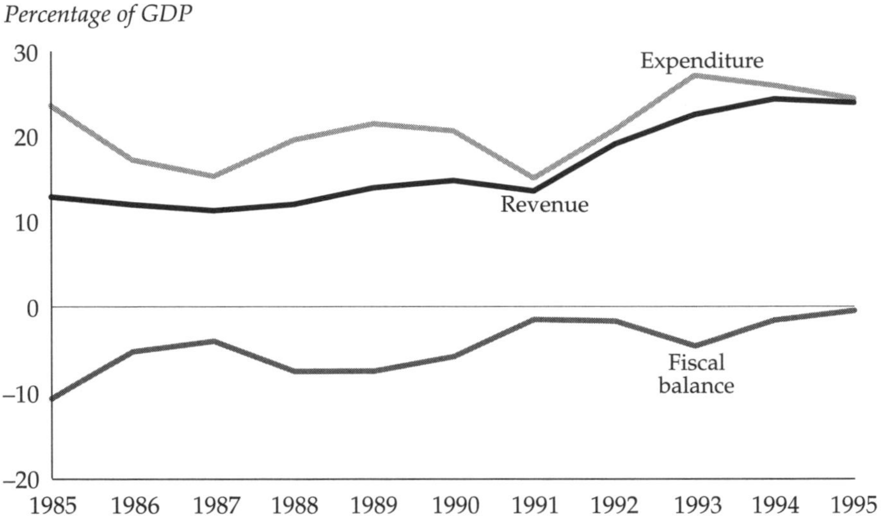

Percentage of GDP

Source: State Bank of Vietnam.

A Successful Structural Adjustment

The monetary and fiscal tightening in the early 1990s represents a classic structural adjustment to bring inflation and the fiscal deficit under control. Vietnam was unusual in that it did not receive any financial support from the International Monetary Fund (IMF) or the World Bank during this adjustment period, owing to the opposition of major shareholders. However, these institutions did offer policy advice and technical assistance. Vietnam's experience with disinflation was also unusual in that it was not accompanied by a recession. GDP growth decelerated to 5–6 percent during 1990–91, but that was still a healthy rate of growth. Once stabilization was achieved, growth accelerated, averaging 9 percent for 1992–95. Because of this high growth and initial reforms of the tax system, government revenue increased rapidly after 1991, and the government was able to restore the investment and social expenditures cut during the austerity period. Thus government expenditures as a share of GDP were higher in 1994 than in 1989, at the beginning of the fiscal adjustment (figure 1.3). Furthermore, because per capita GDP had increased substantially during this period, real per capita government expenditures were nearly twice as high in 1994 as in 1989.

Structural adjustment is usually associated with cutbacks in government services. But Vietnam's experience was that successful adjustment combined with several good years of high growth enabled the government to provide more services than it had previously. The government of

Vietnam also improved its allocation of resources: it reduced expenditures that did not promote development (that is, those for the military or to subsidize production) relative to development spending for infrastructure, health, and education.

The importance of a dualistic economy. The fact that Vietnam was able to halt high inflation without suffering a recession can be attributed to the dualistic nature of the economy at the beginning of 1989. As noted, agricultural land had been distributed to peasant families, a relatively easy reform that could be carried out quickly. Furthermore, Vietnam's private sector was large compared with other socialist economies. This sector had been operating largely underground until 1988.

Stabilization is normally a shock to the economy because interest rates are raised, government subsidies are cut, and devaluation makes imported inputs more expensive. Vietnam's stabilization had the predictable effect on the state sector of the economy, which showed negative growth in 1989. What distinguished Vietnam from most transition economies was that, alongside the state sector, it had large agricultural and private service and manufacturing sectors, in total producing about 60 percent of GDP and employing 85 percent of the labor force. These producers were not receiving credit from the formal sector or subsidies from the government. Thus, for them, 1989 was a year in which inflation fell and prices were liberalized, creating a good environment for expansion. That interest rates were much higher and subsidies were lower did not matter to agricultural households and small private firms, since they were not getting any of the formal credit or budget subsidies to begin with.[7]

International interventions. Two other aspects of Vietnam's reform may help explain the outstanding results: its thorough opening to international markets and the timing of foreign assistance to support its reform. Vietnam's initial conditions were very similar to those of other low-income countries, many of which have carried out macroeconomic policy reform supported by the IMF and the World Bank, but without Vietnam's spectacular results.

Opening itself to international markets included the unification of its multiple exchange rates in 1989. At the same time the official rate was devalued from 900 dong per dollar to 5,000 dong per dollar, the rate prevailing in the black market. The central bank has subsequently kept the official rate very close to the parallel rate. This bold devaluation in 1989 greatly strengthened incentives to export. At the same time administrative controls on exports and imports were relaxed. As a result exports have been a leading growth sector throughout the reform period, with real export growth averaging more than 25 percent per year. Rice exports were a major part of this success in 1989, crude petroleum exports (not part of the reform program) contributed in 1990 and 1991, and a wide range of exports have been on the rise in the past few years, including cash crops (rubber, cashews, coffee), labor-intensive manufactures, and tourist services.[8]

Desai (1998) finds Vietnam to be one of the transition economies most open to foreign trade and investment. By 1995 net exports relative to GNP had reached 79 percent in Vietnam, a high figure for a populous country. The comparable figure for Thailand—well known as an open economy—was 70 percent; Egypt, a large closed economy, had net exports totaling 32 percent of GNP. A number of studies have found that open economies grow more rapidly. Sachs and Warner (1995), for example, estimated that a shift from a closed to an open trade regime adds more than two percentage points to growth. They also identified 35 developing countries that were still closed as of 1994. Vietnam's experience provides additional evidence of the value of trade liberalization. Combined with a large devaluation, it spurred production at a time when fiscal and monetary restraint were contracting aggregate demand. Vietnam's export surge was important not only because it spurred production, but also because it financed the economy's growing import demand. As anticipated, Soviet aid declined very rapidly after 1988, and this was not replaced by financing from other sources.

Another key way in which Vietnam differed from other low-income reformers was that it did not have access to official finance. The current account deficit declined from more than 10 percent of GDP in 1988 to near zero in 1992 (figure 1.4). The collapse of financing did not require any cutback in imports, however, as Vietnam's export growth was sufficient to ensure that imports could grow throughout this adjustment period. It is also remarkable that investment increased sharply between 1988 and 1992, while foreign aid was drying up. In response to stabilization, strengthened property rights, and greater openness to foreign trade, domestic savings increased by 20 percentage points of GDP, from negative levels in the mid-1980s to 16 percent of GDP in 1992. Foreign financial assistance was not offered to Vietnam until the country had an established track record of macroeconomic and trade reform; financing from the World Bank and the IMF resumed in 1993. While the delay was largely political, it perhaps offers a useful lesson. Too much financing in the early stages of reform may delay adjustment rather than support it. In Vietnam's case foreign aid came after good policies were in place.

Widespread Benefits

A final aspect of Vietnam's reform, which may not be replicable in all countries, is that a large number of households benefited quickly. One of the important findings of later chapters is that the underlying distribution of assets in Vietnam was quite equitable. Vietnam has very little capital stock; its main assets are land and human capital. Chapters 2 and 3 reveal that the distribution of land among households is relatively equitable and

Figure 1.4 Savings and Investment, Vietnam, 1985–95

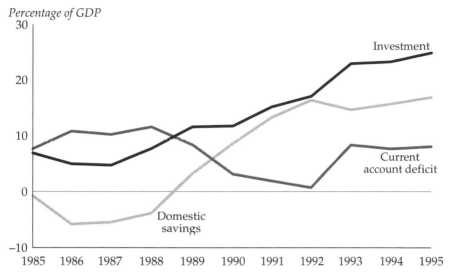

Percentage of GDP

Source: State Bank of Vietnam.

that basic education and literacy are widespread. The vast majority of households were thus able to benefit quickly from market reforms and the opening of the economy to international trade. Put simply, the reforms raised the relative price of rice and other agricultural products, and most households had the land and knowledge to respond to the improved incentives. Higher incomes generated demand for other goods and services, some of which could be met by the private sector. In this way a positive dynamic was established. And since most households benefited right away, the reform was popular and possible to sustain politically.

Lurking Challenges

In summary, Vietnam's macroeconomic performance has been very good since 1989. The country has reduced inflation from 400 percent to single digits. The root problem was a large and inefficient public sector. With military demobilization, layoffs from state enterprises, and reductions in the civil service, about 1.5 million people have left the public sector since 1988, reducing its weight in the labor force from 15 percent to 10 percent. This adjustment was accomplished without a recession because private producers, particularly in agriculture and the service sector, responded quickly to strengthened property rights and price reforms. A growing economy made adjustment easier. The Ministry of Labor found in its surveys that most workers laid off from the public sector were absorbed by the rapidly growing private sector within one year (World Bank 1993b, chapter 3). Robust growth has also raised government revenue, with the result that public expenditures on infrastructure, education, and health are much higher now than at the beginning of adjustment.

Vietnam still faces serious challenges. It is too early to conclude that its shift onto a higher growth path is permanent and not simply a boom. Vietnam's low per capita GNP indicates that it has a large amount of labor relative to other factors of production, such as physical capital (including infrastructure), land, and natural resources. While the distribution of land among households is equitable, the population density on the country's arable land is extreme—1,000 people per square kilometer of agricultural land, one of the highest concentrations in the developing world. Furthermore, population growth remains high.

Absorbing the workers laid off from the public sector may have seemed to many observers to be a daunting task. But it was minor compared with the challenge of employing the new entrants to the labor force. Retrenchment released 1.5 million public sector employees over five years; new workers total about 1 million people per year. Population growth has begun to decelerate; however, rapid population growth in the range of 2–3 percent per year during 1975–90 will result in the ongoing expansion of the labor force for some years. The 9 percent GDP growth seen in recent years is necessary to absorb this expanding pool of workers; any slippage from that rate will result in mounting unemployment.

Absorbing the large number of underutilized workers is both a challenge and an opportunity. Vietnam has the opportunity to follow the same kind of labor-intensive development strategy that has been successful in other East Asian economies. The common features of this strategy have been macroeconomic stability, reliance on the private sector to finance most investment, a strong focus on human resource development, and relative openness to foreign trade and investment (World Bank 1993a).

Vietnam has made substantial progress in each of these areas. Nevertheless, the state sector is still large and significant impediments to foreign trade and investment remain. Progress with structural reforms is thus one of the factors that will influence the country's growth. Divesting state enterprises, improving the environment for private investment, and lowering trade barriers are all structural reforms that will help sustain the 9 percent growth of recent years. It will be easier for the government if it moves on all of these policy fronts at once: if the government retains a large number of commercial enterprises, it will be more difficult to promote private investment or to reduce protection of inefficient industries.

Looking to the future, then, one important issue is whether the reform program will continue to generate robust growth. A growing literature analyzes macroeconomic policies in Vietnam and the priorities for further reform (see, for example, Dapice, Haughton, and Perkins 1996; Dollar 1996; Riedel 1992). It is not the purpose of this book to contribute to that literature. Rather, we take macroeconomic policies as given and address the question of how the benefits of growth are distributed among the population. Vietnam began its transition with well over half its population living below a widely accepted international poverty line. Rapid growth can reduce poverty quickly, but only if growth involves the bulk of the population. The initial reforms in 1988 and 1989 did reach a large number of households. But during 1993–95 growth has been more narrowly concentrated in the urban areas around Ho Chi Minh City and Hanoi.

The Impact of Economic Growth on Poverty Reduction

Vietnam's economic growth has accelerated over the past decade. By the end of the 1980s per capita income growth had climbed to almost 6 percent per year. This strong rate continued through the first half of the 1990s. This growth has probably reduced poverty somewhat. But by how much? The answer depends on the extent to which the poor have shared in the growth process. We cannot know this definitively though, owing to a lack of historical data with which to track the distribution of household living standards. We can, however, combine data on income distribution in 1993 and growth rates from 1984–93 with a set of plausible assumptions about changes in the income distribution, in order to identify a range of estimates for the poverty rate in 1984. In the second half of this section we use a similar methodology to project forward the likely effect of growth on poverty reduction during the rest of the decade.

Income Distribution in Other Transition Economies

The Living Standards Survey revealed that in 1993 the distribution of income in Vietnam was relatively even compared with other developing countries. The Gini coefficient, which measures inequality in the distribution of individual consumption, was 0.34. Recent figures for some nearby countries are 0.32 for Indonesia, 0.38 for China, 0.41 for the Philippines, 0.46 for Thailand, and 0.48 for Malaysia (World Bank 1996, table 5). In order to estimate the impact of growth on poverty reduction during the past decade in Vietnam, we need to make some assumptions about what happened to the distribution of income during that period. Kuznets's well-known inverted-U theory—inequality rises during the early phase of industrialization and then falls—launched a lengthy debate in the field of development economics regarding the likely trends in income distribution as a country grows. Subsequent research has cast doubt on the universality of this pattern of growth (Anand and Kanbur 1993). Indeed, experiences in East Asia have illustrated that economies need not suffer from rising inequality during initial stages of development. Taiwan (China) and the Republic of Korea are two notable examples. There, country circumstances and policy decisions led to widespread participation in rapid growth and, as a result, dramatic levels of poverty reduction. More generally, Bruno,

Ravallion, and Squire (1995) demonstrate that there is no systematic relationship between growth and inequality over time.

On the other hand, countries undergoing the transition from a socialist to a market economy have shown a tendency toward greater inequality. This tendency has been particularly strong in the heavily industrialized countries of Central and Eastern Europe. China's experience demonstrates a different path, which may be particularly relevant for Vietnam given its initial agrarian character. Income distribution improved during the early years of China's reforms (1978–83), when changes in agricultural policies led to dramatic increases in rural income. Distribution became more unequal in subsequent years with the increasing importance of rural enterprises and industry. Gini coefficients are estimated to have declined from 0.28 in 1978 to 0.22 in 1983 and then to have risen to 0.31 in 1989 (World Bank 1992).

China's experience is also noteworthy because of recent analysis indicating that while the proportion of the population living below the poverty line declined throughout the 1980s, the depth and severity of poverty worsened (Ravallion and Chen 1994). The growth process was leaving some of the poorest people in China behind. These findings highlight the need to examine not only the rate of poverty (that is, the headcount index), but also higher-order poverty measures (that is, the poverty gap and the Foster-Greer-Thorbecke index).

Estimates of Poverty Incidence

We can only speculate on how income distribution has changed in Vietnam since before *doi moi*. Many believe that economic reforms have not only led to higher household living standards, but also to greater inequality among households. Yet Vietnam's response to market reform was driven largely by the agricultural sector in the early years of reform, 1988–91, followed by rapid expansion of industry since 1992. It is possible that Vietnam, like China, experienced an initial improvement in distribution followed by a recent worsening. Thus in estimating the likely impact of growth on poverty, we examine several different scenarios, the most plausible of which is that income distribution has become more unequal since the mid-1980s and will continue to become more unequal. In China the Gini coefficient increased at about 1.6 percent per year in 1985–90, once the initial impact of agrarian reform had been absorbed. In our scenarios, a Gini of 0.30 in 1984 increasing to 0.38 by 2000 would be very similar to the Chinese experience. Because of the impact of Vietnam's agrarian reform, the deterioration may not have been quite so sharp between 1984 and 1993, but we believe that this is a reasonable estimate.

We look at other scenarios as well, including one in which the Gini coefficient increases from 0.24 in 1984 to 0.34 in 1993. Such a shift is very large relative to the historical experience of other countries and can thus be taken as a plausible outer bound of an increase in inequality.

Completing our analysis are scenarios in which the Gini declined from 0.38 in 1984 and in which it remained constant at 0.34. The four possibilities provide a range of estimates for the change in poverty incidence between 1984 and 1993.

Specifically, we estimate the impact of growth on poverty alleviation using the following data and specifications:

- Four different Lorenz curves representing different distribution scenarios (with Gini coefficients of 0.24, 0.30, 0.34, and 0.38).[9]
- A poverty line constructed using the "cost of basic needs "methodology" (see Ravallion 1994 for the methodology and chapter 2 of this book for details on calculating Vietnam's poverty line).
- Per capita consumption estimates based on actual growth rates of 1984–94 and on projected annual per capita growth of 6 percent from 1994 onward.[10]

Projections of poverty incidence are based on the structure of the parameterized Lorenz curve that best fits the data and is selected as described in Chen, Datt, and Ravallion (1994).[11] Ravallion and Datt (1992) used a similar method to assess the importance of growth and distributional changes on poverty reduction in India and Brazil during the 1980s. Here, actual poverty is unknown for all years except 1993; so we estimate poverty rates using known growth rates and several possible income distributions.

Results indicate that there was a dramatic decrease in poverty during 1984–93, regardless of which assumption about the change in income distribution is used (table 1.1). Poverty was extremely prevalent prior to reform, and has declined rapidly since. The estimated poverty rate in 1984 ranges from 74 percent to 77 percent under the different distributional assumptions. Estimated higher-order poverty measures—the poverty gap and squared poverty gap indexes—also indicate that the severity of poverty decreased under all distributional scenarios. This magnitude of poverty reduction is similar to that experienced by other developing economies that have grown rapidly, such as Korea and Indonesia between 1970 and 1990 (Johanson 1993).

It may seem counterintuitive that the estimated decline in the poverty rate depends so little on the distributional trends. There is an explanation:

Table 1.1 National Poverty Incidence in Vietnam under Different Distributional Scenarios, Selected Years

	1984				1993	2000			
	Gini	*Gini*	*Gini*	*Gini*	*Gini*	*Gini*	*Gini*	*Gini*	*Gini*
Index	0.24	0.30	0.34	0.38	0.34	0.24	0.30	0.34	0.38
Headcount index	77	74	76	74	55	14	22	27	34
Poverty gap index	25.8	28.9	31.8	34.7	17.0	2.0	5.7	6.2	10.6
Squared poverty gap index	11.0	14.5	16.2	19.8	7.1	0.4	2.0	1.9	4.3

Source: Authors' calculations.

the backward projections generate a mean per capita consumption in 1984 that is well below the national poverty line. Thus regardless of which Lorenz curve is used to assess poverty incidence, poverty levels are high and quite similar—at about 75 percent. In general, when the poverty line is much higher than mean consumption, the headcount index is unresponsive to changes in the Gini. In Vietnam's case, if total consumption in 1984 were distributed evenly over the whole population, everyone would have been below the poverty line. Thus we can conclude that poverty incidence declined significantly between 1984 and 1993, regardless of what happened to the distribution of income.

Changes in the estimated depth and severity of poverty, on the other hand, depend greatly on assumptions about changes in the distribution of income.[12] Thus the backward projections of the poverty gap and squared poverty gap indexes vary substantially depending on the assumption about the change in the Lorenz curve. With most of the population having incomes below the poverty line, the depth and severity of poverty relay important details about the nature of poverty. These details depend on the structure of the Lorenz curve.

Projections of Future Poverty Incidence

What will be the impact on poverty if Vietnam maintains an 8 percent annual growth rate (6 percent per capita) for the rest of the 1990s? Again, we have to introduce assumptions about distributional trends to address this question. Whereas backward projections of poverty incidence are not very sensitive to assumptions about the Lorenz curve, forward projections are. Given 6 percent per capita growth, the projected poverty incidence in 2000 ranges from 14 percent to 34 percent, depending on the Lorenz curve chosen for the analysis. The main point, however, is that the poverty rate will drop substantially throughout the rest of the 1990s if the economy continues to grow at the rate of recent years. Even with a worsening income distribution, the magnitude of poverty reduction would be great. If the distribution is stable or becomes more equitable, the magnitude would be even larger. In the forward projections both the poverty gap and the poverty gap squared also decline rapidly under all the assumptions regarding the shape of the Lorenz curve. Nevertheless, the extent of poverty reduction in the next few years will depend critically on distributional trends.

The main point illustrated here is that, for a country with most of its people living below the poverty line (as in Vietnam in 1984), rapid growth will reduce poverty regardless of changes in the distribution of income. As poverty incidence declines, however, further reductions in poverty will depend increasingly on distributional issues. In Vietnam the speed of poverty reduction in the next decade will depend on the extent to which growth is spread among the population.

Regional growth patterns. One reason for concern about the possibility of increasing inequality in Vietnam is that different regions have grown at different rates during the past few years. The initial impact of reform boosted agricultural production throughout the country. Subsequently, expansion of manufacturing and services has been concentrated more in urban areas than in rural ones, and more in the south than in the north. The Southeast region, around Ho Chi Minh City, had the lowest poverty rate in 1993, 34 percent, and also the highest growth rate, 15.6 percent (table 1.2). The problem is even more acute if urban areas are separated from rural areas. The urban Southeast had a poverty rate of 20 percent in 1993, and a growth rate in 1993–94 of 17.1 percent. Regions also have much different distributions of expenditures, characterized by Ginis ranging from 0.24 to 0.38 (table 1.2). Despite more equitable distributions in the poorer regions, their slower rate of growth poses great challenges for poverty reduction.

The impact of regional growth on poverty reduction can be estimated using the same methodology as above. Holding each region's income distribution constant, and assuming that population growth is 2.1 percent in all regions, we can estimate the impact of regional growth on annual poverty reduction.[13] If each region continued to grow at the rate it did during 1993–94 and aggregate growth remained 8.8 percent (the average for the period), national poverty incidence would decline by 5.8 percent each year. But poverty reduction would be much quicker in some regions than in others. For example, poverty incidence would decline by 15 percent annually in the Southeast, but only by 3–4 percent in the predominantly rural Northern Uplands, Red River Delta, North-Central Coast, and Mekong Delta (table 1.3). If these growth differentials persist, poverty will become much less prevalent in some regions and increasingly concentrated in others. Again, the difference is even more striking if urban areas are separated from rural ones. The projected rate of poverty decline in the urban Southeast, given its 17.1 percent growth rate of 1993–94, is 26 percent per year.

Table 1.2 Poverty Incidence (Headcount Index) and Growth Rate in Vietnam, by Region, 1993–94

Region	Poverty incidence 1993	GDP growth 1993–94 (percent)	Gini coefficient
Northern Uplands	66	7.7	26
Red River Delta	53	7.0	33
North-Central Coast	77	7.1	24
Central Coast	56	7.5	34
Central Highlands	67	9.0	30
Southeast	34	15.6	38
Mekong Delta	46	4.1	31
Average	55	8.8	34

Source: 1992–93 Vietnam Living Standards Survey; Vietnam Ministry of Planning and Investment.

Equal regional growth. What would happen to poverty if regional growth were more equal? Three scenarios are explored here to assess the impact of balanced growth and the redistributive policies that may bring about more equal growth. The first scenario estimates the impact on poverty reduction if all regions had grown at 8.8 percent between 1993 and 1994. While this scenario is implausible, it illustrates the impact of more equitable regional growth on poverty reduction. The second and third scenarios estimate the impact on poverty reduction if all regions had grown at 7.8 percent and 6.8 percent, respectively, between 1993 and 1994. These scenarios are explored because if the government were to implement policies to improve regional equality, a tradeoff might arise in terms of a reduction in aggregate growth.

The annual poverty reduction rate would be high under all scenarios (table 1.3). It would decline by 7.7 percent annually if all regions grew at 8.8 percent, and by 5.8 percent if regions grew at different paces, but generated an aggregate growth rate of 8.8 percent. This simulation shows the potential benefit of more balanced growth, provided the overall growth rate can be maintained. Yet if the government were to adopt aggressive redistribution policies to target growth to the poorest areas, aggregate growth might decline. If it were to drop from 8.8 percent to 7.8 percent, and all regions grew equally, overall poverty reduction would be 6.3 percent per year—higher than the rate obtained from faster but unbalanced growth. If the growth rate were to slow to 6.8 percent in each region, however, the overall decline in poverty would be 4.9 percent per year, less than that achieved through the scenario with more rapid but unbalanced growth. Thus efforts to encourage more equal regional growth will not necessarily benefit the poor if they drive the aggregate growth rate down by more than about 1 percentage point.

Table 1.3 Effect on Poverty Incidence (Headcount Index) of Different Growth Scenarios in Vietnam, 1993–94

| | | Different regional growth | |
| | | --- | --- |
Region	Actual poverty incidence 1993	Projected poverty incidence 1994	Percentage change 1993–94
Northern Uplands	66	63	−4.1
Red River Delta	53	51	−2.9
North-Central Coast	77	75	−3.1
Central Coast	56	50	−11.2
Central highlands	67	60	−11.1
Southeast	34	29	−14.9
Mekong Delta	46	44	−4.2
Average	55	51.8	−5.8

Source: Author's calculations.

A Poverty Alleviation Strategy for Vietnam

One important objective of Vietnam's five-year plan for 1996–2000 is to promote broadly based development, as indicated in the following excerpt:

The living standards of the population, especially those in some rural and mountainous areas, are still very low and are improving too slowly. The gap between rich and poor is inappropriate... Poverty alleviation is one of the important aims of the five year plan 1996–2000. (Government of Vietnam 1995, 7)

Furthermore, the government is planning a wide range of interventions to reach this objective:

Specific measures to be applied under this program include: policy and institutional measures (job creation, infrastructure construction, education, and health care); measures to mobilize funds for poverty alleviation activities (domestic funds and external grants and soft loan assistance); and measures to organize implementing mechanisms, combining socio-economic development activities with poverty alleviation programs (Government of Vietnam 1995, 12)

Which interventions will be successful in promoting broadly based growth is not obvious, however. The government has a growing amount of resources to finance public services. After a period of structural adjustment, real government expenditures per capita were about twice as high in 1995 as in the late 1980s. What should the government do with these resources? How should it choose among the different services that it can provide? In what areas should the government intervene, and in what ways?

8.8 percent GDP growth for all regions		7.8 percent GDP growth for all regions		6.8 percent GDP growth for all regions	
Projected poverty incidence 1994	Percentage change 1993–94	Projected poverty incidence 1994	Percentage change 1993–94	Projected poverty incidence 1994	Percentage change 1993–94
62	−5.6	63	−4.2	64	−2.9
50	−5.3	51	−4.0	52	−2.7
73	−4.7	74	−3.8	75	−2.8
49	−12.6	50	−11.5	50	−10.4
60	−10.9	60	−9.8	61	−9.5
32	−5.7	33	−4.3	33	−2.8
41	−11.4	41	−9.9	42	−8.4
50.7	−7.7	51.5	−6.3	52.2	−4.9

The Role of Government in a Market Economy

When considering government intervention in any sector, one must ask first what are the reasons for intervention, and, second, what intervention, if any, is best given behavioral responses, distortion costs, and information problems.[14] These considerations are important for Vietnam. There are now many high-return investment opportunities, most of which can eventually be undertaken by the private sector. In the short term the government has a role in facilitating private sector investment. Beyond that, the government's role is to intervene where there are large discrepancies between the social return to investment and the private return (such interventions will improve the efficiency of the market economy) and to ensure that distributional goals are met. Finding the right balance between distributional and efficiency objectives is perhaps the most difficult challenge for Vietnamese policymakers.

In choosing among redistributive policies, it will be important to pick those that help the poor in the most efficient way. One means of explicitly considering both efficiency and equity tradeoffs is by creating an *efficiency policy hierarchy* (Knowles and others 1996). This involves ranking possible policy options (those that enhance efficiency by addressing externalities and market failures) according to their direct and indirect (distortionary) costs, and then selecting the option that will achieve distributional objectives at the least cost. A solid understanding of household behavior is essential for developing such a hierarchy. The other chapters in this book focus on the analysis of household data.

When considering household behavior in a range of sectors, there are generally good prospects for public interventions that improve efficiency and promote equity, such as infrastructure investment, agricultural support services, human capital accumulation, and safety nets. Together, these areas make up an effective poverty alleviation strategy. The particular interventions selected in each sector should be assessed considering both the direct and indirect (distortionary) costs of alternatives. Vietnam has a history of quantitative restrictions and interventions, which tend to be more distortionary than price-based (taxes, subsidies) approaches. Thus in the Vietnamese context it is important to focus on the costs of different types of interventions—whether designed to promote efficiency or increase equity. The analyses in the book are designed to provide information that will help policymakers identify the most effective interventions.

One of the main lessons of this work is that household survey data can be useful for identifying interventions that will promote growth and poverty reduction. Ideally, policymakers want to work with panel data that trace how household welfare changes over time as policies and other variables change. But Vietnamese policymakers do not have panel data on household behavior. This situation is common in the developing world.

Even in countries in which several household surveys have been carried out over time, there are rarely panel data with observations over time on the same households. Furthermore, survey questionnaires change, making even basic comparisons over time difficult.

The authors of this book attempt to draw lessons from cross-sectional data on household behavior. This approach is risky, as results can be affected by omitted variables or household-specific effects that cannot be controlled for. While cross-sectional data can reveal associations, they cannot as easily determine causation. The basic methodological approach used throughout the book is to combine the cross-sectional survey data with other information in order to draw inferences—cautiously. Developing panel data sets should be a high priority for Vietnam and any country interested in monitoring the impact of policies. The approaches used throughout this book should be relevant to the wide range of policymakers in the developing world who have to work with less-than-ideal data. Vietnam's policymakers are not going to wait until they have a perfect dataset to begin policy analysis. We show how the cross-sectional data can be used to make informed judgments about the likely effect of different interventions.

Lessons Learned

What are some of the key lessons from this analysis? The chapters that focus on the household economy (3–5) provide useful guidance on the kinds of interventions that are likely to increase the incomes of the poor. While the cross-sectional estimates must be treated with caution, they indicate that the returns to infrastructure and capital are quite high in agricultural and nonagricultural household production. Deficiencies in power, transport, and water management are clearly serious problems for Vietnam. The main urban industrial areas there need infrastructure investment. At the same time, rural infrastructure is one of the important determinants of economic development in some regions. All of the provinces of Vietnam are looking to the central government to finance infrastructure projects that will benefit their areas. Chapters 3–5 indicate that these types of investments could spur growth and alleviate poverty by raising productivity.

Industrialization and urbanization. Vietnam is a labor-rich country whose rapid growth will certainly be accompanied by industrialization and urbanization. As the country industrializes, the pace of urbanization will be an important issue. If people move into the cities too quickly, it will be more difficult to develop an urban infrastructure base in a manner conducive to long-term growth. A recent survey of migrants to the Hanoi area indicates that more than half moved for economic reasons (UNDP 1997). Given that per capita income in rural areas of the Red River Delta is more than five times lower than that in neighboring Hanoi, this movement is hardly surprising. Investments and programs to promote rural and agricultural development can reduce the relative attraction of urban life and slow the pace of urbanization.

Equality and efficiency. One of the interesting findings highlighted in chapters 2 and 3 is that the distribution of land among agricultural households is quite equitable within regions of Vietnam—there are few landless rural households. Still, 61 percent of rural households are poor, primarily because of the extreme population density and the failure to generate the maximum value from agricultural land. Diversification into nonagricultural activities is the only solution to the first problem. The second problem can be addressed through investments in transport and irrigation, and improvements in agricultural extension services.

An important message in chapters 3–5 is that there are interventions that can achieve both efficiency and equity objectives. They would have a high rate of return and a strong direct impact on rural poverty. Simulations in chapter 4, for example, demonstrate that irrigation investments should have high rates of return—in the 20–35 percent range. These benefits will be pro-poor in general but even more so if the irrigation expansion is targeted to households with low per capita holdings. The government has indicated its intention of increasing infrastructure investment in rural and remote areas. These investments must be chosen carefully. Infrastructure investments with a low rate of return are not going to help the poor in the long run. Our analysis indicates that there are high-return rural investments, and that these are the kinds of "win-win" projects (since they promote growth and reduce poverty) that the government should target. In regions where infrastructure investments have low returns, out-migration will have to be an important part of the solution to widespread poverty.

Private sector development. Chapters 3 and 5 paint a vibrant picture of a small-scale private sector both in agricultural and nonagricultural activities. The estimated return to capital for both of these activities is high, well above prevailing interest rates (which themselves are high in real terms). This finding implies that the expansion of credit at market interest rates would benefit private producers. The government has developed a bank for the poor that lends money to poor households at subsidized interest rates. The amount of subsidized credit will always be constrained by the government budget, and there are questions as to how well this credit can be targeted to poor households. Our analysis suggests that distributional objectives could be achieved more efficiently through other approaches with lower direct and, especially, indirect costs. For example, measures that promote the expansion of commercial banking (such as regulatory and tax reform, training of bankers, and outreach of financial services to remote areas) can help private producers, taking the place of ongoing subsidies.

Investment in human capital. Human capital development is critical to ensure that growth is broadly based and involves most households. Several chapters of this book focus on different aspects of human capital accumulation, including education, health, nutrition, and fertility. The common theme running through these chapters is the way in which poverty today breeds poverty in the future by hampering the development of human capital. This research examines the determinants of educational enrollments, health and nutrition status, and fertility and offers insights into which kinds of interventions are likely to be successful in building up the human capital of poor households.

We find that education, as currently provided in Vietnam, may or may not affect living standards. Primary education is strongly associated with farm income and with wages in urban areas. Secondary education increases the productivity of nonfarm activities. But education is not always associated with higher incomes. Secondary education has little additional impact on farm incomes and no effect on wages in rural areas, and primary education has little effect on nonfarm self-employment activities.

When returns to education are low, households begin to remove their children from school. For example, many rural households took their children out of lower secondary school when the market reforms began. Our analysis suggests that this choice was influenced by the poor quality of education and by expanded income-earning opportunities for the 12–17-year-old cohort. The government must understand that a program to expand secondary education by building additional school buildings is not likely to have much impact. Keeping more of the 12–17-year-old group in school will require an increase in the return to this investment. At the school level, school quality could be improved and the curriculum altered. At the macroeconomic level, policies that promote labor-intensive growth and expansion of the private sector will also be critical.

Although private returns to education vary among regions, the social returns to education appear quite strong throughout. In Vietnam there is little evidence that poverty—that is, lack of income—is associated with malnutrition or high fertility. Education and information, however, do play key roles. For example, the educational status of women, and that of their husbands, is a key determinant of fertility. Furthermore, child malnutrition is prevalent among all income groups in Vietnam, even the richest, indicating that low incomes are not the cause. Improving information must be a key part of a successful strategy to alleviate malnutrition. Simply put, income growth alone is unlikely to solve the problems of malnutrition and rapid population growth; yet high fertility and malnutrition are likely to be sources of future poverty. The evidence supports the view that education and knowledge are keys to reducing fertility and malnutrition today, which will strengthen households' income-earning ability in the future.

Household choices. One of the important implicit messages in this book is that the government needs to understand how households make decisions and factor this into its interventions. The applied microeconomic research in the book should enable policymakers to better appreciate the factors that influence household choices. For example, evidence presented in chapter 6 shows that most households are involved in private transfers. The transfers tend to go to the elderly for income support and to the young to build up human and physical capital. Households either receive or give transfers to other households, and for some groups these transfers make up a substantial portion of household income.

Transfers tend to be allocated to vulnerable households, such as those containing the elderly or the disabled, or low-income households, and thus serve as a form of insurance. In addition, private transfers help equalize the distribution of income. They provide a larger boost to the resources of very poor households than do public transfers. Yet while private transfers fill an important insurance role for all households and help raise the consumption of the poorest, they do not obviate the need for public safety nets. The private transfers received by the poorest are not nearly sufficient to lift them out of poverty, and some of the poor do not receive any private transfers. Moreover, such transfers are likely to perform inadequately in the face of community covariate shock.

Public safety nets have several advantages over private ones. For example, they widen the risk-sharing pool, helping to insure against widespread disasters that might impoverish entire private networks. Still, policymakers should recognize that expanding the public safety net might well diminish the private safety net. The government can learn about household vulnerability by studying private transfers and can try to target public safety nets where private ones are unlikely to be sufficient. This is particularly important in Vietnam, since the government has limited fiscal ability to finance a public safety net. Much of Vietnam's current safety net spending benefits households that are not very poor (World Bank 1995). These public transfers may crowd out private ones, and would be much better used if they were effectively targeted to the poorest households.

In sum, the key to maintaining a high rate of poverty reduction in Vietnam is sustaining rapid, broadly based growth for at least another one or two decades. In some cases there may be tradeoffs between short-term growth and redistributive policies that have an immediate impact on poverty. But the extent of the tradeoff is probably not great. Vietnam's current transfer programs are not effectively reaching the poor. If some of these resources were redirected to basic education or to carefully chosen rural infrastructure investments, the likely impact would be both an immediate improvement in conditions for the poor and an acceleration of medium-term growth.

With good policies and a well-designed program of infrastructure investment, industrial and commercial activities should expand in several locations around the country. The inevitable rural-urban migration can proceed without disruption if it is supported by programs that build up rural infrastructure and human capital. On the one hand, this will ensure a supply of healthy, literate workers to the expanding cities; on the other, these activities will raise the productivity and incomes of those who remain in rural areas. Thus policies and investments that promote growth in different regions of Vietnam can be both an effective long-term growth strategy and the best poverty alleviation strategy.

Notes

The authors gratefully acknowledge excellent research assistance from Ky Viet Tran; helpful comments from Paul Glewwe, Martin Ravallion, Dominique van de Walle, and an anonymous referee; and financial support from the World Bank's Research Support Budget (RPO 678-83).

1. A good example of this criticism is the nongovernmental organization (NGO) declaration at the United Nations Conference on Women, held in Beijing in 1995: "The global economy governed by international financial institutions, the World Trade Organization, and multinational corporations proposes structural adjustment programs for countries in the South in the name of fiscal health. The result is increasing poverty, debt, and unemployment."

2. See Fforde and de Vylder (1988) for a description and analysis of Vietnam's development strategy during the early and mid-1980s.

3. The data are from Vietnam's General Statistical Office. Data for 1979–87 are cited in Fforde and de Vylder (1988, 88). All of the data in this chapter for 1988 and later are from official sources and are reported in the appendix tables to World Bank (1993b) and World Bank (1994).

4. Before 1988, national accounts were calculated using the Net Material Product System (MPS). Vietnam subsequently adopted the System of National Accounts (SNA) used by most countries and has calculated GDP in 1989 market prices beginning with data for 1988. The MPS data for the pre-1998 period exclude some services counted as part of GDP in the SNA. More important in the case of Vietnam, production data were aggregated using the rather arbitrary fixed plan prices of 1982. We have made our own estimates of pre-1988 GDP by combining the sectoral growth rates calculated using the MPS with the sectoral weights calculated using the SNA. This approach corrects for the main distortion in the 1982 fixed prices, which undervalued agricultural output relative to industrial output.

5. See Ljunggren (1993) for a discussion of the political and economic factors that led to *doi moi*, as well as a detailed description of the measures introduced during 1988–90.

6. Dollar (1994) analyzes the stabilization measures and the factors that led to their success.

7. Ronnas (1992) used survey data to demonstrate the extent to which the private sector in services and manufacturing was cut off from formal credit channels in this period.

8. Dollar and Ljunggren (1998) provide details on trade reform measures and on the response of exports, imports, and foreign investment.

9. To get a reasonable estimate of national inequality in 1984, we examined the range of inequality among the different regions in 1993. Gini coefficients for the different regions ranged from 0.24 to 0.38. We chose Lorenz curves corresponding to Ginis of 0.24 (North-Central Coast), 0.30 (Central Highlands), 0.34 (national), and 0.38 (Southeast).

10. Consumption is used as a proxy for income, which itself is used as an indicator of individual living standards. Experience with household surveys in low-income countries has indicated that consumption data can be collected more accurately than income data.

11. We tried two different specifications of the Lorenz curve—the general quadratic Lorenz curve (Villasenor and Arnold 1984) and the Beta, Lorenz curve (Kakwani 1980). These are described in Ravallion and Datt (1992). The curves are constructed using the software program POVCAL (Chen, Datt, and Ravallion 1992).

12. We repeated this analysis using a lower poverty line of 800,000 dong (rather than the national average of 1.2 million) to provide more sensitivity when examining the 1984 poverty rates. Using this lower line, the poverty rate was estimated at 30 percent of the population in 1993. The backward projections with different Ginis lead to greater dispersions in poverty rates in 1984 (ranging from 58 to 66 percent). Nevertheless, the difference still appears modest.

13. These regional projections are based on the simplifying assumptions that income distribution within each region remains constant and that the population growth rate is the same in all regions.

14. For a more complete discussion of the role of government (particularly in developing countries), see World Bank (1997).

References

Anand, Sudhir, and Ravi S. M. Kanbur. 1993. "Inequality and Development: A Critique." _Journal of Development Economics_ 41(1): 19–43.

Bruno, Michael, Martin Ravallion, and Lyn Squire. 1995. "Equity and Growth in Developing Countries: Old and New Perspectives on the Policy Issues." World Bank, Policy Research Department, Washington, D.C.

Chen, Shaohua, Gaurav Datt, and Martin Ravallion. 1992. "POVCAL." World Bank, Policy Research Department, Washington, D.C.

———. 1994. "Is Poverty Increasing in the Developing World?" World Bank, Policy Research Department, Washington, D.C.

Dapice, David, Jonathan Haughton, and Dwight Perkins, eds. 1996. _In Search of the_

Dragon's Tail: Economic Reform in Vietnam. Cambridge, Mass.: Harvard University Press.

Desai, Padma, ed. 1998. *Going Global: Transition from Plan to Market in the World Economy.* Cambridge, Mass.: MIT Press.

Dollar, David. 1994. "Macroeconomic Management and the Transition to the Market in Vietnam." *Journal of Comparative Economics* 18: 357–75.

————. 1996. "Economic Reform, Openness and Vietnam's Entry into ASEAN." *ASEAN Economic Bulletin* 13: 169–84.

Dollar, David, and Börje Ljunggren. 1998. "Macroeconomic Adjustment and Structural Reform in an Open Transition Economy: The Case of Vietnam." In Padma Desai, ed., *Going Global: Transition from Plan to Market in the World Economy.* Cambridge, Mass.: MIT Press.

Fforde, Adam, and Stefan de Vylder. 1988. *Vietnam: An Economy in Transition.* Stockholm: Swedish International Development Authority.

Johanson, Frida. 1993. *Poverty Reduction in East Asia: The Silent Revolution.* World Bank Discussion Paper 203. Washington, D.C.

Kakwani, Nanak. 1980. *Income Inequality and Poverty: Methods of Estimation and Policy Applications.* Oxford: Oxford University Press.

Knowles, James, Jere Behrman, Benjamin Diokono, and Keith McInnes. 1996. "Key Issues in the Financing of Vietnam's Social Services." Report prepared for the government of Vietnam and the Asian Development Bank. Abt Associates, Bethesda, Md.

Kuznets, Simon. 1965. *Economic Growth and Structure.* New York: Norton.

Ljunggren, Börje, ed. 1993. *The Challenge of Reform in Indochina.* Cambridge, Mass.: Harvard University Press.

Ravallion, Martin. 1994. "Poverty Comparisons." *Fundamentals of Pure and Applied Economics* 56. Chur, Switzerland: Harwood Academic Press.

Ravallion, Martin, and Shaohua Chen. 1994. "An Update on Rural Poverty in China." World Bank, Policy Research Department, Washington, D.C.

Ravallion, Martin, and Gaurav Datt. 1992. "Growth and Redistribution Components of Changes in Poverty Measures: A Decomposition with Applications to Brazil and India in the 1980s." *Journal of Development Economics* 38: 275–95.

Riedel, James. 1992. "Vietnam: On the Trail of the Tigers." Working paper. Johns Hopkins Univ., School for Advanced International Studies, Washington, D.C.

Ronnas, Per. 1992. *Employment Generation through Private Entrepreneurship in Vietnam.* Geneva: International Labour Office.

Sachs, Jeffrey, and Andrew Warner. 1995. "Economic Reform and the Process of Global Integration." *Brookings Papers on Economic Activity 1.* Brookings Institution, Washington, D.C.

UNDP (United Nations Development Programme). 1997. "Report on Spontaneous Migration Survey in Hanoi." VIE/95/004. Center for Population and Human Resources, New York.

Vietnam, Government of. 1995. *Socio-Economic Development and Investment Requirements for the Five Years 1996–2000.* Hanoi.

Villasenor, J., and B. C. Arnold. 1984. "The General Quadratic Lorenz Curve." Technical report. Colegio de Postgraduados, Mexico City.

World Bank. 1992. *China: Strategies for Reducing Poverty in the 1990s.* Washington, D.C.

———. 1993a. *The East Asian Miracle: Economic Growth and Public Policy.* New York: Oxford University Press.

———. 1993b. "Vietnam: Transition to the Market." Report 11902-VN. East Asia and Pacific Region, Washington, D.C.

———. 1994. "Vietnam: Public Sector Management and Private Sector Incentives." Report 13143-VN. East Asia and Pacific Region, Washington, D.C.

———. 1995. "Vietnam: Poverty Assessment and Strategy." Report 13442-VN. East Asia and Pacific Region, Washington, D.C.

———. 1996. *World Development Report 1996: From Plan to Market.* New York: Oxford University Press.

———. 1997. *World Development Report: The State in a Changing World.* New York: Oxford University Press.

Poverty and Inequality in the Early Reform Period

David Dollar and Paul Glewwe

Despite impressive economic growth in the past few years, as documented in chapter 1, Vietnam remains one of the poorest countries in the world. While lack of data precludes a detailed analysis of poverty and inequality in Vietnam in the 1980s and earlier, the 1992–93 Vietnam Living Standards Survey (VNLSS) offers a wealth of data with which to investigate household welfare at an early point in Vietnam's reform. This chapter provides a broad descriptive analysis of poverty and inequality in Vietnam based on those data. The information presented here establishes a context for more detailed analyses of specific aspects of household welfare in Vietnam in later chapters.

Data Available for Examining Poverty and Inequality in Vietnam

To analyze poverty and inequality, data are needed from a sample of individual households, since average levels of income provide no information about the distribution of income across households and, consequently, are consistent with a wide range of possible levels of poverty. Until the early 1990s data collection in Vietnam closely followed the system developed in the former Soviet Union. At the national level this means that estimates of economic production were based on the Net Material Product System, as opposed to the System of National Accounts (see chapter 1, note 4). Vietnam's use of the Soviet system of household data collection in the 1980s and earlier emphasized separate surveys for different kinds of workers, such as factory workers and farmers. This approach leads to problems for analysis for two reasons: families that have several types of workers may be overcounted when separate surveys are combined, and families with nonworking members (unemployed, retired) are excluded from all such surveys. An additional problem arose in the 1980s because financial constraints in Vietnam's General Statistical Office led to substantial reductions in the number of households sampled; in any given year only a few provinces were surveyed (out of a total of 52 provinces in Vietnam). Yet another problem is due to a major switch in the method of collecting expenditure data—in the 1970s household expenditure diaries were replaced by direct questions asked by interviewers. Such a fundamental change in survey design complicates attempts to assess changes in household welfare as measured by consumption expenditures.

In general, because of these problems and others it is difficult, if not impossible, to use data from past household surveys to analyze changes in poverty and inequality before the early 1990s. Fortunately, this dearth of information ended upon the successful completion of the 1992–93 VNLSS, jointly conducted by the State Planning Committee and the General Statistical Office. This multitopic household survey covered 4,800 Vietnamese households from all regions of Vietnam. The data were collected between October 1992 and October 1993. The survey is patterned after the World Bank's Living Standards Measurement Study (LSMS) household surveys.[1] The VNLSS is the first nationally representative general-purpose household survey (in the sense of collecting income and expenditure data) ever conducted in Vietnam. Preparations are currently under way for a new survey in 1998.

A brief description of the data collected gives a general idea of the wealth of information available from the VNLSS (see the appendix at the end of this book for a detailed description). The household questionnaire collects detailed data on household composition, education, health, employment, migration, housing, fertility, agricultural activities, nonfarm self-employment, food and nonfood expenditures, income, credit and savings, and anthropometric measurements (height, weight, and upper arm circumference). In addition, a community questionnaire was completed in all rural areas (80 percent of the households surveyed) that collected data on demographic structure, economic activities, infrastructure, schools, health facilities, and agricultural activities (including local wage rates). Finally, price data were collected from all sampling areas. For rural areas a separate price questionnaire was completed, while in urban areas comparable price data already collected by Vietnam's General Statistical Office were used.

Household Characteristics and Household Welfare in Vietnam

Before directly analyzing inequality and poverty in Vietnam, it is useful to get an overall picture of Vietnamese households. This section begins by examining the basic characteristics of Vietnamese households, and then examines how those characteristics are related to household welfare.

Characteristics of Vietnamese Households

General descriptive information on Vietnamese households, both for the country as a whole and by geographic region, is presented in table 2.1. (A map showing the location of these regions appears at the beginning of this book.)

Eighty percent of Vietnamese live in rural areas, making it one of the least urbanized countries in the world. Among Vietnam's seven regions, the least urbanized are the Central Highlands and the North-Central Coast, each with more than 90 percent of their population living in rural areas. The most urbanized region is the Southeast, which contains Ho Chi Minh City (formerly known as Saigon), Vietnam's largest city. Nearly half of the population in that region resides in urban areas.

Historically, the predominant religion practiced in Vietnam was Buddhism. Yet its current influence appears relatively weak—about 60 percent of the population indicates no religious affiliation and only about 27 percent identify themselves as Buddhist. Christians (Catholics or Protestants) make up about 9 percent of the population, while 2 percent belong to other religious groups. Both Buddhists and Christians are more common in the south than in the north, probably reflecting the impact of 40 years of socialist ideology in the north. The overwhelming majority of the population (about 85 percent) are ethnically Vietnamese (Kinh). The next largest group is the Chinese—about 2.5 percent of the population. A variety of other groups each constitute 2 percent or less of the total population. The Chinese are heavily concentrated in the south, and several other ethnic groups have relatively high concentrations in particular regions.

Table 2.1 also characterizes the population according to the occupation of household heads. Vietnam is mostly a country of farmers, with about 65 percent of the population living in households whose head works in agriculture. This pattern is evident in all regions except the relatively urbanized Southeast. Each of the remaining occupational categories comprises 10 percent or less of the total population (when classified by the occupation of the household head). Given the prevalence of farm households, it is no surprise that 75 percent of Vietnamese live in households in which the head is self-employed. In light of the socialist tradition, however, it is interesting that 9 percent of the population belongs to households headed by someone working for a private employer; the comparable figure for public employment is only 5.5 percent. These data confirm a point made in chapter 1, that even at an early stage of reform Vietnam had a relatively large private sector. Private sector employment is far more prevalent in the south than in the north.

In some developing countries, such as India, female-headed households tend to be worse off than those headed by men. Table 2.1 shows that female-headed households are fairly common in Vietnam, accounting for about 23 percent of the population.[2] According to VNLSS data, about 45 percent of female heads of household are married but living apart from

Table 2.1 Characteristics of Vietnamese Households, by Region
(percent)

Characteristic	All Vietnam	Northern Uplands	Red River Delta	North-Central Coast	Central Coast	Central Highlands	South-east	Mekong Delta
Total population[a]	100.0	15.6	21.6	12.8	11.9	3.2	12.6	22.4
Urban	19.9	14.8	15.2	8.7	30.6	0.0[b]	44.3	17.9
Rural	80.1	85.2	84.8	91.3	69.4	100.0	55.7	82.1
Religion of head								
Buddhist	27.4	19.7	19.8	3.1	15.2	24.6	47.8	49.5
Catholic	8.2	3.6	4.3	15.3	6.7	16.3	21.2	3.5
Protestant	0.9	0.0	0.0	0.0	2.0	15.9	0.5	0.4
Other	2.2	0.0	0.0	0.0	0.3	0.0	6.0	6.4
None	61.3	76.7	75.9	81.6	75.8	43.1	24.5	40.3
Ethnic group								
Vietnamese	84.5	62.5	91.8	96.8	88.8	47.7	86.7	87.4
Tay	2.0	11.7	0.1	0.2	0.0	0.0	0.4	0.6
Thai	1.0	2.6	0.0	2.8	0.0	7.3	0.0	0.0
Chinese	2.4	0.3	0.0	0.0	0.5	0.0	12.5	3.5
Khome	2.0	0.1	0.1	0.2	0.0	0.7	0.3	8.6
Moung	2.0	1.8	7.9	0.0	0.0	0.0	0.0	0.0
Nung	1.6	10.4	0.0	0.0	0.0	0.0	0.0	0.0
H'mong	0.7	4.3	0.0	0.0	0.0	0.0	0.0	0.0
Dao	0.3	1.6	0.0	0.0	0.0	0.0	0.0	0.0
Other	3.5	4.7	0.1	0.0	10.8	44.4	0.2	0.0
Employer of head								
Government	5.5	3.8	7.1	4.9	7.8	1.3	7.1	4.0
Private	8.6	2.7	6.1	4.4	9.2	10.5	12.9	14.3
Self-employed	75.2	87.4	77.3	85.7	70.2	78.5	56.2	71.3
Retired	6.5	3.5	6.3	3.7	6.1	7.3	12.6	6.9
Other not working[c]	4.2	2.4	3.1	1.3	6.5	7.3	11.1	3.5
Occupation of head								
White collar	4.6	2.7	4.5	7.1	7.7	0.5	4.6	3.7
Sales/service	8.1	4.8	7.3	3.3	13.3	2.4	15.0	8.2
Farming	64.7	77.5	64.6	77.0	54.8	78.9	37.7	67.2
Production	10.9	8.9	13.3	6.4	10.0	7.5	17.8	9.6
Other	1.0	0.2	0.9	1.3	1.5	1.1	1.2	0.9
Retired	6.5	3.5	6.3	3.7	6.1	7.3	12.6	6.9
Other not working[c]	4.2	2.4	3.1	1.3	6.5	2.4	11.1	3.5
Sex of head								
Male	77.5	78.5	78.6	81.8	73.8	82.0	70.3	78.5
Female	22.5	21.5	21.4	18.2	26.2	18.0	29.7	21.5
Schooling of head								
None	11.9	8.7	6.0	5.6	20.3	35.6	12.9	15.3
Primary	37.5	34.5	21.5	31.4	38.4	33.7	43.3	55.4
Lower secondary	33.5	38.6	47.8	42.2	23.8	23.5	28.6	20.5
Upper secondary	12.3	14.1	17.9	14.6	11.3	6.2	11.2	6.4
Technical	2.5	2.6	4.1	4.7	2.1	0.5	0.9	1.2
University	2.2	1.6	2.8	1.5	4.2	0.5	3.2	1.2

a. Percentages refer to people, not households—for example, 80.1 percent of the people (not 80.1 percent of households) live in rural areas.
b. None of the areas sampled in the VNLSS came from urban areas of the Central Highlands. There are a few urban areas in this mostly rural region, but none was selected to participate in the VNLSS.
c. This category includes unemployed heads and heads not in the labor force for reasons other than retirement.
Source: 1992–93 Vietnam Living Standards Survey.

their husbands. Another 40 percent are widowed, and the remainder are roughly evenly divided among divorced women, separated women, and women who have never been married.

Human capital, particularly in the form of formal education, is increasingly considered a fundamental determinant of economic growth (World Bank 1993). Despite its low level of income, Vietnam has reasonably good levels of education among household heads. Only 12 percent of the population lives in households in which the head has no education at all, while another 38 percent lives in households in which the head has a primary level of education. In other words, half the population lives in households in which the head has at least some secondary education. Across regions, the Red River Delta has the highest levels of education, while the lowest levels are found in the remote Central Highlands. Generally speaking, levels of education are higher in the north (Northern Uplands, Red River Delta, and North-Central Coast) than in the south (Central Coast, Central Highlands, Southeast, and Mekong Delta).

Measuring Household Welfare Using per Capita Consumption Expenditures

For both descriptive and analytical purposes it is convenient to have a single indicator of household welfare along which to measure the well-being of households, even at the cost of some simplification. The most obvious candidate is household income per capita. Yet income itself may not be the concept one has in mind, because families with large amounts of savings can draw on them to maintain a relatively high standard of living even if their current income is low. Conversely, families that are heavily indebted may have relatively high incomes but low levels of consumption because part of their income is used to pay off their debts. For these reasons consumption, usually measured in terms of household expenditures, is the best single indicator of household welfare. In this book we measure household welfare in terms of household consumption per capita.[3] In some chapters, however, the focus is on other dimensions of the quality of life—such as health, nutrition, and schooling—that are correlated, though not perfectly, with household consumption.

Because this book makes extensive use of the VNLSS expenditure data to examine household welfare, it is worthwhile to discuss how the total consumption expenditure variable was constructed. (For more details, see the appendix at the end of this chapter.) Total annual household consumption expenditure is the sum of five components:

- Explicit consumption expenditures on food and (nondurable) nonfood items.
- Value of food items produced and then consumed by the household.
- Value of goods received in-kind from employers (housing, food, clothing).

- Estimated rental (use) value of durable goods owned by the household.
- Estimated rental value of the dwelling occupied by the household.

The VNLSS household questionnaire asks for household expenditures on 45 different food items, as well as on the value of foodstuffs produced and consumed by the household. Because the Tet (new year) holiday leads to unusually large expenditures on some food items, additional questions are asked explicitly for Tet and other holidays. Expenditures on 68 non-food items are also recorded, though we exclude a few that are not household consumption (examples include gifts and insurance). Finally, other parts of the survey questionnaire collect data on health, education, and utility expenditures.

In some cases workers receive goods or services from their employers in addition to their wages. The VNLSS collects information on such payments for each worker's principal occupation; this is added to explicit consumption expenditures.[4] Durable goods must also be given special treatment, because their durability implies that they raise household welfare for several years after their purchase, and thus the purchase value of each good is not fully "consumed" in the year it is bought. To spread out this consumption over time, information on current value and purchase value are used to calculate depreciation rates. These rates can then be used (along with the real rate of interest) to calculate an annual use value for 13 kinds of durable goods. Finally, the annual rental value of the largest durable good, housing, must be calculated. This was done by regressing current estimated resale value on a variety of dwelling characteristics. Based on a small number of households that actually rented housing at a market rate, it was assumed that the annual rental value was 3 percent of the current predicted value of the housing.

Summing all the above components of consumption yields a comprehensive measure of household welfare. Note that regional prices have been used for these calculations so that the final measure is real consumption. To account for household size, total consumption is divided by household size to obtain per capita household consumption, the main indicator of household welfare used in this book.[5]

Welfare Levels among Different Vietnamese Households

How do various population groups compare in terms of household welfare and living standards? The relevant information is shown in table 2.2, where welfare is measured by per capita consumption expenditures and the population is divided into five groups of equal size (quintiles) according to this welfare indicator. Consumption levels of urban residents are twice those of rural residents, which is reflected in the increasing proportion of urban residents as one moves from the poorer to the wealthier

Table 2.2 Characteristics of Vietnamese Households, by Expenditure Quintile

(percent)[a]

Characteristic	Quintile 1	Quintile 2	Quintile 3	Quintile 4	Quintile 5	Mean per capita expenditure (thousands of dong)
Urban	5.5	7.5	13.9	21.3	51.3	2,267.6
Rural	94.5	92.5	86.1	78.7	48.7	1,166.8
Region						
Northern Uplands	23.9	20.3	16.4	11.9	5.7	1,011.4
Red River Delta	16.9	23.7	23.6	23.8	19.9	1,395.7
North-Central Coast	22.3	17.2	12.9	8.5	2.9	952.8
Central Coast	11.0	9.5	11.1	11.9	15.9	1,465.5
Central Highlands	4.0	4.3	3.1	2.5	2.0	1,121.2
Southeast	6.0	7.5	10.5	12.7	26.3	2,043.3
Mekong Delta	15.9	17.6	22.4	28.7	27.3	1,510.6
Religion of head						
Buddhist	24.7	26.4	24.5	29.6	31.9	1,497.7
Catholic	8.0	8.3	10.3	7.1	7.5	1,348.3
Protestant	1.7	1.5	0.7	0.0	0.7	1,108.6
Other	1.7	1.9	1.8	2.5	3.1	1,566.3
None	63.9	62.0	62.8	60.8	56.8	1,338.6
Ethnic group						
Vietnamese	70.7	83.4	87.6	91.0	89.6	1,427.9
Tay	4.0	2.4	2.3	1.0	0.5	953.6
Thai	2.2	1.2	0.9	0.5	0.2	882.9
Chinese	0.5	0.3	1.0	2.5	7.9	2,661.8
Khome	3.4	1.9	2.3	2.0	0.6	1,060.0
Moung	3.7	2.9	1.9	0.8	0.5	909.9
Nung	2.8	2.7	1.6	1.0	0.2	930.3
H'mong	3.1	0.3	0.0	0.0	0.0	433.1
Dao	0.9	0.3	0.1	0.0	0.0	655.7
Other	8.9	4.7	2.3	1.1	0.4	779.7
Employer of head						
Government	1.4	1.1	3.2	7.9	14.0	2,241.0
Private	9.7	9.1	8.9	8.5	6.8	1,268.8
Self-employed	82.2	80.3	80.5	72.5	60.2	1,275.9
Retired	3.8	5.6	3.9	7.2	11.9	1,835.8
Other not working[b]	3.0	3.9	3.4	4.0	6.9	1,769.9
Occupation of head						
White collar	0.9	2.4	3.0	5.6	11.3	2,183.6
Sales/service	2.7	3.2	6.4	10.0	18.4	2,097.9
Farming	81.9	75.4	73.2	59.2	33.7	1,122.2
Production	6.3	9.3	9.4	13.2	16.4	1,654.2
Other	1.5	0.3	0.7	1.0	1.4	1,498.1
Retired	3.8	5.6	3.9	7.2	11.9	1,835.8
Other not working[b]	3.0	3.9	3.4	4.0	6.9	1,769.9
Sex of head						
Male	81.3	81.0	81.0	77.1	66.8	1,316.4
Female	18.7	19.0	19.0	22.9	33.2	1,624.9

(Table continues on next page.)

Table 2.2 Characteristics of Vietnamese Households, by Expenditure Quintile (continued)
(percent)[a]

Characteristic	Quintile 1	Quintile 2	Quintile 3	Quintile 4	Quintile 5	Mean per capita expenditure (thousands of dong)
Schooling of head						
None	19.3	14.2	8.4	9.7	8.1	1,127.4
Primary	37.5	39.6	39.6	37.9	33.0	1,310.8
Lower secondary	34.0	34.8	35.0	33.3	30.3	1,339.2
Upper secondary	7.3	9.8	13.7	14.1	16.6	1,611.9
Technical	1.4	1.3	2.6	2.5	4.9	1,985.6
University	0.4	0.4	0.7	2.6	7.3	2,802.6

a. Percentages refer to people, not households.
b. This category includes unemployed heads and heads not in the labor force for reasons other than retirement.
Source: Authors' calculations, based on 1992–93 Vietnam Living Standards Survey data.

quintiles. This finding is not surprising—in virtually every developing country urban areas have much higher per capita expenditure levels than rural areas, even after adjusting for differences in price levels.

There are sizable differences in consumption levels among Vietnam's seven regions. The wealthiest region by far is the Southeast, which contains Ho Chi Minh City. The three poorest regions are the North-Central Coast, the Northern Uplands, and the Central Highlands. These are the three least urbanized regions in Vietnam (see table 2.1). The remaining three regions (Red River Delta, Central Coast, and Mekong Delta) have expenditure levels that are quite similar.

There are few differences by religion, except that the small number of Protestant households is clearly poorer than the rest, reflecting the fact that these households are concentrated in the relatively poor Central Highlands region. The main differences by ethnic group are that the Chinese are much better off than all other groups, with consumption levels almost twice as high as those of the Vietnamese, the second wealthiest group. The remaining ethnic groups are much poorer than both the Chinese and the Vietnamese, the H'mong group being by far the poorest.

When households are grouped by the household head's occupation and employer, differences in welfare levels are also evident. Households in which the head is self-employed or works for the private sector are relatively poor, while households headed by someone who works for the public sector are well off. Households in which the head is retired are also relatively well off, as are households in which the head is not working for some other reason.[6] Turning to occupation categories, farming households are by far the poorest. At the other extreme are households headed by a white-collar worker or by someone in a sales or service occupation.

Perhaps the most surprising finding in table 2.2 is that female-headed households appear to be much better off than households headed by men.

Much of this difference is due to the fact that female-headed households are more common in urban areas (table 2.1 shows that they are most common in the relatively urbanized Southeast region), which are much better off than rural areas. If we look at male- and female-headed households within urban and rural areas (not shown in table 2.2), a different result emerges. In rural areas female-headed households are still better off, but much less so (their per capita expenditures are about 11 percent higher, as opposed to 23 percent higher for Vietnam as a whole), and in urban areas female-headed households are slightly worse off than male-headed households. Finally, it is worth noting that among the two main types of female-headed households—widows and married women living apart from their husbands—widows are worse off, having a per capita income of 1.5 million dong compared with 1.7 million dong for women living apart from their husbands.

We can also examine the welfare levels of households classified by the educational attainment of the head. As expected, households with better-educated heads are better off. Yet the differences are not very large until we come to the university level. For example, households headed by someone with a lower secondary education have per capita consumption expenditures only about 19 percent higher than households with an uneducated head. Moving to upper secondary, the difference is still only 43 percent. In most other countries these differences are much larger. It is interesting to note that although the northern regions of Vietnam have higher levels of education (see table 2.1), they are not as wealthy as the southern regions.

Of course, there are other ways to measure household living standards. Table 2.3 examines several other indicators. Comparing urban and rural areas, the former have higher adult literacy and better access to electricity, potable water, and sanitary toilet facilities. In addition, young children in urban areas are less likely to be malnourished (stunted). While there are wide gaps in most of the indicators, it is worth noting that adult literacy is widespread in Vietnam, even in rural areas. Yet one should note that this literacy is self-reported (the respondent claims to be literate), and thus could overestimate functional literacy.

Table 2.3 also reports the incidence of the different indicators by region. The findings are similar to those seen earlier. Overall, the regions with the highest living standards are the Red River Delta (where Hanoi is located) and the Southeast (which contains Ho Chi Minh City), and that with the lowest living standards is the Central Highlands. Note that the Mekong Delta, which is not particularly poor in terms of consumption levels, has relatively low indicators of well-being. Moreover, nonincome indicators of well-being are not always highly correlated; in particular, stunting among young children is more severe in the three northernmost regions (including the Red River Delta) than in the Central Highlands, and the Mekong Delta region has the second-lowest incidence of stunting.

Table 2.3 Nonincome Indicators of Living Standards in Vietnam
(percent)

Region or quintile	Adult literacy	Electricity	Potable water[a]	Sanitary toilet[b]	Stunting among children aged 0–5[c]
All Vietnam	88.1	47.8	15.1	52.0	50.0
Urban and rural areas					
Urban	93.9	88.3	54.7	73.8	32.7
Rural	86.4	37.8	5.3	46.6	53.1
Region					
Northern Uplands	87.6	35.0	0.6	71.3	58.5
Red River Delta	91.6	76.4	19.0	70.4	53.7
North-Central Coast	90.9	35.6	0.5	49.8	58.4
Central Coast	85.2	58.3	19.2	51.0	46.1
Central Highlands	68.3	23.6	0.8	57.6	52.4
Southeast	92.5	65.6	38.1	68.8	29.8
Mekong Delta	84.8	24.1	17.0	12.3	44.5
Quintile					
1 (poorest)	77.4	22.2	2.9	36.4	59.2
2	87.1	40.8	4.4	50.5	56.7
3	89.7	44.8	8.8	51.6	46.2
4	89.7	56.5	14.8	54.0	44.3
5 (wealthiest)	93.8	74.8	44.7	67.4	27.7

a. Potable water is defined as water obtained from private water taps, public standpipes, and tubewells. Other sources were simple (hand-dug) wells, rivers, lakes, and rainwater.
b. Sanitary toilets are defined as flush toilets or latrines.
c. Stunting is defined as having a height-for-age Z-score of –2 or less. This indicator of childhood nutrition is explained further in chapter 9.
Source: Authors' calculations, based on 1992–93 Vietnam Living Standards Survey data.

The bottom of table 2.3 shows these living standards indicators by per capita expenditure quintile. As one would expect, better off households always do better. Yet for some indicators (such as adult literacy) the poorest quintiles are not far behind the wealthier ones.

Inequality in Vietnam

The Vietnamese government has been very concerned about inequality during the transition to a market economy. Frequently mentioned in speeches at the National Assembly in the early 1990s, for example, was the fear that inequality is on the rise and the need for a development strategy that limits increases in it. In addition to general concerns about inequality, there is also the more specific issue that reform is benefiting certain regions of the country while other areas are being left behind. Unfortunately, there are no data to examine systematically whether inequality has been rising during the transition to market. What can be done with the data at hand is to examine in detail the nature of inequality in 1993, early in Vietnam's period of adjustment and reform.

Measurement of Inequality

Before turning to the VNLSS data, discussion is needed on how to measure inequality in a useful way. The distribution of consumption expenditures is not equal in any country, so the relevant question is: when is one distribution more equal than another? In some cases the answer to this question is clear— if an initial distribution of consumption expenditures is altered by a series of transfers that take money from one person and give it to another with a higher income, the resulting distribution is more unequal than the initial one. This principle, known as the Pigou-Dalton transfer principle, is intuitively appealing for ranking specific distributions as more or less equal than others. It has long been known that this principle is directly related to Lorenz curves (Atkinson 1970), which are commonly used to visually compare distributions of income or expenditures. If one Lorenz curve lies below another, and thus represents a less equal distribution of income or expenditures, that curve can be constructed from the other curve by a series of Pigou-Dalton transfers that take money from one person and give it to another who has a higher level of income or expenditures. In contrast, if the two Lorenz curves cross, it is not clear which distribution is more unequal and it is not possible to construct one curve from the other by a series of Pigou-Dalton transfers.

This discussion suggests that any index of inequality should have the following characteristic: if one constructs a new distribution of income or expenditure through a series of transfers that take money from one person and give it to another with a higher income, the inequality index should show an increase in inequality. A Gini index of inequality, for example, satisfies this standard. Another inequality measure that satisfies this criterion is the Theil (1967) index, which is defined as follows:

$$T = \sum_{i=1}^{N} \frac{Y_i}{Y} \ln \left(\frac{Y_i N}{Y} \right).$$

where Y is the total income (or total expenditures) of the population, Y_i is the income of individual i, and N is the total number of people in the population. The Theil index has one useful property that the Gini index does not have—total inequality is the sum of two components: the weighted average of the degree of inequality within each "group" for any division of the total population into different groups, and inequality in the mean incomes across the different groups. This property is useful because it allows one to divide total inequality into the contribution from inequality within each group and the contribution due to differences in mean income among the different groups. That is, total inequality can be decomposed into two components: within-group inequality and between-group inequality.

Another inequality index introduced by Theil (1967) is the following:

$$L = \sum_{i=1}^{N} \frac{1}{N} \ln \left(\frac{Y}{Y_i N} \right).$$

This index decomposes into the weighted average of the index for each group (except here the weights are population shares, not income shares) and the inequality in the mean incomes of each group. These two inequality measures usually yield similar results. One difference is that the first is more sensitive to inequality at the upper tail of the distribution ("wealthy" outliers) while the second is more sensitive to inequality at the lower tail ("poor" outliers).

Before examining inequality in Vietnam, it is useful to clarify the difference between indicators of inequality and indices of poverty. Both examine the distribution of income or consumption expenditures. The primary difference is that poverty indices do this with reference to a poverty line, while measures of inequality do so only with reference to other members of the distribution. Moreover, poverty indices are concerned only with the population that falls below the poverty line, while indicators of inequality always examine all members of the distribution. Because poverty lines are, at least in the short to medium term, thought of as absolute standards,[7] economic growth will generally reduce poverty. But economic growth can occur without changing the distribution of income or consumption expenditures, and thus may have no effect on overall inequality (and may even lead to greater inequality). In this book both poverty and inequality will be examined, since both are of interest to policymakers.

Factors Associated with Inequality in Vietnam

How unequal are per capita consumption expenditures in Vietnam? One way to answer this question is to compare Vietnam's inequality to estimates of inequality using similar data from other countries. This is done in table 2.4. The main finding is that Vietnam has a relatively low level of inequality, the lowest of the five countries examined. Only Ghana is close to Vietnam in terms of low inequality.

Table 2.5 examines inequality in Vietnam from several different perspectives. More precisely, it groups households in different ways to provide a clearer picture of the nature of inequality in Vietnam. Recall that average per capita expenditures in urban areas of Vietnam are almost twice as high as the average in rural areas (see table 2.2). How much of overall inequality is due to the fact that these average expenditure levels

Table 2.4 Expenditure Inequality in Vietnam and Other Developing Countries

Country, year(s)	Gini coefficient	Theil T	Theil L
Côte d'Ivoire, 1985–86	0.4350	0.3530	0.3254
Ghana, 1987–88	0.3471	0.2141	0.2046
Jamaica, 1989	—	0.3487	0.3203
Peru, 1985–86	0.4299	0.3534	0.3194
Vietnam, 1992–93	0.3440	0.1996	0.1690

— Not available.
Source: Glewwe 1986, 1987; Glewwe and Twum-Baah 1991; Statistical Institute of Jamaica 1989.

Table 2.5 Inequality in Vietnam, 1992–93

Region or group	Inequality indicator Theil T	Inequality indicator Theil L	Between-group inequality (as a percentage of total inequality)[a] Theil T	Between-group inequality (as a percentage of total inequality)[a] Theil L	Population share (percent)
All Vietnam	0.1996	0.1814			100.0
Urban and rural areas					
Urban	0.1960	0.1899	0.0443	0.0398	19.9
Rural	0.1356	0.1295	(22.2)	(22.0)	80.1
Region					
Northern Uplands	0.1096	0.1068	0.0274	0.0275	15.6
Red River Delta	0.1775	0.1556	(13.7)	(15.2)	21.6
North-Central Coast	0.1006	0.0947			12.8
Central Coast	0.1956	0.1968			11.9
Central Highlands	0.1386	0.1420			3.2
Southeast	0.2376	0.2307			12.6
Mekong Delta	0.1642	0.1546			22.4
North and south					
North	0.1583	0.1401	0.0131	0.0132	50.0
South	0.2069	0.1963	(6.5)	(7.3)	50.0
Ethnic group					
Vietnamese	0.1857	0.1679	0.0199	0.0210	84.5
Tay	0.0960	0.0865	(10.0)	(11.6)	2.0
Thai	0.1052	0.1027			1.0
Chinese	0.1780	0.1713			2.4
Khome	0.1514	0.1395			2.0
Moung	0.0720	0.0683			2.0
Nung	0.0680	0.0604			1.6
H'mong	0.0697	0.0736			0.7
Dao	0.0660	0.0647			0.3
Other	0.1713	0.1654			3.5
Employer of head					
Government	0.1831	0.1732	0.0162	0.0146	5.5
Private	0.1678	0.1542	(8.1)	(8.0)	8.6
Self-employed	0.1766	0.1612			75.1
Retired	0.2232	0.2085			6.5
Other not working[b]	0.2316	0.2223			4.2
Occupation of head					
White collar	0.2043	0.1888	0.0348	0.0331	4.6
Sales/service	0.2030	0.1865	(17.5)	(18.3)	8.1
Farming	0.1278	0.1239			64.7
Production	0.1829	0.1742			10.9
Other	0.2343	0.2401			1.0
Retired	0.2232	0.2085			6.5
Other not working[b]	0.2316	0.2223			4.2
Sex of head					
Male	0.1851	0.1690	0.0042	0.0040	77.5
Female	0.2240	0.2061	(2.1)	(2.2)	22.5

(Table continues on next page.)

Table 2.5 Inequality in Vietnam, 1992–93 (continued)

Characteristics	Inequality indicator		Between-group inequality (as a percentage of total inequality)[a]		Population share (percent)
	Theil T	Theil L	Theil T	Theil L	
Education of head					
None	0.1884	0.1885	0.0156	0.0136	11.9
Primary	0.1692	0.1563	(7.8)	(7.5)	37.5
Lower secondary	0.1844	0.1631			33.5
Upper secondary	0.1997	0.1801			12.3
Postsecondary technical	0.2484	0.2272			2.5
University	0.1856	0.1855			2.2

a. The figures in these columns refer to groups as a whole, not just the first two categories within each group.
b. This category includes unemployed heads and heads not in the labor force for reasons other than retirement.
Source: Authors' calculations, based on 1992–93 Vietnam Living Standards Survey data.

are so different, and how much is due to the fact that expenditure levels are unequal within both urban and rural areas? The two Theil inequality indices suggest that the largest source of inequality is that within urban and rural areas—only about 22 percent of overall inequality is due to differences in average expenditure levels between urban and rural areas. In other words, if per capita expenditure levels were doubled for all rural households (making them equal to mean urban per capita expenditures), overall inequality would decline only by about 22 percent.

How much does inequality in mean expenditure levels across the seven different regions in Vietnam contribute to overall inequality? Only modestly—about 14–15 percent of overall inequality. This result implies that if one could introduce policies that equalize expenditure levels across regions, but do not alter the distribution of expenditures within each region, inequality would be reduced by only 14–15 percent. Another useful way to decompose inequality in Vietnam given its recent history is to divide the country into its northern and southern halves. Table 2.5 shows that inequality is substantially higher in the southern half of Vietnam, which may reflect the north's longer history of socialist economic management. Note as well that the south is relatively better off than the north— mean per capita expenditure in the three northern regions is 1.2 million dong, compared with a mean of 1.6 million dong for the four southern regions. While this difference may appear to be large, only about 7 percent of overall inequality is due to north-south differences in mean expenditure levels—variation within the north and south accounts for 93 percent of overall inequality.

Table 2.2 showed substantial differences in mean expenditures across ethnic groups. But since Vietnamese (Kinh) make up 85 percent of the total population, there is not as much scope for ethnic differences to contribute to inequality. In fact, table 2.5 shows that they explain only 10–12 percent of overall inequality in Vietnam. This finding suggests no major role for ethnicity in understanding the nature of inequality in Vietnam. The role for differences by religious affiliation (not shown here) is even smaller—they account for less than 1 percent of overall inequality.

Another dimension on which to examine inequality is by employment characteristics of household heads. Table 2.2 showed that households headed by self-employed and private sector workers were relatively poor, yet table 2.5 shows that the contribution of such differences to overall inequality is not very large—only about 8 percent of total inequality. One reason for this is that three-quarters of the population fall into a single group, the self-employed. A larger source of inequality is differences when households are classified by the occupation of their heads—about 18 percent of overall inequality is due to such differences. This contribution is relatively large given that about 65 percent of the population falls into a single group: households in which the head works in agriculture.

Recall the unexpected finding that female-headed households are substantially better off than male-headed ones. While this difference is not very large, it is worth checking to see the role it plays in overall inequality. Table 2.5 shows that this role is minuscule—only about 2 percent of overall inequality is due to differences in the mean per capita expenditures of male- and female-headed households.

The last decomposition of overall inequality is by the education level of the household head. Differences in education levels account for about 8 percent of overall inequality. Although this figure may appear to be sizable, it is much smaller than that found in other countries. Decompositions for other countries have yielded contributions ranging from 10 percent to 35 percent.[8] This result suggests that part of Vietnam's relatively low inequality may be due to smaller differences in expenditure levels across education groups.[9] It also raises the issue of whether there are substantial returns to education in Vietnam—an issue that is taken up in later chapters of this book.

Poverty in Vietnam

In general, policymakers care about both inequality and poverty. Yet the relationship between them is complex: it is possible for poverty to decline while inequality remains stable or even rises. Chapter 1 showed that there has been a large decline in poverty in Vietnam over the past decade, regardless of what has happened to the distribution of income. The forward projections in that chapter also showed that if the recent growth of 8 percent per year continues, poverty will continue to decline, even if inequality remains stable or rises modestly. The extent to which poverty will continue to decline in the future is an open question, but in any case it is important to set a baseline for future comparisons. This section does so using the 1992–93 VNLSS data.

Measuring Poverty

Poverty means different things to different people. Perhaps the first concept that comes to mind is that poverty is the lack of a certain minimal income necessary to attain a "decent" standard of living. Poverty may also have a wider meaning, encompassing malnutrition, illiteracy, unemployment, substandard housing, and other dimensions of a low standard of living. One approach to measuring poverty is to define a minimally adequate standard of living in terms of a set of "basic needs," such as reasonably good health, adequate calorie intake, access to safe drinking water, and enough schooling to attain functional literacy. One may even include nonmaterial components such as human rights and democratic political processes.

This multidimensional approach, while intuitively appealing, raises as many questions as it answers because many people have some of their minimal needs met, but not others, and it is not clear whether such people should be classified as poor. While one might argue that any person who does not attain the minimal level in all dimensions is poor, real-life situations quickly complicate this approach. For example, some people with high incomes may suffer from poor health, but one would not usually classify them as poor. Similarly, in some low-income families many children are clearly malnourished while other low-income families have well-nourished children. This chapter measures poverty along only one dimension, per capita consumption expenditure. Later chapters focus on other aspects of household welfare.

Another methodological issue with respect to poverty measurement is how to account for the fact that some poor households have consumption levels only slightly below the poverty line, while others have much lower levels of consumption. The most common poverty indicator is the headcount measure: the proportion of individuals living in households whose consumption levels fall below the poverty line. This measure has the disadvantage of ignoring how far below the poverty line households fall. For example, if poor households became poorer over a period of time while all nonpoor households remained nonpoor, the headcount measure would not change, although intuitively one would think that poverty had worsened.

One measure of poverty that overcomes this deficiency is the "poverty gap" measure, which is defined as the average difference ("gap") between the poverty line and the (per capita) consumption level of poor households, divided by the poverty line.[10] This measure of poverty would show an increase in poverty if poor households become poorer while nonpoor households remained nonpoor. Yet even this poverty indicator has been criticized because it does not account for inequality in the gaps. For example, the level of poverty would be the same for two individuals with a gap of, say $500, as it would be for two individuals with gaps of $100 and $900, respectively. The most common way to overcome this deficiency is to use the "squared poverty gap" measure, which simply squares the poverty gaps (and divides them by the square of the poverty line).

In practice, these three indicators of poverty usually give similar results. In this chapter we use all three measures, which can be expressed using the same formula:

$$P_\alpha = \frac{1}{N} \sum_{n=1}^{N} \left(\frac{G_i}{z}\right)^\alpha \text{ where } \begin{aligned} G_i &= z - x_i \text{ if } z > x_i \\ &= 0 \quad \text{ if } z \le x_i, \end{aligned}$$

where z is the (per capita) poverty line and x_i is household per capita expenditures.[11] The headcount index is obtained by setting $\alpha = 0$,[12] while $\alpha = 1$ yields the poverty gap index, and $\alpha = 2$ yields the squared poverty gap index.

The above formula has another advantage that is useful for analyzing poverty, which is that the level of poverty within a given country is the (population) weighted average of the level of poverty measured within each region (or any other categorization that divides the population into different groups). For example, if one-fourth of the population resides in urban areas and the other three-fourths reside in rural areas, national poverty is equal to 0.25 times the incidence of poverty in urban areas plus 0.75 times the incidence of poverty in rural areas. This property allows one to (additively) decompose overall poverty into the amount of poverty pertaining to each group.

Choosing a Poverty Line

Once a poverty index has been chosen and the expenditure data are available, the remaining task is to calculate a poverty line with which to classify households as poor or nonpoor (and, for some indices, measure the poverty gap of each household). Unlike some developing countries, Vietnam does not have any long-standing official poverty line. Thus we propose our own poverty line. While it is impossible to completely avoid subjective judgments, a reasonable approach is to base the poverty line on the cost of attaining a minimal number of calories per person. We do so following the approach of Ravallion (1994).

The VNLSS data provide quantities of most food items purchased by each household, which can be used to calculate total calories consumed. Based on several studies, particularly the work of the World Health Organization (1985), we assume that, averaging over family members of different ages, a typical household member needs 2,100 calories per day. While one could design a food basket that meets this caloric requirement very cheaply,[13] such a basket would be very bland and have little relationship to what poor (or nonpoor) Vietnamese households actually consume. A more reasonable approach would be based on actual spending patterns of poor Vietnamese households. As measured in the VNLSS, the middle 20 percent of Vietnamese households (ranked by per capita expenditures) have caloric intakes of about 2,022 calories per day, which is slightly below the requirement of 2,100 calories. We take the food basket of this group, which reflects the consumption patterns of the poor, and raise it slightly (multiplying by 2,100/2,022) to create a food basket that provides exactly 2,100 calories per person per day. The cost of this basket, adjusted for different prices within Vietnam's seven regions, is the food component of the overall poverty line.

The nonfood component of the overall poverty line must also be calculated. Unfortunately, there is nothing analogous to calories from food consumed on which to base nonfood needs. Ravallion proposes two methods, both of which are based on the following regression:

$$FS_i = \alpha + \beta \ln(EX_i/FP) + e_i,$$

where FS_i is the food share (percentage of total expenditures devoted to food) of household i, EX_i is total expenditures of household i, FP is the food poverty line (cost of the basket of food that provides 2,100 calories), and e_i is an error term. The first method uses the parameter estimates from this regression to estimate how much is spent on nonfood items by a household for whom total expenditures are just equal to the food poverty line. This approach yields a "low" estimate of spending on nonfood items because such a household would reduce its food expenditures below the food poverty line by purchasing nonfood items. The second method uses the estimates of α and β to calculate the expenditure level at which the average household will spend just enough on food to purchase the minimum food requirements. Ravallion calls this a "high" estimate of nonfood needs. Separate regressions were run for urban and rural areas in each of Vietnam's seven regions. The poverty lines used throughout this book are given in table 2.6; they are simple averages of the "high" and "low" lines obtained from these regressions.

Analysis of Poverty in Vietnam

The extent and nature of poverty in Vietnam are examined in table 2.7. The headcount index indicates that nearly 55 percent of the population is poor in the sense that typical expenditure patterns imply that they do not spend enough on food to obtain 2,100 calories per person per day. Poverty is twice as high in rural areas as in urban areas (61 percent compared with 30 percent), and the difference increases as more distributionally sensitive indicators are used—the squared poverty gap index shows a level of poverty 2.5 times higher in rural areas than in urban areas. When these results are combined with the fact that about 80 percent of the population lives in rural areas, 90 percent of poverty in Vietnam is found in rural areas (see the numbers in parentheses in table 2.7). Clearly, future poverty reduction in Vietnam will primarily be a matter of reducing poverty in rural areas.

The incidence of poverty also varies by region. The three regions with the highest poverty are the North-Central Coast, the Central Highlands, and the Northern Uplands. While these three regions together account for about 32 percent of the population, they account for about 41–44 percent of poverty in Vietnam, depending on the poverty measure used. The North-Central Coast region is by far the poorest, no matter which poverty index is used. Although it accounts for only about 13 percent of the population, its share of nationwide poverty is 18–20 percent. The Southeast region, which includes Ho Chi Minh City (formerly Saigon), has the lowest incidence of poverty—it contains about 13 percent of Vietnam's population but only 7–8 percent of overall poverty. Yet even in this region poverty is widespread; the headcount index shows that about 34 percent of the population is poor.

The fact that two of Vietnam's three poorest regions (including the poorest region) are located in the northern half of the country while the wealthiest region is in the southern half suggests an examination of differences in poverty across the northern and southern halves of the country. The three northernmost regions (Northern Uplands, Red River Delta, and North-Central Coast) can be defined as the north and the other four regions can be defined as the south.[14] As one would expect, poverty is higher in the north; the headcount index shows that 63 percent of northerners are poor while 47 percent of southerners are impoverished. The other two poverty indices tell a similar story. Yet these differences are not very pronounced; with exactly half of the population the south still accounts for 43–44 percent of overall poverty in Vietnam.

What is the incidence of poverty by religion and ethnic group? The incidence by religion is similar across all religious groups (including no religion), with one exception: Protestant Christians were somewhat poorer. Yet this group constitutes only about 1 percent of the population. Since

Table 2.6 Urban and Rural Poverty Lines in Vietnam, by Region
(thousands of dong per person per year)

Region	Urban poverty line	Rural poverty line
Northern Uplands	1,359	1,043
Red River Delta	1,506	1,037
North-Central Coast	1,404	1,134
Central Coast	1,563	1,201
Central Highlands	a	1,282
Southeast	1,701	1,266
Mekong Delta	1,377	1,221

Note: These poverty lines are slightly different from those used in World Bank 1995. This is because of some minor technical errors with the poverty lines used in that report.
a. Poverty line is not needed because no households in the VNLSS sample were from the urban areas of the Central Highlands region.
Source: Authors' calculations, based on 1992–93 Vietnam Living Standards Survey data.

Table 2.7 Poverty Indexes in Vietnam, 1992–93

Region, group, or characteristic	Head count index	Poverty gap index	Squared poverty gap index	Population share (percent)
All Vietnam	0.549	0.170	0.071	100
Urban and rural areas				
Urban	0.299 (10.9)	0.085 (10.0)	0.034 (9.5)	19.9
Rural	0.611 (89.1)	0.191 (90.0)	0.080 (90.5)	80.1
Region				
Northern Uplands	0.663 (18.9)	0.210 (19.2)	0.087 (19.2)	15.6
Red River Delta	0.527 (20.7)	0.147 (18.7)	0.054 (16.3)	21.6
North-Central Coast	0.772 (18.0)	0.263 (19.8)	0.113 (20.3)	12.8
Central Coast	0.559 (12.1)	0.190 (13.3)	0.091 (15.2)	11.9
Central Highlands	0.668 (3.9)	0.231 (4.3)	0.108 (4.8)	3.2
Southeast	0.337 (7.7)	0.099 (7.3)	0.041 (7.2)	12.6
Mekong Delta	0.460 (18.8)	0.133 (17.4)	0.054 (16.9)	22.4
North and south				
North	0.632 (57.5)	0.199 (57.7)	0.079 (55.9)	50.0
South	0.466 (42.5)	0.144 (42.3)	0.063 (44.1)	50.0
Ethnic group				
Vietnamese (Kinh)	0.522 (80.3)	0.154 (76.4)	0.061 (72.8)	84.5
Tay	0.704 (2.6)	0.222 (2.7)	0.084 (2.4)	2.0
Thai	0.819 (1.5)	0.286 (1.7)	0.130 (1.8)	1.0
Chinese	0.137 (0.6)	0.037 (0.5)	0.016 (0.5)	2.4
Khome	0.729 (2.7)	0.257 (3.1)	0.121 (3.5)	2.0
Moung	0.801 (2.9)	0.253 (2.9)	0.101 (2.8)	2.0
Nung	0.771 (2.3)	0.206 (2.0)	0.068 (1.6)	1.6
H'mong	1.000 (1.2)	0.591 (2.3)	0.372 (3.5)	0.7
Dao	0.885 (0.4)	0.391 (0.6)	0.194 (0.7)	0.3
Other	0.871 (5.5)	0.383 (7.8)	0.212 (10.4)	3.5
Employer of head				
Government	0.192 (1.9)	0.049 (1.6)	0.021 (1.7)	5.5
Private	0.603 (9.4)	0.196 (9.9)	0.085 (10.2)	8.6
Self-employed	0.588 (80.5)	0.182 (80.5)	0.076 (80.6)	75.1
Retired	0.392 (4.6)	0.121 (4.6)	0.046 (4.2)	6.5
Other not working	0.457 (3.5)	0.137 (3.4)	0.056 (3.3)	4.2
Occupation of head				
White collar	0.253 (2.1)	0.059 (1.6)	0.020 (1.3)	4.6
Sales/service	0.304 (4.5)	0.074 (3.5)	0.026 (3.0)	8.1
Farming	0.645 (75.9)	0.205 (77.7)	0.087 (79.2)	64.7
Production	0.422 (8.4)	0.124 (7.9)	0.049 (7.5)	10.9
Other	0.504 (0.9)	0.216 (1.2)	0.113 (1.5)	1.0
Retired	0.392 (4.6)	0.121 (4.6)	0.046 (4.2)	6.5
Other not working	0.457 (3.5)	0.137 (3.4)	0.056 (3.3)	4.2
Sex of head				
Male	0.572 (80.7)	0.177 (80.7)	0.074 (80.9)	77.5
Female	0.469 (19.3)	0.146 (19.3)	0.060 (19.1)	22.5
Education of head				
None	0.675 (14.7)	0.260 (18.2)	0.127 (21.4)	11.9
Primary	0.569 (38.9)	0.175 (38.5)	0.073 (38.4)	37.5
Lower secondary	0.569 (34.7)	0.170 (33.4)	0.067 (31.5)	33.5
Upper secondary	0.436 (9.8)	0.114 (8.3)	0.042 (7.3)	12.3
Technical	0.306 (1.4)	0.083 (1.2)	0.031 (1.1)	2.5
University	0.144 (0.6)	0.032 (0.4)	0.010 (0.3)	2.2

Note: Figures in parentheses are the percentage of overall poverty attributed to poverty within the particular region, group, or characteristic.
Source: Authors' calculations, based on 1992–93 Vietnam Living Standards Survey data.

these figures are not very interesting, they are not presented in table 2.7. Turning to ethnic groups, the Vietnamese (Kinh) are somewhat less poor than average; although they constitute about 85 percent of the population their share of overall poverty is 73–80 percent, depending on the poverty index used. The Chinese minority has a very low rate of poverty—only about 14 percent of Chinese are classified as poor by the headcount index, and their contribution to overall poverty is a minuscule 0.6 percent. Most of the other ethnic groups are poorer than average. Together they account for 19–27 percent of poverty in Vietnam, although they make up only about 13 percent of the population.

The relationship between employment and poverty is also examined in table 2.7. Households headed by self-employed individuals or private sector workers are poorer than average. Together they account for 90–91 percent of overall poverty, while constituting about 84 percent of the population. At the other extreme, households headed by public sector employees (including employees of state-owned enterprises) have a very low incidence of poverty, almost as low as those recorded for the Chinese. Although such households constitute about 6 percent of the population, they account for only 1–2 percent of the poor. Finally, households headed by someone who is retired or not working for some other reason are less likely to be poor than average, though they are not as well-off as households headed by government workers.

The figures on poverty by the occupation of the head show that households working as farmers (this category also includes fishermen and hunters) are the poorest households in Vietnam. They account for 76–79 percent of overall poverty even though they constitute only about 65 percent of the overall population. Clearly, efforts to reduce poverty in rural areas must reach these farming households. Individuals living in households headed by white collar workers are least likely to be poor, followed by individuals in households where the head is in a sales or service occupation. Together these two groups cover about 13 percent of the population, but their share in overall poverty is only 4–7 percent. Households headed by persons employed in production occupations (construction, manufacturing, artisanal work), as well as those headed by someone who is retired or not working for some other reason, are less likely to be poor than farming households, but not as fortunate as households headed by white collar or sales and service workers.

In accordance with the figures in table 2.2, female-headed households have lower levels of poverty than households headed by males, but the difference is not very large. Still, it is clear that there is no justification for targeting female-headed households in poverty programs simply because they are headed by women (though there may be other reasons to target some or all of them).

Finally, it is instructive to examine poverty among Vietnamese households according to the education level of the head. As one would expect, the higher the level of education, the lower the incidence of poverty, no matter which of the three indices is used. Yet it is worth pointing out that the differences are not large. For example, the incidence of poverty (headcount index) among individuals in households with an uneducated head is about 68 percent, while that for individuals in households headed by someone with an upper secondary education (10–12 years of education) is not much lower, about 44 percent. Only when individuals attain postsecondary education do the levels of poverty decline substantially. This result suggests that education alone may not be a very effective way to reduce poverty. The role of education in generating income will be examined in later chapters of this book.

A Closer Examination of Regional Variation

The main finding of this chapter is that there is relatively little inequality in Vietnam, but a large amount of poverty. Inequality is low relative to other countries. Furthermore, some specific concerns about inequality are not borne out by the data. For example, the contribution of north-south differences to inequality is not very large, and differences in mean incomes among the seven regions are small compared with variation within regions.

The sharpest differences in Vietnam are between urban areas and rural areas. Within rural areas there is a surprising degree of homogeneity in terms of income and poverty. As seen in table 2.8, average real annual expenditures range from 912,000 dong to 1.4 million dong, and the headcount poverty index ranges from 45 percent to 79 percent. This lack of variation belies some of the stereotypes about Vietnam. In particular, there are several reasons to expect the south to be richer than the north. The area around Ho Chi Minh City is clearly less poor than the rest of Vietnam, as these data have shown. Furthermore, the Mekong Delta is the "rice basket" of Vietnam. With about one-fifth of the country's population, it pro-

Table 2.8 Expenditure Levels and Poverty in Rural Areas of Vietnam, by Region

Region	Mean per capita expenditure[a]	Poverty index		
		Headcount	Poverty gap	Squared poverty gap
Northern Uplands	940.8	0.694	0.224	0.094
Red River Delta	1,184.6	0.589	0.167	0.061
North-Central Coast	912.1	0.788	0.269	0.115
Central Coast	1,226.3	0.625	0.219	0.108
Central Highlands	1,121.2	0.668	0.231	0.108
Southeast	1,434.4	0.449	0.133	0.056
Mekong Delta	1,353.7	0.506	0.146	0.059
All rural areas	1,166.8	0.611	0.191	0.080

a. Mean per capita expenditure is in thousands of dong per person per year.
Source: Authors' calculations, based on 1992–93 Vietnam Living Standards Survey data.

duces nearly half of the rice crop, and all of the exportable surplus. Finally, some of the infrastructure left behind by the United States is in pretty good shape. Thus one might expect the south to be much less poor; but in fact the rural poverty rate is not much lower in the south than in the north.

To examine in more detail regional differences in rural areas of Vietnam, consider how different endowments are correlated with rural incomes, and how these endowments vary by region. Table 2.9 reports a regression of the logarithm of real per capita consumption of rural households on a vector of household and community characteristics. Leaving aside the regional dummy variables, each variable has a significant relationship with per capita consumption, with signs in the expected directions. Household consumption is positively correlated with quantity of land farmed, the household head's level of education, and access to infrastructure (irrigation, electricity, and passable roads). The t-statistics are very high: above 8 for years of schooling, quantity of land, and access to electricity; and above 5 for the impassable road variable and the local wage rate (which indicates the extent of economic opportunities outside of the household).

The relatively small regional dummy variables indicate that the most important correlates of regional differences in expenditure levels have been included in the regression. In particular, the dummies for the southern regions are all insignificant (the omitted dummy variable is that for the Southeast region). The dummies for the three northern regions, on the other hand, are significantly negative. Northern households generate about 20 percent less income than southern households that are similar in

Table 2.9 Determinants of Log per Capita Expenditure in Rural Areas of Vietnam

Variable	Coefficient	t-statistic
Constant	6.5948	132.24
Years of schooling of head	0.0187	8.44
Months road is impassable	−0.0256	−5.69
Agricultural land per capita	0.00014	16.34
Percentage of agricultural land irrigated	0.00065	3.29
Male agricultural wage rate	0.0141	5.69
Electricity	0.2208	12.16
Regional dummy variables		
Northern Uplands	−0.1688	−4.00
Red River Delta	−0.1474	−3.66
North-Central Coast	−0.2378	−5.88
Central Coast	−0.0290	−0.69
Central Highlands	0.0141	0.25
Mekong Delta	0.0177	0.49

$R^2 = 0.233$.
Number of observations = 3,256.

Source: Authors' calculations, based on 1992–93 Vietnam Living Standards Survey data.

terms of the characteristics measured. This difference may reflect the north's relative lack of experience with the market economy. The magnitude of the regional dummy is particularly large for the North Central Coast; it indicates that per capita consumption in this area is 24 percent lower than that predicted by the endowments included in the regression.

The purpose of this regression is simply to provide a framework for discussing regional differences. Recall that the variation in rural poverty rates among regions is surprisingly small. Variation by region in the endowments is shown in table 2.10. In general, there is far less dispersion in consumption levels and poverty rates than in the endowment variables used in the regression analysis. This reflects the fact that each region has different advantages and disadvantages that on balance contribute to similar rural income levels and poverty rates.

Beginning in the far south, the Mekong Delta has a surprisingly high rural poverty incidence of 51 percent, not far below the national rural poverty rate of 61 percent. The main advantage of this region is that it has a large amount of agricultural land per capita (more than double the averages of the other regions). There are, however, offsetting disadvantages. The education level—4.5 years of schooling for the average household head—is the second lowest of all the regions. Electrification is low (26 percent of households, compared with 39 percent nationally and 75 percent in the Red River Delta). Also, the share of land irrigated for year-round use is relatively low. Finally, the transport infrastructure is weak, leaving much of the delta relatively isolated (World Bank 1994). Thus the Mekong Delta's exceptional land endowment is offset by below-average human capital and deficiencies in infrastructure. While this region is the nation's rice basket, low education and poor infrastructure may hamper the expansion of economic activity into other sectors.

The other very large concentration of rural population is in the Red River Delta, and this region's endowments are an interesting contrast to those of the Mekong Delta. The rural poverty rate (59 percent) is slightly higher than that in the Mekong, and mean consumption a bit lower.

Table 2.10 Selected Characteristics of Rural Areas in Vietnam, by Region, 1992–93

Region	Schooling of head (years)	Electricity (percentage of households)	Agricultural land per capita (square meters)
Northern Uplands	6.5	36	589
Red River Delta	7.2	75	478
North-Central Coast	7.0	35	549
Central Coast	5.2	56	382
Central Highlands	4.0	21	417
Southeast	5.6	62	522
Mekong Delta	4.5	26	1,219

Source: Authors' calculations, based on 1992–93 Vietnam Living Standards Survey data.

Unlike the Mekong Delta, however, this outcome results from a very poor per capita land endowment combined with relatively good human capital and physical infrastructure. Per capita land endowment (478 square meters) is less than half the Mekong's 1,219 square meters. On the other hand, the average household head in the Red River Delta has 7.2 years of schooling compared with 4.5 years for household heads in the Mekong. In addition, virtually all of the land (87 percent) is irrigated, and electrification reaches 75 percent of households.

The Southeast region has the lowest rural poverty rate (45 percent), though it is not that much different than those of the Red River Delta and Mekong Delta. The advantages enjoyed by this region include more schooling than in other southern regions (though less than in the north) and relatively good transport and power infrastructure. Its proximity to Ho Chi Minh City is also an important advantage. The going wage in this area is well above the national average, suggesting that there are good opportunities outside of the household for generating additional income.

The Central Highlands is reputed to be a poor part of Vietnam, but in fact the incidence of rural poverty (67 percent) is only slightly higher than the national average for rural areas. The region has the lowest levels of schooling and electrification. Its low schooling reflects the high proportion of ethnic minorities, among whom school enrollment is low. Moreover, the land endowment, especially that of irrigated land, is small. The relatively high going wage, however, reflects the fact that there are opportunities outside of the household (particularly on coffee, rubber, and tea plantations). Also, the road network is surprisingly good (a legacy of the war).

The Northern Uplands is another area reputed to be poor. It turns out, however, that the region has endowments of land, irrigation facilities, electric power, and human capital very close to the national average. Thus the incidence of rural poverty is not much higher than the national average.

The region that deviates furthest from the mean in terms of rural poverty is the North-Central Coast. Its one advantage is good human capi-

Share of land irrigated (percentage)	Agricultural wage rate (thousands of dong per day)	Months road is impassable
43	6.1	0.6
87	8.4	0.2
53	8.1	0.8
58	8.6	0.6
8	11.8	0.0
31	13.4	1.2
48	14.7	0.7

tal (7 years of schooling for the average household head). However, the area is extremely densely populated, similar to the Red River Delta, but without that region's extensive irrigation network. The extent of electrification is below average (though better than in the Mekong Delta). Yet these variables alone cannot explain the region's low income. Recall that the dummy variable for this region has a large negative coefficient, indicating that its per capita expenditures are well below the level predicted by the regression based on its endowments. Indeed, the endowments of the Central Coast are not that different from those of the North-Central Coast region, yet the former has a much lower poverty rate. One factor not adequately captured in the regression is that the North-Central Coast region's transport infrastructure is probably the worst in the country. Its main north-south highway is barely passable. Furthermore, the area is particularly susceptible to damage from typhoons.

To summarize, this analysis shows that the different factors that affect rural income in Vietnam are distributed regionally in a manner that is not positively correlated. Thus land per capita is high in the south, and human capital per capita is high in the north. The availability of good transport infrastructure and power tend to go hand in hand in Vietnam, but together they are uncorrelated with the availability of irrigation facilities or human capital, and negatively correlated with the endowment of land.

As noted, this variation in endowments contributes to relatively equitable rural outcomes. The common outcome, however, is that most of the rural population is poor—just for different reasons. This fact complicates efforts to develop an effective poverty alleviation strategy for Vietnam, because it implies that the details of any strategy will have to be tailored to each region. There is no simple solution for reducing poverty in rural areas in Vietnam.

Appendix: Calculation of Total Household Expenditures

The variable for household consumption expenditures is intended to capture, as accurately as possible, all consumption of goods and services by each household in the year preceding the interview. The VNLSS contains expenditure and consumption information on various food and nonfood items. This appendix describes how this information is used to arrive at a measure of household expenditures in the 12 months preceding the interview.

Food Expenditures

Household expenditures on food items is available from sections 11A and 11B of the household questionnaire (in-kind wages received as meals are collected in sections 4B and 4E, but their calculation is described later). In Vietnam the lunar new year (Tet) represents a considerable departure from normal spending patterns. Food expenditure information during Tet and other holidays (hereafter simply referred to as Tet) is collected separately in section 11A. Nonholiday expenditure information is available in section 11B.

It is assumed that Tet expenditures cover a two-week period.[15] For 18 food items or categories, information is available on the quantity and value of market purchases. For these same foods, information is also available on the quantity consumed out of home production and the value of this quantity had it been purchased in the market. The data on the value of market purchases and the value of home production consumed by the household are included in household expenditures, as described below.

Value of annual market purchases. Section 11B contains nonholiday food expenditure information on 45 food items. Data are obtained on the value of purchases made since the first interview, the quantity and value of market purchases in the preceding 12 months, and the quantity and value of foods consumed out of home production in the past 12 months. Information on market purchases in the last 12 months is obtained as follows. The respondents are asked for the number of months during which market purchases were made. They are then asked for the number of purchases made during these months. To allow for differences in purchase frequency, both across food items and across respondents, respondents can provide information on purchase frequency for one of six different recall periods separately for each item. Respondents then provide the information on the average quantity and value of a typical purchase. This information—months of purchase, number of purchases, recall period, and value of a typical purchase—is used to obtain the value of nonholiday market food expenditures in the 12 months preceding the interview.

Value of home-produced foods consumed during the year. Information on foodstuffs produced and consumed by the household is obtained as follows. Respondents are asked for the number of months during which the food item is consumed, the total quantity consumed (during these months), and the value of such consumption if it were to be purchased in the market. Calculation of annual expenditures on home production is then done in a manner similar to that done for food purchased in the market.

Nonfood Expenditures

Nonfood expenditures include expenditures on clothing, footwear, personal care, entertainment and recreation, transportation, housing supplies, housing, furniture, household appliances, other consumer durables, education, and health. Most of this information is from section 12 of the questionnaire, but some of it also comes from sections 2, 3, and 6.

Daily expenses. Section 12A contains information on 14 frequently purchased nonfood items. These include expenditures on cigarettes, tobacco, areca nut, cooking fuel, soap and detergents, and parking fees in the four weeks preceding the interview. Annual expenditures on these items is obtained by multiplying four-week expenditures by 13. The one item excluded from household expenditures is lottery tickets. These expenses are excluded because they enhance well-being only when a household wins the lottery, and in that case the amount won is likely to be reflected in increased expenditures on other goods.

Annual expenses. Less frequent nonfood expenditure information is obtained in section 12B. Information is obtained on expenditures in the two weeks since the first interview, as well as in the past 12 months. This section includes expenditures on cloth, ready-made clothing, blankets, footwear, tailoring services, pots and pans, household supplies, housing materials, motorcycle and bicycle tires, tubes and spare parts, public transportation fees, books and stationery, recreation, and taxes. Since annual expenditures are directly available for each item, no calculations are needed. The following items in this section are excluded because they do not increase economic well-being: income taxes, security funds, social funds (aging, charity), insurance, gifts, and transfers. The following items are excluded because spending on them is likely to be reflected in the current value of the relevant consumer durables, expenditures on which are treated separately: purchase materials to build a new house, other expenses for building a new house, home repairs and maintenance, tires and spare parts for bicycles and motorcycles, and maintenance expenses for vehicles other than gasoline and oil.

Consumer durables. Consumer durables provide a flow of services over many years, thus it is misleading to include annual expenditures on them to measure a household's standard of living over one year. Excluding these expenditures is also inappropriate since they do improve a household's economic well-being. What one would like is a measure of the value of services provided by consumer durables, that is, their "use value" in the 12 months preceding the interview. To obtain a measure of "use value" what is needed is the price at which the durable was purchased, the length of time the household has been in possession of the item, the durable's current value, and the interest rate. Based on these three variables, along with a price index for deriving real values for purchase price and current value, one can construct a measure of the monetary value of services derived from consumer durables. These data are all available from section 12 of the household questionnaire.

One constructs the use value as follows. The first step consists of deriving depreciation rates for each type of consumer durable. The relationship between the real value of a good at the time it was bought (VB) and its real value at the time of the interview (VT) is:

$$VT = VB \, (1 - d)^t,$$

where t is the number of years since purchase and d is the depreciation rate. Since the survey collects information on purchase price, resale value at the time of the interview, and year of purchase, it is possible to derive the implicit depreciation rate for each type of consumer durable for each household. Specifically, the depreciation rate can be derived from the formula above as:

$$d = 1 - (VT/VB)^{1/t}.$$

To minimize the influence of errors and biases in self-reported resale values and purchase prices, the median depreciation rate for each type of consumer durable is used. These depreciation rates were calculated using only consumer durables acquired after 1986. This was done because there are no reasonable price indices for earlier years, which are necessary for converting nominal purchase prices into real values. The second step consists of using the depreciation rate along with the real interest rate to obtain the annual use value of a durable good in order to measure the opportunity cost to the owner of using the good for one year, instead of selling it at the beginning of the year and investing the money at the real interest rate. Therefore, use value is obtained as:

$$\text{Use value} = VT \, (1 + d) \, (d + 0.05),$$

where 0.05 is an estimate of the real interest rate and $VT \, (1 + d)$ is the value of the consumer durable 12 months before the interview.

Utilities. Section 6 contains information on housing characteristics and expenses. Expenditures on electricity and water are obtained from this section. Similar information is also obtained for household payments for garbage disposal services. For all of these expenditures, the information reported is scaled up (if the reporting period is less than a year) to obtain annual expenditure figures.

Rent. For households that rent their dwelling, rental expenditures for the year are clearly their housing expenses. For households that live in dwellings they own, the true cost of living in the owned dwelling is not zero, but the opportunity cost of living in that dwelling. If there is a competitive rental market for dwellings, then the rental amount paid by households that rent their dwelling can likely serve as an accurate measure of the opportunity cost of living in similar dwellings. This information can also be used to impute a rent for those who live in dwellings they own. The usual procedure is to run a regression of rental values on housing characteristics and then use the coefficients from such a regression to impute rental values for those who do not rent their dwellings. Unfortunately, in the Vietnamese case it is not possible to use this procedure because only 309 households live in dwellings that they do not own. More important, only 17 of these households rent from private persons, that is, parties other than the government and relatives, and almost all of these are concentrated in or near Ho Chi Minh City. Thus for all practical purposes there is no competitive rental market for housing in the country. However, a similar approach uses information in section 6 on the value of the dwelling for all households—owners as well as renters. On average, those that rent their dwelling from private persons pay an annual rent that is approximately 3 percent of the current value of the dwelling. This ratio is used as a guide to obtain the "use value" of dwellings. This ratio is also reasonable with respect to the real interest rate prevailing in the economy. Instead of applying this ratio to the reported value of a dwelling, a predicted housing value is derived from a regression of housing value on various housing characteristics. The ratio is applied to that predicted value, since reported values are likely to have substantial random variation related to respondent knowledge and other factors.

Education and health. Household expenditures on education (including expenditures on foreign language courses) for each household member are obtained in section 2 of the survey. Section 3 contains information on health expenses during the 12 months preceding the interview for each member of the household.

In-kind wages. Wages received in-kind are a form of household consumption not measured elsewhere and therefore should be included in household expenditures. In sections 4B and 4E detailed information is available on wages and different types of compensations received for primary employment in the seven days preceding the interview and the 12 months preceding the interview. The latter information is available only when primary employment in the 12 months preceding the interview is different from employment in the seven days preceding the interview. In-kind compensation from secondary employment cannot be included because only total earnings are recorded for secondary employment. Data on in-kind compensation can be reported for different time periods—day, week, month, quarter, half-year, and year. This in-kind wage data is annualized on the basis of labor supply information, that is, by multiplying it by the number of hours, days, or weeks worked in the previous year.

Notes

   1. For a general description of LSMS surveys, see Grosh and Glewwe (1995, 1998).
   2. The head of household is the person identified by the household members as being the head. In most cases it is the person who is the main income earner.

3. For further discussion of the relative merits of income and consumption data for measuring household welfare, see Deaton (1997). In the case of Vietnam using income data yields results similar to those obtained using consumption data. In particular, the figures in table 2.2 were calculated using income data and all the main findings were unchanged.

4. A related issue is the use of publicly provided health and education services, which are subsidized by the government. Calculating the value of these subsidies for each household surveyed in the 1992–93 VNLSS is a major task and is not done here. However, adding the value of these subsidies to total household consumption is unlikely to change the results because parents who send their children to public schools pay a variety of costs that are not much lower than the costs of sending children to private schools (see Glewwe and Patrinos 1998), most health consultations are with private providers, and health and education expenditures together account for only 8–9 percent of total expenditures.

5. Since some household members, such as children, may have fewer material needs than others, such as adults, we would like to use adult equivalence scales to take this into account when dividing total consumption by household size. Unfortunately, there is no generally accepted method for estimating equivalence scales (Deaton 1997), so they are not used. Note that one implication of the lack of credible equivalence scales is that one should not compare households of different sizes to see whether large or small households are better off. To see whether the use of equivalence scales affected other types of comparisons, an admittedly arbitrary set of equivalence scales was used to generate "equivalence-scale-adjusted" figures for table 2.2. No major changes were found in any of the results.

6. The other reasons for not working are as follows: about 60 percent were chronically sick or handicapped, about 20 percent were engaged in housework, about 8 percent reported that they did not want to work, about 4 percent said that no work was available or that they did not know how to look for work, and the rest gave a variety of other reasons. Note that very few could be classified as unemployed.

7. See Sen (1983) for an attempt to define poverty in relative terms.

8. The following numbers are from the studies cited in table 2.4: Côte d'Ivoire, 32–37 percent; Ghana, 10 percent; Jamaica, 9–11 percent; and Peru, 25 percent.

9. Note that the other country in table 2.4 with a relatively low level of inequality, Ghana, also has a relatively low contribution of education to overall inequality.

10. This gap is set to zero for nonpoor households. The average gap includes all the "zero gaps" of nonpoor households.

11. This class of poverty indices was first introduced by Foster, Greer, and Thorbecke (1984).

12. Note that any nonzero number to the power of zero equals one, but zero to the power of zero equals zero.

13. This was first pointed out by Stigler (1945).

14. This division is fairly close to the division of Vietnam into two distinct countries, North Vietnam and South Vietnam, between 1954 and 1975.

15. Consultations during the questionnaire design stage indicated that this was a reasonable assumption to make.

References

Atkinson, Anthony. 1970. "On the Measurement of Inequality." *Journal of Economic Theory* 2(3): 244–63.

Deaton, Angus. 1997. *The Analysis of Household Surveys: A Microeconometric Approach to Development Policy*. Baltimore, Md.: Johns Hopkins University Press.

Foster, James, Joel Greer, and Erik Thorbecke. 1984. "A Class of Decomposable Poverty Measures." *Econometrica* 52(3): 761–65.

Glewwe, Paul. 1986. *The Distribution of Welfare in Côte d'Ivoire in 1985*. Living Standards Measurement Study Working Paper 29. Washington, D.C.: World Bank.

———. 1987. *The Distribution of Welfare in Peru in 1985–86*. Living Standards Measurement Study Working Paper 42. Washington, D.C.: World Bank.

Glewwe, Paul, and Harry Patrinos. 1998. *The Role of the Private Sector in Education in Vietnam: Evidence from the 1992–93 Vietnam Living Standards Survey*. Living Standards Measurement Study Working Paper 132. Washington, D.C.: World Bank.

Glewwe, Paul, and Kwaku A. Twum-Baah. 1991. *The Distribution of Welfare in Ghana in 1987–88*. Living Standards Measurement Study Working Paper 75. Washington, D.C.: World Bank.

Grosh, Margaret, and Paul Glewwe. 1995. *A Guide to Living Standards Measurement Study Surveys and Their Data Sets*. Living Standards Measurement Study Working Paper 120. Washington, D.C.: World Bank.

———. 1998. "The World Bank's Living Standards Measurement Study Household Surveys." *Journal of Economic Perspectives* 12 (1): 187–96.

Ravallion, Martin. 1994. "Poverty Comparisons." *Fundamentals in Pure and Applied Economics* 56. Chur, Switzerland: Harwood Academic Press.

Sen, Amartya. 1983. "Poor, Relatively Speaking." *Oxford Economic Papers* 35(2): 153–69.

Statistical Institute of Jamaica. 1989. "Jamaica Survey of Living Conditions, July 1989." Kingston, Jamaica.

Stigler, George. 1945. "The Cost of Subsistence." *Journal of Farm Economics* 72: 304–14.

Theil, Henri. 1967. *Economics and Information Theory*. Amsterdam: North-Holland.

World Bank. 1993. *The East Asian Miracle: Economic Growth and Public Policy*. New York: Oxford University Press.

———. 1994. "Viet Nam: Transport Sector Review." Report 12778-VN. East Asia and Pacific Region, Washington, D.C.

———. 1995. "Viet Nam: Poverty Assessment and Strategy." Report 13442-VN. East Asia and Pacific Region, Washington, D.C.

World Health Organization. 1985. "Energy and Protein Requirements." WHO Technical Report Series 724. Geneva.

3

Agriculture and Rural Poverty in Vietnam

Thomas B. Wiens

The chapter uses the 1992–93 Vietnam Living Standards Survey to help develop a program that will alleviate rural poverty.

Reforming Institutions in Rural Vietnam

Vietnam is unique among transition economies for the thoroughness, speed, and success of its institutional reforms. The success was particularly manifest in agriculture—domestic supply and demand remained largely in equilibrium while the country transformed overnight from rice importer to major rice exporter. By decree, the government followed the Chinese path of restoring full land use rights and management authority to farm households, eliminating most powers of the commune or cooperative. Private trade and production swelled to more than offset contraction of the state sector. In the absence of external assistance, however, this success came about at the expense of severe unemployment and net disinvestment (mainly failure to maintain or augment infrastructure), which affected urban and industrial areas more than rural areas.

A series of fundamental reforms known as the renovation program (*doi moi*) were implemented beginning in 1988 and were largely complete by the time of the 1992–93 Vietnam Living Standards Survey (World Bank 1993, 1994). Those that had the greatest impact on rural areas included:

- Dismantling the collective system and returning agriculture to family farming on the basis of long-term leases.
- Abandoning administered pricing.
- Devaluing the exchange rate and maintaining a managed float,

exposing the farm sector to levels and fluctuations in international prices.

- Partitioning the single state bank into sectoral banks, including an agricultural bank offering credit not only to state enterprises and collectives but also to individual family farms at positive and roughly nondiscriminatory real interest rates.
- Reducing the size of public sector employment, including the size of the military, and nearly eliminating direct subsidies to state enterprises, including state farms, resulting in the contraction of wage-earning opportunities for rural families and the return of many dismissed employees to farming.
- Giving formal recognition, legal status, and encouragement to the private sector, which absorbed other former state employees.

A 1988 Politburo resolution and its implementing regulations made farm households in the cooperative sector entirely responsible for production and sales decisions, leaving taxes and fees their only obligations to the government. The cooperatives, no longer having direct production management responsibilities, were expected to become service agencies assisting farm households. The government retained the law that land could be owned only by the state but permitted usufruct rights to assume a significance similar to that of ownership rights in nonsocialist countries. Long-term (usually 15 years for agriculture), nontransferable tenure rights were sanctioned, and most farmers in the north received allocations of land (though only a small percentage received formal land use certificates). In the south, although cooperatives were put in place, most never assumed full control over land tenure or management, and the reforms have generally restored the status quo of private farming.

Despite the nominal lack of transferability, a land market developed secretly in which transactions are not formally registered. A 1993 Land Law passed by the National Assembly formalized and rationalized this process already under way, by acknowledging the right to sell or lease land, mortgage or inherit land use rights, and receive compensation for transfers based on market prices, with agricultural land tenure of 20 years for annual crops and 50 years for perennials (renewable). An ancillary legal framework still had to be developed to maximize the utility of legalized land use rights and tenure.

A further series of directives facilitated the development of product markets. A directive abolishing internal barriers to trade was among the earliest liberalizations. No direct legal barriers to entry in domestic wholesale or retail trade remain. Until 1989 prices and procurement of major agricultural commodities were administratively controlled and, following the Soviet and Chinese models, used to subsidize food supplies to urban residents and industrial workers, and to cover the bureaucracy's large overhead. Subsidies for food supplies were phased out in 1988–89, and grain prices were unified at market rates. Excellent rice harvests since 1988 and sharp reductions of excess stock holdings by farmers and the state eliminated shortages in staple food and put downward pressure on market prices, facilitating a smooth transition. As state dominance in the marketing system for rice, fertilizer, and most cash crops diminished, "guidance pricing" relaxed, and private traders resumed their marketing activities, Vietnam became a true market economy.

Until 1990 the Soviet Union was the largest source of finance to Vietnamese farmers. It advanced fertilizer and other inputs to the government, which passed them through to farmers in return for commodities at harvest time. The elimination of this source of national working capital and a drastic contraction of budgetary subsidies to state trading firms have made liquidity the central problem in the agricultural marketing system. Although state trading firms still supply inputs and purchase agricultural products, most trade is now carried out on a cash-and-carry basis at market prices, and the banking system—particularly the new Agricultural Bank of Vietnam—has become the main formal source of working capital. Today the private sector obtains credit largely from personal resources and the informal market, supplemented by pass-throughs from the state trading and processing enterprises. Private producers and traders have access to formal credit, but private borrowing from state banks has been constrained by collateral requirements and limited branches. Real interest rates of formal sector loans were raised to positive levels to combat inflation, though they remain well below informal market rates.

Characterizing Rural Poverty

The causes of rural poverty include geography—natural endowments of land and climate that affect agricultural productivity, density of settlement, level of infrastructure development, and extent of opportunities outside agriculture—and household circumstance—different endowments of land and resources such as human and financial capital. Separating geographic from household influences and further distinguishing natural from human-made causes of poverty should be helpful in both targeting and specifying an effective strategy to reduce poverty.

This section pays equal attention to geographical and household influences. Where possible, geographic factors are measured as average characteristics of the sampled communities. Otherwise, the seven regions—groupings of provinces based on location and ecological characteristics—are taken as proxies for geographical influences. Household expenditure quintiles are taken as proxies for income and poverty status, and the terms "poor" and "wealthy" are used to describe the lowest and highest household quintiles (although more than half of rural households fall below the poverty line).

Location and Economic Environment

Rural poverty is associated with geography (table 3.1). The Northern Uplands, Red River Delta, North-Central Coast, and Central Coast are the poorest regions, with the North-Central Coast the worst-off of the group. The ranking of the remaining regions depends on the poverty measure— percentage of households in the lowest quintile, average income per household, or per capita food availability. Low land productivity, limited commercialization, and lack of off-farm earning opportunities are among the most important factors associated with poverty. To provide a context for a disaggregated look at the 1992–93 Vietnam Living Standards Survey sample, some underlying natural influences are enumerated below:[1]

Northern Uplands. This region is composed of 12 northern provinces with hilly-to-mountainous terrain, mostly outside the Red River Delta. The climate is suitable for a wide range of crops, though low sunlight and temperatures are constraining during January–March, especially at higher altitudes. Except in the lowlands, cropping is extensive, with upland rice, maize, and tubers dominating sloping areas. Poverty is broadly associated with three groups: ethnic minorities in remote areas engaged in subsistence production; households whose holdings of level, irrigable land are small relative to household size, even if sloping or nonirrigable areas are larger; and former state farm workers or military settlers producing perennials or timber in unproductive or remote areas.

Red River Delta. This region comprises seven provinces, including the municipal provinces of Hanoi and Haiphong. The climate is similar to that of the Northern Uplands, though less constrained by cold winter temperatures. Much of the farmland is fertile, irrigated alluvial soil, and rice is the main crop (sometimes followed by maize, tubers, or cabbage). Water is a constraint in the winter, and drainage a problem in the summer, leading to a low multiple-cropping ratio. A population density

Table 3.1 Rural Poverty's Link to Geography in Vietnam, 1992–93
(thousands of Vietnamese dong)

Region	Percentage in lowest quintile	Rural income (per household)	Per capita food consumption	Output per hectare	Crop sales (per household)	Off-farm wage income (per household)
Northern Uplands	30	5,520	620	47,392	525	283
Red River Delta	15	5,351	624	64,366	550	334
Southeast	15	8,212	841	65,347	2,108	1,699
North-Central Coast	31	3,883	571	44,776	418	211
Central Highlands	20	7,217	715	53,696	3,466	766
Central Coast	19	4,752	687	39,225	401	777
Mekong Delta	13	8,208	740	283,205	2,687	1,335

Source: 1992–93 Vietnam Living Standards Survey.

exceeding 1,000 people per square kilometer is the most important regionwide constraint.

North-Central Coast. This region is long and narrow, consisting of six provinces. It suffers from moisture deficit due to blockage by the mountains along the western border, and from exposure to typhoons moving in from the east and southeast. Paddy rice is the main crop, and overall cropping intensity is low for want of irrigation. Population densities are high only along the coast, but arable land is limited and households with small land allocations and limited irrigated area are among the poorest of the rural poor in Vietnam.

Central Coast. This region shares most of the limiting geographic influences of the North-Central Coast, and its agriculture is also similar. Its agricultural productivity is in fact lower, but the territory is less mountainous, being predominantly coastal. It lacks the concentration of subsistence-oriented shifting cultivators found in the North Central Coast and enjoys better access to southern food surpluses, which it pays for with its higher levels of off-farm income.

Central Highlands. This region includes four provinces with high-elevation, mountainous terrain. One of these provinces was not represented in the Vietnam Living Standards Survey data. The Central Highlands have the highest share of ethnic minorities (50 percent), the highest share of its population born outside the region (45 percent), low overall population density and, consequently, large average landholdings. Adequate rainfall, a relatively temperate climate, and lack of irrigation (and low potential for more) favor perennial crops and vegetables, which account for the majority of the land area. This has been a frontier area absorbing population surpluses from the north, and poverty may be associated with the difficulty migrants have in getting established with minimal government assistance.

Southeast. This region consists of five provinces, including the urban province of Ho Chi Minh City, which makes up half of the region's total population. The climate is tropical monsoonal, with warm temperatures and high humidity prevailing during most of the year. The area, partly moist and partly arid, has correspondingly mixed cropping, with perennials and legumes ranking high and irrigated land being relatively scarce. Nevertheless, cropping intensity is high. This region benefits from a high degree of industrialization and urbanization, with concomitant opportunities for off-farm income generation.

Mekong Delta. This region includes six densely populated (400 people per square kilometer) provinces. The tropical monsoonal climate and natural flood irrigation on alluvial soil permit very high cropping intensity and high productivity in annual crops (mainly rice). On unirrigated areas sugarcane, tropical fruit, and other perennials are grown. Farm sizes are relatively large, though unequal, permitting substantial commercial surpluses. Poverty is mainly associated with households' lack of land rights.

Land Quality and Tenure

The limited amount of farmland available to rural households is the main cause of rural poverty in Vietnam. But it is not as important in accounting for interhousehold differences in income in every region. Farm size is largest in the south, where it is an average of 1.2 hectares in the Central Highlands and 1.0 hectare in the Mekong Delta. It is little more than one-third of a hectare in the Red River Delta—roughly equal to the cultivated area per household in nearby provinces of south China. Unequal access to land among households in the same area and the correlation of land access with poverty is notable in the south, especially in the Mekong Delta, where average farm size of the lowest rural quintile (hereafter referred to as poor households) was about 35 percent of that of the highest quintile (hereafter referred to as wealthy households). In the north, where redistribution in the course of land reform was quite thorough, wealthy households have smaller farms than poor households, and in the Red River Delta farm size varies little across quintiles.

Farm area includes irrigated and nonirrigated land in annual crops, land in perennials, ponds, and land with miscellaneous uses such as swidden, wooded, idle (or pasture), (newly) reclaimed, and riverbank land. Irrigated and perennial land, along with ponds (if exploited for raising fish), might be termed "high-productivity land" and the miscellaneous land as "low-productivity," with nonirrigated annual land lying between the two extremes. However, the impact of variations in natural conditions and farming techniques belies the simplicity of this distinction.

Still, these categories are useful in summarily indicating qualitative differences in landholdings by region and across quintiles. Very little farm area is taken up by low-productivity land in either the Red River or Mekong Deltas—most farm area is high-productivity land. On the other hand, the apparent advantages in the Northern Uplands and the Central Highlands of farms that are larger than those of adjacent regions are offset by their possession of much low-productivity and little high-productivity land (although upland area devoted to vegetables around Dalat in the Central Highlands, for example, could have extremely high productivity if appropriate choices as to crops, input levels, technique, and furrow irrigation were made).

Moreover, within the Northern Uplands, Central Coast, and Central Highlands intraregional land quality differences play an important role in accentuating inequality. That is, subsistence or swidden farmers and immigrants farming reclaimed land in the more remote or inland parts of these regions tend to be among the poorest households, whereas the wealthiest farm households are either lowlanders with healthy shares of land in irrigated rice or are specialized in perennial cash crops. By contrast, the quality distribution of land is just as equal in the Red River Delta and North-Central Coast as the overall size of holdings, which has implications for the potential extent of commercialization, specialization, and development of a wage labor market.

The survey distinguished several forms of land tenure:

- Allocated land (29 percent of annual, perennial, and forest land),[2] which was probably distributed in the course of decollectivization by cooperatives or state farms under leases of 15 years or more. Hence such land is nearly absent in the Southeast and the Mekong Delta.
- Long-term-use land (34 percent), which in the north was probably land long allocated for management by individual families, mainly for vegetables and animal feed. In the south, where most of this type of land is found, households probably had no pre-revolutionary claim to it.
- Auctioned land (2 percent), found exclusively in the north, where it was retained by cooperatives and auctioned to households for a definite and limited term. Examples include land seasonally flooded, fishponds, and orchards.
- Private land (20 percent), which was land that was probably never collectivized, and thus is least common in the Red River Delta and the North-Central Coast.
- Land rented in or out (5 percent).
- Swidden land (8.5 percent).
- Sharecropped land (4 percent), identified for perennial crops only and found only in the south.

In view of past experience in Vietnam, the relationship between the form of tenure and farmers' sense of tenure security may be ambiguous and the enabling legal framework incomplete. It is noteworthy that only about 11 percent of land is now held under nominally short-term arrangements. Most of this land is found in the Southeast and the Mekong Delta. Land reportedly farmed under short-term arrangements (not counting swidden) is in fact a larger portion of the total farm area for the wealthy (12 percent) than for the poor (5 percent), and may represent a means whereby better-off farmers expand their scale of operation. Swidden, on the other hand, is common in the Northern Uplands, the Central Coast, the Central Highlands, and the Southeast, and most common among the poor. Finally, reported land sales show no correlation with income, implying that no trend toward land concentration due to forced sales by the poor is yet observable.

Labor and Dependents

Since poverty is defined here mainly in terms of per capita expenditures, a larger family size should increase the likelihood of being poor. And indeed it does—wealthy households tend to be one person smaller than poor households (the correlation with quintile status is –0.14). However, larger households may have greater labor power, the earnings of which could help offset the cost of dependents.

The dependency ratio of household members to labor power also must be examined. It has a higher negative correlation with quintile status (–0.25), and across almost all regions falls from 2.0 for the poorest quintiles to 1.5 for the wealthiest. The exception is the Central Highlands, where there is no correlation, probably because young immigrant households with few dependents are so prevalent. In these measurements household size has not been adjusted to consumer equivalents, but labor power is an estimate of potential labor. The dependency ratio usually varies over the life cycle of the household, rising in the childbearing period and falling as children mature. Although the relationship with poverty will not be explored further here, it should be kept in mind that some of the variation in per capita expenditures may reflect stages in the household life cycle rather than permanent phenomena.

Labor is a productive resource only if it is occupied, and the small size of farms in Vietnam makes it unlikely that farm work will fully employ household labor. Does underemployment or seasonal unemployment contribute to rural poverty? By comparing the reported number of on- and off-farm labor days with an estimate of potential labor days we can construct a rough index of the underemployment rate of the household.[3] It is assumed that time not absorbed in production could be used for economic benefit in another way. But in fact measured underemployment includes women whose time is absorbed in housework and child care, students over 10 years old attending school, and the sick or handicapped. Moreover, leisure time (especially of women and youth) might be expected to be positively correlated with household income, and might also differ according to regional culture. Indeed, a tabulation of rural individual responses to Vietnam Living Standards Survey questions about unemployment and job seeking implies that either complete or seasonal unemployment or active job search among the employed or unemployed are very rare and distributed fairly evenly across quintile groups. For these reasons the relationships of this index to geography and quintile status are hard to predict.

Estimated underemployment is strongly negatively correlated with quintile status in the Red River Delta, Central Coast, Central Highlands, and Southeast but less consistently so elsewhere. In the listed regions, the poorest may have 29–54 percent "idle time," and the richest 0–17 percent. Thus inability to fully use their most abundant resource seems to be a clear handicap of the poor. But the regional differences in underemployment are not obviously related to regional poverty rankings. The wealthiest regions have relatively high index values, and the Northern Uplands, one of the poorest regions, an exceptionally low value, 13 percent compared with 37 percent in the Southeast and 32 percent in the Mekong Delta. In the Northern Uplands the prevalence of swidden and reclamation of formerly forested land suggests that labor power may constrain farm size, rather than farm size constraining labor absorption. In the Mekong Delta a high index value of underemployment (25 percent) among the richest households implies that voluntary unemployment is an important explanation.

Rural households in Vietnam generally depend heavily on off-farm wage and self-employment labor to supplement earnings from farming. The average share of household labor engaged in off-farm wage labor and self-employment ranges from 16 percent in the Northern Uplands to 57 percent in the Southeast, and falls between 27 and 46 percent in other regions. This share is positively correlated with per capita expenditure ($r > 0.2$) in all regions except the Southeast and the Mekong Delta, where many of the poorest households are actually or virtually landless, and where on average, the poor devote more than 40 percent of their labor to off-farm activities. Off-farm activities are least important among the poor in the Northern Uplands and North-Central Coast (8 and 19 percent of labor power, respectively). Thus it is arguable that off-farm activities are a path to wealth accumulation rather than a vent for surplus labor.

No significant relationship was found between the "endowed" labor-land ratio (potential family labor divided by farm size) and either poverty status or percentage of off-farm employment, even controlling for region. This result implies that:

- Variations in demand may be more constraining than variations in supply. For example, the poor are concentrated in communities where relatively few individuals possess jobs in nearby factories (presumably because of the absence of such factories).
- To a large extent farm size has been "adjusted" to the potential labor supply through clearing (in swidden areas), reclamation (in newly settled areas, like the Central Highlands), redistribution by the cooperatives or state farms, land rental, or land sale. This is not to say that this adjustment is sufficient to fully employ the household labor force (except perhaps in the Northern Uplands), but that unequal distribution of land does not account for variations in dependence on off-farm activities.

Infrastructure

If only because of its prevalence in remote and isolated areas, poverty is correlated with deficiencies in infrastructure.[4] The correlation is apparent for a number of quantitative indicators within and across regions, although there are anomalies:

- Sampled rural communities were usually accessible by road (86 percent), and the exceptions, 11 kilometers away from a road on average, were exclusively found in the Northern Uplands, the North-Central Coast, and the Mekong Delta (the Mekong Delta being a unique case, because of the importance of canal and river transport). In all three areas poor communities are on average farther away from the nearest road than are other communities.
- Where there are roads, their condition, as measured by the number of months for which the road is impassable, were best in the Red River Delta and the Central Highlands; and within every region except the Mekong Delta, the poorest communities had the worst roads. But roads were seasonally impassable in only 17 percent of all communities. And, for these, the roads were impassable for an average of 3.5 months per year.
- More than half of all rural communities have local access to public transport, but it is least frequently available to communities in the Northern Uplands, the Red River Delta, the North-Central Coast, and the Mekong Delta (the last relying main on private water transport), and only in the Red River Delta and the Central Coast is access negatively correlated with community income levels.
- The distance to the nearest source of public transport is greatest in the Northern Uplands, the North-Central Coast, and the Mekong Delta (6.3–8.4 kilometers away, on average). In the Northern Uplands, the Red River Delta, and the Central Coast the poorer communities are usually farthest from public transport.
- Electricity is available to some households in 88 percent of rural communities, and to most households in 47 percent of communities. Electrification of the majority of households in a community is most common in the Red River Delta (81 percent of communities) and least common in the Mekong Delta (16 percent). Except in that region, poor communities are less likely than the average to be fully electrified, though the bias is substantial only in the Northern Uplands, the Central Coast, and the Central Highlands.
- About 65 percent of communities had access to either a permanent or periodic local market, though least frequently in the Northern Uplands and the North-Central Coast.

What all this adds up to will be clearer when multivariate relationships have been explored (below). In general, infrastructure deficiencies account in part for the severe poverty in the Northern Uplands and the North-Central Coast and some of the differences in income among communities within regions.

Farm Production

Most rural income, for all except the wealthiest families, comes from farming. Most farm income is derived from crop production, and crop production is dominated by paddy rice production. Nationwide, farmers grow an average of 1.6 crops a year on their landholdings (including land in annual and perennial crops)—that is, the area sown or harvested is about 160 percent of the cultivated area (ranging from a low of 81 percent in the Central Highlands to 208 percent in the Red River Delta). There is no marked difference in cropping intensity by quintile, though in every region the poorest quintile farms less intensively than the second quintile, and in several regions cropping intensity is clearly positively related to income.

Of the cropped area, 77 percent is paddy rice (89 percent of all food-grains and tubers); only 11 percent is used for vegetables, legumes, and annual cash crops. The poorest farmers are concentrated slightly more on foodgrains and tubers (86 percent) than the richest quintile (81 percent). But the biggest difference between class extremes is in the share of rice: 76 percent for the poorest quintile versus 95 percent for the richest.

Most of these differences in land allocations among crops and cropping intensity are more a result of climatic factors than economic choice—more of the poor live in upland areas or the north, and more of the rich live in the warm, productive south (nationwide, the portion of irrigated farm area varies only from 27 percent for the poorest to 34 percent for the wealthiest families). Insofar as diversification is associated with higher income levels—the portion of sown area devoted to annual crops other than foodgrains and tubers rises from 14 percent to 19 percent, moving from lowest to highest quintile, and the absolute area sown doubles—it occurs within a small portion of total farm area and is much less significant than the difference associated with paddy rice production (from 65 percent to 77 percent of sown area, and absolute area almost doubled).

Examining the value of crop production does not change these conclusions. The rural wealthy produce crops valued at 2.5 times those of the poor, and their rice production is 2.3 times higher. Production value for crops other than grains and tubers increases by more than 320 percent moving from the poorest to the wealthiest quintile, and the share of gross value rises from 21 percent to 35 percent. The appropriate inference is that diversification occurs along with generation of substantial surpluses of paddy rice, not at the expense of staple food production. It is obvious, however, that this process increases output value disproportionately.

Both gross crop productivity and input intensity, measured as gross value and cost of production per cultivated hectare, differ systematically among regions and income groups. The regional differences are partly attributable to differences in price, but when these are accounted for it still appears that productivity is substantially higher in the Red River Delta than in the Mekong Delta and lowest in the Central Highlands (due to lack of irrigation). When other locality characteristics are controlled for, rice prices in the Northern Uplands and the Red River Delta are about 30 percent and 20 percent higher than in the Mekong Delta, but these differences are partly offset by much lower maize and tuber prices in these regions.

Otherwise, the average regional differences are not so remarkable. Variation in cost per hectare is regionally correlated with productivity, such that farming appears most profitable in the Red River Delta and least profitable in the Central Coast. Within regions gross crop productivity and income levels are strongly positively correlated, but in most regions cropping costs vary only slightly over the quintiles. As a result the net return to crop production per hectare in all regions is substantially higher for the wealthy than for the poor, even though per hectare crop income of the poor in the North-Central Coast, for example, is almost as high as that of the wealthy in the Mekong Delta (who have much larger farms). Thus farmers in the north—including the poorest—partly offset their natural disadvantages (especially their small farm sizes) by more intensive production. But it cannot be argued that smaller (and poorer) farmers in Vietnam are more productive than larger (and richer) ones, given the country's narrow and low range of farm sizes.

It may seem surprising that the correlation of crop productivity and poverty is not well accounted for by differences in input intensity. In fact, the comparison of means hides an equally surprising dichotomy of practices among farmers. Consider fertilizer use, for example (figure 3.1).

Figure 3.1 Irrigated Area and Fertilizer Use in Vietnam

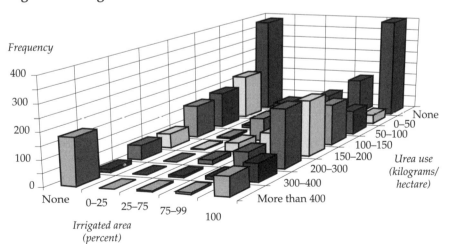

Source: Author's calculations, based on 1992–93 Vietnam Living Standards Survey data.

Most farmers either have area in annual crops that is entirely irrigated or have no irrigated area at all. One might suppose that farmers with irrigation would use fertilizer whereas those with no irrigation would not. But the sample frequencies indicate that there are almost equally large numbers of farmers who have irrigated land and do not use fertilizer and farmers who have no irrigated land and use no fertilizer. These nonusers are most frequently found in the north, especially in the Red River Delta, where nearly 47 percent of farmers use no fertilizer, or in the upland cash crop areas (Central Highlands), where 71 percent of farmers use no fertilizer.

Frequencies of nonuse are highest among the poor in the Red River Delta and North-Central Coast, but more evenly distributed among all income groups elsewhere. Among farmers who use fertilizer, the difference in fertilizer intensity (per hectare) between rich and poor is small in most regions. One might assume that the nonusers represent a less sophisticated group (or a group that is unable to afford inputs), but in fact the nonusers in five regions obtained higher paddy rice yields than most farmers who used fertilizer in varying quantities. A possible inference consistent with this finding is that farmers possessing land that is reasonably fertile can achieve decent yields without using fertilizer, and therefore do not use it. (This might be land whose fertility is renewed during annual flooding.)

Given the heterogeneity of farming conditions and technologies disguised by nationwide means, it is impossible to infer from a tabulation of detailed crop production costs by quintile anything about the causative link between inputs and outputs. But it is apparent that fertilizer is the biggest discrete cost for all income groups. Rents (including contractual obligations to the collective) and taxes together constitute a major burden, amounting to 19 percent of net crop revenue before rents and taxes for the poorest farmers (10 percent of total net income) and 15 percent for the wealthiest. Interest on borrowings for agricultural purposes is not a significant burden. In addition, the small size of depreciation (measured as one-tenth of the value of farm equipment) indicates how unmechanized Vietnamese farms are, although the sharp increase in costs related to mechanization across quintiles also suggests a high propensity to invest in machinery and equipment as rural income grows.

Finally, there is a striking increase in input costs and a corresponding gain in net revenues between the first and second quintiles (figure 3.2), whereas increased net revenues of higher quintiles are not accompanied by much intensification of input use. Thus extensive farming with relatively low input levels tends to differentiate farmers in the poorest quintile from other farmers. If the real constraints to intensified crop production for this group prove to be capital and technique rather than environment, quality of land, and differences in human capital, then concentrating

Figure 3.2 Crop Revenues and Input Costs in Vietnam, by Income Quintile

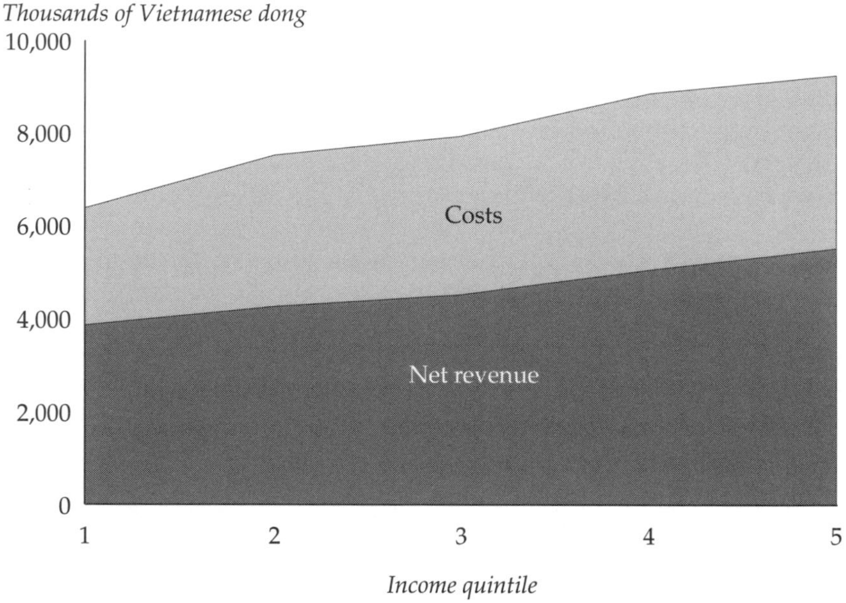

Thousands of Vietnamese dong

Income quintile

Source: Author's calculations, based on 1992–93 Vietnam Living Standards Survey data.

financial assistance and extension on the poorest might prove an economically efficient strategy.

Vietnamese farmers produce first to meet their own consumption requirements and then sell any surpluses. Because of differences between farmgate and retail prices (owing to transport and storage costs, and markups) and variable availability and pricing of food in the market, a safety-first approach to production planning is presumably to their advantage. But surplus is slim in the north and among the poor, so crop sales represent the major part of production in only the Central Highlands, the Southeast, and the Mekong Delta and elsewhere among the wealthy (figure 3.3). This does not mean that any class of farmers is subsistence-oriented: even the poorest farmers market nearly 20 percent of their grain production and much higher proportions of the other crops they grow. For all quintiles sales of paddy rice account for a remarkably stable 44–49 percent of total crop sales. For the poor, the remainder is made up mainly of low-unit-value staples, vegetables, oilseeds, and perennials, whereas the wealthy tend to market higher-unit-value perennials and fruit.

Even wealthy farmers are surprisingly self-sufficient in food production (nationwide, 43 percent compared with 60 percent of the poorest). On average, wealthy farmers can provide their households with a minimum dietary standard of around 2,100 calories per capita per day (roughly equivalent to the minimum daily requirement for energy) from their crop production alone, whereas the poorest farmers provide 1,200 calories. Farmers in the Northern Uplands and the Red River Delta are most self-sufficient in food, regardless of income class, whereas farmers in the Central Highlands (mainly cash crop producers) and the Southeast (having reliable access to food marketed farther south) rely on the market for the major part of their food supplies.

Net Rural Income

The overall income of farm households comprises farm income (crops, livestock, and aquaculture; and processing for self-consumption) and off-farm income (wages, self-employment, remittances, and other sources such as interest and rents). The proportions vary by region and income

Figure 3.3 Crop Production in Vietnam by Use, by Region

Thousands of Vietnamese dong

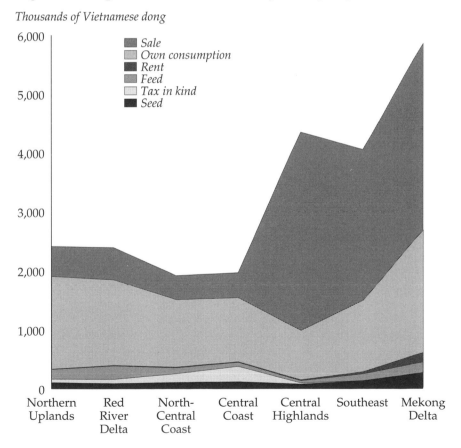

Source: Author's calculations, based on 1992–93 Vietnam Living Standards Survey data.

level: Nationwide, the poorest farmers receive about 65 percent of their income from farming. This value declines to about 46 percent for the wealthiest farmers (figure 3.4). But in the Northern Uplands, 77 percent of the poor's rural income comes from farming, compared with 31 percent and 34 percent in the Southeast and the Mekong Delta, where the percentage of income from farming does not decline among wealthier households.

Credit and Poverty

The rural poor in Vietnam borrow about as often as the nonpoor, but obtain smaller loans, more often from interest-free or lower-interest sources, and use the money more frequently for consumptive purposes. Relative to the size of their main fixed asset (land), the value of their borrowings, and, even more, their liquid assets is extremely low relative to richer households. These generalizations can be verified by cross-tabulating various credit characteristics against the classification of households by per capita expenditure (discussed below).

The frequency of borrowing declined with increasing per capita expenditure, but modestly. Nationwide, about one-third of households in every quintile received interest-bearing loans, but the distribution of such loans among quintiles was quite different in the Northern Uplands, the Red River Delta, and the North-Central Coast from that in the Central

Figure 3.4 Sources of Income for Farm Households in Vietnam, by Income Quintile

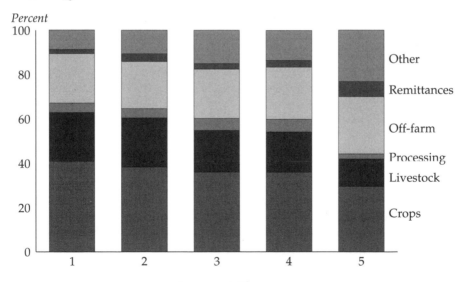

Income quintile

Source: Author's calculations, based on 1992–93 Vietnam Living Standards Survey data.

Coast, Central Highlands, and Southeast: In the far north nearly 30 percent of loans went to the poorest 20 percent of households, compared with less than 10 percent to the richest 20 percent. But in the more southern regions these figures were reversed. Still, the average loan size from every source rose sharply with wealth, so that the highest quintile received loans that were three to seven times as large as those received by the poorest quintile.

To some degree this difference is explained by a geographical pattern of discrimination against the poor, that is, credit availability was generally greater in richer communities than in poor communities. If the average loan per household in the community is taken as a measure of community-wide credit supply, communities where the rich congregated had averages of interest-bearing loans roughly twice those of communities where the poor were concentrated. This pattern is strongest in the center of the country, though weak or nonexistent in the Northern Uplands and the Southeast.

On the other hand, there is evidence of net credit inflows into some poor areas. A high ratio of the average volume of interest-bearing loans per family to the average household savings plus inventories suggests a greater volume of credit than local savings alone could sustain. Using this measure, the rural households in the Northern Uplands (especially among the poorest communities) and, to a much lesser extent, the North-Central Coast appeared to benefit from net credit inflows.

The poor were more likely to look to their relatives, friends, or the cooperatives for loans, and were much less likely to obtain loans from the Agricultural Bank of Vietnam. Indeed, 27 percent of loans received by the highest quintile were from the Agricultural Bank, compared with 8 percent for the poorest quintile. The poor, according to their own reports, were more likely to borrow for consumptive purposes (including house building) than the better-off households. Of the loans sought by the poorest quintile, 37 percent were for productive purposes (not including house building), compared with 67 percent for the wealthiest quintile. When multiple regression was used to control for loan source, loan amount, collateral, purpose, interest period, and region, the quintile status of the borrower had no significant impact on the interest rate charged.

Borrowing at interest can be measured relative to the crop area of a farm, which may be taken as a rough index of the need for capital in farming. In every region, the poorest farmers have much less credit per hectare than the richest—nationwide, the ratio is 1:10. It may be more telling, though, to look at the ratio of a household's total liquid assets (including borrowings) relative to crop area: The poorest were found to have one-twentieth the liquid assets per hectare of the richest farmers, the ratio being the smallest in the Red River Delta, the Central Coast, and the Central Highlands. Thus the distribution across quintiles of household liquid assets other than interest-bearing loans—that is, savings, inventories, remittances, and interest-free loans—is much more unequal than the allocation of interest-bearing credit. Interest-bearing loans represent a much larger portion of the liquid assets of the lower three quintiles of rural households (35–80 percent) than of the richest households (18 percent).

Promoting Crop Production

The essence of a strategy for reducing rural poverty is setting priorities among possible interventions. The emphasis may be on production or on directly improving welfare without affecting income-generating potential; on farming or the absorption of farm labor by nonfarm activities; on intensification or resettlement; on commercialization or improving self-sufficiency; on dismantling discriminatory policies or compensatory measures; on public investments or structural reforms. The analysis that follows is intended to shed some light on the potential for interventions that raise the incomes of the rural poor and the most promising instruments to use. A reasonable place to begin is with farming, in particular, paddy rice farming.

Income from crops accounts for less than half of rural household income, even among the rural poor. The share of income from crops, livestock, and fish raising declines over quintile groups (from lowest to highest), whereas nonfarm income sources grow in importance. Yet we could hypothesize that escape from poverty begins with the ability of a poor household to generate a surplus of its most basic product. Since most of the poor's crop production is absorbed by subsistence requirements, a relatively small increase in food production could lead to a large percentage increase in marketed surplus. This surplus would ease the household's shortage of financial resources and help satisfy household food requirements—both of which could limit the ability to diversify into products intended mainly for cash sale (surplus grain also provides feed for expanding livestock production) or nonfarm activities. Increased cash income also augments local demand for nonfarm goods and services, enlarging the scope of opportunity for nonfarm employment or enterprise. According to this theory, then, increasing production of paddy rice and other staple foods would have priority in a poverty reduction strategy. But how can this be done?

The 1992–93 Vietnam Living Standards Survey data provide sufficient information on crop production to econometrically estimate a paddy rice supply function, as well as a corresponding supply function for on-farm labor. Extending this supply function will permit an estimate of the determinants of net crop income as a whole, but a paddy rice supply function also allows us to look at prospects for crop diversification.

The Paddy Rice Supply Function

Assume that Vietnamese farm households make several major choices with respect to paddy production: the amount of land to allocate to rice relative to other crops, the amount of household or hired labor to employ in paddy production, and the amount to invest in current inputs or equipment, all taking into account real wages and relative crop and input prices, which differ by area.[5] Complete and perfect markets are assumed for consumption commodities, crops, labor, and current inputs to ensure separability of production and consumption decisions (this assumption will be challenged below). Levels of other inputs used or influences on production aside from labor and current inputs are decided in advance of the harvest (and are thus exogenous in their relationship with harvest levels) or not subject to household choice. If the household maximizes a utility function defined over income subject to its fixed resources (land and household labor), a set of product supply functions (and a farm labor supply function, not considered here) can be derived from the optimization conditions (Singh, Squire, and Strauss 1986). The supply function for paddy rice would look much like a production function, except that wage rates and input prices would be used as variables in place of labor and input quantities, and relative price indices for alternative products (composites for annual cash crops, perennial cash crops, fruit, and other food crops) would be included.

If the familiar Cobb-Douglas form, which translates into an equation linear in logarithms, is chosen to approximate the underlying production function, then for ease of estimation and interpretation the supply function should also be log-linear in form. This form has the drawback that it is multiplicative in all variables, so that the absence of any variable (such as nonuse of some exogenous input) implies zero supply or output. This problem has been remedied by including dummy variables representing instances of nonuse or nonoccurrence, on the assumption that in such instances the intercept of the equation differs but all other coefficients remain the same. Also, a variety of other possible influences on total factor productivity in crop production, such as infrastructure, education, health, and agricultural extension contacts, may be included as independent variables in order to assess the importance of government investment programs to crop production. These influences enter into the equations mainly as determinants of the intercept term (which represents total factor productivity)—that is, not in logarithmic form. The equation (before taking logs) is:

$$Q = \gamma \, e^{\Sigma \alpha_i D_i + \Sigma \alpha_j X_j} \, w^{\beta_1} \prod p_m^{\beta_m} \prod F_n^{\beta_n}$$

where Q is paddy rice production, γ is the intercept term, D_i are various dummy variables, X_j are cardinal influences, w is the wage (with paddy price as the numeraire), p_m are the prices of competing crops and current inputs (paddy price as numeraire), and F_n are the fixed (exogenous) factors of production.

The specific variables included in the OLS regression analysis of the supply function, per farm, are:

- Paddy rice production (kilograms; in logs), which is the dependent variable.
- Mean wage received for nonfarm labor (thousands of dong per workday; in logs).
- Cultivated area in annuals and perennials (hectares; in logs).
- Percentage of area irrigated.
- Mean fertilizer price paid (price in equivalent amounts of paddy sold).
- Composite prices for food crops (except paddy), annual cash crops, perennials, and fruit, averaged by community (farmgate value divided by quantity produced, measured in paddy-equivalent).
- Dummy variables representing the absence of a price quote in a community because the commodity is not locally produced or imported to the community.
- Depreciation of farm equipment (10 percent of equipment value; in logs) and other (miscellaneous) expenditures on inputs to cropping, and dummy variables reflecting their absence for some farms.
- Number of employees (and employees squared) hired by nearby factories in each community, as a proxy for opportunities for nonagricultural employment.
- Distance from the community to the nearest road (and distance squared; both in kilometers).
- Number of months for which the nearest road is impassable, as a proxy for road condition.
- Separate variables for road distance and impassable months in the Mekong Delta, where waterways pose a competitive alternative to roads.
- Labor time adjustment, as a health proxy (100 minus the percentage of labor days lost because of poor health; in logs).
- A dummy variable equal to one if most households in the community have electricity (and equal to zero if none or a few have electricity).
- Dummy variables reflecting the schooling of the household head, ranging from none to post–middle school.
- Dummy variables reflecting whether the household had been contacted at least once by an extension source (either government cooperative, nongovernment extension agent, or mass media) and, if so, whether the primary message content was the crop season (planting time) or something else.

- Dummy for farm size, to test for total factor productivity differences between small and large farms.
- Regional dummies (of which only the Mekong Delta proved significant and was retained in all regressions), to distinguish the influence of climatic and other geographic conditions on total factor productivity.

Several permutations of the paddy rice supply function were estimated in order to gain more insight into differences across quintile, region, and farm size (table 3.2). The best overall estimates were evaluated for marginal impacts of inputs to clarify the results. The best equation has an R^2 of 0.71. What support can such an equation lend to hypotheses about sources of increase in crop supply that might be relevant to an antipoverty strategy?

Labor

If the structural assumptions of the implicit household model are correct, the coefficient on the nonfarm wage rate (in paddy equivalents) should reflect the sensitivity of production decisions to rice prices and the wage rate, and the influence of increased labor on production. Higher wage rates should attract labor to nonfarm activities, reducing labor's commitment to farming and hence lowering production. The estimated coefficient is indeed negative and statistically significant, but its low magnitude implies that an increase in the real wage of one kilogram rice-equivalent (about 25 percent over the current average wage) would be associated with a fall in production of 53 kilograms per hectare (a change of less than 2 percent).

When separate supply functions were estimated for each region, the labor coefficient was no longer statistically significant in any region. Apparently, allocation of labor to crops is insensitive to differences in nonfarm wages and/or shifts of labor between cropping and other activities would have little impact on crop production. Given evidence of surplus household labor, these results are not consistent with the supposition that the quantity of labor is a constraint on paddy production, or that intensification of labor use, all else being equal, would have much of an impact on yields.[6] Nor should rural-urban migration be expected to negatively influence food production.[7]

Land and Irrigation

Recall that a household's cultivated area was assumed to be exogenous (that is, not readily adjusted through a rental market), and the portion of area irrigated (adjustable only through previous investments) and regional dummies were included to account for land quality differences (land quality categories, as officially assessed for tax purposes, were tested as dummies, but proved to have no consistent relationships with land productivity). Not surprisingly, cultivated area and irrigation are by far the most important influences on

Table 3.2 Paddy Rice Supply Function Estimates

Dependent variable: ln(paddy)[a]

	Base condition	Quintile 1	Quintile 2	Quintile 3	Quintile 4	Quintile 5
Intercept	1.260*	2.592*	0.039	0.511	2.376**	2.226*
lnRealWage	−0.080*	−0.098*	−0.127*	−0.148*	−0.063	−0.135**
IrrigPercent	0.615*	0.722*	0.614*	0.661*	0.503*	0.576*
lnCultArea	0.525*	0.544*	0.546*	0.505*	0.472*	0.464*
lnRealFertPrice[b]	−0.349*	−0.209*	−0.315*	−0.368*	−0.366*	−0.433*
lnPriceFood[b]	0.111*	0.030*	0.099*	0.205*	0.155*	0.123*
No_FoodPrice[c]	−0.098*	−0.184*	−0.250*	−0.094	0.068	−0.075
lnPriceCash	−0.034*	−0.045*	−0.005	−0.038	−0.039	0.003
No_CashPrice[c]	−0.199*	−0.373*	0.073	−0.185	−0.215	0.041
lnPricePeren	−0.007	0.002	0.005	0.000	−0.006	−0.007
No_Peren[c]	0.007	0.132	0.042	0.020	0.067	−0.019
lnPriceFruit	−0.040	0.064	−0.017	−0.073	−0.212*	−0.032
No_PriceFruit[c]	0.052*	0.101*	0.096*	−0.090**	−0.013	0.139*
lnDepreciation	0.078*	0.055*	0.087*	0.084*	0.053*	0.086*
No_Deprectn[c]	0.020	−0.066	0.047	0.138	0.012	−0.063
lnOtherCost	0.126*	0.115*	0.102*	0.056*	0.144*	0.185*
No_OtherCost[c]	0.573*	0.402*	0.425*	0.250*	0.739*	1.017*
No. Employees	−0.001*	0.004*	0.003*	0.001	−0.001	−0.002*
No.Empl.Squared	0.000	0.000*	0.000*	0.000	0.000	0.000*
RoadDistance	0.043	0.014	−0.006	0.133	0.113	0.002
RoadDistSquared	−0.008	−0.006	−0.001	−0.018	−0.017	−0.008
Impassable Mos.	−0.032*	−0.040*	−0.023**	−0.033*	−0.024	−0.027
RoadDist (7)	−0.030*	0.144**	−0.019	−0.032*	−0.038*	−0.029*
RoadDistSq(7)	0.001*	−0.020**	0.000	0.001*	0.001*	0.001*
Impass Mos.(7)	−0.045*	0.036	−0.042	−0.085*	0.003	−0.087*
lnLabTimeAdjust	0.228*	−0.171	0.427*	0.509*	0.123	0.053
MostlyElectrified	0.168*	0.117*	0.182*	0.185*	0.151*	0.257*
Schooling						
Some primary	0.112*	0.174*	0.125*	0.196*	0.013	0.095
Primary grad	0.116*	0.178*	0.126**	0.169*	0.004	0.085
Some middle	0.125*	0.226*	0.085	0.121	0.071	0.256**
Middle grad	0.081	0.099	0.103	0.160	0.056	−0.069
Post–middle	0.015	0.271	0.043	−0.068	0.044	−0.110
ExtensSource[d]						
Gov't/Coop	1.366*	0.051	−0.011	−0.111	0.010	1.330*
ExtAgent	1.458*	0.292**	0.089	−0.091	−0.029	1.470*
MassMedia	1.352*	0.041	0.033	−0.123	−0.042	1.274*
ExtensContent[e]						
CropSeason	−1.152*	0.114	0.141**	0.284*	0.272*	−1.078*
Other	−1.348*	dropped	dropped	dropped	dropped	−1.287*
Farm size						
< 2.5	−0.526*	−0.181	−0.641*	−0.553*	−0.635*	−0.755*
2.5 – 5.0	−0.283*	0.001	−0.231*	−0.319*	−0.430*	−0.482*
5.0 – 7.5	−0.143*	0.142	−0.128**	−0.166**	−0.250*	−0.245*
7.5 –15.0	−0.102*	0.122	−0.161*	−0.077	−0.122	−0.164
15.0–20.0	−0.131*	0.043	−0.177*	−0.122	−0.116	−0.156
>20.0	dropped	dropped	dropped	dropped	dropped	dropped

(Table continues on next page.)

Table 3.2 Paddy Rice Supply Function Estimates (continued)

Dependent variable: In(paddy)[a]

	Base condition	Quintile 1	Quintile 2	Quintile 3	Quintile 4	Quintile 5
Region 7 dummy	0.651*	0.398*	0.473*	0.916*	0.661*	0.670*
R^2	0.7117	0.6644	0.659	0.6466	0.6899	0.8001
Number of observations	2,956	603	645	613	599	496

* Significant at 5 percent level or better. ** Significant at 10 percent level or better.

a. Paddy rice production in kilograms.

b. All prices (and the wage) are divided by the average market price of paddy in the community—that is, these are relative prices and wage. Prices (in logarithmic form) are average unit receipts for commodity groups in each community (prices received by each individual household would be endogenous variables). Commodity groups include non-paddy food crops (maize, tubers, and vegetables); cash annuals (legumes, sugarcane, fibers, tobacco, and the like); perennials (tea, coffee, rubber, pepper, coconut, and the like); and fruit.

c. Extra dummies are employed equal to 1 when an input or other variable is absent, and the value of the log of input use is set equal to zero in such a case. Thus it is assumed that the production function, in the absence of that input, differs only in its intercept and omission of the input term. If farmers use inputs only if needed (for example, they use fertilizer when natural fertility is insufficient to meet crop needs, or use pesticides only if pests are a problem), this dummy can have a positive coefficient. Absence of a community price observation for a particular community implies that environmental conditions are not "right" for such a crop at prevailing market prices. Thus these dummies may be instruments for environmental conditions that affect paddy as well.

d. Only the tabulation of (the first) extension contact relating to paddy rice in the past twelve months is included here.

e. One "message" is what is the right time to plant paddy this year (which may be crucial to organizing irrigation delivery). If that was the main content, the variable is equal to 1. If the primary content concerned other aspects of paddy cultivation (for example, the appropriate seed varieties), the variable is equal to 2. And if there was no contact (hence no message), the variable is equal to 3. Because of the correlation between source and content (if source is equal to 3, then content is equal to 3), the two coefficients must be added together to get the net effect of an event with a particular source and content.

Source: Author's calculations.

paddy production. Because the market wage rate is well above the value of labor's marginal product, the reverse must be true for land—or else payments for access to land would leave no surplus for the household's survival.

Indeed, the implied value of the marginal product of a hectare of land under cultivation (about two-thirds irrigated) is estimated to average 2.1 million dong—more than twice what households pay on average for land use. Irrigation adds substantially to land value: the difference in paddy yields between no and full irrigation amounts to 2.2 tons per hectare, all else being equal. As paddy area and irrigation status together account for most variation in production, equalizing access to these across income groups (largely achieved in the Red River Delta) would nearly equalize income from crop cultivation among households. Neither the technical feasibility nor the costs of increasing irrigated area have been considered here (see chapter 5), but the gross gains would clearly be substantial.

Fertilizer and Agrochemicals

We saw earlier that a substantial portion of farmers, especially in the Red River Delta, used no fertilizer yet obtained paddy yields greater than those of households that used moderate amounts of fertilizer. An alternative specification of the supply function (detailed results not shown) included, among other things, specific fertilizer and pesticide input variables and dummies representing their nonuse. Positive and significant coefficients on the dummies confirmed that farmers who could avoid using these inputs, perhaps because their land was naturally very fertile (or was replenished by annual flooding) or because there were few local pest problems, were substantially better off than those who could not (they could achieve higher crop yields at less cost).

On the other hand, for the average farmer the estimated benefit-cost ratio—that is, the value in dong of output obtained for every dong of additional input—at the sample mean favored increased input use: 3:1 for urea and 4.7:1 for pesticides. These averages were sufficient to cover the opportunity cost of own or borrowed working capital, even at interest rates of 25 percent per month, but not necessarily enough to compensate the farmer for production risk. A negative interaction term between fertilizer and irrigation suggests that those farmers who combined high levels of irrigation and fertilizer use would often be better off cutting back on fertilizer. Phosphatic fertilizers, although heavily used, showed no significant association with paddy yields. Potash is less frequently applied, and widely varying amounts used showed no significant effect on paddy yields—although yields were 8 percent lower if no potash was used at all. Evidence from alternative estimates suggested that many farmers were unsure about optimal fertilizer use, an important area for agrotechnical extension work.

Returning to the best equation, the average price (paddy equivalents) of all fertilizers was the sole instrument for input prices that could be calculated for most farms. The estimated elasticity coefficient of –0.35 combines the allocative impact of relative price variation with the effect of fertilizer on crop yields. The magnitude of the joint effect is not trivial: a 50 percent increase in the relative price of fertilizer would reduce paddy yields by about 0.5 tons per hectare (a 13 percent decrease at the geometric mean yield of 3.8 tons per hectare). Clearly, the ratio of the price of fertilizer to the price of paddy rice is an indicator of incentives that have a powerful effect on crop production (the impact on income will be considered below).

Capital Services

The relationship between investments in farm equipment and increased output was measured by the inclusion of (the log of) depreciation (calculated as one-tenth of the value of equipment) and "other costs" associated with mechanization, including transport and electricity fees. Payback in paddy yields to such investments is very high: one Vietnamese dong invested in equipment or related other costs is associated with a gross annual return of 4–5 dong worth of paddy, other things being equal. Nevertheless, the average value of all durable farm equipment among sampled farms was only about $5. Mechanization is evidently a means to increase farm income, though not because of its labor-saving impact.

Prices of Competing Crops

If farmers are market-oriented, then variation in the relative profitability of different crops should affect paddy rice production (that is, farmers should diversify out of rice if other crops become more profitable). There are two problems with such a simple generalization. First, it ignores own-consumption demand for paddy rice, which may be relatively price-inelastic. And it ignores the probable wedge between farmgate and retail prices, reflecting transport costs, uncertainty of market prices and availability, and economies to home storage.[8] Such a wedge and the associated price risks tell us why farmers first meet their own consumption requirements before selling their crop. Also, inelastic household demand for rice would limit the scope for diversification even if relative rice prices fell.[9]

The second problem is the implicit assumption that farmers have substantial choice as to how they use their land. But without major investments of labor or cash, most paddy fields are too poorly drained to be suitable for upland (dry land) crops and, vice versa, upland fields lacking irrigation facilities provide very low rice yields. Nor can individual farms readily diversify independently of their neighbors or public authority, as surface irrigation or drainage works usually require public investment. Still, there may be some scope for substitution in the medium to long run. But these econometric estimates do not provide much confirmation. The estimated cross-price elasticity coefficients are either small, statistically insignificant, or have the wrong sign. The coefficients are likely influenced by a specification problem: the high-productivity rice growing areas are distant from areas with comparative advantage in upland, cash, or fruit crops, creating a positive association between high rice productivity and high prices of other crops.

Recall that the underlying farm model assumed three dimensions of household choice with respect to paddy rice production—choice of crop (area), farm labor input, and investment in other inputs and equipment. The findings to this point suggest that only the last of these choices may have a substantial impact on rice production. However, small changes in paddy rice area and production could be associated with large changes in area and production of diversified crops. Thus the estimates do not necessarily undercut arguments for a diversification strategy. Rather, they suggest that it would have little cost in terms of rice area or output.

Nonfarm Employment

Although variations in the wage rate are shown to have little relationship to variations in on-farm labor use, it may be that opportunities for nonfarm employment influence farm labor allocation, though (as argued above) the marginal effect on farm production would be minimal. Note that, whereas the household model assumed a complete and perfect labor market, we are now considering the possibility that the labor market does not clear at going wage rates—rather, access to nonfarm labor opportunities is rationed. The number of employees from the community hired by nearby factories was included in quadratic form as an instrumental variable reflecting the extent of such opportunities. The coefficients were significant, but the effect small. At the mean, an increase in factory hires of one employee in the community was associated with a loss of only 2 kilograms per hectare of paddy yield. The marginal impact actually turned positive when factories hired more than 250 employees in a community.

Infrastructure

The presence and condition of roads and village electrification should influence the ease and scope of marketing, and availability and timeliness of input supply—factors partly (but not necessarily entirely) reflected in the price structure. Electrification should allow farmers to custom process their output, increasing value-added, and also might be a proxy for differences in overall levels of commercial activity. The Mekong Delta was distinguished from other regions in looking at roads because of the importance there of canals for transport. Few of the sampled communities outside the Mekong Delta did not have road access, and only in the Mekong Delta did the relationship between access and productivity appear significant—a decrease of 81 kilograms per hectare in yields for every kilometer of distance from a road. Poor road condition does matter: yields fall by 92 kilograms per hectare (128 in the Mekong Delta) for every additional month that a road is impassable to vehicles.

Why? Possibly because human transport takes labor away from crop management and timely harvesting, or because shortages of inputs or crop losses arise because of impassable roads. (Paved roads also serve as good drying, threshing, and winnowing grounds in Vietnam, thus representing a direct input into rice production.) Rural electrification is also important: village households that are mostly electrified have yields that are 18 percent higher than those of unelectrified villages. Why? Electrification enables better control of water, including farm-level pumping for irrigation or drainage. It also facilitates threshing.

Health and Education

The proxy for health status is an adjustment to the number of labor days in farming for workdays lost because of ill health (of household head). As hired labor can substitute for sick family labor, albeit with some efficiency loss, and as there may be labor surplus, household models predict little effect. Indeed, a 1 percent increase in household labor time in farming because of reduced incidence of sickness is associated with a yield improvement of only 7 kilograms per hectare.

The possibility that endogeneity of health with respect to rice productivity influences this estimate cannot be ruled out, although the direct impact of rice productivity on health is probably small. Thus any biases in the estimated parameters will also be small. As for education, if the household head had received some primary education, a productivity gain of at least 12 percent was observed. Additional education had little or no association with higher crop productivity in rice farming.

Extension

In evaluating the estimates for extension, the (positive) coefficient on "source" must be combined with the (negative) coefficient on "message" to obtain a measure of total relationship. If the message consists of instructions on planting times (which should be well-coordinated to ensure that the irrigation system functions properly), the apparent net impact is in the 20–30 percent range. But it is very small for other messages.[10] Messages delivered by an extension agent other than a government or cooperative functionary have a greater effect on productivity. The latter appear no more effective than messages delivered by the mass media.

Farm Size

It is often suggested that small farms in less densely populated countries have higher crop yields than large farms, either because small farms are more labor- and input-intensive or because their total factor productivity (measured as the intercept term in the production function) is higher. Earlier we demonstrated that poor farmers have lower gross and net crop productivity and invest less in inputs other than labor. Insofar as poor farmers have small farms, this conclusion might be expected to carry over to farm size. Analysis of the paddy rice supply function has to this point indicated that greater labor intensity on small farms is unlikely to generate significantly higher crop yields.

The influence of farm size on total factor productivity in rice production was tested more directly by including dummies for six farm size classes—essentially testing for omitted influences associated with farm size. The estimates show conclusively that the smallest farm sizes (less than 0.25 hectare) have only about 41 percent of the total factor productivity of farms larger than 2.0 hectare, all else being equal, and in general residual (total factor) productivity rises sharply with farm size until 0.50–0.75 hectare is reached. Thereafter, productivity levels off. This tendency holds when quintile is controlled for (by running regressions on quintile subsamples): it is definitely the size of the farm, not characteristics associated with poverty level, that is responsible. But as discussed below, this phenomenon is not so obvious when productivity is measured as net income from all crops.

Regional Differences

Independent of everything else accounted for, total factor productivity in the Mekong Delta is considerably higher (92 percent) than that in other regions. And differences among the other six regions are relatively minor. This finding accords with the regional differences in measures of income and productivity, which were not accounted for by the much smaller differences among means of explanatory variables by region.

Net Value of Crop Output

An alternative to a model specified in terms of physical output of paddy rice is one focusing on net value of output of all crops. This formulation takes into account long-run adjustments within the cropping system and between crops and other farm and nonfarm activities. Its main drawback is that this dependent variable is sensitive to errors in the more numerous variables (input and output quantities and prices required to calculate net income), so the error term may be larger. Moreover, aggregation problems are likely to affect the link between theoretical assumptions and the estimated equation, again tending to enlarge the error term. Nearly 200 observations had to be dropped because of incomplete data on the components of the dependent variable. Finally, the closer the dependent variable is to household income, the more we need worry about explanatory variables being partly endogenous. On the plus side, the estimated signs of coefficients would leave no doubts about the direction of effects on net crop income.

Using the same explanatory variables as in the rice supply equation, we find that the results are generally consistent with those for that equation (table 3.3). The only differences expected were in the signs of the coefficients on relative prices of crops that are substitutes for rice, where differences in value-added rates as well as substitutability and subsistence requirements may affect the net value of crop production, and the signs cannot be predicted a priori. The (log of) farm price of paddy rice appears in the denominator of all (relative) price variables, so its elasticity, calculated as −1 times the sum of all coefficients on prices, is between 0.03 and 0.12. That is, a 10 percent increase in farmgate rice prices, with no change in prices of fertilizer and other crops, was associated with only a 0.3 to 1.2 percent increase in net crop income, because of increased use of fertilizers and other inputs (involving offsetting cost increases), limited substitution or intensification possibilities, and substitution of rice for upland foodgrains.

Table 3.3 Supply Function for Net Value of Crop Output

Dependent variable: ln(net value crops)[a]

	Coefficient	t-statistic	Coefficient	t-statistic
Intercept	0.142	0.266	0.971	1.619
lnRealWage	−0.026	−0.653	−0.070	−1.734
IrrigPercent	0.209	4.223	0.206	4.124
lnCultArea	0.743	29.463	0.682	18.363
lnRealFertPrice[b]	−0.152	−3.181	−0.212	−4.404
lnPriceFood[b]	0.129	4.516	0.125	4.317
No_FoodPrice[c]	−0.456	−6.527	−0.447	−6.383
lnPriceCash	0.049	3.101	0.047	2.934
No_CashPrice[c]	0.201	1.537	0.195	1.490
lnPricePeren	0.020	1.391	0.026	1.818
No_Peren[c]	−0.034	−0.346	−0.001	−0.013
lnPriceFruit	−0.079	−1.755	−0.105	−2.310
No_PriceFruit[c]	−0.145	−4.281	−0.146	−4.297
lnDepreciation	0.080	5.336	0.082	5.405
No_Deprectn[c]	0.034	0.654	0.048	0.899
lnOtherCost	−0.002	−0.152	−0.011	−0.767
No_OtherCost[c]	0.090	1.176	0.058	0.758
No. Employees	0.000	−0.813	0.000	−0.651
No.Empl.Squared	0.000	2.157	0.000	1.920
RoadDistance	0.117	1.624	0.103	1.411
RoadDistSquared	−0.023	−2.252	−0.019	−1.842
Impassable Mos.	−0.011	−1.094	−0.015	−1.459
RoadDist (7)	−0.048	−5.451	−0.053	−6.034
RoadDistSq(7)	0.001	4.792	0.001	5.270
Impass Mos.(7)	−0.027	−1.375	−0.029	−1.434
lnLabTimeAdjust	0.145	1.399	0.127	1.224
MostlyElectrified	0.248	6.414	0.285	7.248
Schooling				
Some primary	0.096	2.003	0.091	1.902
Primary grad	0.181	3.281	0.163	2.942
Some middle	0.199	2.693	0.200	2.708
Middle grad	0.251	3.251	0.240	3.095
Post–middle	0.235	2.659	0.235	2.644
ExtensSource[d]				
Gov't/Coop	0.933	1.260	0.964	1.298
ExtAgent	0.961	1.289	0.965	1.291
MassMedia	0.968	1.309	0.947	1.277
ExtensContent[e]				
CropSeason	−0.873	−1.179	−0.874	−1.178
Other	−1.103	−1.491	−1.101	−1.484
Farm size				
< 2.5			−0.226	−2.345
2.5–5.0			−0.217	−3.035
5.0–7.5			−0.093	−1.462
7.5–15.0			−0.103	−1.680
15.0–20.0			−0.162	−2.658
>20.0			dropped	

(Table continues on next page.)

Table 3.3 Supply Function for Net Value of Crop Output (continued)

Dependent variable: ln(net value crops)ᵃ

	Coefficient	t-statistic	Coefficient	t-statistic
Region				
1	−0.237	−2.942	−0.113	−1.400
2	−0.358	−4.326	−0.279	−3.344
3	−0.576	−6.866	−0.592	−7.030
4	−0.891	−10.403	−0.904	−10.509
5	−0.567	−3.833	−0.563	−3.782
6	−0.605	−7.486	−0.483	−5.917
7	dropped		dropped	
R^2	0.5055	0.4906		
Number of observations	2786	2786		

a. Log of the net value of crop output. Households with negative or missing values omitted.

b. All prices (and the wage) are divided by the average market price of paddy in the community—that is, these are relative prices and wage. Prices (in logarithmic form) are average unit receipts for commodity groups in each community (prices received by each individual household would be endogenous variables). Commodity groups include non-paddy food crops (maize, tubers, and vegetables); cash annuals (legumes, sugarcane, fibers, tobacco, and the like); perennials (tea, coffee, rubber, pepper, coconut, and the like); and fruit.

c. Extra dummies are employed is equal to 1 when an input or other variable is absent, and the value of the log of input use is set equal to zero in such a case. Thus it is assumed that the production function, in the absence of that input, differs only in its intercept and omission of the input term. If farmers use inputs only if needed (for example, they use fertilizer when natural fertility is insufficient to meet crop needs, or use pesticides only if pests are a problem), this dummy can have a positive coefficient. Absence of a community price observation for a particular community implies that environmental conditions are not "right" for such a crop at prevailing market prices. Thus these dummies may be instruments for environmental conditions that affect paddy as well.

d. Only the tabulation of (the first) extension contact relating to paddy rice in the past twelve months is included here.

e. One "message" is what is the right time to plant paddy this year (which may be crucial to organizing irrigation delivery). If that was the main content, the variable is equal to 1. If the primary content concerned other aspects of paddy cultivation (for example, the appropriate seed varieties), the variable is equal to 2. And if there was no contact (hence no message), the variable is equal to 3. Because of the correlation between source and content (if source is equal to 3, then content is equal to 3), the two coefficients must be added together to get the net effect of an event with a particular source and content.

Source: Author's calculations.

A number of explanatory variables that were statistically significant in the rice supply function were no longer so when net crop value became the dependent variable, notably road condition (impassable months), health status (labor time adjustment), and extension visits. The results for schooling suggest that net value of crops does increase progressively with greater education, though with diminishing returns.[11] The disparity in productivity between small and larger farms, noted earlier, fell considerably when net value of crop output was used. Encouragement of land transfers, which led to consolidation of smaller farms, thus might have a minor effect on economic productivity (and thus incomes of the poor), even though it may raise rice yields. Finally, the regional dummies indicated greater variation in total factor productivity among regions, all else being equal, than was indicated by the rice supply equations.

The Cash Farm Economy

The rationale for exploring how to increase crop productivity was a theory of development in which generating a surplus in basic agriculture (food production) would enable the poor to pull themselves out of poverty. It is undoubtedly true that the poorest farmers use a large portion of their crop production for subsistence requirements, leaving a small portion for sale to generate cash income. It may also be true that growth of most diversified farm and nonfarm (nonwage) activities is constrained by shortage of household financial resources and preoccupation with subsistence requirements. But does it follow that for food crops like paddy rice, a small increase in production by the poor can translate to a large percentage increase in cash income and, therefore, that relatively small improvements in food production can fuel a "bootstrapping" process in which other farm and nonfarm activities grow in importance relative to food production? We must consider further how improving farming (as opposed to expanding nonfarm activities) raises income levels of rural households.

As seen earlier, it is not only the poorest farmers who are self-sufficient in food production—the share of household food consumption that is self-produced declines only moderately over the quintiles, from 60 percent for the lowest to 43 percent for the highest. Total family incomes rise across quintiles (by at least 218 percent, from lowest to highest) much more rapidly than the component derived from farming (109 percent) because of the increased importance of nonfarm activity among higher quintiles. Thus demand for food across quintiles also increases at a rate (163 percent, from lowest to highest) exceeding that of income from farming.

The reverse side of the coin is that for about one-third of farms, farming as a whole (crops, livestock, and basic processing) generates a negative cash flow. That is, sales of farm produce are insufficient to cover cash costs. The difference is made up from income derived from off-farm sources (wage labor, self-employment, or others).[12] Again, this phenomenon is relatively stable across quintiles: 27 percent of farmers in the highest quintile have negative cash flow from farming, compared with 35 percent in the lowest. The cross-sectional relationship may be better understood by regressing net cash flow (*NCF*) per hectare on gross value of crops (*GVC*) per hectare and crop production cost (*CPC*) per hectare, yielding the equation (t-statistics in parentheses):

$$NCF = 330 + 0.06\ GVC - 0.67\ CPC$$
$$(0.8)\quad (50.1)\qquad (28.2)$$

$R^2 = 0.5$. Number of observations = 3,328.

A 1 dong increase in the value (not cash receipts, and holding costs constant) of per hectare crop output is associated with only a 0.06 dong increase in cash income, whereas a 1 dong increase in the cost per hectare of crop production is associated with a loss of 0.67 dong in cash income from farming. If this equation were behavioral (which it clearly is not), it would imply that an extra 1 dong investment in fertilizer that resulted in, say, an additional 5 dong of crop value would end up reducing cash income. But other components of household income that have not been held constant in the regression have an elasticity greater than unity with respect to the value of crop output value. The greater demand for home-produced food induced by combined off-farm and on-farm income change exceeds the on-farm income change.

If one held other components of income constant, it is likely that increased crop productivity would generate much more cash income than the above equation implies. But the survey indicates that differences in farm productivity are merely mopped up by increased food demand resulting from growth in cash income from nonfarm sources. The hypothesis that increased food crop productivity (or, for that matter, gross production value) generates a larger surplus of cash income certainly does not account for the present differences in cash availability among rural households. Overall, the evidence suggests that nonfarm income affects farm (cash) income through demand for own-produced food, rather than vice versa.

The finding that the self-sufficiency orientation of rural households does not vary with income is puzzling, since one would expect that increases in income lead rural households to move into commercial (as opposed to subsistence) farming. What determines this orientation? One would expect a greater orientation toward self-sufficiency in areas with poor market development or areas with strong comparative advantage in food crops (such as irrigated deltas). Farms with more off-farm income or too little land and farms in areas where cash cropping is advantageous (perhaps because of higher prices) would tend to be less self-sufficient.

These expectations are confirmed by regressions relating the rate of food self-sufficiency to various proxies for the above relationships. Most of the coefficients have the expected signs and significance for variables indicative of the extent of market development, reliability, and transport costs (distance from road, number of months the road is impassable, electrification status, squared distance from public transport, days per month when markets are open); farm size; extent of nonfarm income; irrigation status; and relative price of cash (nonfood) crops. A statistically insignificant coefficient on gross value of crops per hectare confirms that increased crop productivity in itself has no effect on self-sufficiency orientation.

Finally, some regional differences remain that are at least partly understandable: the low self-sufficiency orientation in the Central Highlands (cash crops, but with good access to food supplies from the Mekong Delta) and the Southeast (near Ho Chi Minh City and relatively industrialized); the high self-sufficiency orientation in the Northern Uplands (mountainous, cut off, and with food deficit), the Red River

Delta, and the North-Central Coast (food deficit regions, distant from the southern surpluses). That the Red River Delta has the highest self-suffi- ciency orientation is at first glance a surprise, as it has a small, if unreli- able, food surplus, and its marketing infrastructure is not that poor. But the extreme equality of land distribution in that region probably means that no one has much in the way of marketable surpluses, dooming the food market (and the labor market) to a limited role.

Overall, the equation suggests that a process of commercialization— decreased self-sufficiency orientation and corresponding increases in crop marketing, leading presumably to diversification or specialization and higher farm productivity—can be spurred mainly by investing in infra- structure that increases market volume and reliability, and decreases mar- keting costs (and further stimulates growth of nonfarm income-earning opportunities). Interventions intending to raise crop productivity will not have this effect. Greater inequality in farm size, insofar as that results from more freedom to transfer land, might also spur commercialization.

Conclusion

We can summarize with some confidence the promise of various instru- ments for increasing productivity in crop farming (and whether greater productivity will raise incomes), given the technologies currently available to Vietnamese farmers. Insofar as the structural relationships have not been misspecified by the estimated functions, the following relationships, which may reflect cause and effect, are supported by the analysis so far:

- Irrigation has a significant effect on land productivity in cropping, and where land is not yet irrigable, the feasibility and costs of investments in irrigation merit study.
- Both short-term farm investments in inputs such as fertilizer and long-term investments in farm equipment offer expected rates of return well in excess of the going interest rates. Attention should be paid to liquidity constraints on farm investment.
- The "price scissors"—the ratio between the price of inputs and the price of outputs (here represented by the fertilizer-rice price ratio)— was an important instrument for manipulating farm incentives under the former administrative price system. Any interventions in the price system that affect the scissors can still be expected to have an impact on crop productivity and net crop income—geographic variations in relative prices of inputs and outputs show strong asso- ciation with output variations.
- However, a change in the farmgate price of paddy rice relative to prices of inputs and all other crops, while affecting paddy produc- tion through incentives to use more or less inputs, may have little net effect on farm incomes.

- Improvements in infrastructure, such as road access (notably in the Mekong Delta), road condition, and especially electrification, have a measurable, positive association with rice production and, less conclusively, with net crop income.
- Education levels have a clear association with rice production, primary education being most important for basic crop yields and secondary education having some additional effect on net income through the development of farm management skills. But the relationship of health to crop production, though statistically significant, appears minor.
- Official extension has a significant association with paddy production, perhaps only because it coordinates planting. The current extension system has no measurable relationship with net crop income.
- Development of the land market (and growth of off-farm employment opportunities), insofar as it enables consolidation of the smallest farms, can be expected to be associated with higher crop yields but less markedly with higher incomes.
- Because of surplus farm labor, developments in the labor market—even substantial increments in off-farm labor demand—are not likely to affect farm productivity or income from farming in the near future. Thus the social rate of return to job-creating investments would likely exceed the private rate of return, because of the gap between nominal wage and opportunity cost of farm labor.
- Households' orientation toward self-sufficiency does not vary with income. Greater farm productivity is absorbed by higher consumption demand, and does not necessarily increase cash income.

Rural poverty in Vietnam is associated with:

- A paucity of productive resources—wealth in the form of land, savings, and other liquid assets, and physical capital.
- Low-quality resources—lack of irrigation, an unfavorable natural environment, lack of education, lack of (or distance from) decent public infrastructure.
- Lack of access to (or absence of) markets, notably product, input, financial, and off-farm labor markets.
- High numbers of dependents relative to productive resources.

These handicaps are not easily remedied. But they have at various times been characteristics of Vietnam's neighbors as well—neighbors as different as China and Indonesia have shown that, with sufficient government focus on rural development, a substantial fraction of the rural poor can climb out of poverty. For the poorest, however, short-run prospects are not so optimistic.

It is not difficult to see how individual families escape from poverty. It may involve finding off-farm employment or succeeding where others fail in a nonfarming enterprise. Farm income, too, might be boosted by a public irrigation project or access to credit permitting intensification. But absent major changes in the production environment, growth of agricultural income plays a passive or dependent role in a family's escape from poverty. An injection of outside cash income raises the family's demand for food, causing it to invest more to intensify its production. But neither agricultural product sales nor net revenues from agriculture will rise very rapidly. This phenomenon is partly the result of factors peculiar to Vietnam: a high income elasticity of demand for basic foods such as rice, low rural income levels, a small range of farm sizes, and limited development of marketing infrastructure.

That agriculture development is not the route out of poverty for the individual rural household does not mean that it is not the key to rural development for the community. Evidence was found that increased agricultural prosperity in the community augments the demand for nonfarm wage labor and for the products of nonfarm enterprises. Hence some part of agricultural growth clearly spills over into more nonfarm opportunities.

The relationship of credit to poverty and the utility of credit as an instrument for dealing with poverty are complex. The poorest households are extremely short of liquidity, even relative to their other meager assets. They could presumably use credit productively, but they are much more likely to use it for consumption and may often prove reluctant to accept the risks attached to credit bearing market interest rates. The poor benefit in some ways from the existing credit system—for example, from cooperatives in poor areas of the north, which supply credit for both consumption and production; a net inflow of credit into some poor areas; and, through choice or necessity, reliance on interest-free credit sources. On the other hand, the Agricultural Bank of Vietnam, focused as it was on productive agricultural lending, has subsidized mainly the wealthier classes through reduced interest rates, higher lending volume offered at below-market interest rates, and acceptance of high default rates. We find in the Vietnam Living Standards Survey, then, the same dilemmas prevalent in rural credit markets elsewhere, and no ready means of using targeted credit to lift the poor out of poverty.

We also must examine the issue of limited demand for household product and labor services. Limited local markets are a serious constraint on the household economy in countries like Vietnam, where the pattern of economic growth has been relatively centralized in major cities or particular regions. Centralized economic growth often has been a corollary of centralization of political power and fiscal resources, leading, among other things, to poorly developed infrastructure in the smaller towns and rural areas. Discriminatory sectoral policies may be embedded in the tax and tariff structures, the eligibility criteria for various kinds of government subsidies, and the structure and functioning of product and input markets (an appropriate subject for another study). Dismantling any policies that cause excessive centralization of public and private investment and that discourage growth of wage labor in both the agricultural and rural non-farm sector would shift incentives in favor of regional growth of incomes and consumption, and expansion of wage labor and entrepreneurial opportunities for farmers.

Precisely because of the poverty of rural households, income elasticities of demand for rural products such as food and simple consumption goods are highest away from the capital and industrial centers. Thus higher rural and small town income translates into expanded markets for raw and processed farm products. Small town expansion also translates into off-farm jobs near the smallholdings, in effect relieving the land access constraint by permitting viable household economies based on a mix of farm and nonfarm activities. In short, raising the productive capacity of the rural poor is not enough—the market for their goods and services must be expanded through regional development and labor-absorbing structural change in the rural economy. This strategy can be thought of as one of bringing the market to the poor, as opposed to bringing the goods and services of the rural poor to (a distant) market.

Is it possible to narrowly target the poorest groups? Clearly it is possible to identify areas where the poor are concentrated, such as the poorest regions and, within such regions, the communities most handicapped by lack of infrastructure and level, irrigable, good-quality land. Within localities, it is possible to target the smallest farm sizes, although this characteristic is imperfectly correlated with poverty. But is it advisable to do so? Some investment programs—such as irrigation, electrification, road building, agrotechnical extension, or postprimary education—would have exceptionally high costs and possibly low returns in poor areas that are remote and mountainous. The poor who are self-sufficiency-oriented and not well integrated into the market economy may be too risk-averse to access credit programs; moreover, the poor have a higher propensity to consume rather than invest their borrowings. And those poor whose farm sizes are very small are not going to use capital as productively as middle-size farms.

The best compromise, it could be argued, would be a strategy that seeks to create general rural prosperity in broad areas where poverty incidence is high or in areas very near impoverished communities. The objective would be to make the most efficient use of public funds to generate the greatest possible income increases, accounting for any multiplier effect, even if first-order beneficiaries were not the poor. This approach should have the maximum impact on nonfarm job creation and enlarge the market for higher-value farm and nonfarm products, creating opportunities for entrepreneurs. Such a strategy should be of substantial benefit to the rural poor without entailing disproportionate sacrifice to the economy as a whole.

Notes

1. This section draws heavily on World Bank (1994).

2. Definitions of the translated Vietnamese terms are somewhat speculative.

3. Women over 15 were counted as 0.89 adult male equivalents, and children between 10 and 15 as 0.64 adult male equivalents, based approximately on average market wage rates by age and sex. Each individual was assumed to offer 300 days a year of potential labor. Family workers engaged in off-farm self-employment were assumed to work full time when businesses were in operation. Because of errors in assumptions, negative underemployment rates are possible and were observed for a few categories of per capita expenditures per region.

4. Although the sampling frame was based on relative population density, particularly isolated communities may have been underrepresented in the sample.

5. There is sufficient variation in input and output prices across Vietnam—because of differences in transport and distribution costs in the context of a poorly developed transport system and newly emerging market distribution system—to estimate the impact of price on supply. To eliminate an endogenous element in determining prices paid or received by the individual household (due to quality and timing differences), all price data were averaged over all farms in each community.

6. There is one caveat: In these regressions irrigation is accounted for independently. Irrigated crops require much more labor than nonirrigated crops. Thus omission of irrigation area (a misspecification) and inclusion of potential family labor as an explanatory variable results in a significant and substantial elasticity estimate for labor. So a labor surplus is conditional on unchanging irrigation area.

7. Until the early 1990s migration in Vietnam was strictly controlled, so there is little scope for analysis of migration using the 1992–93 Vietnam Living Standards Survey. After that survey was completed migration is thought to have increased as restrictive controls were removed. Future research on agriculture in Vietnam will need to incorporate analyses of the relationship between migration and agricultural activities.

8. The existence or size of the wedge cannot be measured from the Living Standards Measurement Survey data because of unknown quality differences between products sold and purchased, and because of uncertain processing losses and conversions between, for example, unmilled and milled rice.

9. Such a wedge implies an imperfect market and a sample with three different types of producers (those with a marketed surplus, a deficit, or neither) who react differently to price changes. Although separability of consumption and production decisions applies to the first two types of producer, a common and single supply function, as assumed here, would not be appropriate (see Singh, Squire, and Strauss 1986, 52–54, for further discussion).

10. One caveat: Farmers differ in their willingness to seek out extension assistance or to act on it if it is supplied exogenously. Insofar as the former is related to the fact of extension contact, this variable may be a proxy for farm managerial ability rather than efficacy of extension work.

11. It seems intuitively plausible that a middle-school education would help farmers master the complexities of profitable farm management, but not necessarily lead them to focus on rice yields.

12. This does not imply that these farms produce output whose value is less than that of their inputs. The cash flow figures exclude the value of self-consumption. When the value of self-consumption is included, only a small percentage of households appear to produce output whose value exceeds that of their inputs.

References

Campell, Robert. 1994. "Consultant's Report." Prepared for the World Bank, Washington, D.C.

Singh, Inderjit, Lyn Squire, and John Strauss, eds. 1986. *Agricultural Household Models: Extensions, Applications, and Policy.* Baltimore, Md.: Johns Hopkins University Press.

World Bank. 1993. "Viet Nam: Transition to the Market." Report 11902-VN. East Asia and Pacific Region, Washington, D.C.

————. 1994. "Viet Nam: Agricultural Marketing Study." East Asia and Pacific Region, Washington, D.C.

4

Infrastructure and Poverty in Vietnam

Dominique van de Walle

The Vietnamese economy has emerged from a long period during which its ability to undertake socially beneficial investments, particularly in infrastructure, was severely constrained. This chapter examines how improving infrastructure might affect average living standards and their distribution in Vietnam.

Different arguments can be made as to why basic infrastructure investments in a country such as Vietnam would reduce poverty.[1] One is that the poor have least access to infrastructure and so will benefit most from new investments. If the nonpoor have captured all the benefits of past infrastructure projects and their needs are fully met, new projects must benefit the poor. Another argument is that the poor are concentrated in sectors of the economy where rates of return to infrastructure investments are high. For example, the poor in Vietnam depend heavily on agriculture, where rural infrastructure investments could have high returns.

This chapter attempts to throw light on these arguments by asking, How large and how pro-poor are the gains from investments in infrastructure—specifically irrigation—likely to be? The household data collected in the 1992–93 Vietnam Living Standards Survey (VNLSS)—contain much information that is useful for examining this question. The chapter addresses the question in depth only for irrigation. The data have partly influenced this choice: the attraction of modeling irrigation is that it is household-specific, and so there is ample scope for identifying interaction effects with other variables and assigning benefits at the household level.

Following the World Bank (1994c), economic infrastructure is here defined to consist of services from public utilities (sanitation, power, communications, and water supply) and public works (road and transport networks and irrigation and drainage systems). Human infrastructure (health, education, and nutrition) is briefly mentioned but is not a focus of the discussion. Economic infrastructure services are often characterized by economies of scale, nonexcludability, problems of information and monitoring, and externalities in consumption and production. For these reasons and because there may be failures in related markets (credit, risk, and labor) and distributional objectives, public intervention is often considered to be necessary (Jimenez 1995). Many of these conditions hold in present-day Vietnam, making arguments for government intervention compelling. But what form that intervention takes—direct provision, subsidization, or regulation—will depend on the type of infrastructure and the nature of the market failure.

Except where noted, the analysis is based on the nationally representative 1992–93 VNLSS. The survey covers 4,800 households (23,790 people), of which 3,840 (19,094 people) are rural, and includes a separate questionnaire on the communes in which sampled rural households are found.[2] The information collected covers many aspects of living standards. The household survey touches on access to and use of infrastructure in the context of household members' activities, income sources, health, education, housing, and so on. The community survey provides detailed information on the availability of infrastructure services in each rural household's commune of residence. It does not cover urban areas. For certain types of infrastructure, the community survey is the sole source of information in the VNLSS. For others, details are also provided at the household level. But these details are often conditional on the household's use and so tend to provide a skewed view of access. For example, for households that do not report an illness or that report an illness that was not externally treated, the survey reveals nothing about the household's access to health facilities. The commune-level data must also be treated with caution. Because communes vary in size, the figures do not provide complete information about household access to infrastructure services. These data were supplemented by a number of field trips to rural areas of the north, center, and south of Vietnam during 1993 and 1994.

Throughout, the chapter uses household consumption expenditure per person as the welfare indicator. Since prices vary spatially, each household's expenditure is deflated by the region-specific poverty line relative to the national poverty line.[3] This provides a measure of household per capita expenditure at what can be termed *all-Vietnam prices*. All monetary units are also converted into real values in this way. The analysis is thus based on real expenditure values representing purchasing power parity throughout the country. For the distributional analysis of irrigation infrastructure and for the figures, individuals are ranked by the converted household per capita consumption expenditure and placed in 14 groups defined by per capita expenditure.

The chapter begins by linking household living standards as revealed in the VNLSS with the level of various infrastructural services. Using standard descriptive techniques, an overall picture of the state of infrastructure, and how access varies by standards of living, is provided. The next section, on crop income, explores in much greater depth one aspect of infrastructure—irrigation—and its association with living standards. Here marginal, as opposed to average, effects of irrigation expansion are estimated and the distributional implications assessed. Farm household crop incomes are modeled as functions of household characteristics, community characteristics, and land, both irrigated and nonirrigated. Estimates of irrigation project costs are also compared with estimated benefits.

Poverty and Infrastructure in Vietnam, 1992–93

This section first looks briefly at the general availability of physical infrastructure in the rural communes to which households belong. It then turns to access to drinking water, sewerage and sanitation, irrigation, and energy sources for both urban and rural households. Some forms of infrastructure that may have important effects on income distribution and poverty—notably communication and transport infrastructure, which can integrate poor areas into the market economy and facilitate the mobility of goods and people—cannot be analyzed using the VNLSS. Though little information on Vietnam's communication networks is available from other sources, some data are available on its transport infrastructure, which is briefly described.

Availability of Physical Infrastructure in Rural Vietnam

About 70 percent of Vietnam's rural population lives in a commune with a passable road, or about 75 percent of the rural nonpoor and 67 percent of the rural poor (table 4.1). Using a lower poverty line (arbitrarily set at close to two-thirds of the national poverty line), 73 percent and 63 percent of those living in nonpoor and poor households, respectively, live in communes with a passable road.

Infrastructure for social services—schools and clinics—is much more widely accessible than other physical infrastructure such as electricity and water. More than 93 percent of the rural population lives in a commune with a clinic, and 88 percent in a commune with a lower secondary school. Every rural commune sampled had a primary school. Facilities tend to be somewhat more prevalent in the north than in the south (table 4.2). Differences between poor and nonpoor are not large.

Thus, according to the VNLSS, communes tend to be quite well provisioned in at least basic social services. But the data also remind us that the quality of social services may leave much to be desired. For example, although all rural communes surveyed report having a primary school, 20 percent of the children who do not attend school say the reason is that the school is too far. And 64 percent of communes complain of poor material conditions as the number one problem facing their primary school.

Forty-three percent of the rural population lives in a commune in which most households have electricity,[4] though the share is much smaller in the south (only 20 percent compared with 56 percent in the north). Pipe-borne water is even less frequently present in communes. Only 5 percent of the rural population resides in a commune in which at least some households have piped water, although this share is somewhat higher in the south. Like access to roads, the availability of electricity and piped water is related to living standards, with the poor less likely to live in a commune with these services. The poverty rate among households living in a commune with this infrastructure is considerably lower than among the population at large.

Some of these data must be interpreted carefully. For example, although the survey indicates that 70 percent of the rural population lives in a commune served by a road that is passable year-round, two caveats should be kept in mind. First, in the south, in coastal areas, and in parts of the north, canals and waterways are widely used to transport goods and passengers, so access to roads may not be the relevant indicator of access

Table 4.1 Rural Poor and Nonpoor with Access to Infrastructure in Vietnam, 1992–93

(percent)

		Rural population living in a commune with infrastructure				Poverty rate among those with infrastructure	
		High poverty line		Low poverty line		High poverty line	Low poverty line
Type of infrastructure	Total	Nonpoor	Poor	Nonpoor	Poor		
Passable road	70.2	74.7	67.3	72.8	62.5	58.6	22.3
Passenger transport	52.3	56.2	49.8	54.0	47.3	58.2	22.7
Electricity[a]	43.1	47.2	40.6	45.8	35.3	57.6	20.6
Pipe-borne water[b]	5.2	7.2	3.9	5.5	4.2	45.8	20.3
Post office	34.4	36.2	33.2	34.9	32.9	59.0	24.0
Lower secondary school	87.9	87.7	88.0	88.7	85.4	61.2	24.4
Upper secondary school	9.7	10.7	9.1	10.2	8.3	57.3	21.5
Clinic	93.3	93.6	93.1	93.7	92.1	61.0	24.8
Total						61.1	25.1

Note: The table combines data from the household and community questionnaires. Those defined as poor using the higher poverty line live in a household with yearly per capita expenditure (deflated by the regional poverty line) less than the national poverty line of 1,209,300 dong. Those defined as poor using the lower poverty line live in a household with yearly per capita expenditure (deflated by the regional poverty line) less than 65 percent of the national poverty line.
a. A commune is considered to have electricity if most households have it.
b. A commune is considered to have pipe-borne water if at least some households have it.
Source: 1992–93 Vietnam Living Standards Survey.

to transport infrastructure. Second, the survey gives little indication of the quality of roads or what passable means. Casual observation during field-work in rural Vietnam suggests that a road that can be traveled by a motorcycle or bicycle may have been considered passable.

For these reasons, the availability of passenger transport may be a more informative indicator of accessibility. Tables 4.1 and 4.2 thus include this variable as a proxy for the presence of a serviceable road or waterway.

Table 4.2 Rural Poor and Nonpoor with Access to Infrastructure in North and South Vietnam, 1992–93
(percent)

| Type of infrastructure | Total | Rural population living in a commune with infrastructure | | | | Poverty rate among those with infrastructure | |
| | | High poverty line | | Low poverty line | | High poverty line | Low poverty line |
		Nonpoor	Poor	Nonpoor	Poor		
Rural north							
Passable road	76.8	89.6	70.4	82.5	62.5	61.1	23.1
Passenger transport	47.2	53.4	44.1	50.0	40.1	62.3	24.1
Electricity[a]	55.9	68.1	49.8	61.1	42.6	59.4	21.6
Pipe-borne water[b]	3.5	6.2	2.2	4.1	2.1	41.9	17.0
Post office	27.7	29.5	26.7	28.4	25.9	64.3	26.6
Lower secondary school	90.6	93.2	89.3	92.5	85.9	65.7	26.9
Upper secondary school	9.3	9.6	9.2	9.4	9.1	66.0	27.8
Clinic	93.9	97.1	92.3	95.3	90.4	65.6	27.3
Total						66.7	28.4
Rural south							
Passable road	58.3	56.5	60.0	57.3	62.4	52.4	20.3
Passenger transport	61.5	59.7	63.2	60.2	66.8	52.3	20.6
Electricity	20.2	21.7	18.8	21.3	15.5	47.4	14.6
Pipe-borne water	8.1	8.4	7.8	7.8	9.7	49.0	22.8
Post office	46.5	44.4	48.6	45.2	52.1	53.2	21.3
Lower secondary school	83.0	81.0	84.9	82.7	84.2	52.1	19.3
Upper secondary school	10.5	12.0	9.1	11.5	6.3	44.1	11.4
Clinic	92.2	89.3	95.0	91.2	96.7	52.4	19.9
Total						50.9	19.0

Note: The table combines data from the household and community questionnaires. Those defined as poor using the higher poverty line live in a household with yearly per capita expenditure (deflated by the regional poverty line) less than the national poverty line of 1,209,300 dong. Those defined as poor using the lower poverty line live in a household with yearly per capita expenditure (deflated by the regional poverty line) less than 65 percent of the national poverty line.
a. A commune is considered to have electricity if most households have it.
b. A commune is considered to have pipe-borne water if at least some households have it.
Source: 1992–93 Vietnam Living Standards Survey.

About half the population lives in communes in which some kind of passenger transport is available. Transport is more frequently found in the south, probably reflecting widespread use of boats as well as road vehicles there. The difference between poor and nonpoor in access to a passable road and transport is more pronounced in the north than in the south, indicating the remoteness of some of the poorest households in the north.

Drinking Water

More than half the people of Vietnam (52 percent) secure their drinking water primarily from wells not equipped with pumps. Another 20 percent obtain their drinking water mostly from rivers, lakes, and other bodies of water, and 11 percent rely on rainwater. There are sharp differences among regions and between urban and rural areas and some variation related to living standards. In rural areas the pattern closely follows the national one. But wells without pumps are more prevalent in the north, where they provide drinking water for 71 percent of rural people (table 4.3). In the rural south people rely somewhat more on surface water (41 percent) than on wells without pumps (33 percent). Almost no rural Vietnamese have access to public standpipes and private taps, while in Ghana, Pakistan, Peru, and Tanzania, countries for which we have comparable data, 14 percent or more of the rural population has access to piped water.[5]

Table 4.3 Sources of Drinking Water in Rural and Urban Vietnam, 1992–93

(percentage of population by household's primary source of drinking water)

	North			South		
Source	Nonpoor	Poor	Total	Nonpoor	Poor	Total
Rural						
Private tap	2.2	0.1	0.8	0.4	0.0	0.2
Public standpipe	1.3	0.1	0.5	0.1	0.5	0.3
Well with pump	2.0	1.4	1.6	10.6	7.6	9.0
Well without pump	68.2	72.2	70.9	31.8	34.1	33.0
River, lake, pond	7.1	15.2	12.5	38.6	43.1	40.9
Rainwater	17.7	9.3	12.1	15.5	11.7	13.6
Other	1.4	1.6	1.5	3.0	3.0	3.0
Urban						
Inside tap	33.2	9.0	24.2	52.9	13.0	44.2
Outside tap	7.9	3.9	6.4	4.1	1.2	3.5
Public standpipe	18.6	11.8	16.1	3.9	2.6	3.6
Well with pump	2.4	1.1	1.9	11.3	5.4	10.0
Well without pump	31.1	61.9	42.6	10.3	39.5	16.6
River, lake, pond	1.2	4.0	2.3	13.6	30.3	17.3
Rainwater	4.8	5.3	5.0	3.9	8.0	4.8

Note: Totals may not add up to 100; the remainder is attributable to other. Private inside and outside taps are aggregated for rural areas. Bottled water is one of the options, though it is rare.
Source: 1992–93 Vietnam Living Standards Survey.

The differences between rural poor and nonpoor in sources of drinking water are not large, though the poor almost always have less access to the more desirable sources. Figure 4.1, which plots how use of a water drinking source varies across expenditure per capita groups, reinforces this conclusion. Though the slopes show a tendency to slightly incline or decline as living standards rise, on the whole the variation across expenditure groups is not dramatic.

The differences between rich and poor are more pronounced in urban areas. Among the national population access to water taps steadily rises beyond the eighth class interval, while use of wells steadily drops from about the sixth (figure 4.2). The better-off are considerably more likely to have access to piped water than the poor (see table 4.3). Still, although piped water systems are limited to urban areas, less than half the urban population has access to tap water (public or private). Again, Vietnam compares poorly with the four comparator countries, where the lowest access in urban areas is found in Pakistan, at 57 percent of households.[6]

There are distinct differences between the north and south in urban water sources. Private indoor taps are more prevalent in the south (44 percent versus 24 percent), while publicly provided standpipes are more standard in the north (16 percent versus 4 percent). Wells with pumps are also more frequent in the south (10 percent versus 2 percent). In the north's urban areas, as in its rural areas, wells without pumps are the most com-

Figure 4.1 Sources of Drinking Water in Rural Vietnam, 1992–93

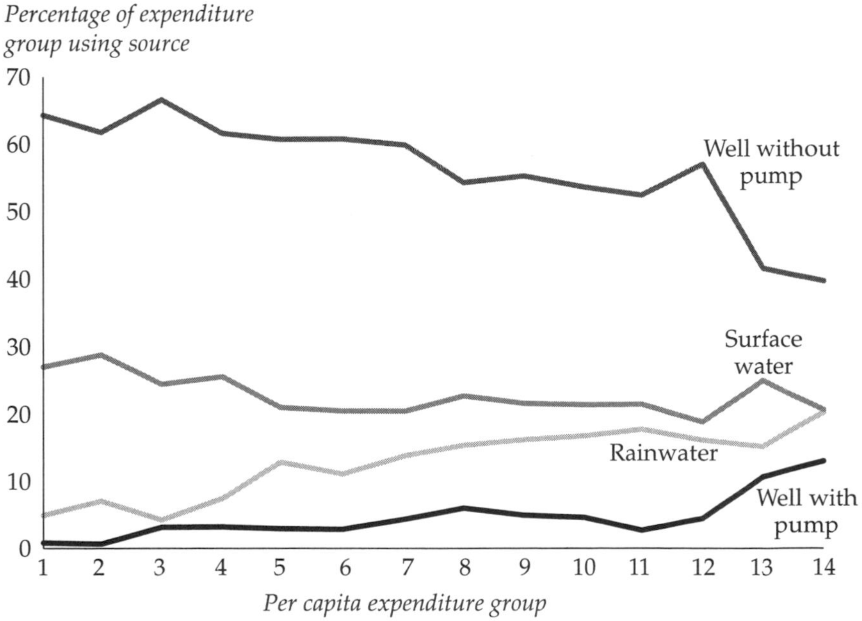

Percentage of expenditure
group using source

Per capita expenditure group

Source: 1992–93 Vietnam Living Standards Survey.

Figure 4.2 Sources of Drinking Water in Vietnam, 1992–93

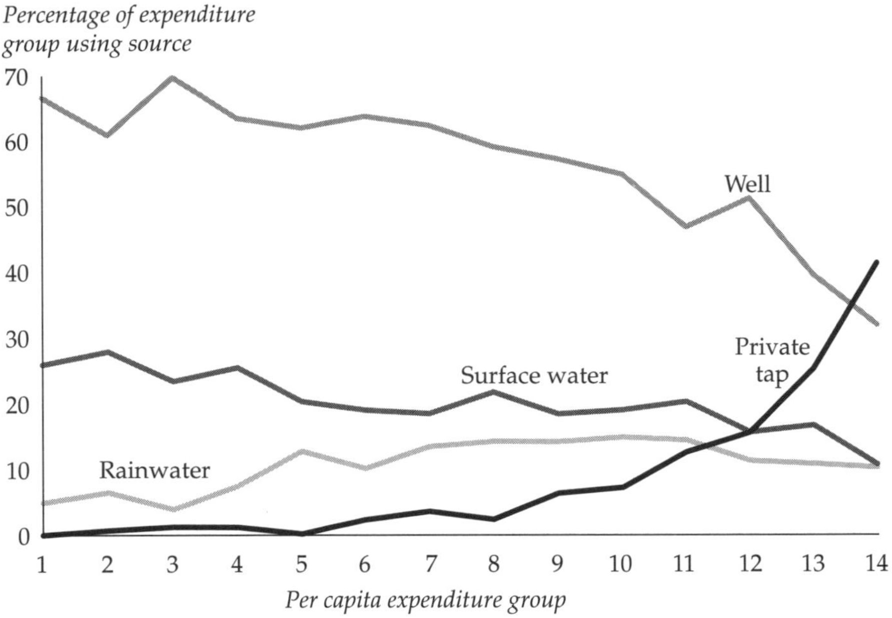

Percentage of expenditure
group using source

Per capita expenditure group

Source: 1992–93 Vietnam Living Standards Survey.

mon drinking water source (43 percent). As much as 14 percent of the south's urban nonpoor population relies on bodies of water, while 30 percent of the poor do so.

When the information on drinking water sources is disaggregated across urban and rural areas of the seven geographical regions, the deltas—particularly the Mekong—stand out among rural areas (table 4.4). While in all other rural regions the population overwhelmingly relies on wells without pumps, households in the Mekong rely primarily on rivers, lakes, and rainwater. In both deltas more than 20 percent depend on rainwater. A large majority of the urban population of the Northern Uplands and the North-Central Coast procures its drinking water from wells (without pumps). Piped water is found primarily in the Red River Delta, Central Coast, and Mekong Delta regions, reflecting the better provisioning of Hanoi, Danang, and Ho Chi Minh City.

The Living Standards Survey data suggest that up to 80 percent of Vietnamese live within 100 meters, and 98 percent within 1 kilometer, of their source of nonpiped drinking water. Close to 79 percent of all households obtain bath and laundry water from the same source. The rest generally live within a kilometer of their source of non-drinking water. Though there may be seasonal variations not captured by these data, such as a need to collect from surface water at greater distances during the extended dry season (World Bank 1990), the data do not support the claim that

Table 4.4 Sources of Drinking Water in Rural and Urban Vietnam, by Region, 1992–93

(percentage of population by household's primary source of drinking water)

Source	Northern Uplands	Red River Delta	North-Central Coast	Central Coast	Central Highlands	South-east	Mekong Delta	National
Rural								
Well with pump	0.4	3.5	0.5	0.8	0.0	7.0	11.4	4.3
Well without pump	72.8	54.7	85.5	83.1	79.4	74.2	9.2	57.4
River, lake, pond	18.3	11.5	6.7	13.5	19.2	5.2	58.3	22.6
Rainwater	5.5	25.7	7.0	0.0	0.0	1.0	20.7	12.6
Other	3.0	1.3	0.2	1.6	0.5	12.0	0.0	2.1
Urban								
Inside tap	0.0	35.9	0.0	36.4	—	64.8	15.5	33.8
Outside tap	0.0	12.1	0.0	7.3	—	2.3	5.2	5.0
Public standpipe	0.0	38.3	0.0	11.1	—	5.0	1.8	10.1
Well with pump	1.3	0.8	0.0	3.9	—	4.4	17.9	5.8
Well without pump	80.0	0.8	100	39.0	—	23.4	7.2	30.1
River, lake, pond	6.5	1.4	0.0	1.0	—	0.0	41.3	9.5
Rainwater	8.3	9.7	0.0	0.1	—	0.2	11.1	4.9

— Not available.
Note: Totals may not add up to 100; the remainder is attributable to other.
Source: 1992–93 Vietnam Living Standards Survey.

water collection represents a severe burden for women and children in Vietnam (UNICEF 1994; NEDECO 1993).

The data tell us nothing about the quality or safety of drinking water, however. Piped water reputedly often goes untreated. Most wells are shallow, and the water prone to contamination. One study found that up to 80 percent of wells were of unacceptable standards and harbored harmful bacteria, though households still preferred them to alternative sources (UNICEF 1994). Sewerage and sanitation conditions lead to a presumption that surface water is rarely safe for drinking, a presumption supported by the country's health profile and the high incidence of water-related diseases. Vietnam's National Programme of Action for Children (NPA) reckons that 21 percent of the rural population have a hygienic and ample water supply, though UNICEF (1994) cautions that this estimate is on the high side.

Sewerage and Sanitation

Industrial and residential wastewater tends to be dumped untreated into sewerage systems and waterways. Waste from flush toilets enters sewers directly or through septic tanks and is eventually discharged into rivers and other bodies of water. Wastewater systems generally manage both flood and wastewater. There is little treatment other than that provided through septic tanks (World Bank 1990). Most sewer systems in the north were built before 1954, and in the south, before 1975. Coverage is limited to a fraction of the population, and performance is poor.

The Living Standards Survey lists flush toilets, double vault composting latrines, pit latrines, other, and no toilet as choices. The first three are considered hygienic and desirable relative to other methods by the Ministry of Health. Other methods, which include bucket and fishpond latrines, toilets hanging over a body of water, and animal and human waste manure tanks, are not officially sanctioned.

Human waste is used extensively in agriculture and aquaculture, a major concern for rural sanitation. A 1989 national study revealed rates of parasitism as high as 90–95 percent in villages where double vault composting latrines are common and excreta is used as fertilizer, compared with rates of 40 percent in similar villages where fishpond latrines are prevalent (World Bank 1990). Although double vault composting latrines are hygienic when operated correctly—including allowing sufficient composting time in a sufficiently large vault—proper use appears to be rare. The NPA estimates the share of the rural population with access to adequate sanitation facilities at 13 percent (UNICEF 1994).

Nationally, 26 percent of the population reports having no toilet, a situation worse than that in Tanzania (5.3 percent of households), Peru (17 percent of the rural Sierra population), and Ghana (25 percent of households).[7] Another 33 percent of the population uses pit latrines, 22 percent uses other methods, and the rest use flush toilets and double vault composting latrines. While not common anywhere in the south, double vault composting latrines are used by 13 percent of the north's rural population and by 21 percent of its rural nonpoor (table 4.5). Pit latrines are by far the most common type of toilet in the rural north, while in the rural south most people report using other methods or no toilet.

People in the urban areas of the Central Coast and the Southeast have the greatest access to flush toilets (table 4.6). But the Central Coast also has one of the worst waste management situations in the country. A household in the urban Central Coast without access to a flush toilet is most likely to have access to no toilet at all. In the rural Central Coast 55 percent have no toilet facilities, the highest share in the country.

The share of the rural population without recourse to any kind of toilet facility steadily declines as living standards rise (figure 4.3). The use of double vault composting latrines in rural areas starts at a low rate and rises with welfare, as does the use of flush toilets. Pit latrines are used primarily in the mountainous areas of the north. In urban Vietnam patterns are less clear except for flush toilets, whose use steadily increases with per capita expenditure (figure 4.4).

Table 4.5 Toilet Facilities in Rural and Urban Vietnam, 1992–93

(percentage of population by type of toilet used by household)

	North			South		
Type of toilet	Nonpoor	Poor	Total	Nonpoor	Poor	Total
Rural						
Flush	4.3	0.5	1.8	3.8	0.8	2.2
Double vault composting latrine	21.4	8.2	12.6	0.7	0.2	0.4
Pit latrine	47.2	44.8	45.6	21.3	18.4	19.8
Other	7.9	16.8	13.8	51.3	39.7	45.4
No toilet	19.2	29.7	26.2	22.9	41.0	32.1
Urban						
Flush	48.1	21.6	38.2	67.7	20.0	57.3
Double vault composting latrine	11.1	12.4	11.6	1.9	2.0	1.9
Pit latrine	23.6	30.8	26.3	6.3	32.3	12.0
Other	0.8	3.3	1.7	13.3	29.9	16.9
No toilet	16.3	31.9	22.1	10.7	15.8	11.8

Source: 1992–93 Vietnam Living Standards Survey.

Table 4.6 Toilet Facilities in Rural and Urban Vietnam, by Region, 1992–93

(percentage of population by type of toilet used by household)

Type of toilet	Northern Uplands	Red River Delta	North-Central Coast	Central Coast	Central Highlands	South-east	Mekong Delta	National
Rural								
Flush	0.1	1.0	0.8	7.3	2.1	5.9	0.9	1.9
DVCL	11.4	13.3	12.0	13.7	2.2	0.2	0.2	8.3
Pit latrine	58.8	54.6	34.3	20.2	53.2	40.2	6.2	36.4
Other	6.5	16.2	25.4	4.2	2.0	18.3	63.3	25.1
No toilet	23.2	14.8	27.4	54.6	40.4	35.4	29.4	28.3
Urban								
Flush	2.0	50.4	3.8	60.7	—	82.8	21.9	47.4
DVCL	10.5	8.1	42.4	6.0	—	0.0	4.6	6.9
Pit latrine	64.8	19.7	31.1	6.4	—	14.4	8.7	19.4
Other	0.9	0.6	11.0	0.5	—	0.0	40.5	9.1
No toilet	21.8	21.2	11.7	26.4	—	2.9	24.3	17.2

— Not available.
Note: DVCL is a double vault composting latrine.
Source: 1992–93 Vietnam Living Standards Survey.

Access to Irrigation

About half the cultivated area under annual crops in Vietnam is irrigated, and much of the rest could be (World Bank 1996). Irrigation needs are supplied largely by surface water (Vu and Taillard 1993), through large-scale systems (networks) and small-scale systems (wells, boreholes). The two major river deltas are characterized by complex hydraulic systems, dating back hundreds of years, that incorporate navigation, flood control, drainage, saline intrusion control, and irrigation functions. The irrigation

Figure 4.3 Sanitation Facilities Used in Rural Vietnam, 1992–93

*Percentage of
expenditure group*

Per capita expenditure group

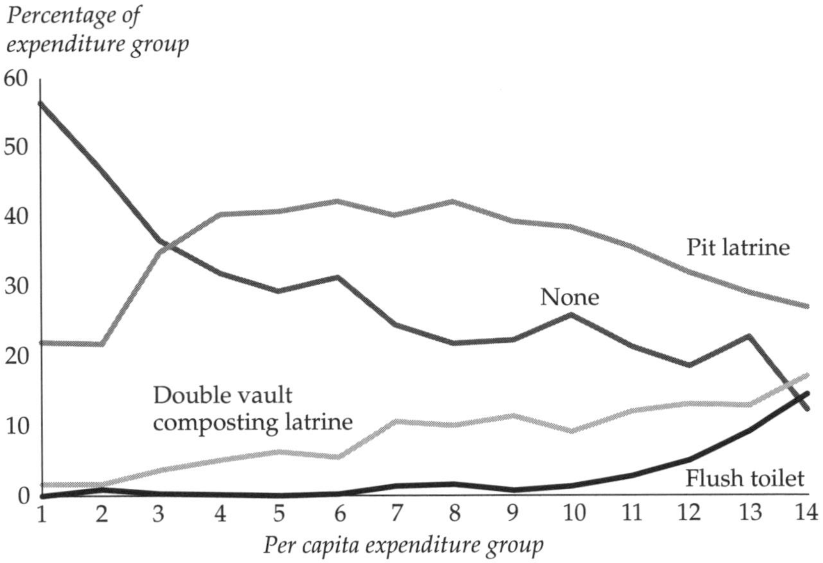

Source: 1992–93 Vietnam Living Standards Survey.

functions rely on a system of canals with pumping stations and on-farm water control arrangements.

Irrigation networks in the deltas and elsewhere are in a state of severe disrepair. Simply rehabilitating existing structures in the nine river basins could expand the irrigated area an estimated 1 million hectares—from 2 million to 3 million (World Bank 1996). Outside the deltas, irrigation—like other physical infrastructure—is less well developed, though there are possibilities for expansion. In some areas this would require constructing storage dams and gravity irrigation systems. In others, developing small-scale irrigation systems (such as systems based on small electric pumps drawing water from reservoirs and

Table 4.7 Average Area of Land per Capita in Rural Vietnam, 1992–93
(square meters)

		North	
Type of land	*Nonpoor*	*Poor*	*Total*
Irrigated, annual crops	414.8	333.4	360.1
Nonirrigated, annual crops	288.9	378.2	348.9
Perennial crops	55.0	50.8	52.2
Other	173.8	126.1	141.8
Total	932.4	888.6	902.9

Note: Calculated over the rural farm population. In the VNLSS *irrigated land* includes all land irrigated through a system of canals or by means of electric or petrol pumps that prevent flood or drought. *Other* includes forest, water surface, and *other* as defined in note 9.

Figure 4.4 Sanitation Facilities Used in Urban Vietnam, 1992—93

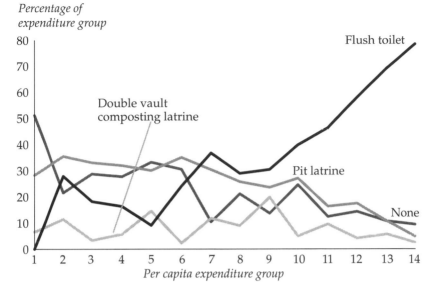

Source: 1992—93 Vietnam Living Standards Survey.

natural bodies of water) would be more feasible (World Bank 1996; Barker 1994).

There is more land per person—and more irrigated land per person—in the rural south than in the rural north (table 4.7). But there are large disparities in the south in land endowments between poor and nonpoor. On average, the southern poor have access to less than half as much land as the nonpoor. Land endowments are relatively equitable in the north, though the poor have less irrigated land.

Regional variation in land per capita is attributable in large part to differences in terrain and population density. The average area of cultivated land per person ranges from 702 square meters in the Red River Delta to 1,977 square meters in the Mekong Delta; irrigated land per person ranges

	South			National		
Nonpoor	Poor	Total	Nonpoor	Poor	Total
825.9	346.0	584.2	590.3	336.8	434.0
1,149.8	660.9	903.5	656.6	454.4	531.9
373.9	212.8	292.7	191.2	94.4	131.5
156.0	29.7	92.4	166.2	100.1	125.5
2,505.7	1,249.4	1,872.8	1,604.3	985.8	1,222.9

Source: 1992–93 Vietnam Living Standards Survey.

from 17 square meters in the Central Highlands to 713 square meters in the Mekong Delta (table 4.8).

Past land reform has ensured relatively low inequality in access to land within regions (figure 4.5; Vu and Taillard 1993). But significant variation in farm size and land quality can be found among regions, and landholdings are more strongly correlated with living standards in some regions than in others. All three regions of the south reveal a pronounced positive association between size of landholding and per capita expenditure levels. In general, the distribution of irrigated land appears to be more equitable than or about the same as the distribution of all land.

Sources of Energy

The north, with coal reserves and hydroelectric power plants, has historically been better endowed with energy than the south, which until recently was plagued by electricity shortages. Throughout Vietnam electricity is also supplied by diesel-powered generators, generally run by local authorities. The two main sources of lighting are electricity (used by 49 percent of the national population) and gas, oil, and kerosene lamps (50 percent). There are pronounced differences between the north and south and across expenditure groups. Electricity networks are better developed and reputedly more reliable in the north, and this is reflected in household usage. Almost half (47 percent) of the north's rural population relies on electricity, compared with less than a quarter (22 percent) in the rural south (table 4.9). For the nonpoor, the share rises to 64 percent in the north and 27 percent in the south. Among the poor, 61 percent in the north and 80 percent in the south use gas, oil, and kerosene. A majority of urban Vietnamese depend on electric lighting, though the share is smaller in the south and

Table 4.8 Average Area of Land per Capita in Rural Vietnam, by Region, 1992–93

(square meters)

Type of land	Northern Uplands	Red River Delta	North-Central Coast	Central Coast	Central Highlands	South-east	Mekong Delta	National
Irrigated, annual crops	229.3	521.2	307.9	325.9	17.1	484.5	713.1	434.0
Nonirrigated, annual crops	697.2	78.7	349.3	321.2	1,015.5	823.1	905.9	531.9
Perennial crops	76.7	31.8	58.9	42.8	398.3	354.9	256.6	131.5
Other	311.0	69.8	112.8	50.3	27.2	101.3	101.5	125.5
Total	1,314.2	701.5	828.8	740.2	1,458.0	1,763.7	1,977.2	1,222.9

Note: Calculated over the rural farm population. In the VNLSS *irrigated land* includes all land irrigated through a system of canals or by means of electric or petrol pumps that prevent flood or drought. *Other* includes forest, water surface, and *other* as defined in note 9.
Source: 1992–93 Vietnam Living Standards Survey.

Figure 4.5 Distribution of Total Land and Irrigated Annual Cropland in Vietnam, 1992–93

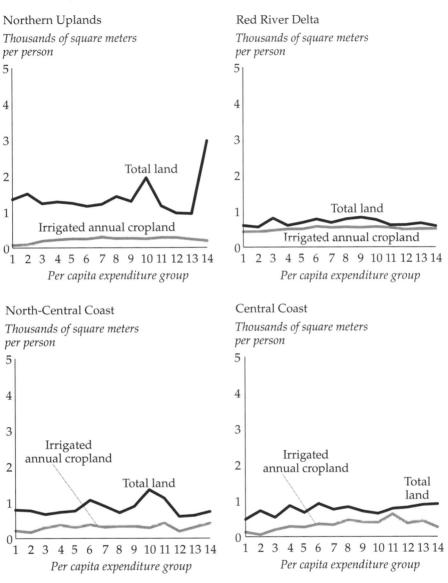

Northern Uplands

Thousands of square meters per person

Total land

Irrigated annual cropland

Per capita expenditure group

Red River Delta

Thousands of square meters per person

Total land

Irrigated annual cropland

Per capita expenditure group

North-Central Coast

Thousands of square meters per person

Irrigated annual cropland

Total land

Per capita expenditure group

Central Coast

Thousands of square meters per person

Irrigated annual cropland

Total land

Per capita expenditure group

(Figure continues on next page.)

among the less well off. On the whole, household access to electricity in Vietnam compares favorably with that in Ghana (69 percent of urban and 9 percent of rural households) and Tanzania (35 percent and 1 percent) but less well with that in Peru (95 percent of the total population).

Figure 4.5 Distribution of Total Land and Irrigated Annual Cropland in Vietnam, 1992–93 (continued)

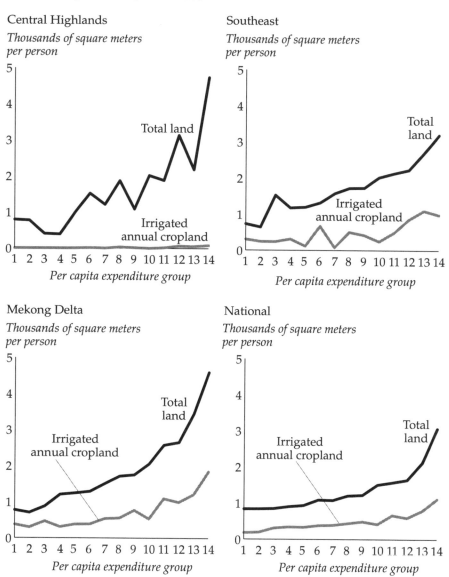

Central Highlands

Thousands of square meters per person

Southeast

Thousands of square meters per person

Mekong Delta

Thousands of square meters per person

National

Thousands of square meters per person

Per capita expenditure group

Source: 1992–93 Vietnam Living Standards Survey.

Electricity is rarely used for cooking. Wood and leaves predominate as cooking fuel in the rural north and wood dominates in the rural south, while in urban areas coal and kerosene are also important (table 4.10). Differences between poor and nonpoor rural groups are small. But in all urban areas the poor are more likely to use wood, and the better off to use coal or kerosene.

Table 4.9 Sources of Lighting in Rural and Urban Vietnam, 1992–93
(percentage of population by household's source of lighting)

	North			South		
Source of lighting	Nonpoor	Poor	Total	Nonpoor	Poor	Total
Rural						
Electricity	63.9	38.0	46.6	27.4	16.4	21.8
Battery lamp, flashlight	1.0	0.4	0.6	4.9	0.6	2.7
Gas, oil, kerosene	34.2	60.9	52.0	67.7	80.3	74.1
Other	1.0	0.7	0.8	0.0	2.7	1.4
Urban						
Electricity	97.0	80.9	91.0	91.0	64.9	85.3
Gas, oil, kerosene	3.0	19.1	9.0	9.0	35.1	14.7

Source: 1992–93 Vietnam Living Standards Survey.

Table 4.10 Cooking Fuel in Rural and Urban Vietnam, 1992–93
(percentage of population by type of cooking fuel used by household)

	North			South		
Type of fuel	Nonpoor	Poor	Total	Nonpoor	Poor	Total
Rural						
Wood	39.3	46.0	43.8	86.7	88.3	87.5
Leaves	51.1	52.7	52.1	9.3	11.3	10.3
Coal	8.9	1.3	3.8	3.7	0.4	2.0
Urban						
Wood	34.7	50.7	40.7	57.9	94.6	65.9
Leaves	5.0	16.1	9.1	2.2	3.2	2.5
Coal	48.7	31.7	42.3	23.8	0.8	18.7
Electricity	3.9	0.4	2.6	1.9	0.0	1.5
Kerosene	7.7	1.1	5.2	13.7	1.4	11.0

Note: Totals may not add up to 100; the remainder is attributable to other and kerosene and electricity in rural areas, and to other and bottled gas in urban areas.
Source: 1992–93 Vietnam Living Standards Survey.

Transportation

Other than information on whether a road passes through the commune, there is little in the VNLSS to illustrate the poor state of the country's transport sector. The public road network consists of about 105,000 kilometers of roads: 11,350 kilometers of national roads, 14,000 kilometers of provincial roads, 25,300 kilometers of district roads, 46,200 kilometers of commune roads, 2,600 kilometers of urban roads, and 5,400 kilometers of special roads (World Bank 1994b). In 1992 about 12 percent of Vietnam's road network was paved, compared with 30 percent of India's in 1985 and 48 percent of Indonesia's in 1990 (World Bank 1994b). Average road density is low, at 0.32 kilometers per square kilometer of land and 1.6 kilometers per 1,000 inhabitants. Not unexpectedly, density is highest in the two deltas and lowest in the more mountainous regions. Like the rest of the country's infrastructure, the road network—dating largely from before the 1970s in the south and before 1954 in the north—is old and in severe disrepair. Thirty percent of all district and 50 percent of commune roads are impassable during the rainy season. Other transport infrastructure (inland waterways, ports, the railway system) is also in poor condition (World Bank 1994b). Waterways play an important part in transport, particularly in the river deltas. But of the 40,000 kilometer network, only 11,000 kilometers are suitable for river transport because of neglect of dredging and other maintenance. Lack of bridges and river piers further impedes mobility.

Summary

The present state of physical infrastructure in Vietnam is clearly poor by most standards. Nearly a third of rural people live in communes without a passable road. Nearly half do not have access to passenger transport. More than half do not have electricity. Barely half of annual cropland is irrigated. All but 5 percent of the rural population lives in a commune where no one has access to piped water. There are also marked differences in access to infrastructure between urban and rural areas, with urban areas generally favored, as well as among regions.

The poor tend to have worse access to infrastructure than the nonpoor. But for many types of infrastructure the poor in rural Vietnam do not have appreciably worse access than the nonpoor: for many types of basic infrastructure access is equally bad for both groups. Ventures to improve basic infrastructure will not automatically be redistributive. It cannot be argued that the nonpoor already have adequate basic infrastructure and the poor have none—so that new investments will necessarily benefit the poor.

What do the data imply about the distributional impact of future investments in infrastructure? The answer will depend on the marginal benefits from infrastructure investments. Take irrigation. If a household's land is fully irrigated, the marginal benefit to that household from expanding total irrigated area would be zero. A general expansion of irrigation would benefit those whose land is not irrigated. If it were true that the rich have fully irrigated land while the poor do not, the benefits would go to the poor. But while the nonpoor have more irrigated land than the poor, they also have more nonirrigated land (see table 4.7 and figure 4.5).

Thus undifferentiated irrigation infrastructure would not appear to be an important redistributive instrument; the poor would benefit but probably less so than the nonpoor.[8] But a number of other factors are correlated with the marginal benefits from irrigation. It is often argued, for example, that smaller farms are more productive, so marginal benefits may be higher for the poor. Or it might be argued that marginal benefits will tend to be higher for those with more human capital, likely to be the not-so-poor. On balance, it is not clear what the outcome would be. Inferring the potential gains from irrigation using cross-sectional data thus requires controls for these other factors. To properly address such questions we need to go beyond descriptive analysis and investigate marginal impacts.

Explaining Crop Income

This section undertakes a detailed assessment of the likely distributional impact of an expansion in irrigated land area. The vast majority of Vietnam's population derives its livelihood from farming (van de Walle 1995a). The extent to which annual cropland is irrigated and water adequately managed is widely recognized as a key factor in agricultural productivity. As noted, about half of annual cropland in Vietnam is currently under irrigation (although the aggregates hide much regional variation).[9] And there is much potential for economically viable expansion of irrigation and rehabilitation of nonfunctioning irrigation networks (Barker 1994; World Bank 1996; Le Thanh Nghiep 1993).

The data from the Living Standards Survey contains detailed information on household land assets and farm incomes and permits a detailed exploration of the impact of irrigation infrastructure on livelihoods in rural Vietnam. This section describes a model of net farm crop incomes as a function of household and community characteristics—as estimated in van de Walle (1996, 1997)—and summarizes the key results. In particular, it explores the marginal effect of irrigated versus nonirrigated land. Next, it uses the resulting parameters to simulate the potential benefits from expanding irrigation and to delve into several policy issues. How large would the income gains from further irrigation investments be? Would those gains be pro-poor? Such questions are of considerable interest given the multiple policy choices that confront policymakers in a country facing heavily constrained budgets and a plethora of real investment and consumption needs.

Determinants of Crop Income

The production function in chapter 3 gives the maximum output at given physical inputs and so is a description of technology. By contrast, the profit function discussed here is a summary of the income gain from combining the technology with a particular market and institutional environment. It assumes that a household's profit from crop production—measured by farm crop income, net of variable costs—depends on output and input prices (p), amounts of nonirrigated (L^N) and irrigated (L^I) annual cropland, and various other fixed factors (z), including other land in agricultural production; education, health, and demographic variables; and location-specific agro-ecological variables.[10] A range of variables are included in z in order to capture characteristics specific to a transition economy in which markets are still underdeveloped. A number of market imperfections in Vietnam—such as missing labor markets in many areas—imply that its production constraints may be quite different from those in other settings. For example, household demographics are likely to be considerably more important to a farm household's productive potential where labor time is not readily bought and sold.

The profit function π (p, L^N, L^I, z) is linearized as follows for household j:

$$(4.1) \qquad \pi_j = \pi(p_j, L^N_j, L^I_j, z_j) = \alpha + \beta^N_j L^N_j + \beta^I_j L^I_j + \gamma z_j + \delta d_j + \varepsilon_j,$$

where d is a vector of regional dummy variables. The error term is assumed to be independently and identically normally distributed. The marginal returns to nonirrigated and irrigated land are given by

$$(4.2) \qquad \beta^N_j = \beta^N_0 + \beta^N_1 d_j + \beta^N_2 z_j + \beta^N_3 L^N_j$$

and

$$(4.3) \qquad \beta^I_j = \beta^I_0 + \beta^I_1 d_j + \beta^I_2 z_j + \beta^I_3 L^I_j$$

The difference in marginal returns between irrigated and non-irrigated land determines the income gains from irrigating a unit of land.

As indicated by equations 4.2 and 4.3, several variables are allowed to have direct effects on the marginal returns from irrigated and nonirrigated cropland, including land itself, demographics, education variables, and the region dummies. Prices of outputs and variable inputs are assumed to vary between but not within communes. Dummy variables for 119 of 200 communes are included in the intercept of the profit function to capture variations in prices and any other spatial, cross-commune variations in omitted or fixed factors such as land and soil quality. The commune dummies will also pick up the influences of geographical and infrastructural variations at the commune level. (The regression model is described in greater detail, and the full results are presented, in van de Walle 1996.)[11]

An important concern with cross-sectional regression analysis of this kind is that estimates will be biased because of endogenous explanatory variables or omitted variables that are correlated with included variables. A number of factors alleviate this concern here. In many agricultural settings land and irrigation are inputs to production chosen by the household and therefore endogenous. But in Vietnam household land use rights have generally been fixed since the 1988 reforms. In the north, communes or cooperatives assigned parcels to households on the basis of family size and number of workers, taking into account land productivity and access to water to ensure equity in both land quality and quantity (Dreyfus 1993; Barker 1994). Between 1988 and the survey period there had been virtually no mobility, investment in irrigation, or land market activity. Thus land and irrigation inputs in the north can reasonably be treated as exogenous at the household level. Endogeneity is more likely in the south, where 1988 land assignments essentially restored the distribution prevailing before the country's reunification. Still, land market transactions and investments in irrigation in the south have been scarce since 1988. The analysis treats land as exogenous in both the south and the north, though the possibility of greater bias in the south needs to be kept in mind when interpreting the results.

Possible omitted variable bias is more worrying. The regressions control for omitted between-commune variance through the commune dummy variables. But there may also be latent heterogeneity in, say, land or soil quality within communes, leading to biased estimates. Testing for this by including land quality variables in the regression revealed no sign of such bias, however, (van de Walle 1997). Again, this could be more of an issue in the south, where salinity and acidity are common problems in the Mekong Delta, though unobserved in the survey data. The chapter returns to this point later.

Ordinary least squares is used on a regression sample consisting of 3,049 farm households, including some urban farm households.[12] The regression results indicate strong, though diminishing, effects of both irrigated and nonirrigated cropland on crop income. Household size has a positive impact on crop incomes, as does its interaction with land variables. But the findings also suggest that the importance of the labor market constraint varies across households and regions, with family labor tending to be a constraining factor in farm production in the north, but less so in the south, particularly for large irrigated farms in the Mekong Delta.[13]

Education, particularly primary education, is also found to be of considerable importance to agricultural productivity. Interaction effects between education variables and land are generally positive. There are significant commune fixed effects and significant spatial differences in the effects of irrigated land, nonirrigated land, and other types of land.

Table 4.11 presents the marginal effect on crop incomes of the key included variables, allowing for all interaction effects. Annual cropland, both irrigated and nonirrigated, and perennial cropland have high significant positive effects on crop income. The impact of irrigated land is more than twice that of nonirrigated land. The returns to perennial land are also higher than those to nonirrigated annual land. Other significant marginal effects are from education, particularly of the household head, which has a significant positive impact on crop income, and from household size. Larger households have higher crop incomes. The finding that family labor continues to play an important part in agricultural production is a recurrent one.

The Benefits from Irrigation: Policy Simulations

Irrigation is not a simple private good, and it would almost certainly be undersupplied by individuals, even without capital market imperfections. Ensuring that electricity is provided to run pumps tends to require public involvement. And since groundwater is a common property resource, in some settings public regulation or operation is necessary (Carruthers and

Clark 1983). Public resources are needed to set things up, coordination is required among networks serving many uses and users, and the benefits are distributed among many people. Some inputs have to be publicly provided, while some can be provided privately, as long as credit is available. Ensuring access to poor farmers has also required public involvement in many countries (Carruthers and Clark 1983). These factors help explain why there could be underinvestment in irrigation in Vietnam.

What are the potential benefits from irrigating a unit of nonirrigated land, holding total cultivable land area constant? How would those benefits be distributed across expenditure groups? And how might they vary with other factors? An attempt is made here to quantify those benefits using the regression model described above.

It is assumed that nonirrigated annual cropland can feasibly be irrigated (though costs may vary widely across regions) and that perennial cropland and other types of land cannot be. Annual cropland may be converted to irrigation through rehabilitation and expansion of existing irrigation networks or through new construction. The analysis considers the distributional impact of irrigating about 10 percent of the annual cropland currently not under irrigation under four possible policy scenarios for distributing the irrigation expansion among farms.

Simulation 1 simply extends irrigation to all farm households that have nonirrigated land. Because some farm households have little or no nonirrigated land, a policy of bringing 10 percent of nonirrigated annual cropland

Table 4.11 Marginal Effect on Net Crop Income, Allowing for Interaction Effects

Variable	Unit	Marginal effect	t-ratio
Irrigated annual cropland	Dong per 100 m²	48,571.5	16.1
Nonirrigated annual cropland	Dong per 100 m²	19,994.0	8.1
Perennial cropland	Dong per 100 m²	21,269.1	4.1
Forest land	Dong per 100 m²	8,722.1	1.9
Water surface	Dong per 100 m²	−86,491.2	0.1
Other land	Dong per 100 m²	10,422.2	1.2
Household size	Dong per person	59,065.9	2.0
Female adults (percentage of household)	Dong per percentage point	−2,366.5	0.1
Male adults (percentage of household)	Dong per percentage point	−1,165.1	0.2
Children aged 7–16 (percentage of household)	Dong per percentage point	1,041.6	0.2
Primary education (head)	Dong per year	191,875.8	3.0
Education above primary (head)	Dong per year	38,584.9	2.0
Primary education (other adults)	Dong per year	35,094.1	2.5
Education above primary (other adults)	Dong per year	22,195.7	1.8
Mean crop income		2,282,069.0	

Note: Based on the crop income regression model (unrestricted version) reported in van de Walle (1996). Marginal effects are evaluated at mean data points.
Source: Author's calculations.

under irrigation allows a maximum of 500 square meters of newly irrigated land per farm household or a mean of about 260 square meters per household.

Farm households tend to have all their annual cropland irrigated or none at all. So a policy of converting nonirrigated land to irrigation may more realistically be implemented in areas where farm households presently have little irrigation. Simulation 2 limits the expansion of irrigation to farms lacking access to irrigated land.

Simulations 3 and 4 target smallholders. As discussed, poor farm households tend to have less annual cropland and less irrigated land than nonpoor households. It is therefore of interest to examine how the distributional effects of bringing 10 percent of the country's nonirrigated annual land under irrigation would differ if those improvements were targeted to households with low total annual cropland holdings. Simulation 3 distributes the irrigation on the basis of low total household holdings of annual cropland, while simulation 4 targets on the basis of low per capita holdings. Once again, the simulations hold total annual cropland constant. Given the existing distribution of irrigated and nonirrigated land across households, simulation 3 results in the irrigation of all the nonirrigated land of households with less than 3,250 square meters of annual cropland, and simulation 4, the nonirrigated land of all those with less than 620 square meters per person.

The expected marginal benefit from irrigation—the change in household crop income from irrigating one unit of nonirrigated land—is estimated by recalculating the value of the function after substituting constrained land changes into the profit function as follows:

$$(4.4) \qquad \Delta\pi_j = \pi(p_j, L^N_j - \Delta L_j, L^I_j + \Delta L_j, z_j) - \pi(p_j, L^N_j, L^I_j, z_j),$$

where, for example, in simulation 1 (and as appropriate for the others)

$$\Delta L_j = 0 \ \ \text{if} \ \ L^N_j = 0$$
$$= L^N_j \ \ \text{if} \ \ L^N_j \leq 500,$$

so that the amount of land shifted into irrigation is appropriate to each household's circumstances—zero for those that have no nonirrigated land and up to 500 square meters for those that do. The results are termed the *simulated total impacts.*

Converting 10 percent of nonirrigated land to irrigation produces an increase in crop incomes equal on average to about 1 percent of mean household expenditure. That implies an elasticity of 0.1. The elasticities vary only slightly across the simulations. But the size of per capita effects and their distribution differ across national expenditure groups depending on how the irrigation is distributed (table 4.12). The results reflect the allocation of the irrigation expansion combined with the existing household distribution of irrigated and nonirrigated annual cropland and the influence of other household and community factors entering the marginal benefit of irrigation function, such as education, household size, and region.

Under simulation 1, with equal distribution to all households subject only to land constraints, impacts are smaller at the lower and upper ends of the distribution but otherwise relatively steady across expenditure groups. Simulation 2 tends to be more generous toward the upper end of the distribution and less so at the bottom end, though the impacts differ little from those under simulation 1. Targeting the irrigation expansion to smallholders results in larger impacts at the lower end of the distribution and the impacts decline much more sharply with rising welfare when targeting is on the basis of per capita rather than household holdings of annual cropland. Under all four simulations the effects are certainly progressive—declining as a share of household expenditure as living standards rise—and so reduce inequality. Progressivity is most pronounced for simulation 4, which confers large benefits on the poorest groups (equal to 4.5 percent of household expenditure for the poorest group, compared with only 0.1 percent for the wealthiest).

Gains are very concentrated regionally (tables 4.13–4.16). The potential benefits of irrigation appear to be strongest in the Northern Uplands, where the simulated total impacts are largest for all simulations (with mean impacts of up to 3 percent of mean household expenditure). Irrigation expansion reduces inequality there, especially when it is targeted to house-

Table 4.12 National Distribution of Impacts of Irrigation Expansion under Four Scenarios

Expenditure group	Thousands of dong per person per year	Share of farm population (percent)
1	0–500	4.1
2	501–600	4.1
3	601–700	6.9
4	701–800	9.6
5	801–900	9.2
6	901–1,000	9.2
7	1,001–1,100	9.1
8	1,101–1,250	11.5
9	1,251–1,400	8.0
10	1,401–1,550	7.3
11	1,551–1,800	7.2
12	1,801–2,200	6.9
13	2,201–3,000	5.0
14	3,001–4,500	2.1
Total		100

Note: In all four simulations 10 percent of nonirrigated annual cropland is converted to irrigation. In simulation 1 irrigation is distributed to all households subject to land constraints; in simulation 2, to households without irrigated land; in simulation 3, to households with low total holdings of annual cropland; and in simulation

holds with low per capita landholdings. But the net gains tend to be relatively steady across expenditure groups in all except simulation 4.

The next largest impacts are found in the North-Central Coast and Southeast. In the North-Central Coast the impacts generally reduce inequality, though by less than in the Northern Uplands. Benefits tend to increase with expenditure class in the North-Central Coast except under simulation 4, which again results in the most progressive distribution of benefits. In the Southeast the impacts tend to be larger for the better-off (except under simulation 4) and flat or only somewhat progressive when expressed as a proportion of household expenditure. Impacts are smallest for the Central Coast and the Mekong Delta, and the benefits far from progressive.

One interesting finding from the above is that benefits tend to be larger where their distribution is more pro-poor. That hints toward targeting irrigation expansion to the Northern Uplands and North-Central Coast, where benefits are both large and well distributed. These are also Vietnam's poorest regions (World Bank 1994a; chapter 2 in this volume).

The regional picture is quite robust across simulations. Nationally, there is little obvious tradeoff between the different ways of distributing the irrigation across regions. Interestingly, however, there is a distinct pattern in the regions in which the simulations have the greatest impact, no doubt reflecting regional differences in how annual cropland is dis-

Simulated total impacts (dong per capita)				Simulated total impacts as a percentage of household expenditure			
1	*2*	*3*	*4*	*1*	*2*	*3*	*4*
9,099.3	6,700.7	11,878.1	19,310.3	2.13	1.57	2.78	4.52
12,645.6	15,513.5	13,267.7	15,314.7	2.29	2.81	2.40	2.77
16,059.4	13,118.9	14,217.7	14,604.0	2.47	2.02	2.18	2.24
14,132.9	12,312.0	15,185.0	16,657.2	1.88	1.64	2.02	2.22
13,750.1	11,443.8	15,974.4	10,287.4	1.62	1.35	1.88	1.21
14,775.1	10,704.2	14,482.1	9,108.2	1.56	1.13	1.53	0.96
12,924.6	9,183.1	11,281.8	11,328.6	1.23	0.88	1.08	1.08
11,396.7	10,261.8	11,310.6	7,977.2	0.97	0.87	0.96	0.68
15,035.7	12,469.1	14,279.8	14,383.4	1.14	0.94	1.08	1.09
14,185.6	13,287.7	13,194.1	9,476.3	0.96	0.90	0.90	0.64
10,240.5	10,226.4	6,653.9	2,836.9	0.62	0.62	0.40	0.17
9,947.0	9,328.1	10,000.7	3,602.2	0.50	0.47	0.51	0.18
10,142.9	11,421.5	5,143.5	3,433.6	0.41	0.46	0.21	0.14
10,935.7	13,185.7	5,215.5	3,900.1	0.28	0.34	0.13	0.10
12,844.6	11,226.5	12,221.3	10,293.6	1.05	0.92	1.00	0.84

4, to households with low per capita holdings of annual cropland.
Source: Author's calculations.

Table 4.13 Distribution of per Capita Impacts under Simulation 1, by Expenditure Group and Region
(dong per capita)

Expenditure group	Northern Uplands Simulated total impact	As a percentage of household expenditure	Red River Delta Simulated total impact	As a percentage of household expenditure	North-Central Coast Simulated total impact	As a percentage of household expenditure
1	27,985.5	6.53	8,335.3	1.88	14,788.3	3.35
2	31,584.0	5.80	5,188.6	0.93	18,062.1	3.28
3	35,212.4	5.37	9,028.8	1.39	15,553.4	2.40
4	34,651.3	4.62	5,162.9	0.68	16,729.4	2.23
5	35,820.9	4.22	6,623.6	0.78	18,529.7	2.19
6	35,807.7	3.81	10,776.5	1.14	20,855.1	2.19
7	30,698.2	2.93	5,547.2	0.53	19,847.3	1.89
8	33,514.2	2.83	11,012.6	0.93	18,230.6	1.54
9	33,915.7	2.58	12,650.2	0.95	22,188.9	1.68
10	30,031.7	2.05	9,656.7	0.67	25,121.2	1.70
11	29,949.4	1.82	8,392.4	0.50	22,120.2	1.35
12	36,663.7	1.86	10,786.7	0.55	26,043.7	1.32
13	29,741.7	1.23	11,884.4	0.47	22,954.4	0.93
14	28,907.6	0.84	8,488.1	0.22	2,900.7	0.08
Total	33,211.4	3.00	8,798.9	0.72	18,767.2	1.96

Note: Under simulation 1 the expansion in irrigation is distributed to all households subject to land constraints. Results are not shown for Central Highlands because there are too few observations.

Table 4.14 Distribution of per Capita Impacts under Simulation 2, by Expenditure Group and Region
(dong per capita)

Expenditure group	Northern Uplands Simulated total impact	As a percentage of household expenditure	Red River Delta Simulated total impact	As a percentage of household expenditure	North-Central Coast Simulated total impact	As a percentage of household expenditure
1	26,082.1	6.08	14,515.3	3.28	14,568.9	3.30
2	41,024.3	7.53	8,358.8	1.49	18,248.0	3.31
3	32,702.6	4.99	8,242.8	1.27	8,442.5	1.30
4	32,412.3	4.32	3,453.1	0.46	12,476.5	1.67
5	34,634.2	4.08	2,869.5	0.34	14,847.7	1.75
6	27,266.9	2.90	4,734.2	0.50	16,719.4	1.75
7	18,956.6	1.81	4,392.2	0.42	14,756.4	1.41
8	34,830.1	2.94	6,677.5	0.57	18,470.4	1.56
9	28,508.3	2.17	5,480.9	0.41	22,731.8	1.73
10	33,139.2	2.26	1,548.1	0.11	24,518.8	1.66
11	36,228.6	2.20	0.0	0.00	20,050.8	1.22
12	28,678.7	1.46	1,006.7	0.05	27,010.3	1.37
13	24,897.8	1.03	4,849.1	0.19	16,223.0	0.66
14	36,872.1	1.07	4,315.9	0.11	0.0	0.00
Total	30,499.2	2.76	4,323.2	0.35	15,755.8	1.65

Note: Under simulation 2 the expansion in irrigation is distributed only to households without irrigated land. Results are not shown for Central Highlands because there are too few observations.

Central Coast		Southeast		Mekong Delta	
Simulated total impact	As a percentage of household expenditure	Simulated total impact	As a percentage of household expenditure	Simulated total impact	As a percentage of household expenditure
1,855.0	0.47	1,216.7	0.30	741.1	0.17
2,989.3	0.54	12,305.0	2.25	−699.6	−0.13
2,645.0	0.41	13,792.3	2.08	6,001.8	0.91
2,704.7	0.36	10,336.9	1.38	4,027.0	0.54
5,195.5	0.61	14,442.1	1.69	3,895.0	0.46
5,480.6	0.57	6,382.4	0.67	4,785.5	0.50
6,768.6	0.64	14,822.4	1.41	3,409.2	0.33
5,822.9	0.50	4,831.1	0.41	4,704.2	0.40
7,073.4	0.54	14,254.1	1.06	4,175.5	0.31
4,587.0	0.31	14,492.9	0.96	8,923.5	0.60
3,201.8	0.20	18,261.2	1.10	7,429.5	0.45
6,518.4	0.33	16,186.4	0.83	7,982.8	0.40
9,928.3	0.41	21,402.4	0.86	7,954.7	0.31
10,387.3	0.31	9,820.4	0.20	11,955.2	0.31
5,151.6	0.42	12,805.3	0.86	5,839.3	0.40

Source: Author's calculations.

Central Coast		Southeast		Mekong Delta	
Simulated total impact	As a percentage of household expenditure	Simulated total impact	As a percentage of household expenditure	Simulated total impact	As a percentage of household expenditure
521.3	0.13	1,302.0	0.33	488.8	0.11
3,641.7	0.66	15,214.6	2.78	2,187.2	0.39
−1,617.5	−0.25	23,844.4	3.60	9,507.0	1.45
2,698.4	0.36	11,907.8	1.59	6,280.3	0.84
5,327.0	0.63	13,564.9	1.59	6,345.0	0.75
6,941.2	0.73	7,792.4	0.82	8,003.3	0.84
3,512.5	0.33	25,629.1	2.43	5,471.4	0.52
4,240.4	0.36	7,473.9	0.63	7,758.6	0.66
3,667.2	0.28	16,530.1	1.23	6,941.2	0.52
1,473.0	0.10	21,100.6	1.40	13,724.1	0.93
1,858.6	0.11	28,771.1	1.74	12,848.4	0.77
4,097.1	0.21	24,500.3	1.26	13,416.3	0.68
13,118.5	0.54	29,843.5	1.20	13,759.6	0.54
17,885.7	0.53	7,788.0	0.16	18,823.8	0.49
4,153.3	0.34	17,769.4	1.19	9,677.5	0.67

Source: Author's calculations.

Table 4.15 Distribution of per Capita Impacts under Simulation 3, by Expenditure Group and Region
(dong per capita)

Expenditure group	Northern Uplands		Red River Delta		North-Central Coast	
	Simulated total impact	*As a percentage of household expenditure*	*Simulated total impact*	*As a percentage of household expenditure*	*Simulated total impact*	*As a percentage of household expenditure*
1	40,040.0	9.34	0.0	0.0	16,744.0	3.79
2	28,688.4	5.26	8,789.7	1.57	18,282.8	3.32
3	41,771.8	6.37	2,980.7	0.46	16,166.5	2.49
4	32,566.1	4.34	3,814.9	0.50	22,552.6	3.01
5	48,170.9	5.68	2,630.6	0.31	30,108.0	3.56
6	30,457.6	3.24	10,523.6	1.12	18,341.9	1.92
7	22,029.0	2.10	3,662.2	0.35	21,273.1	2.03
8	29,176.5	2.46	9,711.9	0.82	23,350.0	1.97
9	31,302.4	2.38	11,247.7	0.85	17,343.6	1.32
10	36,372.9	2.48	8,862.0	0.60	31,239.5	2.11
11	21,393.9	1.30	6,116.1	0.37	24,493.6	1.50
12	30,343.8	1.54	9,582.8	0.49	41,661.6	2.11
13	44,089.7	1.82	14,057.4	0.56	22,001.1	0.89
14	522.3	0.02	6,134.8	0.16	0.0	0.00
Total	32,870.9	2.97	7,061.2	0.58	21,878.8	2.29

Note: Under simulation 3 the expansion in irrigation is targeted to households with low total holdings of annual cropland. Results are not shown for Central Highlands because there are too few observations.

Table 4.16 Distribution of per Capita Impacts under Simulation 4, by Expenditure Group and Region
(dong per capita)

Expenditure group	Northern Uplands		Red River Delta		North-Central Coast	
	Simulated total impact	*As a percentage of household expenditure*	*Simulated total impact*	*As a percentage of household expenditure*	*Simulated total impact*	*As a percentage of household expenditure*
1	66,093.4	15.42	0.0	0.0	23,270.5	5.27
2	51,335.4	9.42	385.7	0.07	15,460.6	2.81
3	31,943.0	4.87	2,162.0	0.33	25,377.8	3.92
4	43,557.8	5.80	4,634.6	0.61	21,889.9	2.92
5	35,629.3	4.20	2,384.4	0.28	13,680.9	1.62
6	26,856.1	2.86	2,441.6	0.26	21,172.2	2.22
7	27,165.8	2.59	2,837.3	0.27	21,864.7	2.08
8	26,032.9	2.20	8,312.0	0.71	21,085.6	1.78
9	37,681.2	2.87	11,383.2	0.86	8,878.4	0.67
10	25,623.7	1.75	3,072.4	0.21	18,073.4	1.22
11	1,761.8	0.11	4,892.5	0.29	4,787.3	0.29
12	8,570.6	0.43	5,237.3	0.27	14,804.9	0.75
13	29,762.1	1.23	2,424.2	0.10	10,597.2	0.43
14	522.3	0.02	6,134.8	0.16	0.0	0.00
Total	31,234.6	2.83	4,660.9	0.38	19,199.2	2.01

Note: Under simulation 4 the expansion in irrigation is targeted to households with low per capita holdings of annual cropland. Results are not shown for Central Highlands because there are too few observations.

Central Coast		Southeast		Mekong Delta	
Simulated total impact	*As a percentage of household expenditure*	*Simulated total impact*	*As a percentage of household expenditure*	*Simulated total impact*	*As a percentage of household expenditure*
201.9	0.05	1,287.6	0.32	1,670.3	0.38
1,763.3	0.32	13,122.9	2.40	1,577.5	0.28
−4,232.3	−0.66	0.0	0.00	6,011.3	0.92
3,308.1	0.44	23,583.0	3.15	1,821.5	0.24
9,489.9	1.12	15,552.6	1.83	2,026.1	0.24
6,740.2	0.71	2,634.5	0.28	4,037.7	0.43
7,292.6	0.69	16,304.3	1.55	652.7	0.06
7,016.3	0.60	9,025.0	0.76	−473.9	−0.04
3,902.9	0.30	27,273.7	2.03	1,390.3	0.10
4,978.5	0.33	4,394.7	0.29	3,578.1	0.24
4,465.9	0.27	10,752.1	0.65	1,530.2	0.09
6,564.8	0.33	11,809.2	0.61	4,639.1	0.23
23,895.0	0.98	7,336.1	0.29	152.4	0.01
9,968.8	0.29	5,342.3	0.11	5,280.6	0.14
6,166.9	0.98	12,051.9	0.81	2,144.9	0.14

Source: Author's calculations.

Central Coast		Southeast		Mekong Delta	
Simulated total impact	*As a percentage of household expenditure*	*Simulated total impact*	*As a percentage of household expenditure*	*Simulated total impact*	*As a percentage of household expenditure*
−12.8	−0.03	1,287.6	0.32	156.1	0.04
12,444.7	2.26	13,122.9	2.40	1,097.9	0.20
−2,818.3	−0.44	0.0	0.00	5,435.2	0.83
572.5	0.08	22,153.2	2.96	−2,719.8	−0.37
3,166.1	0.37	15,552.6	1.83	649.7	0.08
10,350.7	1.08	2,634.5	0.28	1,183.4	0.12
2,006.5	0.19	16,304.3	1.55	−2,227.8	−0.21
4,904.6	0.42	10,021.0	0.84	−473.9	−0.04
5,234.4	0.40	16,070.5	1.20	2,678.8	0.20
6,787.5	0.46	4,394.7	0.29	1,855.4	0.13
4,066.6	0.25	1,635.3	0.10	1,530.2	0.09
6,902.3	0.35	7,262.8	0.37	2,064.8	0.10
25,819.3	1.06	7,336.1	0.29	152.4	0.01
0.0	0.00	0.0	0.00	5,280.6	0.14
5,785.7	0.47	9,284.6	0.62	906.9	0.06

Source: Author's calculations.

tributed. Simulation 1 produces the largest gains in the Northern Uplands and Red River Delta; simulation 2, in the Southeast and Mekong Delta; and simulation 3, in the North-Central and Central Coasts. In each case the two regions are contiguous. Simulation 4 is distinguished by tending to favor the poor with larger absolute impacts and by producing the most progressive distribution of benefits across almost all regions.

At first sight, the simulation outcomes for the Mekong Delta appear surprising. They also appear robust. The Mekong is the country's primary rice-producing region with, as yet, only half its cultivated area under irrigation. But the Mekong Delta's situation is complex, and characteristics of its ecosystem and economy appear to provide credible explanations for the relatively small benefits. As mentioned earlier, irrigation systems in the Mekong Delta have been plagued by sea water intrusion and acid-sulphate soils. As more land has been brought under irrigation in upstream areas in recent years, the level and flow of the Mekong River have dwindled, resulting in salt water intrusion in previously productive irrigated fields downstream (NEDECO 1991; World Bank 1996). That has meant that only one crop can be grown annually or, in the worst case, that rice cultivation has become impossible. Areas where rice can no longer be grown are often converted to aquaculture activities, such as the farming of brackish shrimp. Such activities can be profitable, but are reflected in lower crop incomes. Fully irrigated areas may also suffer from extensive flooding and waterlogging for much of the year. In such areas of the Mekong what is needed is better water management and drainage control, not more irrigation.

The explanation for the Mekong results seems to lie in the heterogeneity of irrigated land in the delta. If the data allowed separation of irrigated areas suffering from salinity and acidity problems from other irrigated land, the results would probably show strong impacts from additional irrigation investments in the Mekong Delta. The results indicate low marginal benefits on average because the benefits are averaged over considerable heterogeneity. Thus the profits from irrigation vary not only among regions, but also within regions.

Household Labor Costs

In defining net crop incomes, no deduction was made for labor inputs by household members, largely because of uncertainty about how to measure the opportunity cost of family labor when alternatives to working on the family farm may not be available and there is a labor surplus.[14] The possibility remains that irrigated and nonirrigated land have different labor input requirements and thus that the estimated net gains from irrigation expansion may be under- or overestimated. Van de Walle (1996) tests the sensitivity of the simulation results to this assumption about own-labor costs by comparing the net marginal effect of irrigating nonirrigated land on the cost of the family labor input with the previously calculated net marginal effect on crop incomes.

Van de Walle (1996, 1997) finds that irrigation tends to increase work on the family farm. Converting nonirrigated land to irrigation raises the market value of family labor time by an estimated 7,279 dong per 100 square meters. Subtracting this amount from the average net impact on crop incomes of converting 100 square meters of nonirrigated land to irrigation reduces the net gain to 21,299 dong, 25 percent less than the earlier results. These calculations assume that the shadow wage of family labor equals the full agricultural wage rate and may considerably overestimate the costs.[15] If the opportunity cost of family labor is assumed instead to be half the market wage, the gain in farm profit from irrigating 100 square meters of nonirrigated land is 24,939 dong, 13 percent less. The earlier results therefore overestimated the marginal effect of irrigation on farm profits by a maximum of 25 percent.

The Cost of Expanding Irrigation

Information on the costs of irrigation expansion is hard to come by, and generalizations across regions and types of irrigation investments are risky. Nonetheless, even a rough sense of the cost-benefit appraisal can be useful. The costs of large-scale irrigation projects have been estimated by several agencies for different regions of Vietnam. Estimated average costs—including for a World Bank irrigation rehabilitation project in the Central Coast and a large number of water resource development projects in the Mekong Delta drawn up as part of the Mekong Delta Master Plan— fluctuate around 85,000 dong per 100 square meters. Although these are averages for several projects, the variance is low.[16]

For these costs, the estimated model indicates an annual gain in net crop income of about 28,600 dong per 100 square meters, falling to 21,300 dong at the maximum shadow wage for family labor. That represents a rate of return of at least 25–35 percent a year, assuming that the project delivers such benefits indefinitely. But even under conservative assumptions of a project life of only 10 years and with the maximum shadow wage for family labor, the rate of return is about 20 percent.[17]

However, although the variance in costs for the projects reviewed was low, these projects are all located in the river deltas or the flat central areas of the country and represent a certain type of large-scale irrigation development. Costs are likely to differ for irrigation projects in the highlands or more isolated regions and for smaller-scale undertakings. For example, low-lift pumps may have lower initial capital costs but higher operating costs (Carruthers and Clark 1983). Naturally, site-specific rates of return must be calculated for each project and compared with economic appraisals of alternative uses of the resources.[18]

Conclusion

Vietnam has poor infrastructure and high poverty. These two facts are intimately linked. The nature of the connections between the two and their implications for the role of infrastructure investments in fighting poverty are complex, however, and difficult to disentangle. This chapter has focused on some aspects of the link between poverty and lack of infrastructure using the Vietnam Living Standards Survey.

Access to infrastructure services is poor for most Vietnamese. Rural areas are less well provisioned than urban, and some regions fare worse than others. There are distinct differences between the north and south. There are also differences among infrastructure services, with the provision of social service facilities generally superior to that of other physical infrastructure. And there are differences between poor and nonpoor: the provision of piped water and electricity reveals considerable disparities. But by and large, basic infrastructure services are generally inadequate for all groups, though generally worst for the poor. As a result, it cannot be surmised that expanding investment in basic infrastructure will primarily benefit the poor. Indeed, there is ample scope for the nonpoor to capture the lion's share of the direct gains from infrastructure investment in Vietnam.

To assess how investing in infrastructure would affect poverty, it is necessary to examine the distribution of the marginal benefits of specific investments. The chapter focuses on irrigation investments using cross-sectional variation to estimate the marginal effects of converting nonirrigated annual cropland to irrigation. It simulates a policy of irrigating 10 percent of currently nonirrigated annual cropland based on a regression model for crop income that includes irrigated and nonirrigated land as explanatory variables. The expansion in irrigation is distributed in four different ways: to all households subject to land constraints, to households without irrigated land, to households with low total holdings of annual cropland, and to households with low per capita holdings of annual cropland.

In general, the results suggest that an undifferentiated expansion of irrigation would be redistributive—with higher proportionate income gains going to poorer households. Targeting the irrigation expansion to households with small per capita landholdings produces the most progressive distribution of gains as well as the largest benefits for the poor. The results for all four scenarios show the largest total impacts on net crop incomes—and the most pro-poor distribution—in Vietnam's two poorest regions, the Northern Uplands and the North-Central Coast.

These substantial potential gains in equity are likely to be accompanied by sizable average rates of return. Even under quite conservative assumptions—a project life of only 10 years and family labor inputs valued at the market wage—the average annual rate of return implied by the estimated gains in farm profits and the investment cost of irrigation would be about 20 percent. Even larger returns might be possible with a more differentiated expansion of irrigation that emphasizes key regions such as the Northern Uplands and with rehabilitation of existing irrigation infrastructure. Conversely, the rate of return would undoubtedly be lower in areas where expanding irrigation is particularly costly.

In a normal setting we wouldn't expect such high rates of return. They may be overestimated. Although tests for biases were conducted (see van de Walle 1996 and 1997), there may still be omitted quality heterogeneity in land, which could lead to overestimation of the benefits from irrigation with the type of data available. But this is not a particularly "normal" setting. High rates of return to irrigation are not implausible in present-day Vietnam, because so little investment in agriculture and rural infrastructure has been possible until recently.

Lack of irrigation infrastructure is clearly not the only constraint to reducing rural poverty in Vietnam. The quantity and quality of families' human resources also matter greatly. And not only do other important constraints exist, but these constraints are inextricably bound to the benefits that households can ultimately derive from irrigation infrastructure. The analysis uncovers important complementarities between education, particularly primary education, and the gains from irrigation. Demographics (particularly household size) are also found to be key. And it can be conjectured that the lack of other infrastructure—roads, electricity, communications—also conspires to reduce the benefits that can be garnered from irrigation alone.

Notes

The author would like to thank Shanta Devarajan, Paul Glewwe, Frannie Humplick, Nauman Ilias, Jennie Litvack, Amit Mohindra, Martin Ravallion, Tom Wiens, and three anonymous referees for their help and useful comments. Financial assistance from RPO BB67883 is gratefully acknowledged.

1. Links between poverty and infrastructure are discussed in World Bank (1994c), Lipton and Ravallion (1995), and Jimenez (1995). For sector-specific discussions see Howe and Richards (1984), Binswanger, Khandker, and Rosenzweig (1993), and Goldstein (1993).

2. Expansion factors are not needed as the survey is self-weighted. The community questionnaire relies on interviews of village leaders, health care workers, teachers, and local government officials.

3. Regional poverty lines are estimated using the cost-of-basic-needs methodology (Ravallion 1994, and detailed in World Bank 1994a). Deflating by region-specific poverty lines is an alternative to using a regional price index. Because the weighting diagram used in deriving poverty lines tends to be more appropriate to the poor than that typically used in spatial price indices, deflating by region-specific poverty lines is often preferred for investigations of poverty.

4. The questionnaire asks whether "most" or "just a few" have electricity.

5. These countries are chosen as comparators because they have Living Standards Measurement Surveys that follow the same methodologies used in the 1992–93 Vietnam Living Standards Survey and ask similar questions. The data on access to piped water in rural areas are as follows: Ghana, 13.5 percent of households (1991–92 Ghana Living Standards Survey); Tanzania, more than 21.5 percent of households (1993–94 Human Resources Development Survey), though this number excludes obtaining water from a neighbor's piped water supply; Pakistan, 15 percent of households (Pakistan Integrated Household Survey 1991–92); and Peru, 43 percent of the rural Sierra population (1991 Living Standards Measurement Survey).

6. Results on access to piped water in urban areas are as follows: Ghana, 73.5 percent of households (1991–92 Ghana Living Standards Survey); Tanzania, more than 56 percent of households (1993–94 Human Resources Development Survey), though this number excludes obtaining water from a neighbor's piped water supply; Pakistan, 57 percent of households (Pakistan Integrated Household Survey 1991–92); and Peru, 91 percent of the urban Sierra population (1991 Living Standards Measurement Survey).

7. Sources are as detailed in note 5.

8. The expected outcome might be different if irrigation could be adequately targeted to the poor, but targeting can often be difficult and costly (van de Walle 1995b).

9. In addition to annual cropland, households derive agricultural income from perennial cropland (used for perennial tree crops), forest land (natural forest or reforested areas used for seeding young plants and growing forest tree crops), water surface (for raising water products), and other land, which includes vacant lots and bald hills (land managed by households but not cultivated for at least 12 months), virgin land (burnt and fallow land), and other (road and dike sides, river banks, and the like).

10. Net crop incomes are defined as total revenue minus total production costs. Total revenue from agricultural land production includes all crops evaluated at harvest prices (missing values are replaced by average community prices), the value of crop by-products consumed or sold (such as thatch, straw, cassava trunks, maize, and jute), land income (rents from other households and government assistance), and income from leasing out farm equipment. Total production costs include hired labor expenses; costs of seeds and young plants; fertilizer, manure, and insecticide costs; animal rental, transport, packaging and storage, equipment rental, repair and maintenance fees, and fuel oil and electricity costs; an accounting depreciation charge for farm equipment owned (5 percent); taxes and fees to the cooperative (such as for irrigation, crop protection, and plowing); land payments, such as rent for land leased and land taxes paid to the government or cooperative. Transformation of homegrown crops (such as producing cured tobacco, peanut oil, and rice noodles) is not included, but treated as family off-farm enterprises using farm inputs. The opportunity costs of household farm labor also are not included. The section on household labor costs discusses the sensitivity of the results to this assumption. Also note that profits from raising livestock are not part of net crop income.

11. Other explanatory variables include household size and composition; gender of the household head; years of primary school (grades 0–5) and of any additional education of the household head; years of primary school (grades 0–5) and of any additional education for all other household members over 17; access to various kinds of land as described in note 9; proportions of annual cropland in various forms of ownership; the stock of household savings; and dummy variables for urban residence and whether a household member was ill in the past year.

12. As discussed in van de Walle (1996), a number of functional form specifications were tried. A linear model with quadratics in land and education variables was found to perform best. Van de Walle (1996) reports two regressions—an unrestricted version that contains all the variables and a restricted model in which all variables with t-statistics below 1 are pruned. All results reported here, including the simulations, are based on the unrestricted model. Full regression details are available from the author.

13. Van de Walle (1996 and 1997) gives supporting evidence for this interpretation. For example, commune-level wage data suggest that labor markets are better developed in the south. Salinger (1993) provides further corroboration of this. The Mekong Delta is characterized by large areas that are either irrigated or not irrigated. As discussed later, irrigation appears to increase the labor input requirement. Labor markets are thus likely to have developed more fully in areas of the Mekong that have large irrigated farms.

14. Recall that nonfamily labor costs are included.

15. The community survey provides information on prevailing commune-level agricultural wage rates by gender and for children, for a number of tasks. Thus wage rates are not household-specific. And there are many missing data. Demographic-specific commune mean agricultural wages are formed over all tasks for which wage rates are recorded and used to value time on all farm tasks by each household member. Missing data at the commune level are replaced by the regional means for men, women, or children, as appropriate.

16. The World Bank project average costs are estimated at about 83,150 dong per 100 square meters when excluding consultant costs and physical and price contingencies. The Mekong Master Plan projects average 85,830 dong, 87,650 dong, and 87,120 dong per 100 square meters (NEDECO 1993).

17. These are internal rates of return that equate the present value of the stream of benefits over the chosen period with initial costs.

18. Proper rates of return would also need to factor in future maintenance and operating costs, which are often significant.

References

Barker, Randolph. 1994. *Agricultural Policy Analysis for Transition to a Market-Oriented Economy in Viet Nam: Selected Issues.* FAO Economic and Social Development Paper 123. Rome: Food and Agriculture Organization.

Binswanger, Hans P., Shahidur R. Khandker, and Mark R. Rosenzweig. 1993. "How Infrastructure and Financial Institutions Affect Agricultural Output and

Investment in India." *Journal of Development Economics* 41(2): 337–66.

Carruthers, Ian, and Colin Clark. 1983. *The Economics of Irrigation*. Liverpool: Liverpool University Press.

Dreyfus, Fabrice. 1993. *Tradition, Idéologies et Pragmatismes: l'Exemple de la Collectivisation et de la Décollectivisation de l'Agriculture au Viêt-nam du Nord*. Montpellier, France: Centre national d'études agronomiques des régions chaudes.

Goldstein, Ellen. 1993. "The Impact of Rural Infrastructure on Rural Poverty." World Bank, South Asia Region, Washington, D.C.

Howe, John, and Peter Richards, eds. 1984. *Rural Roads and Poverty Alleviation*. London: Intermediate Technology Publications.

Jimenez, Emmanuel. 1995. "Human and Physical Infrastructure: Public Investment and Pricing Policies in Developing Countries." In Jere Behrman and T. N. Srinivasan, eds., *Handbook of Development Economics*. vol. 3. Amsterdam: North Holland.

Le Thanh Nghiep. 1993. "Agricultural Development in Viet Nam: Issues and Proposals for Reform." In Mya Than and Joseph L. H. Tan, eds., *Vietnam's Dilemmas and Options: The Challenge of Economic Transition in the 1990s*. Singapore: Institute of South East Asian Studies.

Lipton, Michael, and Martin Ravallion. 1995. "Poverty and Policy." In Jere Behrman and T. N. Srinivasan, eds., *Handbook of Development Economics*. vol. 3. Amsterdam: North Holland.

NEDECO (Netherlands Engineering Consultants). 1991. "Mekong Delta Master Plan: Inception Report." Amsterdam: North Holland.

———. 1993. "Draft Master Plan for the Mekong Delta in Viet Nam: A Perspective for Sustainable Development of Land and Water Resources." Amsterdam: North Holland.

Ravallion, Martin. 1994. "Poverty Comparisons." *Fundamentals in Pure and Applied Economics* 56. Chur, Switzerland: Harwood Academic Press.

Salinger, Lynn B. 1993. "Viet Nam's Agricultural Comparative Advantage and Export Potential." Associates for International Resources and Development, Cambridge, Mass.

Vietnam State Planning Committee, UNDP (United Nations Development Programme), FAO (Food and Agriculture Organization), and World Bank. 1989. "Viet Nam Agricultural and Food Production Sector Review." Mission report. Hanoi.

UNICEF (United Nations Children's Fund). 1994. *Situation Analysis of Women and Children in Viet Nam*. Hanoi.

van de Walle, Dominique. 1995a. "Rural Poverty in an Emerging Market Economy: Is Diversification into Non Farm Activities in Rural Viet Nam the Solution?" World Bank, Development Research Group, Washington, D.C.

———. 1995b. "Targeting and Incidence: An Overview of Implications for Research and Policy." In Dominique van de Walle and Kimberly Nead, eds., *Public Spending and the Poor: Theory and Evidence*. Baltimore, Md.: Johns Hopkins University Press.

———. 1996. "Infrastructure and Poverty in Viet Nam." Living Standards Measurement Study Working Paper 121. World Bank, Washington, D.C.

———. 1997. "Human Capital and Labor Market Constraints in Developing Countries: A Case Study of Irrigation in Viet Nam." World Bank, Development Research Group, Washington, D.C.

Vu, Tu Lap, and Christian Taillard. 1993. *Atlas du Viet Nam.* Montpellier and Paris: Reclus, La Documentation Française.

World Bank. 1990. "Viet Nam: Water Supply and Sanitation Sector Study." East Asia and Pacific Region, Country Department I, Washington, D.C.

———. 1994a. "Viet Nam: Poverty Assessment and Strategy." Report 13442-VN. East Asia and Pacific Region, Country Department I, Washington, D.C.

———. 1994b. "Viet Nam Transport Sector: Serving an Economy in Transition." Report 12778-VN. East Asia and Pacific Region, Country Department I, Washington, D.C.

———. 1994c. *World Development Report 1994: Infrastructure for Development.* New York: Oxford University Press.

———. 1996. "Viet Nam: Water Resources Sector Review." Report 15041-VN. East Asia and Pacific Region, Country Department I, Washington, D.C.

5

Nonfarm Household Enterprises in Vietnam

Wim P. M. Vijverberg

Vietnam is becoming a market-oriented economy. Successive economic reforms have legitimized economic activity in the private sector and boosted production. Policy initiatives are under way to make state enterprises economically accountable, privatizing some and shutting down those that are unprofitable. Entrepreneurship, markets, and efficiency are popular buzzwords. The government must enhance tax revenue to finance growth-facilitating programs and find ways to tax the private sector equitably. Furthermore, because population density is high and the labor force is growing rapidly, the country must generate employment in the nonfarm sector, especially in rural areas, to avoid mass migration flows to cities. Such flows would be economically disruptive and would likely increase urban poverty and congestion.

Vietnam is counting on the self-employed to contribute to economic growth. Studies have shown that average self-employment incomes may well exceed average wage earnings (see, for example, Chiswick 1977; Mazumdar 1981; Teilhet-Waldorf and Waldorf 1983; Vijverberg 1986; and Speare and Harris 1986), contrary to the perception of self-employment as a low-status, low-income, dead-end career. Mazumdar (1981) and Blau (1986) report workers moving out of wage employment into self-employment, and the self-employed are likely found across the whole income distribution, rather than merely at the bottom of it.

This chapter addresses a number of questions concerning the self-employed. First, are they young or old, men or women? Are they members of particular ethnic groups? Are they educated? How important are their self-employment activities to their incomes? We will see that about 60 percent of the self-employed combine their entrepreneurial activities with either wage employment or farming activities, and that there are significant male-female and north-south differences.

Second, do households with nonfarm enterprises have high or low standards of living as measured by per capita consumption expenditures? It turns out that the nonfarm self-employed are underrepresented at the bottom of the income distribution and overrepresented at the top. Also, statistical evidence shows that a more productive household enterprise is associated with a higher standard of living.

Third, how can we characterize family enterprises in the private sector? The enterprises surveyed in the Vietnam Living Standards Survey appear typical of the private sector in Vietnam. About a third of the enterprises are in the retail trade sector, and a little more than a fourth are in manufacturing. Less than half operate year-round. The size distribution is extremely skewed, with many small and few large enterprises populating each sector. Importantly, one in seven enterprises reports paying a license tax; one in four pays some other kind of tax. For an hour of family labor the average enterprise yields between 2,000 and 2,600 dong. This figure compares favorably with the average wage of 1,300 dong.

Fourth, which factors raise incomes of the self-employed, catapulting their households to the top of the living standards distribution? Both physical capital (buildings, vehicles, boats, tools, equipment, and so on) and inventory stocks yield substantial returns that may rise as enterprises grow. Also, additional hours of work raise incomes: people working in nonfarm enterprises are not underemployed, nor is their productivity driven to zero, as some proponents of segmented labor markets believe. Primary schooling does not appear to contribute to enterprise income, but secondary schooling and higher have a fairly small but precisely estimated rate of return, raising incomes by 3.1 percent per year (or between 8,800 and 16,400 dong monthly). There is also a strong age effect distinguishing young and elderly workers from those in the 25–55 age range. Women earn about 40 percent less than men in otherwise equivalent enterprises. Part of that gap is explained by the discrepancy in capital and inventory holdings. Still, regional differences in enterprise incomes persist, even controlling for these variables.

Fifth, are women at a disadvantage? Traditionally, women in Vietnam have been extensively involved in market exchange and family finances (Pelzer 1993, 317–25). The socialist revolution emphasized the employment of women and gender equality. The U.S. presence lowered the female labor force participation rates: in South Vietnam, women were not as deeply involved in market work as they were in the north. Extended periods of war and the general culture of Southeast Asia have promoted high labor force participation rates for women (Kaufman and Sen 1993, 236–37). Still, women are at a disadvantage, even if less so than elsewhere in the world. Women earn less in their family enterprises, in part because they are undercapitalized. And their literacy rates, especially those for older women, are lower than for men, and school enrollment of girls is less than that of boys.

The Current Business Environment

The private sector in Vietnam differs in the north and the south. In the northern economy of the late 1950s the private sector functioned under the suffocating control of the communist regime. In the mining, trade, transport, handicraft, and manufacturing sectors private enterprises were replaced by public enterprises or absorbed into cooperatives: by the mid-1960s the state controlled the vast majority of economic activity. The official statistics of 1971 indicate the state's partial retreat from the construction, transport, and trade sectors, with the share of state enterprises and cooperatives being 78 percent, 83 percent, and 57 percent, respectively (Nguyen Tien Hung 1977, chapter 4). It is also likely that a substantial number of enterprises were engaged in petty production and trade—they were either unregistered and illegal or registered but small and escaping state regulation and control (Fforde and Paine 1987, 97; Ljunggren 1993, 65–66, 78).

By contrast, the south had a flourishing capitalist system until 1975, though one dependent on U.S. involvement. After the fall of the South Vietnam regime in 1975, the policy focus was to bring the private sector under the public umbrella, as was done earlier in the north (Nguyen Tien Hung 1977, chapter 9). In 1976 this policy was accelerated (Ljunggren 1993, 59). Traders were severely restricted in the range of commodities they could trade. Larger enterprises were reorganized into state enterprises, and owners received little compensation for their firms' value. Access to factors of production was controlled more tightly (see, for example, Hy Van Luong 1993, 123). Smaller enterprises were turned into cooperatives (Porter 1993, 44). A new currency, the dong, replaced the old, the piaster, with limitations on the amounts that could be exchanged. These limitations affected larger enterprises more than smaller ones and allowed for state monitoring and control of private investable cash holdings (Nguyen Tien Hung 1977, chapter 9).

Official policy toward private initiative in general and the private productive sector in particular started to turn as early as September 1979 (Beresford 1988, chapter 11; Fforde 1993, 300; Ljunggren 1993, 77–84). Small-scale producers were able to sell their wares on a free market, highway checkpoints were closed in order to encourage a free flow of goods transported by private traders, and regulation and licensing procedures were eased. These changes unleashed substantial productive activity—to such an extent that, in 1983, some political leaders blamed private traders for inflation and unemployment. The government attempted to curtail private trading with steep taxes and licensing fees, and revoked the freedom of industrial enterprises to buy and sell outside official channels. Efforts to push the larger still-private enterprises into cooperatives continued (Hy Van Luong 1993, 119). In 1985 the government implemented another currency change, introducing the new dong, one of which was exchanged for 10 old dong. The state bank strictly limited the amount of convertible currency so as to reduce private wealth and cash holdings—a move that therefore sharply restricted black market activity (Beresford 1988, 169) and private investment in family enterprises.

By late 1986 it had become clear that the economic performance of the state-controlled sector was so poor that a policy reform favoring the private sector was inevitable (Porter 1993, 44): the policy of *doi moi* was born. Small private enterprises with up to 30 employees were now allowed to operate, though with restrictions on the type of commodities they could produce. Further regulatory liberalizations took place in 1988 and 1989, and private enterprises employing up to 1,000 workers sprang up even in the north. In the south businesses that had been nationalized since 1975 were returned to their former owners or relatives of the owners (Turley 1993, 7; Hy Van Luong 1993, 119). Underground enterprises operating in sectors that had been only state monopolies, including gold, silver, precious stones, food and foodstuffs, and credit, were given legitimacy (Vo Dai Luoc 1993, 114); foodstuff traders soon took the market away from state enterprises. By 1990–91 most inputs and outputs were sold on free markets, without rationing or price controls (Fforde 1993, 312). Migration was still restricted, though labor markets were mostly free. Capital and land markets were still weak (Ljunggren 1993, 95; Fforde 1993, 313–14).

Under guidelines approved at the Seventh Party Congress in 1992, 19 state enterprises were to be privatized (or "equitized") under a pilot program, but only 3 were in fact privatized by 1995 (Rondinelli and Le 1995, 33; World Bank 1995, 106). Resistance among workers and managers, difficulty in valuing the enterprises, and problems with regulations, management inexperience, and debt settlement turned out to be significant hurdles. In the early 1990s the nonstate sector was producing more than one-third of total industrial output, more than half of the service sector's output, and more than 90 percent of agricultural output (World Bank 1995).[1] It provided almost two-thirds of all jobs in the manufacturing sector; overall, employment in the state sector fell by 1.1 million jobs between 1988 and 1993, while the nonstate sector generated 5.4 million jobs (Ljunggren 1993, 81–82; World Bank 1995, 33).

In all, the economic and political climate for private enterprises since the reunification of 1975 can be characterized as initially moderate (1976), but then severely repressed (1978), followed by a relaxing of a few restrictions (1981), a renewed clampdown (1983–85), and the beginning (1986) and acceleration (1988–89) of *doi moi*. That review brings us to the Vietnam Living Standards Survey (VNLSS) of 1992–93. The family enterprises surveyed started up in the middle of these events. It would be extremely interesting to examine the sensitivity of start-up decisions to fluctuations in the economic and political climate. Unfortunately, the current sample of enterprises consists only of those that survived until the date of the interview. Examining the frequency distribution of start-up dates of the current VNLSS enterprises, we see that there are few old enterprises in the sample (figure 5.1). There is also evidence that mild relaxations in 1981 and the subsequent clampdown in 1984–85 affected business start-ups. Many businesses have started since 1988, though the number has leveled off in the past year or so. (Note that the decline in 1993 owes to the timing of the survey.) It should also be noted that there is surprisingly little difference between the patterns in the north and the south.

Given Vietnam's history, one might expect that the private sector consists mostly of young enterprises relative to other parts of the world. But this is not the case. The average enterprise age in Vietnam is 7.2 years; in Peru the average age was 10 years in 1985 (Moock, Musgrove, and Stelcner 1990). In Vietnam 33.3 percent of enterprises are younger than 2.5 years, 33 percent are older than 7 years, and 20.6 percent are older than 11 years. In Côte d'Ivoire in 1985–86, 30 percent of the enterprises were less than 2 years old, and 18 percent were 11 years or older (Vijverberg 1991). In Ghana in 1987–89, 36.7 percent of enterprises were less than 4 years old, and 36.3 percent were more than 7 years old (Vijverberg 1995). One may conclude, therefore, that, notwithstanding the unfavorable policy climate of earlier years, the age distribution of (and likely the rate of attrition of) enterprises in Vietnam has been roughly similar to that of freer economies.

Nonfarm Self-employment in the Context of Labor Market Activities

It is standard practice to divide labor market activities into three categories: wage employment (working for someone else), farming (self-

Figure 5.1 Frequency Distribution of Family Enterprise Start-up Dates, Vietnam, 1992–93

Percentage of enterprises

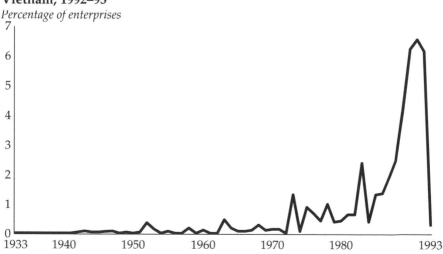

Source: 1992–93 Vietnam Living Standards Survey.

employment in agricultural activities), and nonfarm self-employment (in industries ranging from retail trade and service provision to manufacturing, fishing, and transportation). I look at the labor force first descriptively and then using a multivariate model.

Descriptive Analysis

The following analysis describes the entire population aged six years or older, which is consistent with the structure of the VNLSS questionnaire and the fact that many children and elderly people report participating in labor market activities. There is a long list of interesting features according to which we can characterize the nonfarm self-employed: urban or rural residence, region, sex, ethnicity, age, schooling level, and household poverty level. Many Vietnamese engage in more than one of the three labor market activities. For example, 18.3 percent work for a wage or salary, 52.1 percent work on a farm, 18.3 percent are self-employed in a nonfarm activity, and 29.2 percent are not employed (table 5.1a). These figures add up to more than 100 percent, since each person engaging in two or three forms of employment is counted two or three times. Thus of the 18.3 percent of nonfarm self-employed, only 7.8 percent make it their only activity. Fully 9.9 percent are also active in farming activities, 1.3 percent also have a wage job, and 0.5 percent combine both farming and a wage job. Also note that 23 percent of total labor market hours are spent in nonfarm self-employment activities. As this figure is higher than 18.3 percent, it implies that the nonfarm self-employed devote more hours to that activity than one might have guessed based only on the participation rate.

   Not surprisingly, farming activities are less important in urban areas. Both wage and nonfarm self-employment is more prevalent there. Men hold more wage jobs; women more often engage in self-employment, especially in urban areas. In rural areas nonfarm self-employment is often only a part-time activity. Likewise, in urban areas many of the self-employed also hold wage jobs. But as a percentage of total hours, nonfarm self-employment is much more important. For example, while 32.5 percent of urban women are nonfarm self-employed, they contribute 53.2 percent of all hours that women supply to the labor market.

   We can also decompose these statistics by region (table 5.1b). Farming is much more prevalent in the north, even in the Red River Delta area, than in the south. Nonfarm self-employment activities are equally common in all areas of Vietnam, with the exception of the more remote areas of the Northern Uplands and the Central Highlands. The wage employment pattern across regions is consistent with the degree of urbanization, but the rate of unemployment is sharply different between the north and the south. In terms of hours of work, nonfarm self-employment is more important in the south (with the exception of the Central Highlands): the hours percentage is substantially higher than the participation percentage.

The differences between male and female workers are also more pronounced in the south.

There are also important differences among ethnic groups (table 5.1c). Nonfarm self-employment is mostly an activity of the Vietnamese (Kinh) and Chinese members of the population. And because farming is rarely practiced among Chinese, they do not often combine nonfarm and farm self-employment. We also see ethnic differences in the male-female ratios: nonfarm self-employment is more prevalent among Thai, Muong, Nung, Dao, and "other" men than women. The women in each of these groups engage extensively in farming and consequently put less emphasis on nonfarm self-employment.

Are there gender differences in the employment picture by age group (table 5.1d)? Consider first the rate of unemployment. The higher unemployment rate of 11–20-year-old males corresponds to their higher rates of schooling. From the 21–30 age group onward, the female unemployment rate is somewhat higher. This finding is not surprising for the childbearing years. It is surprising that women's labor force participation rates are so high for all age groups. Recall, though, that these rates describe annual participation rather than participation at the time of the survey. Also, high female labor force participation rates are common throughout East Asia, especially in nearby Cambodia and Thailand (see, for example, Durand 1975; Galenson 1992; ILO 1992). Men in the 21–50 age range work the longest hours of all men, whereas, among women, young women (11–20) and older women (51–70) work slightly longer hours on average than men.

Nonfarm self-employment is more prevalent among women of all ages than for the corresponding age group among men, except for women

Table 5.1a Labor Market Participation in Vietnam, by Rural or Urban Residence and by Gender, 1992–93

Characteristic	Total	Rural			Urban		
		Total	Male	Female	Total	Male	Female
Participation in labor market activities (percent)							
Wage employment	18.3	16.2	21.1	11.5	26.8	31.7	22.5
Farming	52.1	65.0	65.0	65.0	17.1	15.8	18.0
Nonfarm self-employment	18.3	15.5	14.3	16.6	29.3	25.4	32.5
Only activity	7.8	4.2	3.4	5.0	21.6	19.1	23.7
With farming	9.9	9.9	9.2	10.5	4.5	2.8	5.9
With wage employment	1.3	0.9	1.1	0.7	2.9	3.0	2.8
With farm and wage employment	0.5	0.5	0.6	0.4	0.3	0.5	0.1
Not employed	29.2	26.7	26.5	26.8	38.9	38.1	39.7
Hours of work in nonfarm self-employment as a percentage of total hours spent in labor market activities	23.0	16.1	13.7	18.4	47.0	39.8	53.2
Number of observations	20,368	16,152	7,753	8,399	4,216	1,970	2,246

Source: 1992–93 Vietnam Living Standards Survey.

Table 5.1b Labor Market Participation in Vietnam, by Region, 1992–93

| | | North | | |
Characteristic	Total	Northern Uplands	Red River Delta	North-Central Coast
Participation in labor market activities (percent)				
Wage employment	14.2	12.5	17.0	12.8
Farming	65.7	69.9	60.4	71.8
Nonfarm self-employment	17.3	12.5	21.2	16.5
Only activity	5.4	4.0	6.9	4.5
With farming	10.5	7.3	12.6	10.8
With wage employment	0.9	0.8	1.2	0.6
With farm and wage employment	0.5	0.4	0.5	0.6
Male	16.9	12.7	20.0	16.9
Female	17.6	12.2	22.2	16.1
Not employed	24.2	22.3	27.3	21.2
Hours of work in nonfarm self-employment as a percentage of total hours spent in labor market activities	17.8	11.3	23.5	18.6
Male	16.9	10.3	21.6	19.6
Female	18.6	12.1	25.2	19.8
Number of observations	10,065	3,310	4,418	2,537

Source: 1992–93 Vietnam Living Standards Survey.

Table 5.1c Labor Market Participation in Vietnam, by Ethnic Group, 1992–93

Characteristic	Vietnam (Kinh)	Tay	Thai	Chinese
Participation in labor market activities (percent)				
Wage employment	18.9	6.5	8.9	25.2
Farming	54.0	70.4	75.2	7.6
Nonfarm self-employment	19.6	6.7	2.6	30.6
Only activity	8.2	1.7	0.0	26.2
With farming	9.5	4.1	2.6	2.1
With wage employment	1.4	0.7	0.0	2.1
With farm and wage employment	0.5	0.2	0.0	0.2
Male	17.6	5.5	5.4	28.7
Female	21.4	10.5	0.0	32.5
Not employed	29.5	24.6	23.2	41.8
Hours of work in nonfarm self-employment as a percentage of total hours spent in labor market activities	25.4	5.4	2.2	49.2
Male	21.3	2.6	4.3	40.9
Female	29.2	7.9	0.0	59.5
Number of observations	17,298	410	190	512

Source: 1992–93 Vietnam Living Standards Survey.

		South		
Total	Central Coast	Central Highlands	Southeast	Mekong Delta
22.3	17.9	16.0	24.9	23.9
44.6	47.0	64.2	25.0	51.9
19.3	15.2	7.0	21.3	19.7
10.2	10.8	2.3	15.0	8.1
7.0	6.6	4.7	4.3	9.1
1.7	1.7	0.0	1.8	1.8
0.4	0.1	0.0	0.2	0.7
16.0	16.6	4.7	19.0	15.6
22.3	21.8	9.2	23.1	23.6
34.1	33.8	31.4	40.4	31.0
28.6	29.0	8.6	35.5	26.9
21.7	23.3	3.9	29.3	18.4
35.4	34.2	13.5	42.3	35.2
10,303	2,425	602	2,627	4,649

Khome	Muong	Nung	H'mong	Dao	Other
29.7	15.8	5.6	0.8	2.2	12.8
59.4	74.4	83.8	82.1	71.7	69.9
12.7	12.0	5.3	0.0	4.3	3.1
3.0	0.3	0.0	0.0	0.0	1.0
8.7	10.6	4.4	0.0	4.3	2.1
1.0	0.8	0.3	0.0	0.0	0.0
0.0	0.3	0.6	0.0	0.0	0.0
6.5	16.7	5.8	0.0	8.7	3.6
17.7	7.4	4.7	0.0	0.0	2.7
28.0	24.5	15.9	17.9	28.3	28.2
14.1	8.1	2.2	0.0	3.7	3.5
6.0	12.4	2.7	0.0	6.9	4.4
22.1	3.9	1.8	0.0	0.0	2.5
404	387	320	123	46	678

between the ages of 31 and 40. Even for that group, however, the hours percentage is higher than that for men. Women more often combine nonfarm self-employment with farming; men, with wage employment. This difference is likely associated with the types of self-employment activities that people choose. We will see evidence of this later on.

Table 5.1d Labor Market Participation in Vietnam, by Age and Gender, 1992–93

Characteristic	6–10	11–20	21–30	31–40	41–50	51–60	61–70	>70	Total
Male									
Participation in labor									
market activities (percent)									
Wage employment	0.3	15.5	42.2	43.5	35.2	21.6	8.4	3.0	23.3
Farming	14.2	55.9	70.9	70.4	68.1	69.4	55.5	36.2	55.0
Nonfarm self-employment	1.0	11.2	23.2	32.3	29.1	18.0	11.1	4.1	16.6
Only activity	0.9	5.0	8.0	11.1	12.5	8.7	5.8	2.6	6.6
With farming	0.1	5.4	11.7	15.9	12.9	8.7	4.8	1.5	7.9
With wage employment	0.0	0.7	2.3	3.8	3.0	0.3	0.4	0.0	1.5
With farm and wage									
employment	0.0	0.1	1.2	1.5	0.7	0.3	0.0	0.0	0.6
Not employed	84.5	32.4	4.4	1.2	3.5	13.7	34.8	60.1	28.1
In school	85.3	47.3	1.7	0.3	0.1	0.0	0.0	0.0	27.7
Hours of work in nonfarm self-employment as a percentage of total hours spent in labor market activities	6.3	13.9	17.3	23.8	26.5	19.5	20.3	19.4	19.3
If working, total hours of work	883	1,356	1,815	1,885	1,823	1,487	1,279	827	1,610
Number of observations	1,648	2,645	1,788	1,456	762	619	537	268	9,723
Female									
Participation in labor									
market activities (percent)									
Wage employment	0.1	13.1	22.4	24.2	19.7	9.3	2.2	0.4	13.8
Farming	12.7	56.6	70.9	72.0	70.6	66.1	46.7	16.8	55.0
Nonfarm self-employment	1.3	16.6	28.6	31.1	31.4	20.8	16.3	4.1	19.9
Only activity	1.1	7.8	11.9	13.1	12.1	10.0	10.9	2.5	8.9
With farming	0.2	7.7	14.8	14.5	16.8	9.5	5.2	1.6	9.5
With wage employment	0.0	0.8	1.3	2.7	2.4	1.0	0.2	0.0	1.2
With farm and wage									
employment	0.0	0.3	0.6	0.8	0.1	0.3	0.0	0.0	0.3
Not employed	86.0	29.5	6.8	4.0	7.6	19.4	41.3	88.3	29.5
In school	86.0	36.7	0.7	0.4	0.0	0.0	0.0	0.0	21.9
Hours of work in nonfarm self-employment as a percentage of total hours spent in labor market activities	7.6	21.4	25.9	27.7	31.0	30.2	38.1	30.6	26.6
If working, total hours of work	843	1,390	1,662	1,805	1,748	1,517	1,295	797	1,570
Number of observations	1,526	2,716	1,961	1,684	916	793	617	432	10,645

Source: 1992–93 Vietnam Living Standards Survey.

Table 5.1e Labor Market Participation in Vietnam, by Years of Schooling, 1992–93

Characteristics	0	1–5	6–9	10–12	>12
Participation in labor market activities (percent)					
Wage employment	10.0	12.7	20.2	26.4	55.3
Farming	40.5	51.7	63.1	67.7	37.8
Nonfarm self-employment	8.0	14.0	22.5	28.5	24.8
Only activity	3.1	6.2	9.9	11.7	11.5
With farming	4.2	6.8	10.8	14.3	5.6
With wage employment	0.4	0.8	1.4	1.8	6.6
With farm and wage employment	0.3	0.2	0.5	0.7	1.1
Male	5.3	10.6	19.8	27.0	25.1
Female	9.5	17.1	25.5	30.2	24.5
Not employed	52.5	37.7	18.2	9.4	14.2
Hours of work in nonfarm self-employment as a percentage of total hours spent in labor market activities	16.5	21.6	24.0	26.2	22.6
Male	10.5	15.7	19.7	24.0	22.3
Female	19.9	26.7	28.5	28.5	23.0
Number of observations	3,012	8,469	3,479	4,619	789
Participation in labor market activities among those older than 20 years (percent)					
Wage employment	12.9	19.7	26.6	29.2	58.7
Farming	54.8	69.7	68.3	70.4	39.7
Nonfarm self-employment	11.7	22.6	30.7	30.8	25.9
Not employed	35.9	14.4	6.9	5.2	10.0
Number of observations	1,735	4,043	1,705	3,619	731

Note: Years of schooling includes completed academic, vocational, and postsecondary training, and excludes apprenticeship, technical, and professional training.
Source: 1992–93 Vietnam Living Standards Survey.

As for schooling, at the lowest levels the unemployment rate is high, though many of these unemployed are children who are still in school (table 5.1e). But even among adults over 20, a high percentage of those with no schooling do not work in the labor market. Further disaggregation by age shows that a large number of them are elderly. About 66 percent of those without any schooling are more than 50 years old, of this subgroup 80.9 percent are women. At higher levels of schooling both wage employment and nonfarm self-employment become more prevalent, and fewer people remain unemployed. Farming remains important until the group with 10–12 years of schooling is reached, even for those who engage in nonfarm self-employment. The number that combine nonfarm self-employment with a wage job jumps significantly for those with more than 12 years of schooling. This is again an indication that the nature of self-employment activities varies systematically across people.

In sum, nonfarm self-employment is more prevalent among women, among people aged 21–50, among the more educated, among the Chinese and Vietnamese (Kinh) populations, and in urban areas. But these conclusions are based on simple crosstabulations. It remains to be seen whether factors such as ethnicity, schooling, and region of residence each have an independent effect on the incidence of self-employment and the patterns revealed in tables 5.1a–e are more than the simple result of correlations among these variables. We need a multivariate model that incorporates all relevant factors simultaneously.

Multivariate Probit Model

In the tabulations above, the individual was the unit of analysis. But many enterprises employ several family members, thus suggesting it is the household unit rather than the individual household member who decides to operate an enterprise.[2] Using a probit model, I generate parameter estimates linking the determinants to the likelihood that a household operates a nonfarm enterprise (table 5.2). A positive estimate implies that the particular variable raises this likelihood.

Of the sample of 4,800 households, 36 percent operated an enterprise at the time of the survey, and 45 percent did so at some point in the 12 months before the interview. Both of these figures are relevant: the difference consists of firms that do not operate currently because of seasonal factors or have gone out of business because of negative profits. Note, though, that since the survey ran continuously for slightly more than a year, some of the enterprises operating currently are seasonal. The parameter estimates indicate whether a household is inclined to operate an enterprise year-round or seasonally.

The first group of variables considers residence, using the north and the rural areas as the basis of comparison. The second group describes rural communities through a number of indices. These indices are not available for urban areas: for urban households, they are coded as "0." In general, one would expect schools, roads, markets, public transportation, electricity, and piped water to be more widely available in urban areas. Thus the parameter estimates of the urban region variables in the first group measure the average effect of all these amenities. As such, they may be compared with the cumulative effect of all measured characteristics of the rural communities. For the average rural community this sum equals 0.4932 for the first column of estimates and –0.0332 for the second. Thus, with the exception of urban localities in the North-Central Coast (with parameter estimates of 0.3305 and –0.1893) and possibly the Southeast, urban households are more likely to operate a nonfarm enterprise than are rural households, even holding all other factors that appear in the table constant.

In rural communities the decision to run an enterprise is influenced by the presence of a regularly operating local market, the level of local wages, the availability of secondary schools, and the spread of electricity and piped water in the community. These are direct and indirect measures of

Table 5.2 Probit Estimates of Whether a Household Operates a Nonfarm Enterprise

Variable	Mean	Range	Enterprise operated at time of interview		Enterprise operated at some time during past 12 months	
Intercept			−1.1759	(4.91)	−0.1982	(0.89)
Residence						
South	0.460	0–1	0.0240	(0.41)	−0.1233	(2.16)
Urban Northern Uplands	0.027	0–1	1.1034	(4.35)	0.3632	(1.52)
Urban Red River Delta	0.043	0–1	1.1732	(4.75)	0.3030	(1.31)
Urban North-Central Coast	0.013	0–1	0.3305	(1.16)	−0.1893	(0.72)
Urban Central-Coast	0.033	0–1	1.1627	(4.63)	0.4437	(1.87)
Urban Southeast	0.047	0–1	0.7688	(3.12)	−0.0071	(0.03)
Urban Mekong Delta	0.040	0–1	1.0184	(4.14)	0.3218	(1.40)
Rural community characteristics[a]						
Availability of lower and upper secondary school	1.373	0–2	0.2684	(2.19)	0.0439	(0.40)
Agricultural extension index	1.273	0–2	−0.1490	(3.34)	−0.2575	(6.00)
Presence and quality of roads	0.745	0–1	−0.2278	(1.71)	−0.3782	(2.90)
Availability of public transportation	7.343	0–80	0.0003	(0.18)	0.0004	(0.28)
Utilization of electricity and piped water	0.373	0–1.33	0.1963	(1.78)	0.1317	(1.24)
Presence and frequency of local market	0.461	0–1	0.3963	(3.51)	0.3109	(2.94)
Presence of market in nearby community	0.193	0–1	0.2058	(1.55)	0.1397	(1.14)
Local wage index	7.021	0–19.7	0.0248	(2.96)	0.0396	(4.85)
Dummy = 1 if local wage index unknown	0.013	0–1	0.9331	(5.36)	1.2077	(5.92)
Household characteristics[b]						
Number of:						
Women aged 16 years and older	1.595	0–7	0.0984	(2.56)	0.0637	(1.69)
Persons aged 16–25 years	0.919	0–7	−0.0766	(1.89)	−0.0881	(2.23)
Persons aged 26–35 years	0.742	0–6	0.0459	(1.01)	0.0141	(0.32)
Persons aged 36–45 years	0.487	0–4	0.0749	(1.55)	0.0159	(0.34)
Persons aged 46–55 years	0.302	0–3	0.0522	(0.96)	−0.0237	(0.45)
Persons aged 56–65 years	0.283	0–3	−0.0459	(0.91)	−0.1305	(2.65)
Persons aged over 65 years	0.247	0–3	−0.2018	(4.09)	−0.2418	(5.07)
Persons with 1–3 years schooling	0.445	0–6	0.0848	(2.14)	0.1314	(3.43)
Persons with 4–5 years schooling	0.531	0–7	0.1175	(3.07)	0.1697	(4.56)
Persons with 6–9 years schooling	1.102	0–7	0.1290	(3.71)	0.2053	(6.06)
Persons with 10–12 years schooling	0.508	0–9	0.1812	(4.39)	0.2237	(5.52)
Persons with postsecondary schooling	0.239	0–7	−0.0826	(2.01)	−0.1488	(3.65)
Persons with technical training	0.105	0–5	0.0354	(0.63)	0.0262	(0.46)
Persons with completed apprenticeships	0.228	0–7	0.1673	(4.58)	0.1537	(4.14)
Characteristics of the parents of head and spouse[c]						
Average years of schooling	2.851	0–17	−0.0015	(0.21)	0.0149	(2.18)
Dummy = 1 if years of schooling unknown	0.225	0–1	−0.0241	(0.37)	−0.0127	(0.20)
Major occupation: farmer	0.783	0–1	−0.5125	(6.81)	−0.4749	(6.29)
Major occupation: manager	0.005	0–1	0.5956	(1.27)	0.3569	(0.76)
Major occupation: proprietor	0.028	0–1	0.6675	(3.22)	0.6905	(3.23)

(Table continues on next page.)

Table 5.2 Probit Estimates of Whether a Household Operates a Nonfarm Enterprise (continued)

Variable	Mean	Range	Enterprise operated at time of interview		Enterprise operated at some time during past 12 months	
Major occupation: supervisor	0.002	0–0.5	−0.2808	(0.39)	−0.2605	(0.36)
Dummy = 1 if major occupation						
unknown	0.002	0–1	0.0860	(0.13)	−0.0445	(0.07)
Log-likelihood value			−2,741.84		−2,945.79	

a. As a group the rural community characteristics are statistically significant at the 0.01 percent level in both models.

b. As a group the household characteristics are significant at the 0.01 percent level in both models.

c. These variables describe the parents of the head and spouse (if applicable), unless these parents live in the household, in which case the variables describe the grandparents. As a group the parental characteristics are statistically significant at the 0.01 percent level.

Source: Author's calculations, based on 1992–93 Vietnam Living Standards Survey data.

the dynamics of the local economic environment. Agricultural extension services make farming more attractive and thus deter nonfarm self-employment activities. Availability of public transportation (measured roughly as how often public transportation is available each day) does not matter. The presence and quality of a local road have an unexpected negative effect. However, we can dismiss this result because in the south roads are not as important for transportation as are inland waterways, and because the questionnaire did not define for the survey participants what constituted a viable road. A community without the need to transport commodities is more likely to call a dirt path a road than a community that struggles to transport heavy loads over that same dirt path.

The list of household characteristics includes sex, age, and education, and, additionally, incidence of technical and (completed) apprenticeship training. The results drawn from the univariate descriptive statistics are confirmed here: there are significant age and education effects, and a household with more women is more likely to engage in nonfarm self-employment. People with past apprenticeship training are also more likely to operate nonfarm enterprises.[3]

A history of entrepreneurship in the family might predispose some to operate an enterprise themselves. Therefore the estimated model includes measures of schooling and occupation for the household head's and spouse's parents. Some parents may still live in the household and would thus be likely to participate in the decision to operate an enterprise. In that case information on them is endogenous to the estimated model. But such parents are also asked about *their* parents' backgrounds, which we can use as relevant information (that is, as instruments).

The impact of parental schooling is uncertain: the first column shows an insignificant effect; the second column shows a positive effect that is consistent with the impact of the household's own educational attainment.

The occupational variables reveal a strong intergenerational effect. Compared with laborers (which, in their many forms, are the excluded category), sons and daughters of proprietors are more likely to operate a nonfarm enterprise, and sons and daughters of farmers, less likely.[4]

Nonfarm Self-employment and the Incidence of Poverty

Before turning to nonfarm household enterprises, we should ask how labor market patterns relate to poverty. As we move from the lowest to the highest quintile, participation in wage employment and nonfarm self-employment rises, and participation in farming diminishes (table 5.3). The trends are almost flat, though still significant, for the first three (poorest) quintiles. They accelerate for the fourth and especially the fifth quintile. The difference between male and female involvement in nonfarm self-employment widens as well, both in participation and in hours devoted to labor. Nevertheless, the difference between the first and fifth quintile in wage employment is only 6.1 percentage points, compared with a difference of 15.8 points for nonfarm self-employment. Thus, unlike experiences in other countries (such as Côte d'Ivoire or Ghana), wage employment does not lift a household into the highest quintile.

Given the differing histories of the north and the south, and the differing position of women in the two regions, it is worthwhile to disaggregate our survey data along these lines. In the north wage employment rises sharply with quintile levels; in the south it falls slightly. In the north farming slowly decreases in importance until the fourth quintile; in the south it remains constant. The involvement in nonfarm self-employment rises with income in both regions, but whereas there is male-female equality in the north until the fourth quintile, in the south women are more engaged in nonfarm self-employment at all levels.

In sum, people engaged in nonfarm self-employment activities live in households that tend to be better off than households with wage employees and, in particular, the farming class. Women are not at any clear disadvantage: while self-employed women in the south are slightly worse off than their male counterparts, in the north they are slightly better off.

Characteristics of Nonfarm Enterprises

We now turn our attention to the nonfarm enterprises themselves, as described by respondents in the VNLSS. Enterprises are categorized by industry on the basis of respondents' descriptions of their activities (table 5.4). About 32.5 percent of the enterprises are in retail trade, 13.8 percent are categorized as fisheries, and 27 percent are in manufacturing. To create homogeneous subsamples, manufacturing industries are broken down into food (including beverage and tobacco), textiles (including leather products and footwear), and other manufacturing. Food commerce (including lodging facilities) and services are the two remaining larger groups. By nature, the service industry is quite heterogeneous, covering everything from financial services to repair and cleaning services. The remaining category, "other," contains primarily transportation, communication, construction, wholesale trade, and some hunting and agricultural services.

About three-quarters of the enterprises were operating at the time of the survey interview, with significant variation across industries. Retail trade, food commerce, and service enterprises were more likely to be open for business at the time of the interviewer's visit—they were open more

Table 5.3 Labor Market Activity and the Standard of Living in Vietnam, by per Capita Expenditure Quintile, 1992–93

Labor market involvement	1	2	3	4	5
All Vietnam					
Participation in labor market activities (percent)					
Wage employment	15.9	16.1	17.2	19.9	22.0
Farming	64.3	64.1	61.5	56.2	32.0
Nonfarm self-employment	11.5	13.9	16.8	20.5	27.3
Only activity	2.4	4.2	5.5	8.1	17.5
With farming	7.6	8.4	10.0	10.6	7.1
With wage employment	1.0	0.8	1.0	1.3	2.3
With farm and wage employment	0.5	0.5	0.4	0.5	0.4
Male	10.6	13.0	15.7	17.6	24.3
Female	12.4	14.6	17.9	23.3	30.0
Not employed	28.2	27.3	27.3	27.6	34.9
Hours of work in nonfarm self-employment as a percentage of total hours spent in labor market activities	10.6	14.4	18.7	24.9	41.7
Male	9.8	12.3	15.0	20.2	35.7
Female	11.3	16.5	22.5	29.1	47.3
Number of observations	3,781	3,906	4,048	4,268	4,365
North					
Participation in labor market activities (percent)					
Wage employment	10.8	11.6	14.2	16.2	22.7
Farming	72.3	72.9	68.9	63.5	38.1
Nonfarm self-employment	11.8	14.4	18.2	20.7	26.2
Male	12.2	14.1	18.6	20.0	23.2
Female	11.3	14.5	17.8	21.6	28.9
Not employed	24.0	22.3	22.9	23.0	31.7
South					
Participation in labor market activities (percent)					
Wage employment	24.5	23.2	20.6	23.0	21.7
Farming	51.1	50.4	53.0	51.2	29.5
Nonfarm self-employment	11.3	13.2	15.3	20.3	27.7
Male	7.9	11.3	12.2	15.5	24.7
Female	14.2	14.8	17.7	24.6	30.4
Not employed	35.3	34.9	32.4	31.4	36.3

Source: Author's calculations, based on 1992–93 Vietnam Living Standards Survey data.

days per month and more months per year, and were open year-round. These enterprises depend on a regular clientele and are likely less profitable when they operate sporadically. Sixty percent of the enterprises operate from a fixed location; fishery and "other" (mostly transportation) enterprises are more mobile, as one might expect. There is regional variation: in particular, retail trade, food commerce, and services are more likely to be urban operations in the south.

Labor Force

The median enterprise typically uses fewer hours of family labor than the average enterprise—the size distribution is strongly skewed to the left (figure 5.2). Even when the right tail of the distribution is truncated at 12,000 hours per year, there are still many more small than large enterprises. Retail trade, food commerce, and other manufacturing activities provide the most jobs.

Family workers average around seven years of schooling, with higher levels among those working in services (9.1 years) and textile manufacturing enterprises (8.2 years). There is some age variation among industries, but the more interesting differences are in the percentages of male and Chinese workers. As in other countries, such as Peru, Côte d'Ivoire, and Ghana, most family workers in retail trade, food commerce, and textiles manufacturing are women. In contrast, we see a high percentage of men in the fishery sector, in services, and in the "other" category, especially transportation. The Chinese self-employed are more concentrated in food commerce, services, and "other" enterprises.

As the variable for number of workers indicates, 84 percent of enterprises employ one or two workers, from the family or elsewhere; but only 6.9 percent hire at least one wage worker. This pattern was also found in a sample of Hanoi entrepreneurs (Le and Rondinelli 1993) and is a common feature of household enterprises elsewhere (Vijverberg 1990 for Côte d'Ivoire; Vijverberg 1996 for Pakistan and Ecuador). The "other manufacturing" category stands out as one in which a significantly larger share of enterprises hire outside workers (22.4 percent). A typical enterprise that hires workers will hire an average of 3.5 paid employees—more than the median number hired (2.0). Again, the distribution is skewed to the left. The number of enterprises reporting wages paid out is closely comparable, but as these two pieces of information derive from different (though adjacent) modules of the survey, there is no exact correspondence.

Are the characteristics relating to enterprise size typical of Vietnam's private sector? To get some idea, we can pool all enterprises surveyed explicitly in the VNLSS and all enterprises that employ a surveyed wage worker[5]—and then compare the proportion of enterprises surveyed within each size class. We find that the survey sample includes more small enterprises. This result is not surprising, since half of the enterprises with more

Table 5.4 Characteristics of Nonfarm Family Enterprises in Vietnam, 1992–93

(percent, unless otherwise specified)

Variable	All industries	Fishery	Food manufacturing	Textiles manufacturing
Number of observations	2,795	386	256	235
Percentage	100.0	13.8	9.2	8.4
Basic characteristics				
Open at visit	76.5	57.8	71.5	79.6
Days per month (mean)	23.1	18.3	21.3	23.2
Months per year (mean)	8.1	5.9	8.2	8.1
Year-round	42.3	15.5	42.4	32.8
Fixed location	59.7	17.6	83.2	93.2
Rural	69.2	93.0	85.2	71.5
Urban	30.8	7.0	14.8	28.5
North	50.6	59.3	67.6	51.9
South	49.4	40.7	32.4	48.1
Labor				
Annual hours of family labor				
Mean	2,212	1,800	1,761	1,812
Median	1,460	834	1,095	1,460
Years of schooling (mean)	7.0	5.6	7.5	8.2
Age (mean)	32.8	29.9	32.8	28.5
Female	55.1	28.9	54.0	72.2
Vietnamese (Kinh)	90.9	89.8	92.7	93.9
Chinese	3.9	0.2	2.7	4.1
Number of workers employed				
1	59.1	57.0	47.7	60.9
2	24.9	21.2	34.4	25.5
3–5	13.2	15.8	14.5	11.9
6–10	2.1	4.7	2.0	1.7
>10	0.8	1.3	1.6	0.0
Mean number of workers employed	1.82	2.09	2.13	1.64
Hire one or more wage worker	6.9	8.8	6.3	4.3
Conditional mean (number of wage workers hired)	3.5	3.5	5.6	2.1
Conditional median (number of wage workers hired)	2.0	3.0	2.5	1.5
Pay out wages	7.4	9.1	8.2	4.7
Conditional mean (wages paid, dong)	7,106	12,767	13,488	1,413
Conditional median (wages paid, dong)	2,283	4,618	2,233	550
Own capital				
Buildings	14.6	0.8	25.5	16.2
Vehicles	18.2	6.5	16.8	6.8
Tools and equipment	48.5	55.2	71.7	76.5
Boats	7.2	31.4	2.8	0.0
Other capital	21.5	20.5	22.3	17.9

Other manufacturing	Retail trade	Food commerce	Services	Other
263	909	191	219	336
9.4	32.5	6.8	7.8	12.0
79.1	80.4	89.0	87.7	73.5
23.3	24.8	27.8	23.7	22.1
8.0	8.7	9.5	9.4	7.7
37.5	50.6	69.6	59.3	33.6
78.3	59.5	83.2	77.2	30.4
71.9	62.9	46.6	48.9	69.4
28.1	37.1	53.4	51.1	30.6
57.4	46.1	37.7	35.2	51.2
42.6	53.9	62.3	64.8	48.8
2,677	2,446	3,162	1,817	2,015
1,911	1,877	2,581	1,460	1,460
6.9	6.7	6.9	9.1	7.5
32.5	34.6	35.8	35.6	32.0
43.1	75.2	73.0	38.8	32.0
94.2	92.5	89.5	89.3	83.1
2.7	4.1	7.8	6.6	6.1
30.0	65.0	57.1	81.7	56.3
25.1	26.8	27.3	11.4	23.5
28.1	7.6	14.1	6.4	17.3
6.8	0.4	0.5	0.5	2.1
1.9	0.2	1.1	0.0	0.9
2.64	1.50	1.79	1.31	1.94
22.4	2.1	5.8	2.3	11.6
3.3	2.3	4.2	2.2	3.6
3.0	1.0	2.0	3.0	2.0
25.5	2.6	6.8	2.7	13.1
5,490	9,225	2,512	3,499	4,135
3,446	875	2,337	4,239	1,744
20.3	15.2	26.8	17.4	6.0
9.5	23.5	15.7	10.1	39.5
60.2	32.2	50.3	57.5	32.0
0.8	6.1	0.0	0.0	5.1
15.6	25.4	40.8	17.8	10.5

(Table continues on next page.)

Table 5.4 Characteristics of Nonfarm Family Enterprises in Vietnam, 1992–93 (continued)

Variable	All industries	Fishery	Food manufacturing	Textiles manufacturing
Have inventories of unsold goods	34.2	7.3	26.2	45.5
Conditional mean (thousands of dong)	1,506	279	833	487
Conditional median (thousands of dong)	182	79	60	46
Have positive total capital resource	85.3	80.2	92.4	92.3
Conditional mean (thousands of dong)	5,097	6,925	6,481	3,692
Conditional median (thousands of dong)	359	151	506	463
Make annual capital investment	18.9	37.1	24.6	12.8
Conditional mean (thousands of dong)	5,127	13,505	927	614
Conditional median (thousands of dong)	121	149	139	195
Taxes				
Pay license tax	13.7	6.0	11.3	8.1
Conditional mean (thousands of dong, annually)	129	164	85	71
Conditional median (thousands of dong, annually)	62	129	55	30
Pay other tax	23.0	13.7	22.7	9.8
Conditional mean (thousands of dong, annually)	792	525	836	477
Conditional median (thousands of dong, annually)	210	110	121	139
Enterprise profitability (thousands of dong, annually)				
Total costs				
Mean	18,585	3,899	14,645	4,941
Median	2,357	12	2,683	321
Revenue[a]				
Mean	19,960	9,594	15,306	6,421
Median	4,345	1,054	4,062	1,503
Revenue[b]				
Mean	31,283	16,355	33,312	7,445
Median	6,820	1,850	6,985	2,532
Profit[a]				
Mean	1,361	5,685	661	480
Median	1,199	950	705	855
Profit[b]				
Mean	9,053	10,677	16,243	1,890
Median	2,657	1,726	3,356	1,777
Net revenue[a]				
Mean	3,351	3,000	3,001	1,939
Median	1,333	1,635	948	897
Net revenue[b]				
Mean	4,113	4,493	3,095	2,258
Median	1,835	1,194	1,480	1,328

a. Reported by enterprises operating during the past 12 months.
b. Reported by enterprises operating at the time of the second survey visit.

Other manufacturing	Retail trade	Food commerce	Services	Other
43.0	47.3	51.8	32.0	12.8
2,445	1,956	374	651	2,937
413	265	94	203	199
85.8	85.1	93.2	80.8	80.0
6,633	3,967	4,732	5,356	4,946
463	230	236	550	779
27.8	8.7	15.7	16.9	22.0
1,200	4,445	957	1,593	2,403
91	53	153	128	183
9.1	19.1	24.6	10.1	13.4
196	133	100	99	154
109	70	44	76	66
13.3	31.9	35.6	13.2	25.6
790	753	1,110	687	924
279	263	245	307	313
11,799	31,648	22,045	5,350	24,635
885	9,949	10,076	459	845
13,994	31,309	23,334	6,399	25,701
2,650	10,879	13,090	2,477	3,893
21,807	45,921	26,689	10,615	45,207
2,777	16,111	15,196	3,296	6,584
2,194	−339	1,289	1,023	1,065
1,348	1,136	2,158	1,361	1,852
7,229	9,659	3,377	4,818	14,584
1,539	3,199	3,790	2,163	3,924
3,448	3,302	5,511	2,600	4,245
1,301	1,521	2,639	1,395	1,877
4,151	4,115	5,254	3,616	5,505
1,699	1,998	3,118	1,816	2,820

Source: 1992–93 Vietnam Living Standards Survey.

**Figure 5.2 Distribution of Hours of Family Labor, Total Capital
Resources, and Annual Enterprise Income, Vietnam, 1992–93**

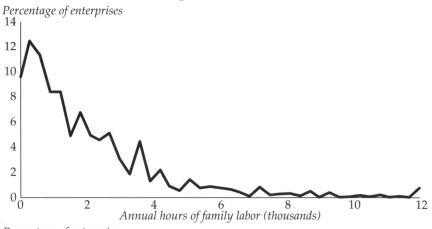

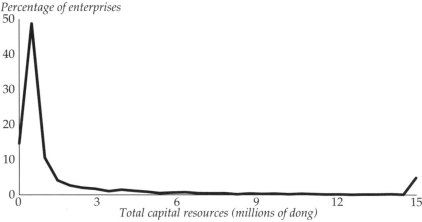

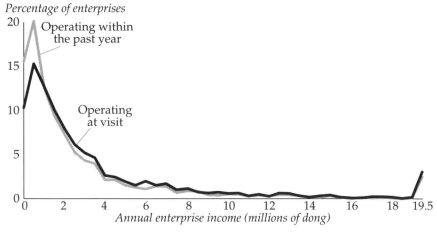

Source: 1992–93 Vietnam Living Standards Survey.

than 50 employees are mixed government-private enterprises, joint ventures, completely foreign-owned enterprises, or cooperatives—categories that are unlikely to be sampled with the Vietnam Living Standards Survey instrument. With this consideration in mind, one may conclude that the survey's sample of enterprises is indeed typical of the private sector.

Capital Stocks

About half of the entrepreneurs surveyed report that they own tools and equipment. This number is lower among retailers and, predictably, higher (but still less than 100 percent) among manufacturing enterprises. Unsold inventory holdings are also sporadic, even in retail trade and food commerce, where inventories can be an integral part of doing business. Among the 34.2 percent reporting positive inventories, the average value is 1.5 million dong, compared with the median value of 182,000 dong.

Total capital resource is the sum of total (physical) capital and unsold inventory holdings: 85.3 percent report a positive amount, with a strongly left-skewed distribution (figure 5.2). Every industry contains a few large enterprises and many small ones, judging size by capital stock. About a fifth of the entrepreneurs surveyed have invested in equipment, land, vehicles, or machinery (using the specific phrase of the questionnaire). The average amount is large compared with the average value of capital stock. But the median value is modest, 121,000 dong annually, considering that this value is the median only among the 18.9 percent of enterprises that made any purchases.

Taxation

Do enterprises pay taxes? Only 13.7 percent pay a license tax, with the rate rising significantly in the more visible retail trade (19.1 percent) and food commerce (24.6 percent) industries. The amounts paid are roughly similar across industries. Only 23 percent of all industries pay other taxes, again with larger proportions of the retail trade (31.9) and food commerce (35.6) sectors paying them. The values of these taxes are more varied than for license taxes. As one might expect, larger enterprises are more likely to pay tax. Survey results indicate that among small enterprises about 3 percent pay a license tax and 10 percent pay other taxes; among large enterprises 40 percent pay a license tax and 50 percent pay other taxes.[6]

In principle, enterprises are subject to a turnover tax, which has 19 different rates, and a profit tax of between 25 and 45 percent depending on the sector. But because many entrepreneurs do not keep books well, this tax is often replaced by a presumptive tax of between 1 percent and 3 percent of sales, which is comparatively low. In addition, enterprises may pay land taxes if they are involved in the transfer of land-use rights (although that tax may not have been in effect when the Living Standards Survey was taken), import duties, or fees related to licensing new enterprises and changing existing enterprises (World Bank 1995, 49–53, 71–75). Because enterprises have a greater incentive to overstate than understate their tax payments and because the percentage of tax-paying enterprises is low, small-scale private enterprises seem to be beyond the grasp of the government of Vietnam. There may also be a perception among small-scale entrepreneurs that the benefits of legitimacy are outweighed by the cost of complying with complicated registration procedures and the tedious tax code. Simplifying these procedures might well increase tax revenue. Full compliance in the payment of taxes may not raise license (or other) tax revenue by a factor of seven, or four (as implied by compliance rates documented in the survey), since larger enterprises are already more likely to pay taxes; but a doubling or more of the tax revenue should be within the realm of possibility.

Profitability

The VNLSS lists 12 enterprise operating cost categories and reports an average cost of 18.6 million dong and a median cost of 2.4 million dong over the length of a year. Part of this spread is a result of the fact that some enterprises are in business for only part of the year. Moreover, 8.9 percent of the enterprises report no operating expenditures. Sixty percent of these are in the fishery sector.

There are two sales revenue measures. The first category of sales revenue refers to revenue (including payments in kind and home-consumed goods) received between the first and second survey visit. Only those enterprises operating at the time of the second visit were able to provide that information. The second measure refers to typical monthly sales revenues over the past year. All enterprises operating at some point during the 12 months before the second visit responded.

Enterprises still operating at the time of the second survey interview received more sales revenue and were more profitable. Enterprises in retail trade, food commerce, and the "other" category reported the highest sales, though they also had higher costs. Judging by the mean values, the most profitable enterprises were therefore found in the food manufacturing, "other," and fishery sectors, with retail trade and other manufacturing following closely behind. Within the "other" sector, detailed tabulations show that it is mostly the transport sector and especially the wholesalers that fare so well.

There is a substantial discrepancy between profits of currently operating firms (mean 9.1 million dong, median 2.7 million dong) and profits of all firms operating during the past year (mean 1.4 million dong, median 1.2 million dong). Obviously, an entrepreneur might decide to discontinue operation because a firm has become unprofitable. Furthermore, cost and revenue data pertaining to the past 12 months suffer from greater recall error than data gathered about events in the two weeks between the survey visits. Finally, the profit values are subject to considerable uncertainty, since profit is the difference between sales revenue and operating costs and both of these are measured with some error. The median values of profits are quite plausible, the mean values less so.

In recognition of these problems, the interviewer also asked the entrepreneurs how much money they had left after expenses were paid. This value, combined with payments in kind and the value of home consumption, is called "net revenue" in table 5.4. It is the entrepreneur's best guess of the firm's profitability. The difference between mean and median values of net revenue again points out a left-skewed distribution (see figure 5.2). Moreover, it is clear that enterprises operating at some point during the year but not during the visit were not as profitable as those currently operating, as one might well expect. The most profitable enterprises are found in food commerce and the "other" category.

Enterprise Performance and Household Poverty

How does the economic well-being of households relate to the performance of their enterprises? Judged by their labor inputs, enterprises grow larger as households move into higher quintiles, though the effect is not dramatic until they enter the fifth quintile (table 5.5). The relationship between enterprise size and a household's poverty level is more pronounced when we consider total capital resources or total operating costs. Consider also, though, that some enterprises belonging to poor households in the first or second quintiles are larger than those in the third, fourth, or even fifth quintiles. Nevertheless, differences in the quintile-level means are still statistically significant. One exception is the capital investment variable: because of the large standard deviation of this variable (not reported here), it is not clear that more prosperous households indeed invest more than poorer ones, even though the means presented here give this impression.

Sales revenue exhibits a rising trend over quintiles. The profit variable rises in its median value, but noise in the measure for some enterprises distorts the mean value, veiling some of the trend. The net revenue variable is much smoother, and thus we shall concentrate on it.

Because our focus is on poverty, we are interested in knowing how important nonfarm enterprises are in meeting households' income needs. For this, we examine the ratio of a household's income from its nonfarm enterprises to its consumption expenditure. This ratio does not have to equal one for the household to break even, since the household may have other income sources. Further, the calculation contains imputed values for the rental value of the residence, the use value of consumer durables, and the value of home-produced consumption items. Thus household expenditure is not a good short-term value of a household's cash flow needs—even if it is a good long-term value of cash flow needs.

Table 5.5 Family Enterprise Characteristics in Vietnam, by Quintile, 1992–93

Variable	1	2	3	4	5
Annual hours of family labor					
Mean[a]	1,705	1,686	1,907	2,153	2,930
Median	973	1,054	1,278	1,703	2,199
Number of workers					
Mean[a]	1.60	1.73	1.65	1.82	2.04
Median	1.00	1.00	1.00	1.00	1.00
Total capital resource					
Percent	79.9	82.9	81.2	88.2	89.2
Conditional mean[a]	337	921	1,790	2,954	12,454
Conditional median	53	164	250	428	1,018
Capital investment					
Percent	16.4	20.7	19.5	19.3	18.4
Conditional mean	189	972	8,149	3,780	8,481
Conditional median	49	84	77	196	192
Total costs					
Mean[a]	7,351	6,761	11,123	16,237	35,972
Median	334	729	1,904	2,882	7,319
Revenue[b]					
Mean[a]	6,193	7,717	10,603	17,068	40,197
Median	1,400	2,052	3,598	5,026	11,193
Revenue[c]					
Mean[a]	7,159	15,247	18,277	25,292	56,398
Median	3,168	3,987	5,548	6,642	13,872
Profit[b]					
Mean[d]	−1,179	956	-540	831	4,426
Median	518	797	853	1,395	2,894
Profit[c]					
Mean[a]	−3,659	6,291	5,416	7,715	16,890
Median	1,462	1,840	1,903	2,498	4,520
Net revenue[b]					
Mean[a]	1,065	1,632	2,512	3,097	5,922
Median	534	708	1,000	1,440	3,030
Net revenue[c]					
Mean[a]	1,427	2,500	3,151	3,303	6,667
Median	909	1,023	1,318	1,763	3,502

a. Differences in the means are statistically significant at the 1 percent level.
b. Monthly value, measured over the past 12 months.
c. Monthly value, measured during the period between the two survey visits.
d. Differences in the means are statistically significant at the 5 percent level.
Source: Author's calculations, based on 1992–93 Vietnam Living Standards Survey data.

For 10 percent of the households that had an enterprise during the 12 months before the survey, income from that enterprise accounts for 4 percent or less of their expenses (table 5.6). For the median household, enterprise income covers 27.1 percent of expenses, and for 10 percent of such

Table 5.6 Income from Nonfarm Family Enterprises as a Share of Household Expenditure
(percent)

Area and region, or area and quintile	Tenth percentile		Median		Ninetieth percentile	
	Net revenue[a]	Net revenue[b]	Net revenue[a]	Net revenue[b]	Net revenue[a]	Net revenue[b]
Regional variations						
All Vietnam	4.0	5.7	27.1	34.6	103.1	115.9
Rural north	3.2	4.7	22.6	31.5	92.9	115.9
Northern Uplands	3.3	4.4	13.8	20.3	54.6	71.0
Red River Delta	3.3	5.4	21.8	28.8	87.0	112.2
North-Central Coast	2.8	2.8	36.8	26.3	107.1	139.1
Rural south						
Central Coast	2.3	4.9	23.0	29.2	93.9	121.5
Central Highlands	4.0	5.8	31.4	39.5	65.2	75.4
Southeast	5.5	7.1	41.7	46.6	146.6	179.1
Mekong Delta	3.8	4.5	22.3	30.8	82.6	115.9
Urban north	7.4	9.4	40.2	43.2	113.8	114.5
Northern Uplands	7.3	13.3	29.7	36.0	82.7	76.1
Red River Delta	8.9	8.0	37.1	35.9	143.7	138.0
North-Central Coast	2.7	8.2	16.8	33.8	75.5	112.0
Urban south						
Central Coast	9.4	11.1	37.5	42.3	94.9	94.9
Southeast	11.5	15.1	55.6	55.4	133.4	131.8
Mekong Delta	6.4	6.7	43.6	50.5	115.2	119.3
Differences by real per capita expenditure quintile						
All Vietnam	4.0	5.7	27.1	34.6	103.1	115.9
Rural	3.2	4.7	22.6	31.5	92.9	115.9
1 (poorest)	2.8	3.7	18.8	29.4	83.3	95.4
2	3.5	4.4	21.9	31.4	81.3	138.4
3	3.1	4.6	19.3	27.0	108.4	158.6
4	3.3	5.5	25.1	31.3	83.6	95.2
5 (wealthiest)	3.7	5.4	31.4	39.7	128.7	139.1
Urban	7.4	9.4	40.2	43.2	113.8	114.5
1 (poorest)	3.6	4.6	28.7	60.4	93.7	141.1
2	6.4	6.4	31.8	50.9	115.4	117.6
3	13.2	12.9	47.9	48.7	122.9	123.4
4	8.5	11.1	38.3	40.8	106.7	108.6
5 (wealthiest)	9.2	10.1	40.0	42.6	114.4	118.7

a. Revenue from nonfarm family enterprises, as a share of income earned over the past 12 months.
b. Revenue from nonfarm family enterprises, as a share of income earned between the two survey visits.
Source: Author's calculations, based on 1992–93 Vietnam Living Standards Survey data.

households enterprise income exceeds household expenditures by 3.1 percent or more. Households with currently operating enterprises rely more on that income. There is a small regional difference. Broadly speaking, nonfarm enterprises in urban areas (with the exception of urban localities in the North-Central Coast) contribute more to households' needs than do those in rural areas (with the possible exception of the rural Southeast). Overall, there is great variation among households: for some, the income from nonfarm enterprises is trivial compared with their consumption expenditures, while for others this income pays for all consumption expenditures. The typical household, though, needs additional income.

Do poorer households with a family enterprise report a lower or higher ratio of enterprise income to consumption expenditure? In rural areas the median household relies more on enterprise income when we move into higher quintiles, but trends at the tenth and ninetieth percentiles are unclear. In urban areas a weak upward trend appears at the tenth percentile and at the median, but not at the ninetieth percentile. Thus there is weak evidence that better-off households depend more on the income of their family enterprise.[7] This result reinforces the conclusion reached earlier: it is not just engaging in nonfarm self-employment activities that allows people to achieve higher standards of living; the level of effort (and income earned) also matters.

There is a more direct way to show that enterprise income is positively associated with the level of well-being. Consider only those house-

Table 5.7 Income from Nonfarm Enterprises and Household Well-being in Vietnam, 1992–93

Quintile of net revenue	Conditional quintile of real household expenditure[a]				
	1	2	3	4	5
All households with nonfarm enterprises					
1 (poorest)	8.81	4.94	3.37	1.89	0.97
2	4.98	5.17	4.89	3.41	1.57
3	4.11	5.17	3.78	4.52	2.40
4	1.80	3.55	5.03	5.26	4.38
5 (wealthiest)	0.28	1.20	2.91	4.94	10.66
Rural households with nonfarm enterprises					
1 (poorest)	7.76	5.04	3.36	2.46	1.36
2	5.04	4.01	4.98	3.62	2.39
3	4.07	4.46	4.59	4.01	2.84
4	2.52	4.72	4.14	4.27	4.40
5 (wealthiest)	0.58	1.81	2.91	5.69	8.99
Urban households with nonfarm enterprises					
1 (poorest)	9.19	4.52	3.39	2.10	0.81
2	5.81	4.19	5.16	2.42	2.42
3	3.55	5.32	4.84	3.55	2.74
4	1.13	4.52	4.35	6.13	3.87
5 (wealthiest)	0.32	1.45	2.26	5.81	10.16

Note: The real household expenditure quintiles are recomputed for each subsample and are therefore referred to as conditional quintiles.
a. Tabulations are based on net revenue earned over the past 12 months.

holds operating a nonfarm enterprise. Rerank these according to their real per capita consumption expenditures and sort them into quintiles. Then, compare this outcome with the quintile ranking of their enterprise income (table 5.7). We see that there are few prosperous households operating unprofitable enterprises and few poor households operating profitable enterprises. These trends tend to show in the middle part of the tabulations as well. Statistically, the trend is strongly significant (at less than a 0.1 percent significance level): higher enterprise income is associated with a higher level of well-being in both urban and rural areas.

Determinants of Nonfarm Enterprise Income

Defining enterprise income as the difference between sales revenue and spending on market-purchased inputs, we can speculate about the determinants of enterprise income. First, the entrepreneurs provide some of the inputs themselves, such as capital and labor, and finance the stock of inventory. These inputs are presumably productive, raising enterprises' output. They are not purchased in the market and so should also raise enterprise income. Second, enterprise characteristics may have an impact. Business

		Conditional quintile of real household expenditure[b]		
1	*2*	*3*	*4*	*5*
7.54	5.63	3.39	2.37	1.02
6.14	5.37	3.77	3.45	1.28
3.96	4.92	4.16	4.16	2.81
1.79	2.69	5.13	5.63	4.60
0.51	1.41	3.39	4.41	10.29
7.70	5.27	2.78	3.16	1.73
5.37	4.60	4.70	3.74	1.63
4.22	4.60	4.60	3.74	2.88
2.68	4.12	4.41	4.60	4.22
0.67	1.44	2.59	4.79	9.49
9.21	4.03	3.65	2.11	0.96
6.14	4.99	3.65	3.07	2.11
3.65	4.41	5.18	3.84	3.07
0.58	4.80	5.57	5.76	3.26
0.38	1.73	2.11	5.18	10.56

b. Tabulations are based on net revenue earned between the two survey visits.
Source: Author's calculations, based on 1992–93 Vietnam Living Standards Survey data.

location and age may be related to the nature and newness of the technology, and the capital embodying that technology. The type of industry will determine profitable opportunities and the degree of competition. Third, the characteristics of family workers may be important. Age, sex, level of education, apprenticeship training, and culture as measured by ethnicity may affect the productivity of individual workers and therefore the overall performance of the enterprise. Finally, enterprise income may vary by region, distinguishing urban from rural areas and each of the seven regions of Vietnam. These variables capture unmeasured price differences, variations in demand conditions, market size, and agglomeration economies.

Defining the Model

Given this list of determinants, we undertake a multivariate analysis of enterprise income. Several methodological issues arise (see, for example, Vijverberg 1991, 1993, 1995a, 1995b). The list of income determinants presented above contains at least two groups of variables that are subject to entrepreneurs' choices. First, entrepreneurs will be more inclined to start a new firm in, or redirect their existing firm toward, an industry that offers more profitable opportunities. Thus the industry can be an indicator of expectations of their firm performance—that is, there is an endogenous link with the explanatory variable. Further, if entrepreneurs are free to vary the amounts of inputs, they will choose profit-maximizing quantities. The quantity of inputs then also becomes a signal of an enterprise's profitability. In a related sense, one might also consider apprenticeship training to be a signal of expected profitability. Thus input quantity and industry may influence enterprise performance, but these variables are likely to be simultaneously determined with enterprise income—causing estimation bias. To avoid such bias, we leave these variables out of the equation. In line with econometric terminology, I will refer to a full-blown model as the structural form and to a model without the input, industry, and apprenticeship variables as the reduced form.

There is also an interesting economic interpretation of the difference between the structural and reduced form estimates. Take, for example, the effect of education. In the structural form education contributes to enterprise income if entrepreneurs can make their inputs more productive. In the reduced form education raises enterprise income through this productive effect and through an allocative effect, reflecting better entrepreneurial choices about the quantity of inputs and the industry of specialization. The difference between the two effects therefore represents the allocative effect of education.[8]

A second issue is that household members choose whether or not to operate an enterprise, implying that the sample of enterprises observed in the Living Standards Survey is not randomly distributed among the population of Vietnam. This may induce estimation bias (Lee 1978; Heckman

1979), with the implication that one could not use the parameter estimates to predict how profitable an enterprise might be in a randomly selected household. For this survey sample, however, there is no evidence that the parameter estimates are biased.[9]

A third issue is that economic theory offers no guidance as to whether we should measure enterprise income as hourly, daily, weekly, monthly, or annual values. We do not know what the relevant period of production is, and this period may vary among enterprises in different industries or even within the same industry. We shall consider both hourly and monthly values—if the estimated effects are robust, they will show up in both sets of estimates.

A related issue concerns the form of the empirical model. While economic theory suggests that the impact of inputs is nonlinear because of diminishing returns, it does not mandate one particular form. We shall estimate the hourly income model in a log-linear form with the log of inputs entering quadratically, and a linear monthly income model with inputs entering quadratically. It may be that the log-quadratic model is less sensitive to outliers, a check on the data did not point out outlier problems that resulted from coding errors, however.

Estimating the Model

In the hourly income model the hours of work variable is removed from the list of explanatory variables since it is used to create the explained variable. The following discussion outlines general trends in the estimates. It is useful to know the mean values of the dependent variables. The average hourly income is 2,560 dong for currently operating enterprises and 2,056 dong for all enterprises operating in the past 12 months; the average monthly income is 457,000 dong and 396,000 dong, respectively.

Inputs appear only in the structural form models, and in quadratic form, which makes them more difficult to interpret. But consider the hourly income regressions, and define "small," median, and "large" enterprises as those that use inputs corresponding to the twenty-fifth, fiftieth, and seventy-fifth percentiles. For currently operating enterprises the amounts are as follows: for small enterprises, hours = 117 per month, capital = 15,000 dong, inventory = 0; for median enterprises, 213, 193, 0; for large enterprises, 304, 963, 96. For enterprises operating during the past 12 months: small, 122, 10, 0; median, 213, 147, 0; and large, 304, 772, 46. According to our estimates of currently operating enterprises, a 1 percent increase in the capital stock raises hourly income by 0.012, 0.082, and 0.092 percent for small, median, and large enterprises, respectively (table 5.8). Results for enterprise operating within the past 12 months are very similar. This result implies that, in a medium-size enterprise, 1,000 dong of additional capital generates an increase of about 0.45 dong per hour or 96 dong per month. Thus the productivity of capital appears higher in larger firms.

Table 5.8 Determinants of Hourly Enterprise Income, Vietnam, 1992–93

Variable	Currently operating enterprises		Enterprises operating within the past year	
	Structural form	Reduced form	Structural form	Reduced form
Intercept	–0.088 (0.53)	–0.037 (0.25)	–0.362 (2.41)	–0.398 (2.94)
Enterprise inputs				
ln(capital)	–0.066 (2.89)		–0.081 (3.95)	
ln(inventory)	–0.130 (4.39)		–0.093 (3.42)	
lnC*lnC	0.014 (6.35)		0.018 (8.21)	
lnC*lnI/10	–0.075 (2.81)		–0.095 (3.60)	
lnI*lnI	0.024 (6.04)		0.023 (5.81)	
Enterprise characteristics[a]				
Fixed location	0.027 (0.43)	–0.017 (0.29)	0.102 (1.96)	0.091 (1.89)
1.42 < agebus ≤ 3	0.014 (0.18)	0.027 (0.33)	0.081 (1.23)	0.083 (1.20)
3.0 < agebus ≤ 5	0.016 (0.19)	0.041 (0.49)	0.134 (1.95)	0.132 (1.83)
5.0 < agebus ≤ 11	0.053 (0.62)	0.074 (0.86)	0.145 (2.01)	0.124 (1.66)
11.0 < agebus	–0.066 (0.77)	–0.061 (0.72)	0.005 (0.07)	–0.034 (0.46)
Fishery	0.018 (0.18)		–0.144 (1.86)	
Food manufacturing	0.070 (0.74)		–0.065 (0.76)	
Textiles manufacturing	–0.221 (2.48)		–0.333 (4.16)	
Other manufacturing	–0.289 (2.95)		–0.289 (3.26)	
Food/hotel commerce	–0.023 (0.27)		0.088 (1.04)	
Transportation/ communication	0.155 (1.30)		0.152 (1.45)	
Services	–0.068 (0.75)		–0.114 (1.37)	
Other industries	0.132 (1.14)		0.125 (1.37)	
Family worker characteristics[b]				
Years of primary school	–0.019 (0.83)	–0.005 (0.19)	–0.018 (0.88)	–0.000 (0.00)
Years of secondary school	0.025 (2.91)	0.033 (3.86)	0.018 (2.32)	0.031 (3.90)
Years of apprenticeship	0.106 (2.50)		0.068 (1.84)	
Age ≤ 15	–0.694 (4.11)	–0.801 (4.54)	–0.728 (5.37)	–0.813 (5.75)
25 < age ≤ 35	0.412 (5.54)	0.415 (5.54)	0.269 (4.40)	0.294 (4.69)
35 < age ≤ 45	0.467 (5.79)	0.512 (6.27)	0.336 (4.87)	0.424 (6.00)
45 < age ≤ 55	0.265 (2.57)	0.266 (2.56)	0.118 (1.31)	0.190 (2.11)
55 < age ≤ 65	–0.023 (0.18)	–0.045 (0.34)	–0.064 (0.52)	–0.006 (0.05)
65 < age	–0.406 (2.22)	–0.380 (2.06)	–0.501 (2.81)	–0.475 (2.58)
Female	–0.211 (3.09)	–0.417 (7.35)	–0.203 (3.56)	–0.360 (7.38)
Chinese	0.038 (0.35)	0.174 (1.50)	–0.009 (0.09)	0.165 (1.60)
Other ethnicity	0.148 (1.34)	0.095 (0.83)	0.187 (2.18)	0.107 (1.23)
Regional location[c]				
Urban	–0.049 (0.90)	0.016 (0.30)	0.083 (1.71)	0.185 (3.84)
Northern Uplands	–0.201 (2.29)	–0.256 (2.87)	–0.153 (2.21)	–0.207 (2.86)
North-Central Coast	–0.267 (2.62)	–0.190 (1.83)	–0.179 (2.36)	–0.168 (2.12)
Central Coast	–0.151 (1.87)	–0.051 (0.62)	–0.185 (2.66)	–0.083 (1.14)
Central Highlands	0.174 (1.08)	0.280 (1.89)	0.248 (1.57)	0.407 (2.71)
Southeast	0.367 (4.65)	0.457 (5.53)	0.399 (5.62)	0.545 (7.28)
Mekong Delta	0.029 (0.42)	0.109 (1.51)	0.033 (0.53)	0.151 (2.31)
R^2/number of observations	0.211 / 2,032	0.144 / 2,032	0.223 / 2,647	0.139 / 2,647

Note: Dependent variable is ln(monthly enterprise income/monthly hours of work).
a. Among the dichotomous variables, the omitted categories are "operating from a varying location," "age of business less than 1.42 years," and "retail trade."
b. Among the dichotomous variables, "15<age ≤ 25" and "Vietnamese (Kinh) ethnicity" are omitted.
c. Among the dichotomous variables, "rural residence" and "Red River Delta" are omitted.
Source: Authors' calculations, based on 1992–93 Vietnam Living Standards Survey data.

But this conclusion is not supported when monthly income is the dependent variable (table 5.9). Then, a 1,000 dong increase in capital raises monthly income by 16 dong or 26 dong, depending on the subset of enterprises used. Further, there is little difference between small and large enterprises; if anything, returns fall slightly with enterprise size. If these numbers appear small, consider that they imply that a 1,000-dong investment yields 192 or 312 dong annually, which are substantial returns. Note also that while the hourly and monthly regression models do not yield the same rate of return estimates, both indicate large returns.

Under the definition stated above, only large enterprises have inventories. According to table 5.8, hourly incomes rise by 0.02 percent (first column) or 0.037 percent (third column) for each 1 percent increase in inventories. And these returns rise rapidly for larger enterprises. But table 5.9 concludes that returns decline slightly: 1,000 dong of additional inventories yields 64 dong (first column) or 100 dong (third column) in monthly income.

The monthly income models also include hours of work. The estimates of the marginal contribution of an hour of work range from 369 to 392 dong across the three enterprise sizes and the two columns of estimates. Note that this is a generic hour of work, as each regression equation also controls for the quality of the worker. As such, it is not fully comparable with the observed average hourly wage of 1,350 dong among salaried employees in the VNLSS sample, since this average is not quality-adjusted.

Whether the enterprise operates from a fixed location does not appear to influence its profitability. Enterprise age is represented by five dummy variables that divide the sample into five roughly equal parts. Its effect is more complex: age shows no effect among currently operating enterprises, but in the annual sample both the newest and the oldest enterprises are less profitable than those operating for 1.42 to 11 years. We can explain this result by start-up problems among the newest enterprises and technology obsolescence among the older ones.

The industry variables allow a comparison with the omitted category of retail trade: incomes are lower in the textile and other manufacturing sectors and may be lower in the fishery, food manufacturing, and services sectors.

Family worker characteristics are computed as the average across all family workers participating in the enterprise, weighted by their respective hours of work. Only years of schooling is measured as the maximum level of education attained among the participating family workers, assuming that the most educated member automatically acts as a leader and confers the benefits of his or her education on the other members. Education is measured by the number of years in primary school, and then schooling at the secondary level and beyond. Primary schooling adds little to enterprise income: in all but one estimated model the effect is small and statistically insignificant.[10] On the other hand, secondary schooling has a statistically significant productive effect: one year yields an income

Table 5.9 Determinants of Monthly Enterprise Income in Vietnam, 1992–93

Variable	Currently operating enterprises		Enterprises operating within the past year	
	Structural form	Reduced form	Structural form	Reduced form
Intercept	218.8 (4.32)	345.4 (4.36)	137.8 (3.50)	270.4 (4.22)
Enterprise inputs				
Hours of work	0.368 (4.56)		0.350 (5.50)	
Capital	0.017 (6.71)		0.029 (9.30)	
Inventory	0.103 (4.81)		0.071 (6.12)	
Hours*hours/10^4	0.800 (1.68)		0.775 (2.08)	
Hours*capital/10^5	−0.479 (1.96)		−1.138 (2.27)	
Hours*inventory/10^5	−4.029 (2.54)		−2.936 (1.53)	
Capital*capital/10^6	−0.031 (2.66)		−0.056 (2.10)	
Capital*inventory/10^6	0.278 (2.61)		0.149 (1.10)	
Inventory*inventory/10^6	−1.297 (3.28)		−0.687 (1.63)	
Enterprise characteristics[a]				
Fixed location	−1.9 (0.10)	15.0 (0.53)	8.5 (0.60)	32.1 (1.36)
1.42 < agebus ≤ 3	−3.6 (0.13)	4.2 (0.09)	30.2 (1.69)	29.6 (0.89)
3.0 < agebus ≤ 5	−13.3 (0.49)	−12.1 (0.25)	34.0 (1.81)	17.7 (0.51)
5.0 < agebus ≤ 11	16.7 (0.61)	−24.5 (0.53)	45.0 (2.33)	18.5 (0.49)
11.0 < agebus	−16.5 (0.59)	28.1 (0.58)	29.1 (1.43)	56.6 (1.46)
Fishery	−23.6 (0.67)		−56.7 (2.74)	
Food manufacturing	−51.1 (1.92)		−52.1 (1.95)	
Textiles manufacturing	−105.1 (3.97)		−99.7 (5.27)	
Other manufacturing	−67.9 (2.40)		−45.5 (2.01)	
Food/hotel commerce	4.9 (0.11)		45.7 (0.92)	
Transportation/ communication	50.6 (1.03)		39.3 (1.16)	
Services	−103.5 (3.66)		−93.8 (4.29)	
Other industries	120.7 (1.76)		73.4 (1.76)	
Family worker characteristics[b]				
Years of primary school	−1.0 (0.17)	13.0 (1.35)	3.2 (0.61)	16.0 (1.90)
Years of secondary school	8.7 (2.82)	16.4 (2.79)	4.8 (2.12)	8.8 (1.73)
Years of apprenticeship	19.7 (1.38)		7.5 (0.65)	
Age ≤ 15	−78.6 (1.71)	−91.2 (1.21)	−77.3 (2.60)	−127.4 (2.54)
25 < age ≤ 35	30.2 (1.23)	1.5 (0.03)	9.4 (0.54)	−5.3 (0.14)
35 < age ≤ 45	53.5 (2.01)	31.2 (0.60)	30.0 (1.43)	−0.5 (0.01)
45 < age ≤ 55	5.2 (0.18)	−49.0 (0.94)	−16.1 (0.74)	−69.0 (1.67)
55 < age ≤ 65	−11.9 (0.34)	−42.4 (0.73)	−5.8 (0.20)	−29.8 (0.56)
65 < age	−116.2 (2.77)	−156.4 (2.41)	−103.1 (2.73)	−127.0 (2.02)
Female	−56.6 (2.78)	−105.9 (2.98)	−53.9 (3.58)	−111.0 (3.81)
Chinese	83.4 (1.38)	180.8 (1.36)	73.6 (1.44)	135.3 (1.01)
Other ethnicity	−12.5 (0.36)	31.1 (0.62)	19.5 (0.75)	5.1 (0.13)
Regional location[c]				
Urban	−15.1 (0.85)	47.1 (1.55)	17.9 (1.22)	65.0 (2.29)
Northern Uplands	−113.9 (4.41)	−201.4 (4.69)	−75.2 (3.92)	−154.5 (4.43)
North-Central Coast	−56.5 (1.74)	−72.8 (1.29)	−40.4 (1.99)	−86.6 (2.14)
Central Coast	−48.9 (1.78)	−54.2 (1.13)	−40.7 (2.00)	−45.3 (1.09)
Central Highlands	−12.1 (0.24)	−53.9 (0.65)	−9.8 (0.26)	−12.1 (0.21)

(Table continues on next page.)

Table 5.9 Determinants of Monthly Enterprise Income in Vietnam, 1992–93 (continued)

Variable	Currently operating enterprises		Enterprises operating within the past year	
	Structural form	Reduced form	Structural form	Reduced form
Southeast	160.4 (4.39)	150.0 (2.38)	116.2 (4.23)	178.4 (3.08)
Mekong Delta	2.6 (0.10)	−5.2 (0.12)	12.5 (0.65)	28.7 (0.73)
Pseudo-R^2 / number of observations	0.145 / 2,054	0.042 / 2,054	0.188 / 2,676	0.043 / 2,676

Note: Dependent variable is monthly enterprise income.
a. Among the dichotomous variables, the omitted categories are "operating from a varying location," "age of business less than 1.42 years," and "retail trade."
b. Among the dichotomous variables, "15<age≤25" and "Vietnamese (Kinh) ethnicity" are omitted.
c. Among the dichotomous variables, "rural residence" and "Red River Delta" are omitted.
Source: Author's calculations, based on 1992–93 Vietnam Living Standards Survey data.

increase of 1.8 to 2.5 percent, or 4,800 to 8,700 dong monthly. The combined productive and allocative effect is larger: about 3.1 percent, or 8,800 to 16,400 dong monthly. With the caveats noted earlier, it appears that the allocative effect of education is roughly the same as its productive effect.

Apprenticeship training and age are two other human capital measures. Apprenticeship training may have a positive impact, but the statistical significance varies among the models. The age effect is measured with a series of age dummy variables, allowing a comparison with workers in the 16–25-year-old age group. There is a strong age effect: both the youngest and oldest workers are less productive, as one might expect. Prime-aged (age 26–55) workers may be most productive, but the evidence is not robust between the hourly and monthly income models.

Women earn less. That there is both a productive and an allocative effect stands out clearly in the estimates: the structural form models each show a negative parameter estimate, which doubles when we switch to the reduced form estimates. The doubling implies that men have more favorable enterprise characteristics that are omitted in the reduced form equation: larger capital stocks (among currently operating enterprises, 4.2 million dong more on average), more inventories (on average, 118,000 dong more), industries with higher incomes (more women work in textiles), and more apprenticeship training (0.1 year more). The raw male-female difference in average earnings is 147,000 dong monthly or 40 percent hourly for currently operating enterprises, and 123,000 dong monthly and 32 percent hourly for the annual sample. These statistics are similar to the parameter estimates found in the reduced form models. Therefore, the male-female income gap is not a result of schooling, age, ethnicity, region, or age of enterprises taken as a group, but rather is due in part to allocative choices that households make involving female-run enterprises.

The last group of variables concerns regional location. We compare urban areas against the excluded rural areas and compare each of the six listed regions against the Red River Delta. There is no clear positive effect of operating in an urban area, as other studies have reported (but the income data used here have been deflated with a region/time price index). Incomes in the Southeast are clearly higher than they are in the Red River Delta; those in the Northern Uplands and the North-Central Coast and Central Coast are lower. In view of the mean values of the dependent variables, the regional effects are considerable.

Considerations for Public Policy

The economy of Vietnam still has a strong agricultural orientation. The nonagricultural sector is relatively small: one-fourth of those working hold a wage job at some point during the year. About 25 percent of these wage employees work in the public sector, some in farming, and a similar proportion engages in nonfarm self-employment. This part of the nonagricultural private sector is thriving. Compared with the other enterprises in this sector, rates of return to capital are high and incomes compare well with the average earnings of waged workers. No selectivity bias was found in the empirical model of enterprise income determination, meaning that the favorable results generated with the current sample of enterprises should extend to the whole population of Vietnam. Finally, this paper presents evidence of a positive association between the (short-term) productive performance of the family enterprise and the household's long-term standard of living.

Taken together, these results imply that market forces provide a favorable environment for expanding nonfarm household enterprises in Vietnam. Thus the main policy recommendation is to remove artificial barriers that inhibit the formation and expansion of small enterprises. Several specific recommendations can be made:

- Registration procedures are cumbersome. A prospective entrepreneur must submit many forms and certificates that must be evaluated by several layers of the bureaucracy, taking up to 60 days (World Bank 1995, 49–57). Both the certificates and the application are costly. The agency in charge of this procedure may see itself as advising inexperienced entrepreneurs, but it is most likely that entrepreneurs prefer a simple business registration procedure that assigns them nothing more than a tax identification number. Similarly, entrepreneurs are currently required to apply for permission to expand or change the focus of their enterprise, which stymies enterprise growth.
- The government should split the advisory function from the licensing process. It should stimulate private enterprise by sponsoring community seminars on entrepreneurship and management at introductory and advanced levels, either directly or through the Vietnam Chamber of Commerce and Industry. Doing so would also

send a clear message of support for private entrepreneurship that would further break down remaining ideological inhibitions against free market operations.

- Organizing local, consistently operating markets will give households an incentive to start or expand an enterprise; developing transportation and marketing networks will open up more distant markets. Access to a market raises the probability that a household will operate a nonfarm enterprise. Of the entrepreneurs in the Hanoi sample (Le and Rondinelli 1993, 11), three-quarters mentioned as obstacles difficulties with selling their products in a competitive market, the low level of purchasing power of their potential customers, and the lack of market information. The government should also facilitate business contacts among entrepreneurs (Liedholm and Mead 1986; World Bank 1995, 84).

- There is some (weak) evidence that availability of utility services (electricity, water) in rural areas is a factor in a household's decision of whether to operate a nonfarm enterprise. In principle, providing reliable utility services should stimulate enterprise start-up and enhance enterprise profitability.

- The government could offer subsidies or tax relief as an enticement to start up enterprises. But these initiatives must be very carefully administered, to avoid substantial distortions in market incentives.

- Few family enterprises appear to be paying taxes, either for licenses or in other forms. It may be that entrepreneurs are put off by the complex registration procedures and the complicated tax code. Abiding by the tax system requires substantial bookkeeping efforts. It may also be that enterprises simply do not bother with these requirements because they can avoid them easily without much probability of retribution. Moreover, one-third of the Hanoi sample complained about high and unfair taxes (Le and Rondinelli 1993, 11). The system makes tax evasion appealing, which lowers tax revenue and distorts production incentives because of sectoral differences in rates. A simpler tax structure is needed, and it is important to hold even small enterprises accountable for the taxes they owe. Tax revenue will also grow if a portion is dedicated to finance public policy initiatives that benefit small enterprises. The analysis presented in this chapter suggests that the total tax revenue raised from small enterprises is likely to at least double if full compliance is achieved.

- Facilitating the availability of credit will allow both new and existing enterprises to expand. At present, the private sector is at a disadvantage when it comes to credit allocated by state-run banks, and a large portion of private credit is arranged through informal channels (Rondinelli and Le 1995, 34; World Bank 1995, 68). At the same time, only a small percentage of private savings is held in government banks. The banking sector is not fulfilling its financial intermediation function because people do not trust banks with their savings—which is not surprising, given the government's currency manipulations in the 1980s and the bankruptcy of a number of credit cooperatives in 1990–91. Thus facilitating credit availability implies a simple abolishment of discriminatory lending practices and a complex policy of building up the banking sector.

- Vietnam's legal structure is still developing. Regulatory changes occur frequently and are not always uniform or, in the eyes of entrepreneurs, fair (World Bank 1995, chapter 3). The economic goal also differs ideologically from leaders' political goals. All of this creates uncertainty among prospective and active entrepreneurs, and lowers entrepreneurial initiative. Economic stability and security are key to high private sector investment.

- Because the legal structure is still developing, there are loopholes in regulations and enforcement. Injustice persists, which especially hurts the disadvantaged groups of society. It also creates conditions that lead to inequality in income and wealth. It is important that the legal structure become clear, manageable, and enforceable, and that it be put in place soon.

It is easy to find motivations for public policies that give preference to particular regions such as the Northern Uplands, the North-Central Coast, and the Central Coast, where enterprise incomes are lower, even when holding other factors constant. All of the policy measures listed above could be applied with greater intensity in the regions that are found to be at a greater disadvantage, but facilitating connections with distant markets may have a higher priority.

In a related sense, stimulating family enterprises in rural areas may well generate the kind of employment that could keep people from migrating to the cities. Given Vietnam's high population density and large agricultural population, this chapter offers encouraging findings that small-scale enterprises are productive and that rural industrialization programs can be successful as a result.

This chapter shows the existence of a large male-female enterprise income gap of 40 percent. Half of this disappears when we control for factors like capitalization and the type of sector in which the enterprise is engaged. To alleviate this portion of the income gap, policymakers should ensure that women have equal access to training for diverse careers and to technology, credit, and so on. The other half of the income gap is unexplained—we may refer to this portion of the gap as "discrimination." Some scholars may point out, however, that women may be less efficient because household responsibilities interfere with enterprise activity. To the degree that discrimination is an issue, policymakers can ensure that female entrepreneurs are not discriminated against in receiving public sector contracts and, furthermore, that there is a receptive legal forum where female entrepreneurs can file complaints.

Finally, households with nonfarm enterprises appear at the top of the distribution of the standard of living more often than at the bottom. This finding may affect public policy initiatives in two different ways, depending on whether the overriding goals emphasize economic growth or economic equality. A public policy emphasis on assistance to existing enterprises would satisfy the objectives of growth; if poverty is an overriding concern, policy should focus on the establishment of new enterprises and assistance to the smallest. This chapter gives hope that either type of action will be successful.

Notes

Comments by David Dollar, Paul Glewwe, Jennie Litvack, and several anonymous referees are greatly appreciated. The author accepts responsibility for any errors in the paper.

1. Other sources put the contribution of the nonstate sector at almost one-half of manufacturing output (Ljunggren 1993, 81–82), or at 84 percent of the output in the industrial and commercial sectors combined (Le and Rondinelli 1993, 8). Note that statistics on the nonstate private sector are likely to be inaccurate and incomplete. Because of poor bookkeeping practices, the activity of household enterprises is not captured well in the statistics, and some productive activity and income is concealed to avoid taxation (World Bank 1995, 24).

2. This assumption is certainly subject to debate, particularly as a bargaining model has recently gained popularity. This model views each individual as a separate decisionmaker, rendering household-level outcomes as results of more or less cooperative agreements among household members.

3. One might argue that people take up apprenticeship training in order to prepare themselves to operate their own enterprise. The variable is included here on the assumption that apprenticeships prepare one for a craft or occupation and that the decision to engage in this craft through one's own enterprise is made separately.

4. Alternatively, it could be argued that these occupational variables contain information about the economic environment that is poorly measured by the other variables and that the parameter estimates reveal environmental conditions, rather than intergenerational effects. It is not easy to discard this alternative hypothesis. But it is interesting to note that of the heads and spouses in the VNLSS sample, 28 percent do not currently live where they were born and another 23 percent had moved elsewhere for at least 12 months before returning to their birthplace. In urban areas 59 percent of heads and spouses on average stated that they were not born where they now live and that they had spent 44 percent of their life at their current location. Thus, since migration takes people away from their parents' environment, the estimated effect of the parental occupation variables are more likely an intergenerational effect.

5. As every person in Vietnam has an equal probability of being sampled by the Living Standards Survey, an enterprise with 100 employees is five times more likely to appear in the sample than an enterprise with 20 employees. Thus for enterprises

found through the wage employee sample, the frequency is weighted by the number of people that work there according to the wage employee.

6. Size is defined by net revenue, total revenue, total capital resource, or total physical capital.

7. In Côte d'Ivoire it is the rural households with nonfarm enterprises that tend to be better off than the average rural household, whereas urban households with an enterprise tend to be worse off than the average urban household (Vijverberg 1990, 534). Ivorian wage earnings are highly unequal, and poor urban households are more likely to depend on enterprise earnings. Thus while the analysis of Ivorian households differs in methodology, it is clear that the self-employed in Vietnam are in a better position.

8. Because the structural form is estimated with bias, by implication, the allocative effect (the difference between the reduced and structural parameter estimates) is estimated with bias as well. The direction of this bias is difficult to predict.

9. The technique developed by Lee (1978) and Heckman (1979) was applied, using the probit model introduced earlier as the selection model. The parameter estimates of the lambda variable in the enterprise income equation were statistically insignificant in eight tests, yielding seven t-statistics below 1 and one of 1.61.

10. For only one-fifth of the enterprises is the amount of education less than five years. Thus the effect of primary schooling is determined by only a small portion of the sample.

References

Beresford, Melanie. 1988. *Vietnam: Politics, Economics, and Society.* London: Pinter.

Blau, David M. 1986. "Self-Employment, Earnings, and Mobility in Peninsular Malaysia." *World Development* 14(7): 839–52.

Chiswick, Carmel U. 1977. "On Estimating Earnings Functions for LDCs." *Journal of Development Economics* 4 (March): 67–78.

Durand, John D. 1975. *The Labor Force in Economic Development: A Comparison of International Census Data, 1946–1966.* Princeton, N.J.: Princeton University Press.

Fforde, Adam. 1993. "The Political Economy of 'Reform' in Vietnam: Some Reflections." In Börje Ljunggren, ed., *The Challenge of Reform in Indochina.* Cambridge, Mass.: Harvard University Press.

Fforde, Adam, and Suzanne H. Paine. 1987. *The Limits of National Liberation.* London: Croon Helm.

Galenson, Walter. 1992. *Labor and Economic Growth in Five Asian Countries.* New York: Praeger.

Heckman, James J. 1979. "Sample Selection Bias as a Specification Error." *Econometrica* 47(1): 153–62.

Hy Van Luong. 1993."The Political Economy of Vietnamese Reforms: A Microscopic Perspective from Two Ceramics Manufacturing Centers." In William S. Turley and Mark Selden, eds., *Reinventing Vietnamese Socialism.* Boulder, Colo.: Westview.

ILO (International Labour Organisation). 1992. *Yearbook of Labour Statistics*. Geneva: International Labour Office.

Kaufman, Joan, and Gita Sen. 1993. "Population, Health, and Gender in Vietnam: Social Policies under the Economic Reforms." In Börje Ljunggren, ed., *The Challenge of Reform in Indochina*. Cambridge, Mass.: Harvard University Press.

Le Ngoc Hung, and Dennis A Rondinelli. 1993. "Small Business Development and Economic Transformation in Vietnam." *Journal of Asian Business* 9(4): 1–23.

Lee, Lung-Fei. 1978. "Unionism and Wage Rates: A Simultaneous Equations Model with Qualitative and Limited Dependent Variables." *International Economic Review* 19(2): 415–34.

Liedholm, Carl, and Donald C. Mead. 1986. "Small-Scale Industry." In Robert J. Berg and Jennifer Seymour Whitaker, eds., *Strategies for African Development*. Berkeley: University of California Press.

Ljunggren, Börje. 1993. "Market Economies under Communist Regimes: Reform in Vietnam, Laos, and Cambodia." In Börje Ljunggren, ed., *The Challenge of Reform in Indochina*. Cambridge, Mass.: Harvard University Press.

Mazumdar, Dipak. 1981. *The Urban Labor Market and Income Distribution*. New York: Oxford University Press.

Moock, Peter, Philip Musgrove, and Morton Stelcner. 1990. *Education and Earnings in Peru's Informal Nonfarm Family Enterprises*. Living Standards Measurement Study Working Paper 64. Washington, D.C.: World Bank.

Nguyen Tien Hung, G. 1977. *Economic Development of Socialist Vietnam, 1955–1980*. New York: Praeger.

Pelzer, Kristin. 1993. "Socio-Cultural Dimensions of Renovation in Vietnam: Doi Moi as Dialogue and Transformation in Gender Relations." In William S. Turley and Mark Selden, eds., *Reinventing Vietnamese Socialism*. Boulder, Colo.: Westview.

Porter, Gareth. 1993. *Vietnam: The Politics of Bureaucratic Socialism*. Ithaca, N.Y.: Cornell University Press.

Rondinelli, Dennis A., and Le Ngoc Hung. 1995. "Creating a New Business Climate in Vietnam: Challenges of Privatization and Economic Reform." *Business & the Contemporary World* 1(25): 39.

Speare, Alden, and John Harris. 1986. "Education, Earnings and Migration in Industry." *Economic Development and Cultural Change* 34(2): 223–44.

Teilhet-Waldorf, Saral, and William H. Waldorf. 1983. "Earnings of Self-Employed in an Informal Sector: A Case Study of Bangkok." *Economic Development and Cultural Change* 31(3): 587–607.

Turley, William S. 1993. "Introduction." In William S. Turley and Mark Selden, eds., *Reinventing Vietnamese Socialism*. Boulder, Colo.: Westview.

Vijverberg, Wim P. M. 1986. "Consistent Estimates of the Wage Equation When Individuals Choose among Income-Earning Activities." *Southern Economic Journal* 52(4): 1028–42.

———. 1990. "Nonfarm Self-Employment and the Informal Sector in Côte d'Ivoire: A Test of Categorical Identity." *Journal of Developing Areas* 24(4): 523–42.

———. 1991. "Profits from Self-Employment: A Case Study of Côte d'Ivoire." *World Development* 19(6): 683–96.

————. 1993. "Educational Investments and Returns for Women and Men in Côte d'Ivoire." *Journal of Human Resources* 28(4): 933–74.

————. 1995. "Returns to Schooling in Non-Farm Self-Employment: An Econometric Case Study of Ghana." *World Development* 23(7): 1215–27.

————. 1996. "Non-Farm Enterprises in LSS Surveys." University of Texas at Dallas, Department of Economics.

————. 1998. "Schooling, Skills and Income from Non-Farm Self-Employment in Ghana." In Paul Glewwe, ed., *The Economics of School Quality Investments in Developing Countries: An Empirical Study of Ghana.* London: Macmillan.

Vo Dai Luoc. 1993. "The Fight Against Inflation: Achievements and Problems." In William S. Turley and Mark Selden, eds., *Reinventing Vietnamese Socialism.* Boulder, Colo.: Westview.

World Bank. 1995. "Viet Nam: Economic Report on Industrialization and Industrial Policy." Report 14645-VN. East Asia and Pacific Region. Washington, D.C.

6

Private Transfers in Vietnam

Donald Cox, James Fetzer, and Emmanuel Jimenez

Vietnam faces many problems in its transition from socialism to capitalism. Leading policy issues include protection of workers laid off from state enterprises, encouragement of domestic savings for capital formation, and development of human capital. Though much of the current policy debate focuses on government or markets, a third institution, the family, is also relevant for Vietnam. Private income transfers between households might function like publicly provided safety nets—for example, in helping to protect displaced workers from the consequences of unemployment. Parental transfers could help finance investment in human capital, a key determinant of economic growth. And incentives for private saving, another channel for economic growth, could be affected by private, informal old-age support systems.

There are reasons to believe that private transfers play a greater role in Vietnam than in the transition economies of Eastern Europe. Vietnam's Confucian heritage and agrarian history have likely strengthened family ties. And the command economy has a much shorter history in Vietnam than in, say, Russia, so reliance on state transfers might be less deeply ingrained. Despite their potential importance for policy, we know little about private transfer patterns in Vietnam because until recently we did not have the requisite household survey data. The 1992–93 Vietnam Living Standards Survey (VNLSS) is now available, however, and it contains information necessary for investigating private transfers.

This chapter uses the VNLSS to provide a snapshot of private transfer activity. We investigate private transfer patterns along several dimensions, such as age, household resources, household demographics, and regional characteristics. We find that private transfers are substantial and widespread in Vietnam, and that they sometimes function like means-tested public transfers. They are targeted to vulnerable groups, such as low-income households or households affected by illness. But they are also given disproportionately to the well-educated. A substantial portion of elderly households receive private transfers, suggesting that they function in part as old-age support.

Each of these patterns is related to the policy concerns listed above, and public transfer schemes should be designed taking into account possible private transfer responses. Public transfers can crowd out private transfers, diluting the effectiveness of public income redistribution. Suppose that for altruistic reasons parents are transferring income to a child living away from home.[1] Suddenly the child becomes unemployed. The parents respond by increasing their altruistic transfers. Private transfers function like insurance—the child's consumption does not fall as much as his earnings because private transfers fill part of the income shortfall. Now suppose an unemployment insurance system was in place when the child was laid off. Since the child's consumption is partly insured by this public program, the parents need not contribute as much support to him. In this way an expansion of public transfers can cause private transfer networks to diminish.

As a result of this crowding out, the child's parents share in the benefits of the public transfer program because it lessens their burden of support.[2] And the child does not reap the full benefits of the program because it causes private transfers to fall. Thus the response of private transfers to the expansion of public transfers creates a targeting problem. Part of the benefits of unemployment insurance accrue to parents, who could be from upper income brackets. Of course, many unemployed people may have no relatives who are willing or able to provide help. These people benefit fully from unemployment insurance. In addition, public transfer systems enable much larger numbers of households to pool risk.

Crowding out can occur with other programs as well.[3] Suppose, for example, that a child supports his retired parents, and then a public pension program is created. The child's burden is eased because his parents now receive public transfers—and private transfers are again crowded out by public ones.

A second reason private transfers might be relevant for policy is their possible connection to capital formation and growth. Private transfers can vary over the life cycle, especially if capital market imperfections exist. For example, if children have difficulty financing their education or on-the-job training, parents may offer private transfers. Later in life the children may provide old-age support to parents. The life-cycle dimension of private transfers ties them to economic growth. The more private transfers flow from old to young, as opposed to young to old, the better it is for economic growth. There are a couple of reasons for this. The most obvious connection is that private transfers targeted toward students enhance the aggregate stock of human capital. But there is a further and perhaps more subtle connection between private transfers and economic growth. A strong private old-age support system might stifle incentives to save for retirement. So the finding that private transfers are targeted to the elderly could be interpreted as a symptom of weak incentives for private saving. While much of the logic of these behavioral models is appealing, the actual magnitude and patterns of private transfers are empirical questions.

Description of the Data Set

The VNLSS is well-suited for analyzing private transfer behavior because it contains information about money and goods transferred between households, as well as potential determinants of these transfers. Some private transfers are measured at the individual level and some at the household level. Since the household is our unit of analysis, we aggregate individual transfers to arrive at a household figure.

In the "income" section of the household questionnaire respondents are asked to report on income that the household receives from a variety of sources. In the first section of this module respondents are asked, "During the past 12 months, has any member of your household received money or goods from persons who are not members of your household?" If respondents answered yes, they were asked the names of all donors, which household member received the money, the relationship of the donor to the recipient, where the donor lives, whether part of the transfer was to be repaid, and the amount. Respondents report both cash and in-kind amounts by answering the question, "How much money have household members received from this person in the past 12 months, including the value of all payments in kind?"

In the next section of this module respondents are asked a set of questions about income from miscellaneous sources: "What is the value of all income received by members of your household in cash and in kind from [income source] during the past 12 months?" Among the fourteen sources listed were the categories "Gifts, including gifts related to weddings, funerals, birthdays, etc. (money and value in kind)" and "Dowry or inheritance." The structure of the module makes clear that this income comes from other households.

In the next module respondents are asked about loans: "Do you or members of your household owe money or goods to anyone? ...a relative, friend, etc." Respondents who answer "yes," report the type of creditor (moneylender, government bank). Among the possible sources of credit are relatives and other private individuals. We count these loans as transfers. Respondents are asked about loan amounts ("How much money have the members of the household borrowed from [source] under this loan?") and timing ("In what month and year did the household member borrow this money or these goods?"). Loans make up about 22 percent of the value of aggregate transfers.

Outflows of private transfers are reported in the final section of the expenditure module. After answering several questions concerning detailed expenditure components, respondents are asked: "During the past 12 months, has any member of your household provided money or goods to persons who are not members of your household?" If respondents answered yes, they were asked the names of all donors, which household member gave the money, the relationship of the recipient to the donor, where the recipient lives, whether part of the transfer was to be repaid, and the amount. ("How much money have household members sent to this person in the past 12 months, including the value of all payments in kind?")

Transfers received and transfers given are not strictly comparable because there are more categories for receipts (such as dowries and loans). Transfers from abroad are another source of imbalance between receiving and giving. We expect reported receipts to exceed gifts.

Respondents are asked to report their income and income received by others in the household. There are four possible sources of income:

- *Wages.* Respondents report wage income from primary and secondary jobs held in the seven days prior to the survey, and income from other jobs held in the 12 months prior to the survey.
- *Agricultural operations.* A separate section of the VNLSS records information for calculating income from agriculture. We calculate profit from operation of the farm by subtracting total expenses from total revenues. Total revenues include those from the sale of crops, crop by-products, livestock, and livestock products. Both cash and barter payments are included in the calculation. Also included are revenues from the rental of agricultural land and the value of agricultural production consumed. Expenses include payments for agricultural labor, equipment rental and repairs, fuel, irrigation, fees for land-use rights, and taxes.
- *Business activities.* Households report revenues and expenses associated with up to three family-owned businesses. Revenues include income from the sale of products in the past 12 months (cash and in-kind). Household consumption of business production is counted as revenues. Revenues and expenses are adjusted for partial ownership by multiplying each by the household's share of a jointly owned business. We did not count expenditures on buildings and land as expense flows, and instead calculated depreciation expenses for these. We assumed a service life of 30 years for buildings and land, and one of 10 years for other durables such as equipment. We used straight-line depreciation.
- *Other.* Households are asked to report income from a variety of sources, such as interest income and public transfers. These questions are contained in a separate module that deals with miscellaneous income sources. Questions about private transfer receipts, discussed above, are also included in this module.

The survey contains several questions about employment status. Those not currently working are asked if they would like to find a job, and those who are currently employed are asked if they experienced a spell of unemployment in the past year. The survey also includes questions dealing with the demographic composition of the household: the ages and educational attainment of individuals, the number and ages of children, the location of the household, and migration history.

We deleted observations with zero or negative income or expenses, and households whose total resources, taking borrowing and saving into account, were grossly inconsistent with their consumption expenditures. For example, we deleted households whose income plus borrowing was less than a third of their total expenditures, or those whose resources were more than three times their consumption (see the appendix for details).

Descriptive Evidence

Private transfers in Vietnam are both widespread and significant. One way to gauge the extent of transfers is to look at total gross transfers received and given.

Scope and Magnitude of Transfers

More than half (51 percent) of the sample received private transfers, and almost three-quarters (72 percent) gave them (table 6.1). About 38 percent did both, and about 15 percent did neither. We refer to that 15 percent as "others."[4]

Since some households both gave and received, we characterized households as net donors or net recipients according to whether outflows of private transfers exceeded or fell short of inflows. Forty-two percent of the households were net recipients and 43 percent were net givers. Twelve percent of net recipients received transfers from abroad (see table 6.1).

Participation in making or receiving transfers varies considerably by geographic region. Overall, participation ranges from a maximum of slightly more than 90 percent in the Mekong Delta, to 60 percent in the North-Central Coast.

The Central Coast has the highest incidence of recipients, while the North-Central Coast has the lowest (figure 6.1). The Mekong Delta has the highest proportion of givers while the North-Central Coast has the lowest (figure 6.2).

Private transfers account for a significant portion of household income.[5] For the overall sample, gross transfer receipts make up 12 percent of household income (see table 6.1, column 1).[6] The corresponding figure for the sample of net recipients is 26 percent (see table 6.1, column 2). Net transfer receipts for this sample total 23.6 percent of household income. On the other side, net donors give away 4.3 percent of their income (see table 6.1, column 3).

Gross transfers received for the whole sample, 775,000 dong, are an order of magnitude higher than transfers given, 199,000 dong, but the two

Table 6.1 Characteristics of Households in Vietnam, by Private Transfer Status

Characteristic	All households	Net recipients	Net donors	Other
Income				
Income	6,453	6,965	6,849	4,008
Income before public transfers	6,266	6,778	6,629	3,909
Income before private transfers	5,877	5,318	7,103	4,008
Income before transfers	5,689	5,130	6,883	3,909
Income from public transfers	187	187	220	98
Receives net income from Social Security Fund (proportion)	0.156	0.159	0.171	0.104
Net income from Social Security Fund	172	170	206	87
Receives income from other social subsidies (proportion)	0.105	0.119	0.095	0.094
Income from other social subsidies	18	21	18	14
Area of land	915	791	1,124	675
Employment				
Head is employed (proportion)	0.824	0.781	0.846	0.880
Spouse is employed (proportion)	0.637	0.552	0.711	0.664
Head was unemployed in past year (proportion)	0.015	0.013	0.012	0.027
Number of employed household members	2.725	2.533	2.919	2.701
Head engages in individual economic activity (proportion)	0.138	0.147	0.130	0.132
Head engages in entrepreneurial activity (proportion)	0.062	0.062	0.067	0.047
Education (proportion of household heads with)				
0–5 years of high school	0.474	0.478	0.445	0.540
6–8 years of high school	0.145	0.135	0.149	0.161
9–13 years of high school	0.381	0.387	0.406	0.299
University education	0.053	0.057	0.058	0.028
Technical school education	0.116	0.127	0.127	0.059
Other characteristics				
Age of household head (years)	45.331	46.365	45.119	43.159
Proportion of households with head's age less than 30	0.136	0.152	0.104	0.182
Proportion of households with head's age greater than 60	0.189	0.219	0.169	0.164
Proportion of households with female head	0.268	0.323	0.215	0.271
Proportion of households with married head	0.817	0.770	0.869	0.798
Proportion of households with married female head	0.117	0.133	0.109	0.100
Household size	5.026	4.872	5.208	4.938
Number of children under 1 year	0.107	0.122	0.089	0.115
Number of children 1–7 years	0.851	0.787	0.846	1.037
Number of children 8–15 years	1.008	0.894	1.112	1.028
Children under 30 away from home	0.532	0.586	0.523	0.411
Proportion of households in urban areas	0.198	0.244	0.178	0.130
Proportion of households with head ill in past year	0.729	0.770	0.698	0.706
Days household members ill in past year	10.897	12.004	9.718	11.176
Work days missed because of illness	6.769	7.426	5.795	7.681

(Table continues on next page.)

Table 6.1 Characteristics of Households in Vietnam, by Private Transfer Status (continued)

Characteristic	All households	Net recipients	Net donors	Other
Proportion of households with retired head	0.075	0.099	0.062	0.045
Proportion of households with head attending school	0.002	0.003	0.001	0.000
Proportion of household with Chinese head	0.021	0.030	0.017	0.007
Region of residence				
Proportion of households living in Northern Uplands	0.167	0.162	0.169	0.171
Proportion of households living in Red River Delta	0.272	0.276	0.305	0.174
Proportion of households living in North-Central Coast	0.137	0.127	0.113	0.232
Proportion of households living in Central Coast	0.099	0.112	0.067	0.154
Proportion of households living in Central Highlands	0.027	0.027	0.017	0.054
Proportion of households living in Southeast	0.106	0.112	0.108	0.085
Proportion of households living in Mekong Delta	0.191	0.184	0.221	0.130
Transfers				
Proportion giving net transfers	0.428	0.000	1.000	0.000
Net transfer given (amount)	109	0	254	0
Proportion receiving net transfers	0.416	1.000	0.000	0.000
Net transfer received (amount)	685	1,647	0	0
Proportion giving gross transfers[a]	0.724	0.685	1.000	0.070
Gross transfers given (amount)	199	171	294	11
Proportion receiving gross transfers[a]	0.512	1.000	0.200	0.070
Proportion receiving gross transfers from abroad	0.050	0.115	0.005	0.000
Gross transfers received (amount)	775	1,819	40	11
Domestic transfers received (amount)	276	632	28	8
Transfers received from abroad (amount)	286	686	3	0
Dowries received (amount)	41	96	1	0
Loans received (amount)	172	405	8	3
Sample size	3,823	1,590	1,635	598

Note: Income and transfers are measured in thousands of dong.
a. Households both giving and receiving: 38.1 percent; households neither giving nor receiving: 14.5 percent.
Source: 1992–93 Vietnam Living Standards Survey.

measures are not directly comparable. Transfers received contain two components not contained in transfers given: dowries (41,000 dong) and loans from relatives (172,000 dong). Further, households receive a large amount of transfers from abroad (286,000 dong).

Still another way to gauge the importance of private transfers is to look at their impact on the distribution of household income. We subtracted both private and public transfers from household income, and then ranked households by quintile. Public transfers include net income from the Social Security Fund (payments for pension and disability) and other social subsidies (payments to victims of natural disasters and to special groups such as orphans, the elderly, and the handicapped). The poorest quintile has 4.1 percent of total income (table 6.2). Including private transfers, the lowest quintile's income share rises to 5.6 percent—an increase of 37.8 percent. The effect of public transfers is smaller: after

Figure 6.1 Vietnamese Households Receiving Private Transfers, by Region

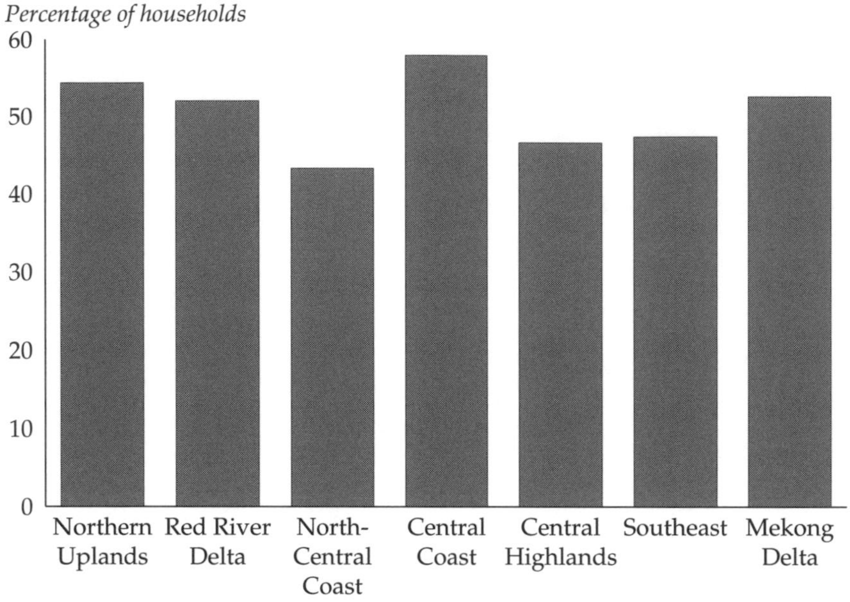

Percentage of households

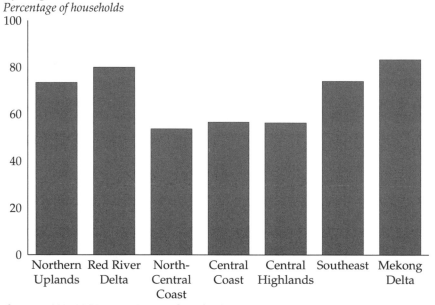

Source: 1992–93 Vietnam Living Standards Survey.

Figure 6.2 Vietnamese Households Giving Private Transfers, by Region

Percentage of households

Source: 1992–93 Vietnam Living Standards Survey.

Table 6.2 Effects of Public and Private Transfers on the Distribution of Income in Vietnam
(percentage of population)

Income quintile (dong per household)	Before transfers	After private transfers	Change	After public transfers	Change	After private and public transfers	Change
Lowest (below 1,940)	4.086	5.632	0.378	4.691	0.148	6.140	0.503
Second (1,941–3,136)	8.855	8.921	0.007	9.082	0.026	9.131	0.031
Third (3,137–4,738)	13.576	13.432	–0.011	13.737	0.012	13.590	0.001
Fourth (4,739–7,572)	20.955	20.503	–0.022	20.920	–0.002	20.495	–0.022
Highest (over 7,572)	52.527	51.512	–0.019	51.570	–0.018	50.643	–0.036

Source: Authors' calculations, based on 1992–93 Vietnam Living Standards Survey data.

adding them to pretransfer income, the lowest quintile's share of income rises by only 15 percent.[7]

Transfer Patterns

What patterns do private transfers display? Do they act like publicly provided transfers in equalizing the distribution of income and providing assistance to households that are especially vulnerable? How do they vary by age? Below we describe the salient patterns of private transfers. We first subtract transfers received from total household income and add transfers given. Income before private transfers are made is 5.3 million dong per year for net recipients (see table 6.1). The corresponding figure for net givers is much higher—7.1 million dong per year. The income of those neither giving nor receiving private transfers is much less—4 million dong per year.

Recipient households appear much more vulnerable than do donors. They are more frequently headed by someone who was ill, for example; and retired heads are far more prevalent among net recipients than among net donors. Private transfers also tend to flow from young to old (table 6.3).

Transfer receipts are by far most frequent among those aged 71 and over. More than two-thirds receive transfers, and the amounts received are relatively large. This pattern suggests that private transfers provide

Table 6.3 Transfers over the Life Cycle in Vietnam

Age of household head	Percentage receiving transfers	Average amount received (thousands of dong)	Average amount received among recipients (thousands of dong)
15–30	50.5	512	1,012
31–40	46.1	616	1,337
41–50	48.5	788	1,625
51–60	55.7	1,104	1,982
61–70	54.2	773	1,428
71 and over	68.0	1,331	1,958

Source: Authors' calculations, based on 1992–93 Vietnam Living Standards Survey data.

old-age security, as in Peru (Cox and Jimenez 1992). The portion of private transfers allocated to the young in Vietnam is much smaller than that in industrial countries, indicating that private transfers are not concentrated as much on financing human capital investment as in richer countries. [8]

The generational patterns are similar for urban and rural subsamples. In each case transfers from young to old predominate. For example, among urban households 42 percent of transfers flow from children to parents; 17 percent of transfers flow in the opposite direction (figure 6.3). The corresponding figures for rural households are 41 percent and 18 percent (figure 6.4).

Urban households are more likely to receive private transfers than rural ones, and urban households receive two-and-a-half times more on average (table 6.4).

Multivariate Analysis

While the unconditional means reported above are useful for getting acquainted with patterns of private transfers, they are inadequate for analyzing the underlying determinants of private transfers. For this reason we turn to a multivariate analysis of transfer behavior.

Figure 6.3 Sources of Private Transfers in Urban Vietnamese Households

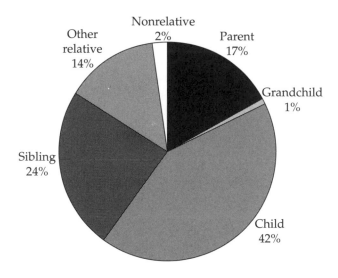

Source: 1992–93 Vietnam Living Standards Survey.

Figure 6.4 Sources of Private Transfers in Rural Vietnamese Households

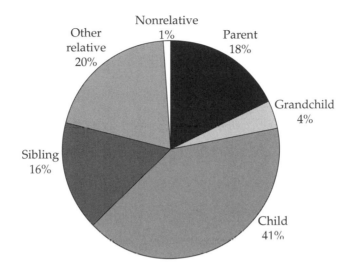

Source: 1992–93 Vietnam Living Standards Survey.

Specification of Transfer Functions

We estimate the incidence of transfers received and, conditional on receipt, the amount received. We include the following household characteristics in the specification of each equation.

Household resources. Household resources are measured by total income (before private transfers), including income from agricultural activities, businesses, wages, and nonlabor sources, such as interest and rent. Also entered separately is net income from the Social Security Fund and from other social subsidies.

In addition to these measures we include several other variables correlated with household resources: the level of education of the household head, which proxies permanent income, dummies indicating the employment status of the household head as well as those of other household members, and the amount of land owned.

Table 6.4 Transfers among Rural and Urban Households in Vietnam

Region	Number	Percentage receiving transfers	Average amount received (thousands of dong)	Average amount received among recipients (thousands of dong)
Urban	757	62.0	1,986	3,206
Rural	3,066	48.6	476	980

Source: Authors' calculations, based on 1992–93 Vietnam Living Standards Survey data.

Age. The simple descriptive evidence presented above suggests that age matters for transfer behavior. We enter a quadratic in the age of the household head and interact age with income. One reason the timing of transfers over the life cycle is likely to be important has to do with liquidity constraints (Cox 1990). If households are subject to binding borrowing constraints, for example, transfer receipts would be concentrated early in life, when current resources are low. In contrast, if transfers serve mainly as old-age support, as the descriptive evidence above indicates, they would be received later in life. Impediments to the acquisition of financial and durable assets, such as the threat of inflation, theft, or natural disasters, could contribute to the formation of private old-age support systems (Nugent 1985). Also, loss of confidence in the banking sector due to the collapse of the rural banking system in the early 1990s probably encouraged the formation of private transfer networks.

Demographic characteristics. We include a vector of household demographic characteristics in addition to age: gender of the household head, marital status, family size, and the number of children by age. Many studies indicate that transfers are targeted to female-headed households (for a review of the evidence, see Cox and Jimenez 1990). Marital status has also been found to be an important determinant of transfers (Cox 1987). And, holding household resources constant, we might expect more transfers to be targeted to larger families, since there would be more mouths to feed. We also include the number of young children living outside the household as a regressor.[9]

Health variables. To find out whether private transfers respond to economic distress caused by health problems, we include two health indicators in the transfer function. The first is the number of days household members were sick in the past 12 months. The second is the number of work days missed by household members because of sickness in the past 12 months.

Regional variables. In light of the descriptive evidence indicating regional differences in transfer behavior, we enter a set of regional dummies in the transfer functions. Further, we calculate three region-specific economic indicators: average regional income, the average unemployment rate, and the variance of the log of income. The first two variables proxy the economic condition of the region, and their expected signs, a priori, are ambiguous. On the one hand economic distress could galvanize households and increase transfer activity. On the other hand such distress could weaken networks if, for example, concerns about future earning potential cause transfer donors to retrench. The log of variance variable is included because, other things being equal, the more unequal income is before transfers the more likely it is that participation in transfers will occur. Of course, this interpretation of the regional variables makes the implicit assumption that transfers do not cross regional boundaries, which need not be true.

Multivariate Results

We consider private transfer behavior in two stages: first, the transfer decision and, second, conditional on a transfer occurring, the amount. The first stage is analyzed with a probit model and the second with ordinary least squares performed on the nonlimit observations (table 6.5).[10]

Household resources. The probit results indicate that transfers are targeted toward low-income households. For example, increasing pretransfer income from 3 million dong to 9 million dong would reduce the probability of transfer receipt by more than 6 percentage points for a household headed by a 35-year-old. But the ordinary least squares results indicate that, conditional on receiving a transfer, the same boost in income would actually raise the amount of private transfers received by 141,000 dong. One possible explanation for the positive income effect has to do with the exchange motivation for private transfers. An increase in pretransfer income enhances the bargaining power of someone involved in exchange, which in turn may lead to larger private transfers (Cox 1987).

We also entered the two measures of public transfers described earlier, net income from the Social Security Fund and other social subsidies. Having the mean value of Social Security Fund income reduces the probability of receiving transfers slightly (the effect is only marginally statistically significant). The ordinary least squares point estimates for Social Security Fund income and other social subsidies are large enough to suggest the possibility of crowding out, but the coefficient estimates are extremely imprecise.

If the household head is employed, the probability of receiving a transfer is reduced by 2.4 percentage points, and if the household has multiple earners that probability is reduced by 9 percentage points. These variables are also inversely related to the amount of transfers, and the coefficients are large, though the employment variable does not enter significantly. (The next section provides a better sense of the magnitudes of these coefficients because we use them to simulate the effect on transfers if the household head loses his or her job.)

Evidence of the connection between private transfers and human capital accumulation is given by the schooling variables. Having at least a secondary education increases the probability of receiving a transfer by about 4 percentage points compared with the reference category—five or fewer years of education. And having a university education has a large, positive, statistically significant effect on the amount of private transfers.

There are several ways to interpret the education effects. The first has to do with liquidity constraints. Holding current income constant, more

Table 6.5 Probit and Ordinary Least Squares Estimates: Transfers Received

Variable	Probit			Ordinary least squares		
	Coefficient	t-ratio	Mean	Coefficient	t-ratio	Mean
Income variables						
Income before public and private transfers	−0.000049	−3.28	5,689.04	−0.13	−1.02	5,130.38
Receives net income from Social Security Fund	0.072565	0.79	0.16	−427.20	−1.22	0.16
Net income from Social Security Fund	−0.000122	−1.90	172.23	−0.04	−0.10	169.96
Receives income from other social subsidies	0.083444	1.05	0.10	−286.60	−1.45	0.12
Income from other social subsidies	0.000060	0.29	15.24	0.13	0.31	17.51
Area of land	−0.000001	−0.14	915.16	0.03	0.89	790.93
Income times head's age	0.000001	2.08	261,590.80	0.00	1.86	242,382.80
Employment variables						
Head is employed	−0.061586	−0.81	0.82	−425.49	−1.04	0.78
Multiple earners in household	−0.237079	−3.71	0.82	−357.28	−0.99	0.77
Education						
Head completed 6–8 year of high school	0.033925	0.50	0.14	−95.15	−0.34	0.13
Head completed 9–13 years of high school	0.125921	2.07	0.38	566.93	2.25	0.39
Head has technical school education	0.093764	0.98	0.05	−359.07	−1.10	0.06
Head has university education	0.142182	1.94	0.12	924.42	2.22	0.13
Other characteristics						
Age of household head	−0.043536	−3.67	45.33	−58.10	−0.74	46.37
Head's age squared	0.000415	3.49	2,270.21	0.45	0.59	2,394.31
Female head	0.117917	0.92	0.27	563.16	1.52	0.32
Married head	−0.164622	−1.35	0.82	417.18	1.25	0.77
Married female head	0.075253	0.52	0.12	531.89	0.84	0.13
Household size	0.023021	1.27	5.03	101.82	1.17	4.87
Number of children under 1 year	0.107893	1.45	0.11	−428.85	−2.00	0.12
Number of children 1–7 years	−0.043573	−1.44	0.85	−145.06	−1.34	0.79
Number of children 8–15 years	−0.032673	−1.20	1.01	−84.79	−0.55	0.89
Children under 30 away from home	0.101909	4.14	0.53	195.00	1.73	0.59
Days household members ill in past year	0.005118	2.18	10.90	−0.37	−0.04	12.00
Work days missed because of illness	−0.000580	−0.18	6.77	2.54	0.22	7.43

Table 6.5 Probit and Ordinary Least Squares Estimates: Transfers Received (continued)

Variable	Probit			Ordinary least squares		
	Coefficient	t-ratio	Mean	Coefficient	t-ratio	Mean
Other characteristics						
Head is retired	0.025196	0.23	0.07	282.88	0.54	0.10
Head is attending school	0.617044	1.06	0.00	77.09	0.04	0.00
Head is Chinese	0.346611	2.11	0.02	4,428.60	1.96	0.03
Regional variables						
Mean income of						
region: urban-rural	0.000041	0.71	5,689.04	0.53	1.64	5,948.02
Employment rate of						
region: urban-rural	−1.194911	−0.57	0.82	9,597.97	0.85	0.82
Variance of income of						
region: urban-rural	0.185221	3.03	1.18	283.27	0.98	1.19
Urban household	0.027224	0.22	0.20	−153.44	−0.23	0.24
Northern Uplands	0.071701	0.49	0.17	−56.77	−0.12	0.16
Red River Delta	−0.083583	−0.51	0.27	673.84	1.10	0.28
North-Central Coast	−0.574696	−2.27	0.14	−353.96	−0.30	0.13
Central Coast	0.046922	0.31	0.10	204.91	0.36	0.11
Southeast	−0.444974	−2.25	0.11	−343.42	−0.48	0.11
Mekong Delta	−0.178600	−1.28	0.19	−319.20	−0.58	0.18
Constant	1.726408	0.84	—	−9,209.07	−0.83	—
Mean of dependent variable		0.42			1,647.37	
R^2		—			0.19	
Chi-squared test (38)		233.36			—	
Sample size		3,823			1,590	

Source: Authors' calculations.

education means higher permanent income and hence higher desired consumption. If households are liquidity-constrained they may not be able to borrow enough to fill the gap between optimal consumption and income. Thus private transfers are more likely to fill some of that gap. Another interpretation for the positive education effect is that a well-educated household is likely to have received private transfers for education in the past. If receipts of private transfers are positively correlated over time, well-educated households would still be more likely to receive private transfers during the sample period. In addition, the education variable could be picking up the effects of connections with high-income relatives.

Age. Age patterns for private transfers are important because they are related to economic growth. The more transfers are targeted to the young, the better the conditions for growth. Empirical estimates indicate that private transfers are targeted toward both the very young and the very old, while the probability of receipt is lowest for the middle-aged. These findings suggest that private transfers are used both to finance human capital investment and to provide old-age support.

Figure 6.5 Probablility of Receiving Net Transfers, as a Function of Household Head's Age

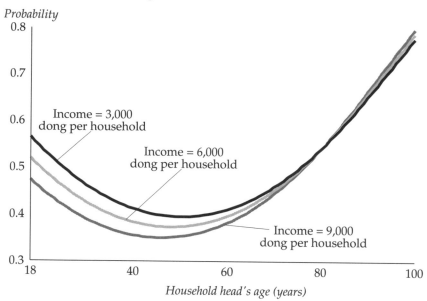

Source: 1992–93 Vietnam Living Standards Survey.

The age profile for the probability of receiving transfers is pronounced. Holding other right-hand-side variables at their sample means, an 18-year-old's predicted probability of receiving a transfer is 0.52. The predicted probability falls to a trough at age 48 (0.375), then rises: that for a household headed by a 70-year-old, for example, is 0.45. The estimated interaction between income and age is positive and statistically significant, and the age profile is more pronounced for low-income households, suggesting that capital market imperfections are more severe for this group (figure 6.5).

Demographic characteristics. Consistent with most studies of private transfer behavior, we find that transfers tend to be targeted toward female-headed households. The probit results indicate that if a household is led by a woman the probability of receiving a transfer rises by almost 7 percentage points, and the transfer amount by nearly 1 million dong.

There are several possible explanations. One is that, even controlling for household resources, the female headship variable could be a proxy for household resources—female-headed households are often economically disadvantaged. For example, women might have experienced career interruptions that reduced income in the past. So the female effect could be consistent with the altruistic motivation for private transfers. An alternative explanation has to do with the provision of services exchanged between households. For example, if women are more likely to provide care for children or elderly adults from other households, and they are being compensated for these services, they are more likely to receive transfers.[11]

Having additional children has little effect on transfers because the negative coefficients for the child variables roughly offset the positive coefficient on household size. But having an additional child under 30 living outside the household increases the probability of receiving transfers by about 4 percentage points.

Health variables. An increase in the number of days that household members were sick increases the probability of receiving transfers. This effect is consistent with findings for Peru (Cox and Jimenez 1992) and suggests that private transfers respond to some household emergencies. But most of the effect of illness works at the probit stage; its effect on transfer amounts is negligible.

Regional variables. Of the three region-specific resource measures, only one, the regional variance of income, is statistically significant.[12] Doubling the average log variance of income increases the probability of receiving a transfer by 8.5 percentage points. Two regions stand out as being much different than the others: the North-Central Coast and the Northern Uplands. All else being equal, the probability of receiving a transfer is 27 percentage points lower in the North-Central Coast than in the Central Highlands, for example. Note that these conditional region effects contrast with the unconditional ones discussed above.

Some of the variables used as regressors in table 6.5 may not be exogenous to the amount of private transfers received. In particular, the amount of transfers a household expects to receive may influence the amount of income earned and the probability of the household head being employed. We do not have the data to correct statistically for this problem. We know of little evidence, however, connecting private transfers and labor supply incentives in developing countries. Recent evidence indicates that this link is weak in the United States (Joulfaian and Wilhelm 1994). Still, such issues should be kept in mind when interpreting results. Induced labor supply effects would strengthen the results, since recipient income coefficients would be influenced in the direction predicted by greater crowding out.

Private Transfer Effects of Employment Loss

Here we use our empirical results to address the question, "How might private transfers respond to income shortfalls?" The example we consider is one in which the household head, currently earning 3 million dong and living in a household where someone else also earns 3 million dong, loses his employment and earnings. Suppose further that this household is average in every respect, except that it is not receiving any private transfers. We use the estimated probit and ordinary least squares equations to gauge the private transfer response.

The ordinary least squares regression results (second column of table 6.5) indicate that the predicted transfer amount for this hypothetical household would be 1.7 million dong, which is not far from the sample average among recipients, 1.6 million dong, and more than half of the hypothetical shortfall in earnings. These calculations suggest that the potential for private transfers to cushion the effects of unemployment may be quite large.

But what are the chances of becoming unemployed and receiving private transfers as a result? To answer this question we turn to the probit results, which imply that, for our hypothetical household, such an event increases the probability of receiving a private transfer by about 4.8 percentage points. Given that the household was originally part of the 58 percent of the sample not receiving transfers (and assuming that there are no fixed effects in the probability of receiving private transfers), the chance that the household would now receive a transfer is 4.8/58 = 8.3 percent. So private transfers are potentially important for alleviating the effects of job loss, but because not every household will receive them, their impact in expected value terms is not very large.

Conclusion

We find that private transfers follow patterns suggesting that they are responsive to household resources, age, education, and a variety of other characteristics. Private transfers tend to be targeted toward vulnerable households: the young, the old, low-income households, and households affected by illness. Private transfers help equalize the distribution of income. They are also sensitive to regional indicators of living standards.

The finding that patterns of private transfers are often similar to those of means-tested public transfers raises the possibility that the two are substitutes and that increases in the former could crowd out the latter. The potential scope for crowding out in Vietnam appears particularly large, since private transfers are widespread. The specter of crowding out presents policymakers with difficult targeting problems. One obvious solution would be to run means tests on all forms of income, including private transfers. But implementing such a scheme would likely prove a formidable challenge. Another avenue would be to focus on transfers that are less prone to crowding out. Measuring differential rates of crowding out of various public programs is a difficult but potentially valuable avenue for future research. For example, Cox and Jimenez (1995) estimate that if an unemployment insurance system were introduced in the Philippines, private transfers would fall so much that the intended beneficiaries of the program would be scarcely better off. In contrast, they find that the degree of crowding out associated with pensions is much lower.

Another finding that could prove important from a policy perspective is that private transfers are a significant old-age support. Households headed by someone over 70, for example, rely on private transfers for more than 20 percent of their income on average. Part of the pattern is surely related to the filial piety inculcated by Confucian teachings. But one consequence may be to discourage life-cycle saving, which in turn could impede capital formation. Further investigation of the connection between private old-age support and saving incentives is an important priority for future research.

As Vietnam liberalizes its economy, changes in markets, policies, and institutions will affect the magnitude and characteristics of private transfer patterns. We cannot make predictions because we do not have time series data. And even if we did, we would not know the extent of the structural changes. This is yet another area for future research. However, the experience of other countries may be useful in providing some clues as to the direction of change. For example, evidence over time from other economies in transition, such as Poland and Russia, indicate that severe economic dislocations significantly diminish the amounts of private transfers received (Cox, Okrasa, and Jimenez 1997; Cox, Eser, and Jimenez 1997). Thus when household incomes fall because of downturns in the macroeconomy, the private insurance market will fail to protect the poor. This is unlikely to happen in Vietnam in the immediate future because the country is making the transition to a more market-oriented economy gradually and the economy is growing. Moreover, a greater portion of private transfers probably originate from overseas and thus may not covary with domestic income.

Over the longer term sustained income growth will likely change institutions more significantly. Improvements in capital markets will obviate the need for private transfers. But these improvements may take a long time. Private transfer patterns in the Philippines, which has a per capita income more than four times that of Vietnam, are still consistent with attempts to correct for capital market imperfections (Cox and Jimenez 1995). Another institutional change may be reform of the pension system. Jensen (1996) estimates that in South Africa, where there was a large exogenous increase in public pensions for poor black households, there was substantial crowding out, as private transfers from migrant children to the elderly declined.

Appendix: Sample Selection Criteria

We deleted observations with unrealistic values for income from the sample. A value for income is considered unrealistic if it differs greatly from total expenditures. First we measured the total amount of money brought in by the household, "net inflows." Net inflows comprise real income, the amount received from land sold, other income not already included in real income, and the amount the household received from borrowing—all net of transfers given. Net inflows should not be much greater than total expenditures, except possibly for wealthy households. Also, net inflows

Table 6A.1 Selection Criteria

Criterion	Number of observations deleted
Total number of records	4,800
Zero nominal income	162
Duplicate income numbers	2
No data except income	1
Discrepancies between net inflows and total expenditures	759
Total expenditures are less than the seventy-fifth percentile and net inflows are three times total expenditures	52
Total expenditures are above the tenth percentile and net inflows are less than one-third total expenditures	669
Real income is negative	308
Net inflows net of savings are more than four times total expenditures	42
Negative pretransfer income	54
Remaining sample	3,823

Source: Authors' calculations.

should not be much smaller than total expenditures, except possibly for poor households. Households with negative income levels are also excluded since the variance of the log of income cannot be calculated. The criteria used to select this sample are shown in table 6A.1.

Notes

The authors are grateful to Paul Glewwe and Jaikishan Desai for assistance with the data set used in this study, Zekeriya Eser for constructing the measures of household income, John Jordan for assistance with the estimation, and David Dollar, Paul Glewwe, Jennie Litvack, Dominique van de Walle, and three anonymous referees for helpful comments.

1. Becker's (1974) seminal analysis posits that altruistic feelings prompt households to make transfers. Alternatively, households may have an exchange motive for making transfers, with different implications for crowding out (see note 2). The data do not allow us to test strictly between these competing hypotheses.

2. An alternative to the altruistic theory of private transfers is that they are part of a two-way exchange (Bernheim, Shleifer, and Summers 1985; Cox 1987). The exchange theory posits that financial transfers are used to purchase in-kind services, such as parents giving money in exchange for help and companionship from their children. A critical difference between the exchange and altruistic theory of transfers is that, with exchange, public transfers need not crowd out private ones. In fact, the exchange theory predicts a possible "crowding in" effect of public transfers. For example, consider the case in which a child receives money from his parents in exchange for periodic help with housework. A windfall increase in public transfers (or income from any other source) would enhance the child's bargaining position with his parents, possibly resulting in his receiving even more money from the parents.

3. Private savings and insurance purchases can also be crowded out by public transfers. For empirical evidence from the United States, for example, see Engen and Gruber (1995) for the case of unemployment insurance and private savings, and Cutler and Gruber (1996) for a study of public and private insurance. For discussions of the connection between public transfers and labor supply, see Moffitt (1992) and Sahn and Alderman (1995).

4. We ignore trivial inflows of transfers by imposing a minimum cutoff of 30,000 dong for classifying gross transfer recipients.

5. Income and transfer figures are adjusted for price differences across regions.

6. Private transfers from other countries are not strictly comparable because of discrepancies in survey methods. With this caveat in mind, note that the corresponding aggregates for private transfers in other countries are as follows: urban Peru—4 percent (Cox and Jimenez 1992); urban Philippines—12 percent (Cox and Jimenez 1995); Poland—4 percent (Cox, Okrasa, and Jimenez 1997); United States—3.9 percent (Cox 1990).

7. If we focus on the poorest by looking at the bottom 5 percent, we obtain the same qualitative results. Private transfers boost income more than public ones do. Private transfers raise this group's share from 0.366 to 1.349. Public transfers raise it from 0.366 to 0.553.

8. Since most Vietnamese finish their formal education by age 18, and most universities in Vietnam are public, few interhousehold transfers are expected to go to students. But private transfers to students are not the only way to enhance human capital. Transfers enabling young workers to invest in on-the-job training are another form.

9. The VNLSS only records the number of children under age 30 living outside the household.

10. An alternative specification would be to model transfer amounts using Heckman's (1979) generalized tobit. But this specification poses difficult identification problems in the context of private transfer behavior. In particular, to identify the generalized tobit, we need one or more variables that are contained in the probit but not in the equation for transfer amounts. Since theories of private transfers provide little guidance for such a specification, we opt for the simpler framework, while recognizing that our estimates could be subject to sample-selection bias as a result.

11. For further discussion of the connection between female status and exchange-related private transfers in the United States, see Cox (1987).

12. In the regressions, Central Highlands is the excluded reference variable.

References

Becker, Gary S. 1974. "A Theory of Social Interactions." *Journal of Political Economy* 82 (November/December): 1063–94.

Bernheim, B. Douglas, Andrei Shleifer, and Lawrence H. Summers. 1985 "The Strategic Bequest Motive." *Journal of Political Economy* 93(December): 1045–76.

Cox, Donald. 1987. "Motives for Private Income Transfers." *Journal of Political*

Economy 95 (June): 508–46.

———. 1990. "Intergenerational Transfers and Liquidity Constraints." *Quarterly Journal of Economics* 105(February): 187–217.

Cox, Donald, Zekeriya Eser, and Emmanuel Jimenez. 1997. "Family Safety Nets during Economic Transition: A Study of Interhousehold Transfers in Russia." In Jeni Klugman, ed., *Poverty in Russia: Public Policy and Private Responses.* EDI Development Studies. Washington, D.C.: World Bank.

Cox, Donald, and Emmanuel Jimenez. 1990. "Social Objectives through Private Transfers: A Review." *The World Bank Research Observer* 5(July): 205–18.

———. 1992. "Social Security and Private Transfers in Developing Countries: The Case of Peru." *The World Bank Economic Review* 6(1): 155–69.

———. 1995. "Private Transfers and the Effectiveness of Public Income Redistribution in the Philippines." In Dominique van de Walle and Kimberly Nead, eds., *Public Spending and the Poor: Theory and Evidence.* Baltimore, Md.: The Johns Hopkins University Press.

Cox, Donald, Wlodek Okrasa, and Emmanuel Jimenez. 1997. "Family Safety Nets during Economic Transition: A Case Study of Poland." *Review of Income and Wealth* 43(June): 191–209.

Cutler, David M., and Jonathan Gruber. 1996. "Does Public Insurance Crowd Out Private Insurance?" *Quarterly Journal of Economics* 111(May): 391–430.

Engen, Eric, and Jonathan Gruber. 1995. "Unemployment Insurance and Precautionary Savings." Massachusetts Institute of Technology, Department of Economics, Cambridge, Mass.

Heckman, James J. 1979. "Sample Selection Bias as a Specification Error." *Econometrica* 47(January): 153–61.

Jensen, Robert T. 1996. "Public Transfers, Private Transfers and the 'Crowding Out' Hypothesis: Theory and Evidence from South Africa." Princeton University, Department of Economics, Princeton, N.J.

Joulfaian, David, and Mark Wilhelm. 1994. "Inheritance and Labor Supply." *Journal of Human Resources* 29(fall): 1205–34.

Moffitt, Robert. 1992. "Incentive Effects of the U.S. Welfare System: A Review." *Journal of Economic Literature* 30(March): 1–61.

Nugent, Jeffrey. 1985. "The Old-Age Motive for Fertility." *Population and Development Review* 11(March): 75–97.

Sahn, David E., and Harold Alderman. 1995. "Incentive Effects on Labor Supply of Sri Lanka's Rice Subsidy." In Dominique van de Walle and Kimberly Nead, eds., *Public Spending and the Poor: Theory and Evidence.* Baltimore, Md.: Johns Hopkins University Press.

7

School Enrollment and Completion in Vietnam: An Investigation of Recent Trends

Paul Glewwe and Hanan Jacoby

Education is thought to have played a key role in the economic success of the high-performing market economies of East Asia (World Bank 1993a). If true, that bodes well for Vietnam's long-term growth prospects because its population is relatively well educated. Yet this apparent advantage may have eroded in recent years, as both public and private investment in education have declined substantially. During the initial phase of Vietnam's transition to a market economy, in the late 1980s and early 1990s, school enrollment rates declined. And school quality had begun to deteriorate even earlier, a trend that continued into the initial transition years.

Several important education policy issues in Vietnam require careful study—the declines in enrollment that began in the late 1980s, poor school quality, the high education costs incurred by households, the role of private schools, and the job opportunities for graduates (see Knowles and others 1996; and World Bank 1995 and 1996 for detailed discussions). The most visible sign of problems in recent years has been the downward trend in enrollment rates, especially at the secondary level. Declines in enrollment in Vietnam are particularly serious because the government views the public provision of education as a key mechanism for promoting equity. As discussed in chapter 1, the Vietnamese government places a high priority on producing equitable social outcomes.

This chapter investigates the causes of Vietnam's recent decline in school enrollment, an issue that is closely linked with many other education policy issues. It begins by describing Vietnam's education system and then examines recent trends in school enrollment. The rest of the chapter analyzes several possible explanations for these trends using data from the 1992–93 Vietnam Living Standards Survey (VNLSS).

An Overview of the Current Education System

Formal education has a long history in Vietnam, one that is well over a thousand years old.[1] Its current form clearly shows the influence of the French colonial rule from 1858 to 1954. Since the country was unified in 1975, several reforms of the management structure have been undertaken at the national level. During the 1980s four separate agencies were responsible for education. These reponsibilities were consolidated in 1987 and again in 1990, and since 1990 all education functions have been the responsibility of a single entity, the Ministry of Education and Training. While the central government is responsible for policymaking and for supervision of all education programs, the day-to-day administration of primary education is carried out at the district or commune level, and secondary education is administered at the provincial level.

Funding for education is the joint responsibility of all levels. The central government provides teacher and administrator salaries and funds for scholarships, and local governments provide the remaining funds, such as school construction costs and "salary enhancements" for teachers. In reality local funding often amounts to funding by parents. They are expected to purchase books, pencils, and writing materials for their children and also bear other local funding responsibilities in the form of additional fees.

In principle, children can enter the education system at a relatively young age in Vietnam. In many urban areas childcare for children up to three years of age is provided in creches, and kindergartens are available for children between the ages of three and five. Yet in many rural areas creches and kindergartens are not available, so schooling does not begin until enrollment in primary school. The five grades of primary education in Vietnam begin at age six. Students who finish grade 5 go directly to lower secondary school, grades 6–9, with no need to pass a formal examination. To successfully complete grade 9, students must pass a formal examination. Students must also pass an entrance examination before they can enter the upper secondary level, grades 10–12. Most students who complete lower secondary education do not go on to upper secondary. Those who do must pass yet another examination at the end of grade 12 to earn an upper secondary diploma.

Some students who complete lower secondary school enter vocational and technical training schools, which offer courses ranging from six months to three years. There are also schools of professional education, which offer training in agriculture, economic management, medicine and pharmaceuticals, teaching, and the like. These are open to students with a lower secondary or upper secondary education. Finally, higher education at universities and colleges is available for students who successfully complete upper secondary education and pass an entrance examination.

This chapter is concerned primarily with general education, particularly primary and secondary education. Two education issues of particular concern in Vietnam are the recent introduction of school fees and the decline in school quality. Until 1989 the official policy was to charge no school fees. Schools and teachers were to be fully funded by the government, and textbooks were to be provided without charge. But funding difficulties in the 1970s and 1980s are said to have reduced school quality in recent years (see World Bank 1993b; and MOET, UNDP, and UNESCO 1992). Buildings deteriorated, textbooks became scarce, and teacher motivation declined as a result of low salaries. Another consequence of scarce funding was increased use of double and even triple shifts in both primary and secondary schools.

Data on school quality in Vietnam are scarce, and there appears to be no data on changes in school quality over time. The community questionnaire from the 1992–93 Vietnam Living Standards Survey provides information on school quality in rural areas. As seen in table 7.1, these data show that 85 percent of rural primary school teachers have had formal teacher training, a respectable share for a country as poor as Vietnam. But student-teacher ratios at the primary level are somewhat high at 35.

Perhaps more illuminating in table 7.1 are the school problems that communities consider to be the most serious. They cited poor condition of school buildings and inadequate teacher pay as problems in three-fourths of primary schools and two-thirds of lower secondary schools. They also cited inadequate supplies as a major concern in nearly half of primary and lower secondary schools. In general, problems appear most acute at the primary level and least acute at the upper secondary level. Note that lack of spaces or desks for students is not a major concern; it is the quality of schools, not access to them, that is the problem in rural Vietnam. Indeed, all 120 rural communes sampled in the VNLSS had primary schools, and 88 percent had lower secondary schools.[2]

In September 1989 Vietnam introduced a system of school fees. Grades 1–3 remained free of charge, but grades 4–5 required fees equal to the value of 1 kilogram of rice per month. Lower secondary student fees

Table 7.1 School Quality Indicators for Rural Areas of Vietnam, 1992–93

Indicator	Primary	Lower secondary	Upper secondary
Teachers with teacher training (percent)	85	—	—
Student-teacher ratio	35	—	—
Percentage of communities citing problems			
Low-quality teachers	26	18	6
Deteriorating facilities	78	68	21
Not enough places or desks	10	6	1
Inadequate supplies	42	49	16
Inadequate teacher salaries	71	67	25
Distance from community (kilometers)	0	1	7

— Not available.
Source: 1992–93 Vietnam Living Standards Survey.

were equivalent to the value of 2 kilograms of rice per month, and upper secondary fees were set at the cost of 3 kilograms of rice per month. Students from families certified by their village or by the neighborhood People's Committee as too poor to pay were exempted from the fees. School fees are collected by the school principal and used for maintenance, purchases of supplies and equipment, and supplements to teacher salaries. A requirement that students pay for their textbooks was also introduced in September 1989. Students from families certified as too poor to buy textbooks were allowed to borrow them from the school library.

By 1993 school fees were no longer charged for grades 4 and 5, but monthly fees of about 4,000 dong were charged for lower secondary school students and about 7,000 dong for upper secondary students.[3] Substantially higher fees were charged in major urban areas, such as Ho Chi Minh City. Full exemptions from secondary school fees were granted to handicapped children, boarder students in minority areas, orphans, children of deceased or seriously wounded soldiers, and children in mountainous or remote areas. Fifty percent reductions were given to children of less seriously wounded soldiers, children of government workers disabled on the job, ethnic minority students, and children of families certified as poor by local authorities.

Recent Trends in Education

Recent trends in education in Vietnam are shown in table 7.2. In the mid-1980s the gross primary enrollment rate was about 104 percent. It rose to 106 percent in 1987, but then dropped to 102 percent by 1989. Gross primary enrollment fully recovered in the early 1990s, reaching a new high of 114 percent in 1994. Total primary enrollment data show a similar pattern.

Much more dramatic changes occurred at the secondary level. The gross secondary enrollment rate was in the low forties during the mid-1980s, but began dropping steadily in the late 1980s, falling to 33 percent by 1990. The rate increased to 35 percent in 1993 and then jumped to 41

Table 7.2 School Enrollment in Vietnam in Selected Years, 1980–94

Level of schooling	1980	1984	1985	1986	1987
Gross enrollment rate (percent)					
Primary	109	104	103	104	106
Secondary	42	40	43	—	44
Tertiary	2.3	—	1.7	—	—
Total enrollment (thousands)					
Primary	—	8,166	8,255	8,485	8,666
Lower secondary	—	3,086	3,253	3,264	3,291
Upper secondary	—	792	860	918	926
Higher education	—	124	121	127	133

— Not available.

percent in 1994, the latest year for which data are available. Total enrollment data show sizable declines at the lower secondary level and even sharper declines at the upper secondary level. Lower secondary enrollment dropped by 18 percent from 1987 to 1990, and in 1990–92 it increased only slightly, despite population growth of about 2.2 percent a year.[4] Upper secondary enrollment fell even more precipitously, dropping 43 percent from 1987 to 1990 and holding steady at this lower level from 1990 to 1992. Enrollment significantly increased in 1993 and 1994 for both lower and upper secondary education, but only in 1994 did lower secondary enrollment surpass the level prevailing in 1985–87, and upper secondary enrollment in 1994 remained below the peak levels of 1986 and 1987.

Overall, secondary school enrollment declined dramatically in Vietnam in the late 1980s, and it had only partially recovered by 1994. There are several possible explanations for these trends, and later sections of this chapter will assess their plausibility. One hypothesis is that the transformation to a market economy opened up new employment opportunities that raised the opportunity cost of schooling (relative to the returns to schooling). In rural areas the shift from the commune system to family farming gave households a greater incentive to employ older children, who might otherwise be in school. This explanation is consistent with the timing of the decline, which began in the late 1980s. It is also consistent with the larger declines at the secondary level, since only a small share of children of primary school age in Vietnam work.

A second hypothesis is that the quality of both primary and secondary schools deteriorated to such a point that parents decided that the benefits of schooling fell below the opportunity costs. Unfortunately, there are few, if any, data on school quality over time with which to assess this hypothesis. Still, one piece of evidence consistent with this conjecture is that the largest declines took place at the upper secondary level, which requires students to pass an entrance examination to enroll. Reduced school quality at the primary and lower secondary levels would generally lead to reduced success among students attempting to enter

1988	1989	1990	1991	1992	1993	1994
104	102	103	—	108	111	114
40	35	33	—	33	35	41
1.6	1.6	1.6	—	1.5	1.5	—
8,635	8,583	8,862	9,106	9,431	9,885	10,049
3,038	2,759	2,708	2,268	2,804	3,175	3,679
844	691	528	529	577	727	863
132	139	124	152	163	226	354

Source: For gross enrollment, UNESCO, various years; for total enrollment, World Bank 1996.

upper secondary school, assuming standards for admittance did not also decline.

A third hypothesis concerns the job prospects of school graduates. Better-educated workers are more likely to work for the government; of all people aged 30–50 in the VNLSS sample, only about 1 percent of those with a lower secondary education or less worked for the government, compared with about 12 percent of those with an upper secondary or higher education. In recent years the prospects of getting a government job have declined, as nearly 800,000 public sector (including parastatal) workers were laid off from 1989 to 1993. The same data show that, among people aged 20–30 with an upper secondary education, only about 5 percent work for the government. Of course, this hypothesis assumes that the decline in government jobs was not offset by new job opportunities for educated workers in the emerging private sector.

A fourth hypothesis is that the introduction of school fees and charges for textbooks in 1989 discouraged parents from sending their children to school. This hypothesis is consistent with the large declines in 1989, but does not explain the declines from 1987 to 1988. Of course, these four hypotheses are not mutually exclusive; each could have contributed to the decline in school enrollment.

Descriptive Analysis

This section provides a descriptive analysis of the VNLSS data, with an eye toward assessing the plausibility of the four hypotheses offered above to explain the decline in school enrollment in Vietnam since the late 1980s.

Changes over Time in School Enrollment and Labor Force Participation

Although the survey data are cross-sectional (rather than longitudinal), they contain some information on past schooling outcomes. For people who have finished their schooling, the survey records the year in which they left school. That information, combined with a person's current age, can be used to calculate school enrollment rates in past years by age cohort. The survey data also indicate how long people have been employed in their current main job, and how long they were employed in their previous main job, if any. This job history information can be used to calculate labor force participation rates for a given age cohort in past years.[5]

Figure 7.1 shows school enrollment and labor force participation rates for two cohorts of children, those aged 6–11 (primary school age) and those aged 12–17 (secondary school age).[6] For both cohorts labor force participation began to increase around 1986 and rose substantially thereafter until hitting a peak in 1991. The increase in labor force participation for children aged 12–17 is particularly dramatic: their participation rose from

Figure 7.1 School Enrollment and Labor Force Participation among Children Aged 6–11 and 12–17 in Vietnam, 1980–92

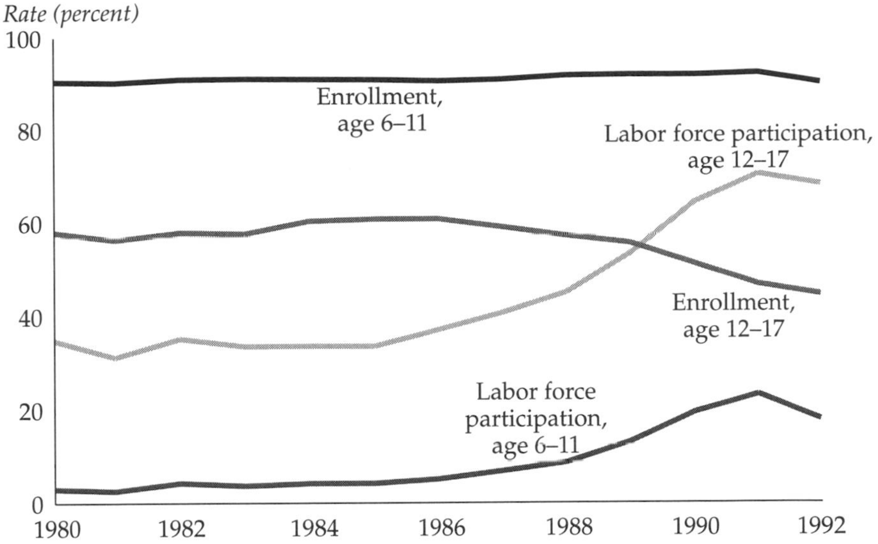

Source: Authors' calculations, based on 1992–93 Vietnam Living Standards Survey data.

about 35 percent in the early to mid-1980s to about 70 percent by the early 1990s. The increased labor force participation of the younger cohort does not appear to have affected its school enrollment, which holds steady at about 90 percent. In contrast, school enrollment rates dropped substantially for the older cohort, from about 60 percent in the early to mid-1980s to almost 40 percent by 1992, which suggests that older children were increasingly drawn out of school and put to work.

Consider again the four hypotheses offered to explain the recent declines in school enrollment. While the data may appear to support the conjecture that the decline coincided with the introduction of school fees, a closer look casts doubt on the importance of this hypothesis. Recall that school fees were introduced in 1989, and at that time they applied to grades 4 and 5. Yet primary school enrollment rates show no change in 1989. Moreover, the decline in school enrollment among children of secondary school age began well before 1989 and continued into 1990 and 1991 even though school fees remained at their 1989 levels.

The hypothesis that the return to household-based farming provided a new incentive for families to pull their children out of school applies mainly to rural areas, while the hypothesis that the reduction in the government workforce has reduced the returns to education applies primarily to urban areas, where most government jobs are found. Figure 7.2 presents school enrollment and labor force participation rates for children aged

Figure 7.2 School Enrollment and Labor Force Participation among Children Aged 12–17 in Urban and Rural Vietnam, 1980–92

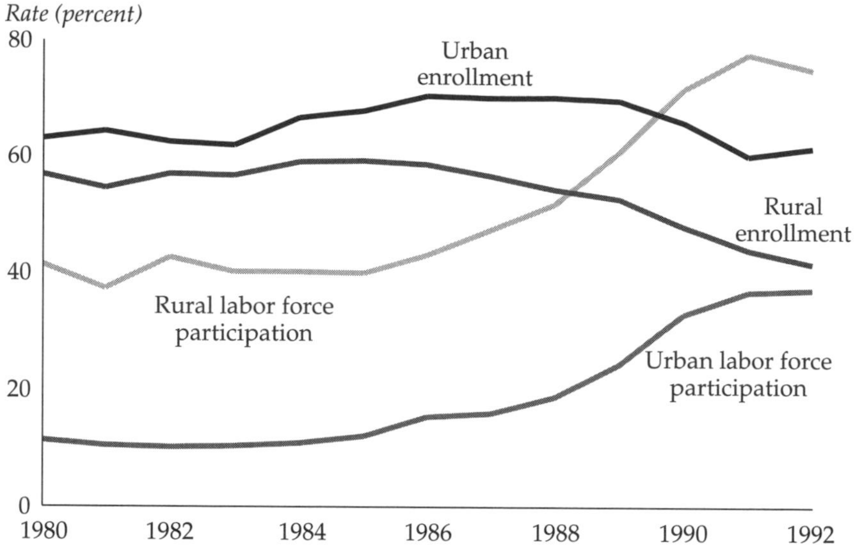

Rate (percent)

Source: Authors' calculations, based on 1992–93 Vietnam Living Standards Survey data.

12–17 separately for urban and rural areas. Labor force participation for this cohort increased dramatically in both areas, yet the increase in rural areas is clearly larger (from about 40 percent to 75–80 percent) than that in urban areas (from about 10 percent to 35–40 percent). Moreover, although school enrollment dropped in both urban and rural areas in the late 1980s and early 1990s, the fall is much larger in rural areas, and it was not preceded by an increase like that that occurred in urban areas. This finding, along with the fact that 80 percent of the population in Vietnam lives in rural areas, suggests that the decollectivization of the commune system accounts for much more of the decline in school enrollment than does the reduction in the government workforce.

Another possible reason that secondary school enrollment did not decrease substantially in urban areas is that losses in government jobs may have been compensated for by new employment opportunities in the emerging private sector, particularly jobs paying higher wages to workers with secondary education. Chapter 4 showed that nonagricultural employment yielded higher incomes to workers with secondary education than to those with less education, but made no distinction between urban and rural areas. This distinction is made in table 7.3, which presents parameter estimates of the effect of schooling on earnings based on simple wage regressions using the VNLSS data. Of particular interest are returns to schooling in the private sector. The estimates show that in rural areas there

Table 7.3 Effect of Years of Schooling on Wages in Vietnam, 1992–93

	Urban		Rural	
Level of schooling	*Government*	*Private*	*Government*	*Private*
Primary	0.075	0.066	−0.005	0.018
	(1.28)	(2.27)	(−0.07)	(1.02)
Lower secondary	−0.050	0.011	−0.043	0.003
	(−1.47)	(0.47)	(−1.34)	(0.18)
Upper secondary	0.036	0.077	0.051	−0.033
	(1.45)	(2.20)	(1.44)	(−1.05)
University	0.059	0.009	0.038	0.001
	(3.22)	(0.07)	(1.08)	(0.01)
Vocational and technical	0.031	−0.008	0.070	−0.004
	(1.24)	(−0.14)	(1.91)	(−0.08)
R^2	0.320	0.302	0.186	0.255
Sample size	451	354	310	759

Note: The dependent variable is the log of hourly wages. Other variables included in the regression are years of work experience and its square, sex, and regional dummy variables. The sample used contains wage earners only. Figures in parentheses are asymptotic t-statistics.
Source: Authors' calculations, based on 1992–93 Vietnam Living Standards Survey data.

are no significant returns to any type of education among private sector wage earners. This result further illustrates the lack of incentives to enroll in secondary schools in rural areas, which is consistent with the third hypothesis. In urban areas private sector jobs yield significant payoffs to primary and upper secondary education, though not to lower secondary. This finding suggests that new opportunities in urban labor markets may have offset the negative effect of reduced government employment on urban secondary school enrollment.

Further insights into the plausibility of the four hypotheses can be gained by examining school enrollment and labor force participation trends across regions. Figures 7.3 and 7.4 show that all seven regions experienced declines in school enrollment starting about the mid-1980s, but some had larger drops than others. The Red River Delta and Southeast regions show modest declines of only about 10 percentage points, while at the other extreme the Mekong Delta and Northern Uplands show declines of about 25 percentage points. These trends differ with those for labor force participation, as seen in figure 7.5. In particular, while the Mekong Delta had the lowest enrollment rate for 12–17-year-olds in 1992, its labor force participation rate for that age cohort in 1992 was the third lowest. That suggests that factors other than income-earning opportunities may explain enrollment differences across regions. One such factor could be changes in school quality.

A possible implication of deteriorating school quality, as mentioned earlier, is an increase in the failure rate on the entrance exam for upper secondary school (grades 10–12). Thus one avenue through which enrollments may have declined is an increase in the number of grade 9 graduates who failed this exam. If that were the case, the share of children

Figure 7.3 School Enrollment Rate among Children Aged 12–17 in Northern Regions of Vietnam, 1980–92

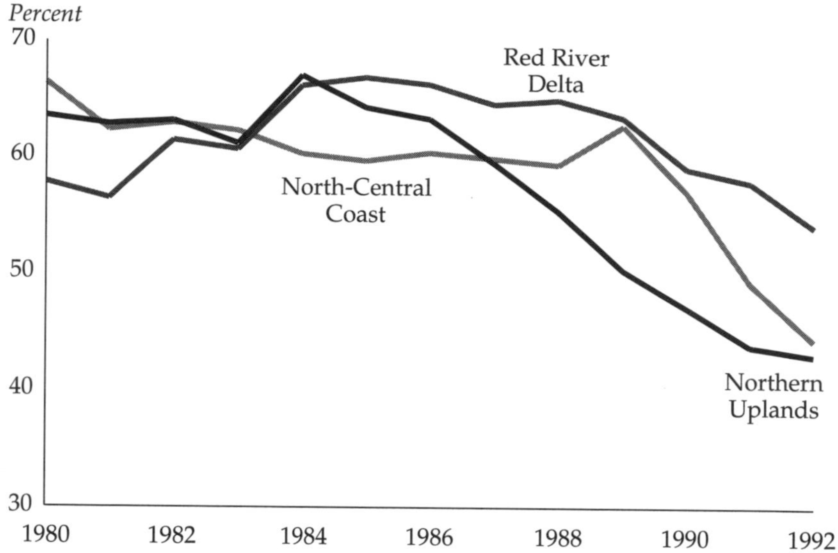

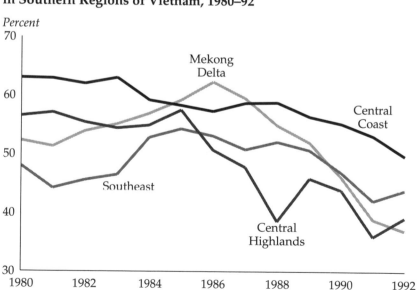

Source: Authors' calculations, based on 1992–93 Vietnam Living Standards Survey data.

Figure 7.4 School Enrollment Rate among Children Aged 12–17 in Southern Regions of Vietnam, 1980–92

Source: Authors' calculations, based on 1992–93 Vietnam Living Standards Survey data.

Figure 7.5 Labor Force Participation among Children Aged 12–17 in Vietnam, by Region, 1980–92

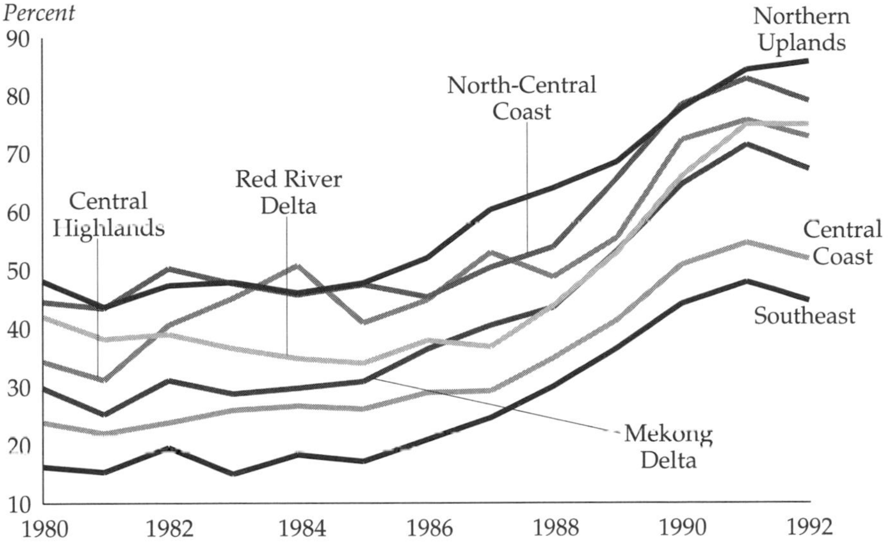

Source: Authors' calculations, based on 1992–93 Vietnam Living Standards Survey data.

leaving school with exactly nine years of schooling should have increased. What do the data show? This can be seen in figure 7.6. In 1985–87 about 25 percent of dropouts had completed lower secondary school (grade 9) but did not continue on to upper secondary education. This share fell to less than 20 percent in the late 1980s and continued falling to about 15 percent in the early 1990s. Over the same period about 20 percent of school leavers had finished some or all of their upper secondary education (most finished all of it). Overall, these numbers are not consistent with an increase in the failure rate on the upper secondary school entrance examination. Yet that does not mean that a decline in school quality had no role in reducing school enrollment, since it may have operated through a reduction in the value of lower secondary schooling.

Finally, it is worth checking whether the reductions in school enrollment affected primarily the poor or occurred among all income groups (recall from chapter 2 that there is a negative correlation between the education of the household head and poverty). The data show no declines in enrollment among the younger cohort (age 6–11), and further investigation (not reported here) revealed no patterns across quintiles. In contrast, figure 7.7 shows that in the early to mid-1980s the gap widened across the different quintiles among the older cohort (ages 12–17), with school enrollment

Figure 7.6 School Leavers by Last Grade Attained, Vietnam, 1985–92

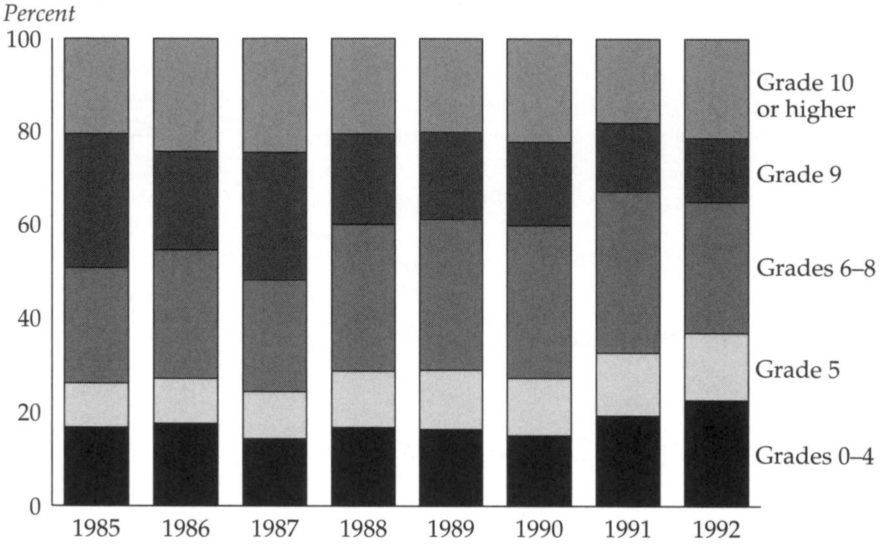

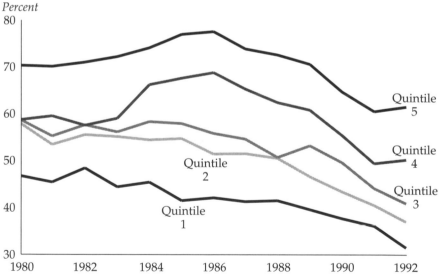

Source: Authors' calculations, based on 1992–93 Vietnam Living Standards Survey data.

Figure 7.7 School Enrollment Rate among Children Aged 12–17 in Vietnam, by Income Quintile, 1980–92

Note: The quintiles are based on household expenditure; quintile 1 contains the poorest 20 percent of households, and quintile 5 contains the wealthiest 20 percent. Since data on expenditure are available only for the current year, the underlying assumption is that there was little movement of households into different quintiles over time. The greater the tendency for households or individuals to move across quintiles over time, the greater the likelihood of observing a spurious increased dispersion over time.
Source: Authors' calculations, based on 1992–93 Vietnam Living Standards Survey data.

increasing for the two richest quintiles (4 and 5) and falling for the two poorest (1 and 2). More interesting is the small narrowing of the gap between the richer and poorer quintiles from the mid 1980s to the early 1990s (though in 1992 the dispersion increased). This finding suggests that the declines in school enrollment in Vietnam since the mid 1980s were not experienced primarily among the poor but instead affected all income groups.

Regional Variation in School Enrollment, Fees, and Quality

Looking at regional variation in school enrollment, fees, and quality in 1992–93 may yield further insights into the causes of Vietnam's recent decline in enrollment. Factors that explain differences in enrollment among regions may also explain changes over time. Table 7.4 presents net and gross enrollment rates in Vietnam by level of schooling, region, and income level.[7] The differences between urban and rural enrollment rates reveal typical patterns, with urban rates exceeding rural rates. But these differences are small at the primary level and only moderate at the lower secondary level.

Regional variation at the primary level also is not very pronounced, despite the large regional differences in household expenditure levels (see table 2.2 in chapter 2). Most unusual in this respect is the Mekong Delta, which has the second lowest net primary enrollment rate even though it has the second highest per capita expenditure. Secondary school enroll-

Table 7.4 School Enrollment Rates in Vietnam, by Quintile and Region, 1992–93

Quintile or region	Primary		Lower secondary		Upper secondary	
	Net	Gross	Net	Gross	Net	Gross
All Vietnam	86	111	39	50	6	8
Urban	94	110	63	77	15	18
Rural	85	111	34	44	3	5
Quintile						
1 (poorest)	75	100	18	24	1	1
2	88	114	28	35	1	2
3	89	114	41	52	5	8
4	91	117	46	59	9	12
5 (wealthiest)	82	112	64	82	10	13
Region						
Northern Uplands	85	108	34	42	6	6
Red River Delta	91	107	57	70	10	15
North-Central Coast	91	115	43	55	3	5
Central Coast	85	112	46	58	5	8
Central Highlands	72	113	15	22	0	0
Southeast	93	116	46	59	6	7
Mekong Delta	79	111	25	35	4	6

Source: 1992–93 Vietnam Living Standards Survey.

Table 7.5 Share of Schools for Which Quality Problems Cited in Rural Vietnam, by Region, 1992–93

(percent, except where otherwise indicated)

Problem	Northern Uplands	Red River Delta	North-Central Coast	Central Coast	Central Highlands	South-east	Mekong Delta
Primary							
Low-quality teachers	26	19	11	8	0	10	64
Deteriorating facilities	89	75	78	67	100	80	72
Not enough places or desks	5	13	22	0	25	0	8
Inadequate supplies	47	41	56	42	25	50	28
Inadequate teacher salaries	74	69	50	92	75	90	68
Lower secondary							
Low-quality teachers	16	16	0	8	0	0	48
Deteriorating facilities	89	63	61	58	100	70	64
Not enough places or desks	5	13	22	0	0	0	12
Inadequate supplies	63	50	61	8	75	50	44
Inadequate teacher salaries	47	72	44	92	50	100	68
Upper secondary							
Low-quality teachers	5	0	0	0	0	0	24
Deteriorating facilities	11	22	17	8	50	30	28
Not enough places or desks	0	0	0	8	0	0	0
Inadequate supplies	16	13	6	0	50	40	20
Inadequate teacher salaries	16	25	17	17	25	30	40
Memo items							
Primary teachers with teacher training	97	95	98	83	95	89	52
Primary student-teacher ratio	31	35	33	36	31	36	38

Source: 1992–93 Vietnam Living Standards Survey, community questionnaire.

ment rates vary much more across regions, and again, enrollment rates in the Mekong Delta are low relative to mean household expenditure, especially at the lower secondary level.

School quality data for rural areas by region and level of schooling are shown in table 7.5.[8] In rural areas of the Mekong Delta the large share of primary schools that cite poor teacher quality as a problem and the low share of primary teachers who have had training both indicate particularly low school quality relative to that in other regions. Yet the Mekong Delta fares better on other school quality indicators at the primary level. At both lower and upper secondary levels teacher quality is again cited as a problem much more often in the Mekong Delta, but the region does not appear worse in other respects.

If teacher quality is a key indicator of school quality, then the low enrollment (relative to the income level) in rural areas of the Mekong Delta may be explained, at least in part, by low teacher quality. This finding also suggests that declines in school quality over time may have played an important role in reducing enrollment in the late 1980s and early 1990s.

Table 7.6 Expenses and School Fees at Public Schools in Vietnam, by Region, 1992–93

(dong per student per year)

Level of schooling and type of expenses	Northern Uplands	Red River Delta	North-Central Coast	Central Coast	Central Highlands	South-east	Mekong Delta
Primary							
Tuition only							
Urban	140	1,679	2,958	2,651	—	55,531	1,134
Rural	95	324	804	1,362	849	5,298	1,981
Tuition, PTA, other							
Urban	13,390	72,157	31,166	87,413	—	141,735	40,185
Rural	10,143	16,136	13,284	17,192	19,622	17,972	13,781
All costs							
Urban	55,440	137,376	60,375	197,998	—	355,377	196,782
Rural	32,751	40,295	40,545	64,985	67,097	115,389	93,683
School fee (rural only)[a]	7,131	22,000	13,472	7,042	21,250	19,667	43,629
Lower secondary							
Tuition only							
Urban	24,688	21,059	18,600	33,090	—	115,366	30,445
Rural	20,065	23,465	20,364	26,719	32,333	28,569	26,787
Tuition, PTA, other							
Urban	54,480	119,926	63,900	184,427	—	287,005	135,070
Rural	30,884	48,601	36,996	81,149	72,827	45,137	52,048
All costs							
Urban	116,329	202,015	162,200	351,677	—	645,200	465,900
Rural	67,013	104,170	90,663	192,880	217,047	174,237	260,745
School fee (rural only)[a]	27,126	54,313	42,241	50,591	49,625	34,000	142,246
Upper secondary							
Tuition only							
Urban	29,778	119,583	24,000	168,500	—	222,214	47,000
Rural	29,500	34,840	38,545	59,000	34,250	51,083	48,667
Tuition, PTA, other							
Urban	43,223	292,500	34,000	404,658	—	467,214	181,286
Rural	68,563	106,880	125,818	154,945	66,750	103,667	129,000
All costs							
Urban	155,222	418,167	159,000	652,447	—	888,214	549,000
Rural	147,313	230,080	209,909	306,167	210,500	275,667	632,889
School fee (rural only)[a]	52,794	110,207	128,294	87,857	68,875	131,471	367,292

— Not available.

a. These data are from the community questionnaire.

Source: 1992–93 Vietnam Living Standards Survey.

But one should be cautious about drawing time-series inferences from cross-sectional data.

Consider now school expenses and fees (table 7.6), beginning with primary schooling. Recall that the official policy in 1993 was to not charge tuition at the primary level, with the possible exception of Ho Chi Minh City (urban areas of the Southeast). Excluding urban areas of the Southeast, mean tuition expenses per child per year are about 5,000 dong or less. But adding parent-teacher association (PTA) fees and miscellaneous costs makes primary schooling much more expensive, about 10,000–20,000 dong in rural areas and as much as 87,000 dong in urban areas excluding the Southeast, where the cost is 142,000 dong).[9] The cost is even higher after adding the costs of uniforms, books, transportation, and food or lodging— up to 115,000 dong in rural areas and 55,000–197,000 dong in urban areas (again excluding the urban Southeast, where the cost is 355,000 dong). Clearly, low or zero tuition does not necessarily mean low schooling costs.

At the lower and upper secondary levels tuition is much higher than at the primary level. Recall that official annual tuition rates for lower secondary were to be about 35,000 dong in rural areas and 45,000 dong in urban areas (excluding the urban Southeast).[10] These rates are somewhat higher than those reported in the VNLSS (see table 7.6), but the difference could reflect discounts for minorities and poor families. The official upper secondary tuition fees of 60,000 dong in rural areas and 80,000 dong in urban areas are fairly consistent with those reported in the survey when the exceptions for certain students are taken into account. But in urban areas the mean tuition paid exceeded the official fees of 80,000 dong in three of seven regions: Red River Delta, Central Coast, and, as expected, the Southeast. For the first two regions, the higher-than-expected fees may reflect high tuitions paid in Hanoi and Danang.

While tuition is substantial at the lower and upper secondary levels, it still accounts for only part of total costs. When PTA and miscellaneous fees are added, the annual costs for a lower secondary student are 31,000–81,000 dong in rural areas and 54,000–184,000 dong in urban areas (excluding the urban Southeast). Adding expenses for books, uniforms, transportation, and food and lodging almost doubles the cost. Finally, the costs for upper secondary students are about 50–100 percent higher than those for lower secondary students. These figures suggest that the decision to charge tuition at the secondary level probably did not raise schooling costs by a large percentage for most students, which raises further doubt about the hypothesis that school fees explain much of the recent decline in school enrollment.

One aspect of the data in table 7.6 merits particular attention. In each rural commune, the survey community questionnaire asked for the cost of attending primary and lower and upper secondary schools. Presumably, this cost includes only payments directly to the schools, such as tuition and PTA and miscellaneous fees, and excludes goods purchased in the market, such as books, uniforms, and transportation. From table 7.6 it appears that the school fee numbers reported in the community questionnaire are generally close to what people in rural areas reported paying for tuition, PTA, and miscellaneous expenses on the household questionnaire. But there are two exceptions. In the Central Coast households report paying fees substantially higher than the school costs reported in the community questionnaire at all levels of schooling. In the Mekong Delta the reverse is true; costs as reported in the community questionnaire are about three times what people report paying in the household questionnaire. This discrepancy is noteworthy because the community questionnaire data support the hypothesis that school fees may have caused the particularly large decline in enrollment in the Mekong Delta, while the data from the household questionnaire offer no such support.

Summary

The data on changes in school enrollment over time and regional variations in enrollment offer support for some, but not all, of the hypotheses offered to explain the decline in school enrollment in the late 1980s and early 1990s in Vietnam. The first hypothesis, that the opportunity cost of staying in school rose sharply when communes were decollectivized, is consistent with the greater decline in enrollment in rural than in urban areas among children of secondary school age. The second hypothesis, that decreasing school quality reduced enrollment, is consistent with current regional variation in teacher quality; in particular, the relatively low enrollment rates in the Mekong Delta may reflect its unusually low teacher quality. Yet declines in school quality did not increase the failure rate on the upper secondary school entrance examination. Moreover, school quality is lowest at the primary level, yet primary enrollment has been much more stable than secondary enrollment.

The third hypothesis, that reduced prospects for government employment led to major reductions in school enrollment, is consistent with the modest declines in enrollment in urban areas (where most government employees are located), but does little to explain nationwide trends for a population that is 80 percent rural. The last hypothesis, on the role of increased school fees, also garners little support. Not only did the declines in school enrollment precede the introduction of school fees, but fees do not appear to be a major part of the direct cost of schooling. Evidence from regional variation in school fees is mixed at best.

Of course, all the evidence in this section is based on relatively simple descriptive statistics, so the conclusions drawn should be regarded as tentative. The following section presents evidence based on regression analysis, which is better suited for disentangling the different factors that determine school enrollment and completion decisions.

Regression Analysis

Although the descriptive analysis above shed some light on the possible causes of the recent decline in school enrollment in Vietnam, there is a limit to what can be learned from cross-tabulations. The next step is to simultaneously control for the multiple determinants of school enrollment behavior in the context of a multivariate regression. Needless to say, causal inferences should be drawn with caution from a cross-sectional regression analysis because of the likely presence of unobserved heterogeneity.

Another limitation of cross-sectional data is that only current variables are observed. The constraints households faced when they made their education decisions cannot be observed, except to the extent that they are reflected in current data. Longitudinal data would be better suited to the task at hand, but such data are rarely available in developing countries, and none exist for Vietnam. Thus the following analysis should be viewed primarily as exploratory—as one that points to areas for future investigation rather than providing a basis for specific policy recommendations.

This section focuses on lower secondary schooling in rural areas because of the finding that this is the main source of the increase in dropouts in Vietnam.[11] But it also examines primary school enrollment in rural areas.

An Empirical Model of School Continuation Decisions

Consider a simple economic model of the school continuation decision, such as the choice between completing lower secondary school or dropping out. Without specifying the household's objective function or constraints in a formal model, assume that the continuation decision rule depends on the current costs of schooling, both direct (school fees) and indirect (time) costs, the expected future benefits from schooling, and current household income. Current income enters the decision rule under the plausible assumption that households in Vietnam do not have access to perfect capital markets with which to finance their children's schooling; credit-constrained households must finance human capital investment at least in part out of current income (see Jacoby 1994). Parental preferences for educated children also influence school enrollment decisions.

The data on the direct costs of schooling (school fees and the like) come from the household survey and, for rural areas only, the community questionnaire as well, though there are some inconsistencies between the two (as explained in the preceding section). Time costs could be obtained from the community questionnaire, which provides distance to the nearest school at each level when there is no school in the commune.[12] But measuring the value of an hour of a child's time poses a challenge, since few children of school age in the sample work for wages. Instead, the analysis uses commune-level wage rates for adult male agricultural labor, as well as household land holdings, as proxies for the value of children's time.[13] Yet land area is also an indicator of wealth, which typically would be positively correlated with the demand for schooling, at least for credit-constrained households. This positive correlation should disappear once household income is controlled for, which is done using per capita household expenditure. Even so, land may still have an ambiguous effect because it may serve as collateral for obtaining credit, which would have a positive effect on school enrollment. Finally, the analysis includes a set of demographic variables to indicate the number of siblings that would be competing with the child in question for household resources.

The expected benefits from schooling are also difficult to capture in cross-sectional data. But the survey data include measures of school quality at the commune level, again only for rural areas, which are indicators of the returns to schooling. The analysis also includes child height-for-age (the standardized Z-score) in the decision rule for starting primary school, since nutritional status may affect the rate of return to schooling.[14] Dummy variables for parental education and ethnic group are also added to control for preferences for schooling.[15] Because there are no data on wages or school quality for urban areas, the entire analysis is restricted to rural areas. Recall, however, that 80 percent of Vietnam's population is rural.

A final set of regressors are regional dummy variables. Although these variables are not suggested by economic theory, they are useful because they indicate whether the large regional differences in school continuation rates observed at the lower secondary level (see table 7.4) persist after controlling for a broad set of factors. Means and standard deviations of all these explanatory variables are reported in table 7.7 for two of the four age cohorts used in the regression analysis (because the descriptive statistics are very similar across cohorts, they are provided only for the youngest and oldest cohorts).

The statistical model used for the school continuation decision follows the sequential probit approach of Mare (1980). That is, separate probit regressions are estimated for each school continuation decision conditional on completion of the previous level.[16] Note that such a model ignores the possibility that students who complete a given level are "better" than students who drop out because of some unobserved factor, such as academic ability or family preferences for education. Such unobserved heterogeneity could lead to serious selection bias in the estimates. But because the analysis is exploratory, it does not appear worthwhile to undertake the computationally burdensome solutions to this potential problem (see Lillard and Willis 1994).

Another econometric issue to contend with is the potential endogeneity of household expenditures and child height-for-age. Families that decide to continue sending their children to school may forgo current consumption to do so.[17] In this sense school continuation may "cause" low consumption. At the same time low consumption (low income) may impede school continuation. This simultaneity would tend to attenuate the expected positive income or wealth effect. To avoid possible bias in the parameter estimates, appropriate instrumental variables are required. But many instruments that immediately spring to mind, such as farm assets, are likely to be invalid in a subsistence agrarian economy, since they may also reflect the value of children's time. Information is available, however, on income from miscellaneous sources (such as the government social fund, inheritance, and gambling winnings) that should be correlated with expenditure but uncorrelated with the income contributed by school age children.

Table 7.7 Descriptive Statistics of Explanatory Variables

	Sample aged 9–14		Sample aged 17–22	
Variable	Mean	Standard deviation	Mean	Standard deviation
Female child	0.49	0.50	0.48	0.50
Siblings aged 0–5	0.67	0.87	0.32	0.63
Siblings aged 6–11	1.61	0.93	0.58	0.80
Siblings aged 12–18	1.66	1.11	1.66	1.11
Mother's years of education	4.95	3.43	3.84	3.17
Father's years of education	6.47	3.41	6.08	3.37
Height-for-age Z-score	–2.16	1.07	—	—
Log per capita expenditure	6.91	0.49	7.14	0.45
Land per capita	5.57	2.25	5.85	2.15
Adult male agricultural wage rate	10.22	4.45	10.33	4.39
Regional dummy variables				
Northern Uplands	0.16	0.37	0.14	0.35
North-Central Coast	0.14	0.35	0.15	0.35
Central Coast	0.10	0.31	0.10	0.31
Central Highlands	0.04	0.21	0.02	0.13
Southeast	0.09	0.29	0.10	0.30
Mekong Delta	0.24	0.43	0.22	0.41
Ethnic dummy variables				
Chinese	0.01	0.07	0.01	0.09
Tay	0.02	0.13	0.02	0.13
Khmer	0.02	0.15	0.01	0.12
Muong	0.02	0.15	0.02	0.15
Nung	0.02	0.15	0.01	0.11
Other	0.07	0.25	0.02	0.12
Primary school variables				
Cost (thousands of dong)	12.97	9.06	13.62	10.03
Student-teacher ratio	34.70	9.33	34.84	9.03
Share of teachers with training	0.83	0.27	0.86	0.23
Poor-quality teachers	0.28	0.45	0.24	0.43
Lack of supplies	0.41	0.49	0.40	0.49
Poor-quality building	0.79	0.41	0.76	0.43
Lower secondary school variables				
Cost (thousands of dong)	44.88	22.56	45.28	21.45
Distance (kilometers)	0.60	2.50	0.35	1.26
Poor-quality teachers	0.19	0.39	0.17	0.38
Lack of supplies	0.50	0.50	0.46	0.50
Poor-quality building	0.71	0.45	0.66	0.47
Upper secondary school variables				
Distance (kilometers)	6.98	5.27	6.11	4.65
Poor-quality teachers	0.07	0.26	0.04	0.20
Lack of supplies	0.16	0.37	0.12	0.33
Poor-quality building	0.21	0.41	0.19	0.39

— Not available.

Source: Authors' calculations, based on 1992–93 Vietnam Living Standards Survey data.

To obtain instrumental variables for height-for-age, the analysis follows the approach described in Glewwe and Jacoby (1995), using the distances to the nearest hospital, dispensary, pharmacy, and clinic as instruments, as well as interactions between these distance variables and the male agricultural wage in the commune. The theoretical justification for the interaction terms is twofold: the effect of distance to a health facility on (the demand for) child health may be stronger when wages (time costs) are higher, but it could also be weaker if wages reflect wealth. Under the assumption that the error terms in the school continuation decision rule and in the first-stage regressions for the endogenous variables are jointly normally distributed, estimation can be done using the two-stage conditional maximum likelihood method of Rivers and Vuong (1988). That is, the first-stage residuals can be inserted into the second-stage probit, along with the endogenous variables, to get consistent estimates of the equations of interest. Of course, if joint normality fails to hold, the estimates may be inconsistent, but little can be done about endogeneity because there is no two-stage estimator based on less restrictive distributional assumptions.[18]

Four separate school continuation decision rules are estimated, two for each level. These are the decisions to start primary school, finish primary conditional on starting, start lower secondary school conditional on finishing primary, and finish lower secondary conditional on starting. Each decision rule is estimated on a separate sample of the appropriate age cohort. Thus, for example, the sample for the primary enrollment decision is all children aged 9–14,[19] while for the lower secondary completion decision it is all 17–22-year-olds who started lower secondary.

Results

Tables 7.8 and 7.9 present estimation results for the four decision rules. In rural areas most Vietnamese children enroll in primary school. Only 8 percent failed to do so in the sample of 2,864 children aged 9–14. The primary school enrollment probit uses 2,468 of these children for whom there are complete data. Among the household-level variables, father's and mother's education are statistically significant determinants of starting primary school, but most others are insignificant.[20] Before instrumenting, the log of per capita expenditure is also highly significant.[21] Yet after instrumenting, its larger positive coefficient is significant only at the 10 percent level. Similarly, while child height-for-age appears to have a strong positive effect on primary school enrollment in the standard probit regression (not reported here), it has a negative, though insignificant, coefficient after instrumenting using the two-stage conditional maximum likelihood method.[22] Note that the joint significance test of the two first-stage residuals is equivalent to a joint Hausman test of exogeneity; exogeneity cannot be rejected.

The coefficient on land area owned per capita is unexpectedly positive and highly significant. Perhaps household resources are not fully cap-

Table 7.8 Determinants of Enrollment in and Completion of Primary School

Variable	Enrollment		Completion	
	Coefficient	t-statistic	Coefficient	t-statistic
Constant	−9.228	−1.78	−31.883	−1.71
Age (years)	0.091	2.32	0.095	−0.23
Female child	0.085	0.69	−0.030	−0.32
Siblings aged 0–5	−0.045	−0.44	0.574	1.64
Siblings aged 6–11	0.094	1.15	0.337	1.20
Siblings aged 12–18	−0.104	−1.57	−0.109	−2.22
Mother's years of education	0.101	3.55	0.067	2.67
Father's years of education	0.070	2.33	−0.028	−0.40
Height-for-age Z-score	−0.361	−0.68	—	—
Height-for-age Z-score residual	0.595	1.12	—	—
Log per capita expenditure	1.167	1.67	4.661	1.67
Log per capita expenditure residual	−0.570	−0.77	−4.242	−1.52
Land per capita	0.072	4.64	0.066	3.57
Adult male agricultural wage rate	−0.044	−2.02	−0.102	−2.67
Regional dummy variables				
Northern Uplands	−0.688	−1.75	−0.437	−2.14
North-Central Coast	0.076	0.20	0.560	1.02
Central Coast	−0.162	−0.39	−0.624	−1.24
Central Highlands	−0.006	−0.01	−1.567	−1.92
Southeast	−0.005	−0.01	−0.589	−1.33
Mekong Delta	0.203	0.44	−0.586	−1.42
Ethnic dummy variables				
Chinese	0.066	0.10	0.175	0.20
Tay	−0.016	−0.05	−0.095	−0.23
Khmer	−0.716	−2.81	0.730	1.43
Muong	—	—	−1.060	−4.37
Nung	0.478	1.35	−1.075	−2.12
Other	−0.709	−2.99	−0.318	−0.71
Primary school variables				
Cost (thousands of dong)	−0.002	−0.20	−0.040	−1.89
Student-teacher ratio	0.014	1.66	−0.004	−0.63
Share of teachers with training	0.939	2.11	1.501	2.41
Poor-quality teachers	−0.447	−2.33	−0.666	−2.15
Lack of supplies	−0.170	−1.02	−0.304	−3.23
Poor-quality building	−0.299	−1.42	−0.493	−2.06
Lower secondary school variables				
Cost (thousands of dong)	−0.005	−1.48	0.001	0.54
Distance (kilometers)	−0.003	−0.18	−0.005	−0.25
Poor-quality teachers	0.408	1.43	0.602	2.06
Lack of supplies	0.193	1.18	0.104	0.69
Poor-quality building	0.124	0.62	0.419	1.93
Upper secondary school variables				
Distance (kilometers)	−0.013	−0.97	−0.032	−3.22
Poor-quality teachers	−0.448	−2.02	−0.277	−1.39
Lack of supplies	0.095	1.34	0.625	1.16

(Table continues on next page.)

Table 7.8 Determinants of Enrollment in and Completion of Primary School (continued)

Variable	Enrollment		Completion	
	Coefficient	*t-statistic*	*Coefficient*	*t-statistic*
Poor-quality building	−0.067	−0.31	−0.082	−0.44
Sample size	2,468		2,120	
Log likelihood	−381.74		−730.62	

— Not available.

Note: Standard errors are corrected for heteroskedasticity using the Huber-White method. For first-stage estimates of two-stage conditional maximum likelihood results, see appendix tables 7A.1 and 7A.2.

Source: Authors' calculations, based on 1992–93 Vietnam Living Standards Survey data.

tured by per capita expenditure, so that land area picks up an unexplained component of income, or wealth, rather than the value of children's time. Another possibility is that land serves as collateral, allowing parents to borrow to pay for schooling. The effect of the commune-level agricultural wage is negative and significant, suggesting that the opportunity cost of time is an important determinant of primary school enrollment.

Among the school quality variables, with one exception (upper secondary school teacher quality), only local primary school characteristics are significant. Thus, if one is willing to view school variables as exogenous, there is little evidence that parents take into account lower and upper secondary school characteristics, including distance, in making decisions on primary schooling. But primary school teachers who lack teacher training, or are otherwise judged as poor in quality, do depress primary school enrollment. Finally, neither primary nor lower secondary school costs, measured as the commune-level median household school expenditure, has a significant impact on primary school enrollment decisions.[23]

Turn now to the results of the primary school completion regression, which was estimated on a sample of 2,120 children aged 14–19 (see table 7.8). Almost a fifth of those who start primary school never finish, and the results suggest some reasons why. In addition to family background variables (such as parental education, household expenditure, and sibling dummy variables), school quality appears to play an important role in primary school completion decisions. Primary schools with insufficient supplies, in bad physical condition, and with poorly trained or otherwise low-quality teachers, are less likely to retain students. Interestingly, students for whom an upper secondary school (but not a lower secondary school) is farther away are also less likely to complete primary school. There are also one or two apparently anomalous results for the lower secondary school characteristics, such as the variable on teacher quality.

As for the cost of school, higher primary school fees discourage completion of this level of schooling, with the effect approaching significance at the 5 percent level. Local labor market conditions matter as well: a higher commune-level agricultural wage significantly discourages prima-

Table 7.9 Determinants of Enrollment in and Completion of Lower Secondary School

Variable	Enrollment		Completion	
	Coefficient	*t-statistic*	*Coefficient*	*t-statistic*
Constant	−64.352	−1.68	−12.226	−2.60
Age (years)	−0.057	−0.92	0.130	4.41
Female child	0.070	0.53	−0.111	−1.35
Siblings aged 0–5	1.178	1.60	0.116	0.98
Siblings aged 6–11	0.943	1.53	0.115	1.46
Siblings aged 12–18	0.091	1.44	−0.085	−1.92
Mother's years of education	0.005	0.15	0.040	2.25
Father's years of education	−0.187	−1.25	0.106	2.59
Log per capita expenditure	9.641	1.72	1.467	2.13
Log per capita expenditure residual	−9.272	−1.64	−0.876	−1.30
Land per capita	0.111	1.92	−0.009	−0.40
Adult male agricultural wage rate	−0.109	−1.63	0.036	2.57
Regional dummy variables				
Northern Uplands	−0.502	−2.34	−0.054	−0.28
North-Central Coast	1.271	1.27	0.106	0.50
Central Coast	−1.653	−1.66	−0.464	−2.32
Central Highlands	−3.584	−1.58	−2.210	−5.71
Southeast	−2.051	−1.94	−1.094	−5.57
Mekong Delta	−1.760	−2.50	−1.305	−6.59
Ethnic dummy variables				
Chinese	−0.771	−0.91	−0.562	−1.21
Tay	1.519	1.41	−0.198	−0.77
Khmer	2.182	1.88	−0.330	−0.86
Muong	−0.283	−0.79	−0.344	−1.15
Nung	−0.863	−2.43	0.139	0.71
Other	−0.766	−1.86	0.053	0.22
Primary school variables				
Cost (thousands of dong)	−0.061	−1.73	−0.018	−2.38
Student-teacher ratio	0.001	0.21	−0.006	−1.12
Share of teachers with training	1.156	1.05	−0.306	−0.86
Poor-quality teachers	−1.334	−2.13	−0.119	−0.76
Lack of supplies	0.113	0.58	0.009	0.08
Poor-quality building	−0.581	−1.82	−0.261	−1.82
Lower secondary school variables				
Cost (thousands of dong)	−0.010	−1.61	0.001	0.40
Distance (kilometers)	0.010	0.42	−0.119	−3.08
Poor-quality teachers	0.489	1.50	−0.294	−1.36
Lack of supplies	−0.496	−1.37	−0.093	−0.71
Poor-quality building	0.658	1.43	0.092	0.61
Upper secondary school variables				
Distance (kilometers)	−0.047	−2.44	0.022	1.84
Poor-quality teachers	−0.130	−0.73	−0.294	−1.70
Lack of supplies	1.210	1.39	0.241	1.69
Poor-quality building	0.002	0.01	0.133	0.85

(Table continues on next page.)

Table 7.9 Determinants of Enrollment in and Completion of Lower Secondary School (continued)

	Enrollment	*Completion*
Sample size	1,738	1,359
Log likelihood	–638.54	–755.03

Note: Standard errors are corrected for heteroskedasticity using the Huber-White method. For first-stage estimates of two-stage conditional maximum likelihood results, see appendix table 7A.2.

ry completion. But again, the land variable has a "perverse" positive sign, suggesting a wealth effect. Finally, in both the enrollment and the completion regressions the Mekong Delta dummy variable is not significantly different from zero, indicating that the explanatory variables account for this region's relatively low net primary enrollment rate.

For the lower secondary school enrollment regression, the sample shrinks to 1,738 primary school graduates aged 14–19 (see table 7.9). About 85 percent of these graduates entered lower secondary. The household-level variables, except parents' education, yield results similar to those in the previous regressions. The indicators of primary school quality appear to be more important than those of secondary schools in determining entry into secondary school. Deteriorating primary school buildings and poor- quality primary school teachers depress secondary school enrollment. This finding suggests that students who attended poor-quality primary schools are ill prepared for lower secondary school and thus tend not to enroll. Greater distance to upper secondary school discourages lower secondary enrollment, but distance to lower secondary has no significant effect. Both primary and lower secondary school fees also discourage lower secondary enrollment, but both effects are significant only at about the 10 percent level. The results are the same for the commune wage rate.

After controlling for all these factors, lower secondary enrollment in the Mekong Delta is no lower than that in most of the rest of Vietnam (although it is significantly lower than that in the Red River Delta, the omitted region, and the North-Central Coast). Interestingly, the analysis would have led to the opposite conclusion if household expenditure had been treated as an exogenous variable.[24] This is true even though the exogeneity of expenditure is hardly rejected (the significance of the Hausman test is exactly 10 percent).

Perhaps of greatest interest are the results of the lower secondary school completion regressions for a sample of 17–22-year-olds. More than 40 percent of the 1,359 individuals in the sample do not complete lower secondary school. Both parents' education and per capita expenditure (the second even after instrumenting) significantly encourage completion. By far the most significant of the school variables is distance to the nearest lower secondary school, which has the expected negative effect on the probability of completion. But distance to the nearest upper secondary school has the "wrong" sign and is nearly significant at the 5 percent level. The other lower secondary school characteristics are insignificant.

Oddly, the commune agricultural wage has a strongly significant positive effect on completion rates at the lower secondary level. Land area per capita has no significant effect. And somewhat implausibly, while lower secondary school fees do not attract a significant coefficient, primary school fees significantly discourage lower secondary school completion. Finally, note that the regional dummies are strongly jointly significant in this regression, much more so than in all the other regressions. This finding suggests that our household- and commune-level variables do a relatively poor job in explaining regional differences in lower secondary school completion rates. Moreover, the regional dummies indicate sharply lower secondary school completion in the south of Vietnam.

These regressions, tentative as they are, provide a mixed bag of evidence in support of the four hypotheses on the decline in school enrollment in Vietnam. If changes in the opportunity cost of children's time are an important part of the story, school enrollment should be lower in areas where agricultural work pays higher wages. The data show this to be the case at all schooling levels except where one would most expect it, for completion of lower secondary. The data also support the hypothesis that school quality and availability affect enrollment, so deteriorating school quality could have contributed to the recent decline. But again, no definitive conclusions on this score can be drawn from a cross-sectional analysis alone. Finally, support for the school fees hypothesis also is decidedly mixed. Although the school cost variables are sometimes significant at the 10 percent level, cross-sectional variation in rural school fees explains little of the variation in school enrollment or completion rates. From this evidence, it is hard to conclude that the recent rise in fees precipitated a large decline in school enrollment in Vietnam.

Conclusion

While Vietnam has a high average level of education for such a poor country, school enrollment there appears to have broadly declined during the recent economic transition and subsequent growth. This chapter examined several explanations for this curious decline in enrollment. The evidence suggests that changes in the opportunity costs of schooling played an important role, particularly in rural areas, where such changes may have resulted from the decollectivization of the commune system. The timing of the decline in enrollment and its concentration in rural areas are consistent with this hypothesis, as are some (but not all) of the cross-sectional regression results. This chapter also found some evidence, particularly from the regression estimates, pointing to the deterioration in school quality as a cause of the enrollment decline, but the evidence is not always consistent, nor does it always have a firm foundation (due to lack of time-series data on school quality). One finding that probably can be ruled out is that the rise in school fees in 1989 significantly reduced school enrollment in Vietnam.

Taken together, these findings suggest that public investment in school quality, perhaps financed by higher school fees, might increase school enrollment and completion at the primary and secondary levels. If fees can be designed so as to exempt the poor, improving school quality could lead to more equitable outcomes in education, a result consistent with the Vietnamese government's emphasis on equity. But before any recommendation is made that the Vietnamese government restore secondary school enrollments to pretransition levels, the question must be asked whether those levels were in any sense "optimal," that is, efficient, to begin with. Were "too many" children enrolled in secondary school in the early 1980s?

In a rural labor market as distorted as that under the Vietnamese commune system, decollectivization should have led to enormous gains in allocative efficiency. For households that can now sell their rice in a thriving export market, it may no longer make sense to keep productive family members in school. The estimates in chapter 3 suggest that primary schooling raises agricultural productivity in rural areas, but secondary schooling provides no additional benefits. It may be that secondary school attainment in rural Vietnam will continue to languish until households perceive a greater return to secondary education in agriculture, or until nonagricultural employment opportunities that provide significant returns to secondary education, such as household businesses (see chapter 4), greatly expand.

Appendix

Table 7A.1 First-Stage Estimates for Primary Enrollment Regression

Variable	Height-for-age Z-score		Log per capita expenditure	
	Coefficient	t-statistic	Coefficient	t-statistic
Constant	−1.989	−5.84	6.569	50.14
Age (years)	−0.041	−3.07	−0.005	−0.90
Female child	−0.011	−0.27	0.007	0.47
Siblings aged 0–5	−0.112	−4.35	−0.123	−12.44
Siblings aged 6–11	−0.085	−3.45	−0.079	−8.39
Siblings aged 12–18	−0.068	−3.17	0.004	0.45
Mother's years of education	0.006	0.64	0.020	5.85
Father's years of education	0.034	3.95	0.030	9.17
Land per capita	0.008	0.79	0.006	1.53
Adult male agricultural wage rate	−0.006	−0.51	0.007	1.58
Regional dummy variables				
Northern Uplands	−0.059	−0.61	−0.028	−0.75
North-Central Coast	−0.205	−2.61	−0.202	−6.70
Central Coast	0.063	0.63	0.312	8.04
Central Highlands	−0.042	−0.28	0.338	5.81
Southeast	0.396	3.74	0.235	5.77
Mekong Delta	0.470	4.33	0.164	3.93
Ethnic dummy variables				
Chinese	−0.009	−0.04	0.067	0.67
Tay	0.137	0.82	−0.100	−1.55
Khmer	−0.385	−2.55	−0.234	−4.03
Muong	0.020	0.12	0.003	0.04
Nung	0.228	1.09	0.107	1.33
Other	−0.019	−0.16	−0.080	−1.71
Primary school variables				
Cost (thousands of dong)	0.005	1.73	0.008	6.79
Student-teacher ratio	−0.000	−0.07	0.003	3.01
Share of teachers with training	0.322	1.92	−0.038	−0.60
Poor-quality teachers	−0.078	−1.01	0.060	2.03
Lack of supplies	−0.158	−2.73	−0.047	−2.12
Poor-quality building	−0.043	−0.57	0.077	2.67
Lower secondary school variables				
Cost (thousands of dong)	−0.000	−0.10	−0.001	−1.85
Distance (kilometers)	0.010	0.81	0.005	0.94
Poor-quality teachers	0.035	0.39	−0.005	−0.14
Lack of supplies	0.135	2.22	0.063	2.69
Poor-quality building	0.069	1.09	−0.035	−1.45
Upper secondary school variables				
Distance (kilometers)	0.012	1.80	0.003	1.23
Poor-quality teachers	−0.231	−2.41	−0.033	−0.89
Lack of supplies	−0.175	−2.27	−0.192	−6.48
Poor-quality building	0.026	0.42	−0.002	−0.07

(Table continues on next page.)

Table 7A.1 First-Stage Estimates for Primary Enrollment Regression (continued)

Variable	Height-for-age Z-score		Log per capita expenditure	
	Coefficient	t-statistic	Coefficient	t-statistic
Identifying variables				
Nonlabor income	0.004	0.51	0.008	2.95
Distance to hospital	−0.035	−3.05	−0.020	−4.52
Distance to dispensary	0.042	2.60	0.022	3.52
Distance to pharmacy	−0.053	−3.32	−0.011	−1.74
Distance to clinic	−0.008	−0.29	−0.033	−2.91
Wage * distance to hospital	0.003	3.61	0.002	4.80
Wage * distance to dispensary	−0.005	−3.55	−0.002	−4.23
Wage * distance to pharmacy	0.005	2.87	0.001	1.46
Wage * distance to clinic	−0.002	−0.68	0.005	4.12
R^2	0.101		0.370	
Sample size	2,514		2,514	

Source: Authors' calculations, based on 1992–93 Vietnam Living Standards Survey data.

Table 7A.2 First-Stage Estimates for Primary Completion and for Secondary Enrollment and Completion Regressions

Variable	Primary completion		Lower secondary enrollment		Lower secondary completion	
	Coefficient	t-statistic	Coefficient	t-statistic	Coefficient	t-statistic
Constant	6.704	47.25	6.798	43.96	6.694	36.44
Age (years)	0.011	2.13	0.010	1.82	0.017	2.75
Female child	−0.022	−1.34	−0.018	−0.99	0.003	0.12
Siblings aged 0–5	−0.123	−10.06	−0.130	−9.35	−0.124	−7.10
Siblings aged 6–11	−0.102	−10.30	−0.108	−9.89	−0.105	−7.31
Siblings aged 12–18	−0.000	−0.03	−0.008	−0.75	−0.024	−2.18
Mother' years of education	0.005	1.52	0.005	1.33	0.005	1.14
Father's years of education	0.026	7.83	0.026	7.32	0.022	5.47
Land per capita	−0.002	−0.54	−0.009	−1.92	−0.002	−0.34
Adult male agricultural wage rate	0.013	4.54	0.011	3.65	0.010	2.88
Regional dummy variables						
Northern Uplands	0.005	0.16	0.018	0.52	0.051	1.23
North-Central Coast	−0.183	−5.96	−0.175	−5.48	−0.185	−5.04
Central Coast	0.175	4.72	0.179	4.59	0.128	2.92
Central Highlands	0.286	4.36	0.406	5.23	0.390	4.04
Southeast	0.141	3.58	0.189	4.51	0.189	4.05
Mekong Delta	0.124	3.11	0.126	2.88	0.140	2.83
Ethnic dummy variables						
Chinese	0.181	1.68	0.130	1.17	0.261	2.38
Tay	−0.150	−2.09	−0.184	−2.22	−0.119	−1.28
Khmer	−0.166	−2.46	−0.189	−2.15	−0.153	−1.75
Muong	−0.031	−0.45	−0.022	−0.28	0.021	0.26
Nung	−0.001	−0.02	0.044	0.35	−0.026	−0.17
Other	−0.142	−2.49	−0.024	−0.32	0.045	0.46
Primary school variables						
Cost (thousands of dong)	0.007	6.11	0.006	4.77	0.008	5.20
Student-teacher ratio	0.000	0.13	−0.000	−0.34	−0.001	−0.98
Share of teachers with training	−0.193	−3.07	−0.188	−2.67	−0.159	−1.99
Poor-quality teachers	0.104	3.75	0.106	3.57	0.097	2.91
Lack of supplies	0.002	0.09	−0.029	−1.23	0.011	0.40
Poor-quality building	0.068	2.35	0.053	1.71	0.056	1.60
Lower secondary school variables						
Cost (thousands of dong)	0.000	0.42	0.001	1.70	0.001	1.31
Distance (kilometers)	0.003	0.50	0.002	0.31	0.025	2.73
Poor-quality teachers	−0.077	−2.43	−0.049	−1.46	−0.062	−1.61
Lack of supplies	0.035	1.56	0.062	2.52	0.007	0.24
Poor-quality building	−0.060	−2.56	−0.082	−3.34	−0.099	−3.52

(Table continues on next page.)

Table 7A.2 First-Stage Estimates for Primary Completion and for Secondary Enrollment and Completion Regressions (continued)

Variable	Primary completion		Lower secondary enrollment		Lower secondary completion	
	Coefficient	t-statistic	Coefficient	t-statistic	Coefficient	t-statistic
Upper secondary school variables						
Distance (kilometers)	0.002	0.97	0.003	1.36	−0.001	−0.37
Poor-quality teachers	−0.014	−0.35	−0.011	−0.21	0.024	0.43
Lack of supplies	−0.185	−6.17	−0.153	−4.72	−0.099	−2.64
Poor-quality building	−0.041	−1.73	−0.030	−1.14	−0.018	−0.60
Nonlabor income	0.013	4.98	0.011	4.44	0.018	4.17
R^2	0.312		0.320		0.314	
Sample size	2,120		1,738		1,359	

Note: Dependent variable is log per capita expenditure.
Source: Authors' calculations, based on 1992–93 Vietnam Living Standards Survey data.

Notes

The authors are grateful to David Dollar, Jennie Litvack, and several anonymous reviewers for comments on previous versions of this chapter.

1. This section draws heavily on World Bank (1995) and MOET, UNDP, and UNESCO (1992).

2. For the 12 percent of communes without a lower secondary school, the average distance to the nearest lower secondary school was 5 kilometers.

3. In 1992–93 one U.S. dollar was equivalent to about 10,000 dong.

4. The enrollment figure for lower secondary education is extremely low for 1991. It may be erroneous, or it may reflect some temporary condition that occurred that year.

5. There are two reasons calculations of past labor force participation may be less accurate than those of past school enrollment. First, if a person has had more than two consecutive jobs, the data do not show when he or she began working; however, this should be less of a problem for relatively young cohorts, whose work experience does not go back very far in time. Second, the school enrollment estimates are based on an answer to a simple question about a discrete event ("When did you finish your schooling?"), while labor force participation estimates are based on one or more questions about years of work experience in current and past jobs that some people may find difficult to answer, such as children who gradually began helping on their parents' farm.

6. The official age of primary school attendance is 6–10. Another year has been added because many children start one to two years late and others repeat at least one year of school. Even so, some children aged 12–17 are still in primary school (though the chapter refers to this age cohort as children of secondary school age).

7. The difference between net and gross enrollment rates is that the former exclude children who are out of the age range of the particular level of schooling, while the latter include all children enrolled at that level, regardless of age. Thus net rates are almost always lower than gross rates.

8. Recall that school quality data are available only for rural areas.

9. The miscellaneous costs are primarily additional fees for clubs, extra classes, and the like. They exclude expenses not paid directly to the schools, such as the purchase of books and uniforms, transportation costs, and any food or lodging expenses.

10. These annual figures assume that children pay tuition 10 months per year.

11. This is not to deny that enrollment also declined at the upper secondary level, but the main reason for this decline is that more students dropped out at the lower secondary level.

12. The community questionnaire also provides travel times (which are highly correlated with distance), but this information is less useful because some of the travel times are by bicycle or another form of transport while others are by foot. Moreover, there can be substantial differences in distance among households in the same commune, and this variation is not reflected in the data provided by the community questionnaire.

13. Land area could be correlated with the value of children's time if labor markets are incomplete, or if child labor is not perfectly substitutable with hired labor.

14. In an earlier study, Glewwe and Jacoby (1995) found that malnourished children in Ghana delay enrollment into primary school. It argued that, at the normal age of enrollment, malnourished children have a lower rate of return to schooling than do well-nourished children.

15. Ethnic group membership may also affect the returns to schooling if, for example, there is discrimination against minorities in the labor market, though this effect should be less important in an economy where 80 percent of the labor force is self-employed.

16. Another statistical model of school attainment is the ordered probit (see Lillard and King 1987; and Glewwe and Jacoby 1994). But this model restricts the effect of the regressors to be equal across grade levels, which seems implausible for such variables as grade-specific school quality and fees.

17. Even though direct school costs are included in consumption expenditures, indirect costs (particularly forgone income from children's employment) would lead to reduced expenditures.

18. Another difficult problem is that both the presence of schools and health clinics and the quality of schools in the commune may be endogenous, because the government may allocate education expenditures according to unobserved characteristics of students that affect enrollment and completion decisions (see Rosenzweig and Wolpin 1986). Data limitations (particularly the lack of longitudinal data) do not allow this issue to be addressed. On a more positive note, migration of households to take advantage of better facilities is unlikely to be an issue since migration in Vietnam was tightly controlled until the early 1990s.

19. Although in principle children should begin primary school at age six, it is common for some to enter at age seven and even at age eight. The sample here starts at age nine, by which time almost all decisions to enroll have been made; starting at a younger age would confound the enrollment decision with the decision on the age at which to enroll, conditional on enrollment.

20. Standard errors are corrected for heteroskedasticity and clustering at the level of the commune using the Huber-White method.

21. The coefficient on log per capita expenditure when all variables are treated as exogenous is 0.581, and the t-statistic is 4.77. These results are not shown in table 7.7.

22. The distance variables and their interactions with the commune-level agricultural wage are highly jointly significant in the first-stage regression for height-for-age ($F[8, 2468]=4.72$). The coefficient on miscellaneous income in the first-stage regression of household expenditure is also highly significant (t-statistic of 2.95).

23. Using school costs from the community questionnaire produced similarly insignificant results. The school cost data from the household questionnaire are preferred because of the unusually large school costs in the community questionnaire for some Mekong Delta communes.

24. When household expenditure is specified as exogenous, the Mekong Delta dummy variable is negative, with a t-statistic of –3.42, and the parameter estimate is twice those for the other regional dummy variables.

References

Glewwe, Paul, and Hanan Jacoby. 1994. "Student Achievement and Schooling Choice in Low-Income Countries: Evidence from Ghana." *Journal of Human Resources* 29(3): 843–64.

———. 1995. "An Economic Analysis of Delayed Primary School Enrollment in a Low-Income Country: The Role of Early Childhood Nutrition." *Review of Economics and Statistics* 77(1): 156–69.

Jacoby, Hanan. 1994. "Borrowing Constraints and Progress through School: Evidence from Peru." *Review of Economics and Statistics* 76(1): 151–60.

Knowles, James, Jere Behrman, Benjamin Diokno, and Keith McInnes. 1996. "Key Issues in the Financing of Vietnam's Social Services." Abt Associates, Bethesda, Md.

Lillard, Lee, and Elizabeth King. 1987. "Education Policy and Schooling Attainment in Malaysia and the Philippines." *Economics of Education Review* 6: 167–81.

Lillard, Lee, and Robert Willis. 1994. "International Educational Mobility." *Journal of Human Resources* 29(4): 1126–66.

Mare, Robert. 1980. "Social Background and School Continuation Decisions." *Journal of the American Statistical Association* 75(370): 295–305.

MOET (Ministry of Education and Training), UNDP (United Nations Development Programme), and UNESCO (United Nations Educational, Scientific, and Cultural Organization). 1992. "Vietnam Education and Human Resources Sector Analysis." Hanoi.

Rivers, Douglas, and Quang Vuong. 1988. "Limited Information Estimators and Exogeneity Tests for Simultaneous Probit Models." *Journal of Econometrics* 39: 347–66.

Rosenzweig, Mark, and Kenneth Wolpin. 1986. "Evaluating the Effects of Optimally Distributed Public Programs: Child Health and Family Planning Interventions." *American Economic Review* 76: 470–82.

UNESCO (United Nations Educational, Scientific, and Cultural Organization). Various years. *Statistical Yearbook*. Paris.

World Bank. 1993a. *The East Asian Miracle: Economic Growth and Public Policy*. New York: Oxford University Press.

———. 1993b. "Vietnam: Transition to the Market." Report 11902-VN. East Asia and Pacific Region, Washington, D.C.

———. 1995. "Vietnam: Poverty Assessment and Strategy." Report 13442-VN. East Asia and Pacific Region, Washington, D.C.

———. 1996. "Vietnam: Education Financing Sector Study." East Asia and Pacific Region, Washington, D.C.

8

Access to Health Care during Transition: The Role of the Private Sector in Vietnam

Paul Gertler and Jennie Litvack

Vietnam has historically shown a strong commitment to its population's health. Before *doi moi* (economic reforms) Vietnam financed and delivered medical care publicly. An extensive network of public health care facilities delivered curative health services free of charge, and health workers and community outreach organizations provided comprehensive preventive health care. Pharmaceutical supplies were subsidized by the Soviet Union. Relative to the national income level, Vietnam had achieved remarkably good access to health care even for the poor.

Vietnam's health sector began facing challenges after reunification in 1975, when the vast public health care network in the north was spread throughout the south. The expansion, coupled with the years of weak and sometimes negative growth in the 1980s, strained government's ability to finance the extensive hospital and clinic network as well as the preventive outreach programs at the central, provincial, and district levels. Health services at the commune level (basic curative care and preventive care) were financed through commune resources. But during the late 1980s the collapse of the cooperatives greatly reduced local financing of commune health centers, limiting their ability to deliver important primary health care services. The collapse of the Soviet Union in 1991 resulted in the loss of Vietnam's drug supply system, compounding the financial crisis in the health sector.

In the late 1980s *doi moi* opened the door to private financing and delivery of health care in hopes of improving health services. In addition, public hospitals and, to a much smaller degree, health centers began charging patients for consultations and drugs in order to mobilize private financing for the public sector system. Doctors and nurses opened up private practices, often in parallel with their public practice, and private pharmacies and drug vendors sprang up throughout the country. The expansion of the private sector occurred very quickly and with minimal government regulation to ensure quality, especially in pharmaceutical supplies and dispensing practices.

The government hoped that the opening of the private sector coupled with increases in the real budget for the public sector health system would reverse the decline in the health sector. This chapter examines the effectiveness of this dual policy as of 1993—in particular, the extent to which private providers are filling gaps left by the contraction of the public sector in the mid-1980s.[1] The analysis draws largely on the Vietnam Living Standards Survey (VNLSS) data.

Structure and Performance of the Health Sector

The health status of Vietnam's population is remarkably good compared with that in countries at similar levels of income and in neighboring countries enjoying otherwise higher living standards (table 8.1). In 1990 life expectancy in Vietnam was similar to life expectancy in countries with incomes 5–10 times higher (such as Malaysia, the Philippines, and Thailand) and about 10 years longer than that in countries with comparable incomes (such as Bangladesh and India). Similarly, Vietnam's infant and child mortality rates were about half those in countries with similar incomes and close to those in much richer countries. Yet Vietnam's health status was high relative to that of its neighbors in 1960, suggesting that its gains in health status in the ensuing three decades were only average for the region.

Table 8.1 Health Status Indicators in Selected Asian Countries, 1960 and 1990

		Life expectancy at birth (years)		
Country	1992 GDP per capita (U.S. dollars)	1960	1990	Percentage change
Vietnam	170	57	67	17.5
Nepal	170	44	56	27.3
Bangladesh	220	46	56	21.7
India	310	47	58	23.4
Pakistan	420	49	56	14.3
China	450	43	69	60.5
Sri Lanka	540	58	72	24.1
Indonesia	670	46	59	28.3
Philippines	770	59	64	8.5
Papua New Guinea	950	47	52	10.6
Thailand	1,840	52	68	30.8
Malaysia	2,790	58	71	22.4
Korea, Rep. of	6,790	53	72	35.8

— Not available.
Source: World Bank 1993.

Before *doi moi* Vietnam had developed a public health care system that achieved widespread coverage through a vast network of health care facilities, trained health staff, and preventive outreach programs. Even today Vietnam's infrastructure of health facilities provides a level of coverage far exceeding that in most developing countries (table 8.2). Vietnam has more doctors per 1,000 people than almost every other country in the region, and hospital bed coverage comparable to that in China, Malaysia, and Sri Lanka.

The public health sector began to deteriorate following reunification, and the decline accelerated during the 1980s. Commune health centers and district hospitals were unable to replace broken equipment and suffered severe shortages of medical supplies. The facilities were unable to recruit and keep qualified medical staff as salaries declined in real terms and relative to new labor market opportunities. The collapse of the Soviet Union meant that subsidized drugs in large quantities were no longer available, which led to severe shortages at public facilities. The symptoms of deterioration can be seen in the drop in the use of public facilities (figure 8.1). According to Ministry of Health statistics, the number of public sector outpatient consultations and inpatient admissions fell substantially in the late 1980s.

At the same time that the public sector contracted during the transition period, out-of-pocket expenditures increased because of the expansion of the private sector and the increase in fees at public facilities. Private sources account for the lion's share (84 percent) of health care expenditure in Vietnam (table 8.3). Not only does the public sector contribute a small share (16 percent) of total health care expenditure, it spends a very small absolute

Child mortality rate (deaths per 1,000 live births)			Infant mortality rate (deaths per 1,000 live births)
1960	1990	Percentage change	1990
105	55	−7	44
279	135	−51.6	—
251	137	−45.4	103
235	127	−46.0	90
222	163	−26.6	97
210	43	−79.5	38
140	22	−84.3	—
214	111	−48.1	74
103	62	−39.8	41
204	169	−17.2	55
149	36	−75.8	27
106	20	−81.1	15
133	10	−92.5	16

Table 8.2 Health Care Infrastructure in Selected Asian Countries, 1991

Country	1992 GDP per capita (U.S. dollars)	Doctors per 1,000 people	Hospital beds per 1,000 people
Vietnam	170	0.84	2.2
Nepal	170	0.06	0.3
Bangladesh	220	0.15	0.3
India	310	0.41	0.7
Pakistan	420	0.34	0.6
China	450	1.37	2.6
Sri Lanka	540	0.14	2.8
Indonesia	670	0.14	0.7
Philippines	770	0.12	1.3
Papua New Guinea	950	0.08	3.4
Thailand	1,840	0.20	1.6
Malaysia	2,790	0.37	2.4
Korea, Rep. of	6,790	0.73	3.0

Source: World Bank 1993.

amount per capita—about $2. Both in level and in share, Vietnam's public spending is the lowest in the region. That Vietnam nevertheless spends a larger share of GDP per capita on medical care than many neighboring countries reflects people's willingness to pay out of pocket for medical care.

One way to get a better understanding of the role of the private sector is to look at Vietnam's national health accounts (table 8.4). The national accounts decompose total expenditure into sources and uses of funds. Two points are particularly noteworthy. First, as mentioned, private out-of-pocket expenditures amounted to about 84 percent of total expenditure, or about five times public expenditure. Second, 90 percent of public funds are spent on hospital services, and only a very small amount on primary and

Figure 8.1 Utilization of Public Sector Health Services in Vietnam, 1987–93

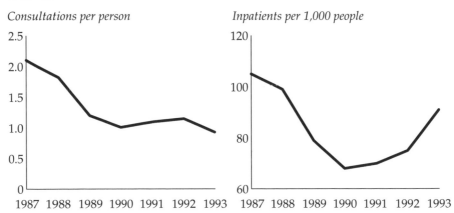

Source: World Bank 1995.

Table 8.3 Annual Health Care Expenditures in Selected Asian Countries, 1991

Country	1992 GDP per capita (U.S. dollars)	Expenditures as a percentage of GDP	Expenditures per capita (U.S. dollars)	Public expenditures as a percentage of total
Vietnam	170	7.4	12	16.2
Nepal	170	4.5	7	48.9
Bangladesh	220	3.2	7	43.8
India	310	6.0	21	21.7
Pakistan	420	3.4	12	52.9
China	450	3.5	11	60.0
Sri Lanka	540	3.7	18	48.6
Indonesia	670	2.0	12	35.0
Philippines	770	2.0	14	50.0
Papua New Guinea	950	4.4	36	63.6
Thailand	1,840	5.0	73	22.0
Malaysia	2,790	3.0	67	43.3
Korea, Rep. of	6,790	6.6	377	40.9

Source: World Bank 1993.

preventive services. About 4.5 percent is spent on primary care through commune health centers, and about 2.1 percent on preventive and communicable disease control activities.

Most remarkable in the national health accounts data is that an astounding 80.1 percent of health care expenditure goes to drugs—all of it out of pocket. About 60 percent of drugs are purchased from private drug vendors, and the rest from public facilities. Not only do the people using private providers purchase drugs from the private sector, so do many of those using public facilities. The main reason is that the state budget allocates only a small amount for drugs to be provided free of charge as part of treatment at public facilities. As a result, there are severe drug shortages

Table 8.4 Uses and Sources of Health Sector Funds in Vietnam, 1993
(as a percentage of total health expenditure)

Use	Public	Private	All
		Source	
Public	16.2	3.5	50.8
Hospitals	14.8	2.9	44.0
Drugs[a]	—	31.5	31.5
Primary care	0.4	0.0	4.5
Preventive health care	0.4	—	1.4
Other	0.7	0.1	0.7
Private	0.0	49.3	49.3
Providers	0.0	0.7	0.7
Drugs	0.0	48.6	48.6
All	16.2	83.8	100

— Not available.
a. Public sector expenditures on drugs could not be separated out from other public uses of funds.
Source: World Bank 1995.

in the public sector, as the 1993 VNLSS indicates. While the spending share for pharmaceuticals suggests that drug utilization dominates health care services in Vietnam, the public sector plays little direct role in providing, financing, or regulating drugs.

Access to Health Care

Clearly, the health care financing reforms introduced as part of *doi moi* have had a far-reaching effect, transforming the provision of health care into a largely private market. Today the public sector no longer monopolizes the delivery of health care. Although it still provides all inpatient care, it is no longer the main provider of outpatient services or drugs. A wide range of providers deliver care—not only public hospitals and commune health centers, but also private doctors, paramedics, pharmacies, and drug dispensaries. How has this privatization affected access to medical care?

One measure of access is the contact rate—the share of people who are sick who contact the health care system for treatment. Data from the VNLSS indicate that contact rates are quite high: the number of people who were sick in the month before the survey but reported seeking no treatment for their illness is quite low. The contact rate is slightly less for the poorest income quintile than for the richest (figure 8.2).

While overall contact rates vary little with income, the composition of utilization differs sharply between the poor and the better-off. Most striking is the dominant use of self-medication, especially by the poor (see figure 8.2). Overall, about two-thirds of ill people self-medicate. But while the

Figure 8.2 Contact Rate with the Health Care System in Vietnam, 1993

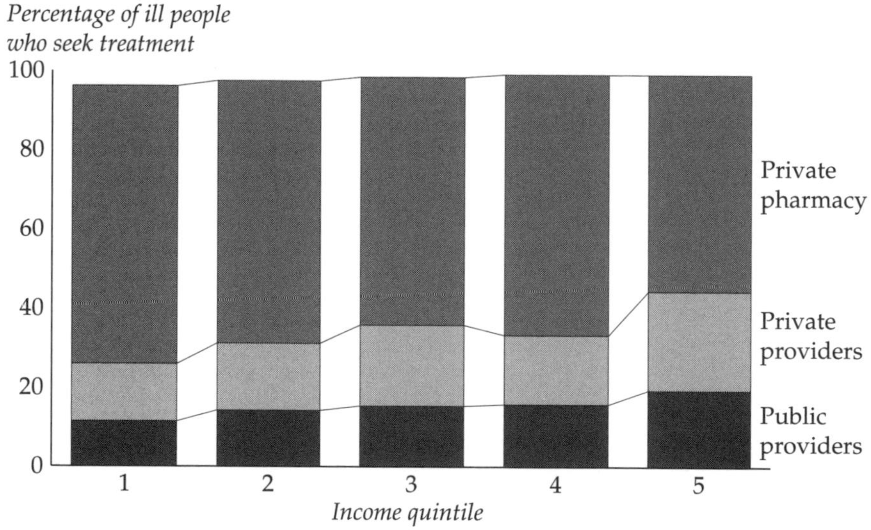

Percentage of ill people who seek treatment

Source: 1993 Vietnam Living Standards Survey.

share of ill people who self-medicate is about 55 percent for the richest quintile, it is more than 70 percent for the poorest. This high rate of self-medication is cause for great concern, as most drug purchases are unsupervised or, at best, prescribed by pharmacists with limited diagnostic information. That most Vietnamese, especially the poor, seem to skip professional diagnosis and treatment in favor of self-diagnosis and self-treatment is both inefficacious and detrimental to health. It also limits contacts with medical professionals, who typically use curative contact to also deliver preventive services and messages (such as on nutrition, family planning, safe water, and immunizations).

Also striking is that among the minority who choose treatment from health care providers, more turn to the private sector (19 percent) than to the public (15 percent). Although this private sector preference shows up among both rich and poor, the importance of the private sector grows with income. Nearly twice as many people in the richest quintile use a private provider as in the poorest quintile.

Utilization patterns in the public sector also vary considerably across income groups (figure 8.3). Commune health centers are the most important source of treatment for the poorest quintile, while people with higher incomes tend to use commune health centers less and rely more heavily on higher-quality hospital care. People in the wealthiest quintile have four times as many outpatient hospital contacts as do people in the poorest quintile. The frequency of hospital inpatient visits is much lower but also rises with income, with the wealthiest quintile having twice as many as the

Figure 8.3 Utilization Rates of the Public Sector Health Care System in Vietnam, 1993

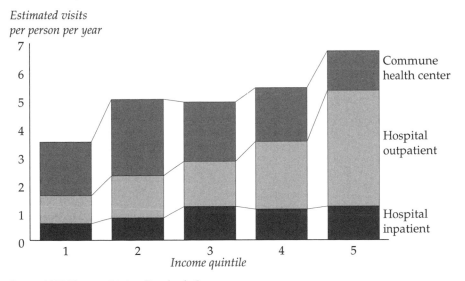

Source: 1993 Vietnam Living Standards Survey.

poorest. Not surprisingly, richer people's greater use of public sector services translates into their benefiting more from public expenditures than do the poor. And richer people's greater use of high-quality hospital services means that the benefit incidence of public expenditures is even more skewed toward the rich than the utilization patterns in figure 8.3 indicate.

There is a substantial difference in quality of care between commune health centers and hospital outpatient services. In a commune health center not only is there likely to be a severe shortage of drugs, but the probability of being treated by a trained doctor is less than 10 percent. By contrast, in a hospital the likelihood of consulting a doctor is more than 90 percent. This disparity suggests that the poor, who are served primarily by commune health centers, generally receive lower-quality care than the nonpoor, who are served primarily by hospitals and private providers.

A major reason that the poor use commune health centers more and hospitals and private providers less is that hospitals and private providers tend to be located in urban areas, while the poor live mostly in rural areas. The coverage of basic health facilities in rural Vietnam is remarkably widespread: 94 percent of rural residents responding to the VNLSS reported having a commune health center in their commune (figure 8.4). Such coverage implies good potential access by the poor: indeed, there is almost no difference in reported availability between the poor and the better-off. Not surprisingly, access to hospitals is more limited, with only about 7 percent of rural residents living in a commune with a hospital. The distance to the nearest hospital for those communes without one averages more than 11 kilometers. The doctors in rural communes work primarily in public hospitals or commune health centers, though they may offer "private" services outside the commune health center's hours. Rural areas are served primarily by commune health centers and private pharmacies, with physicians, physicians assistants, nurses, and midwives providing most of the care.

Policy Reform

Doi moi presents an opportunity for improving the quality and accessibility of health services. Nevertheless, two problems are arising. First, scarce public resources are spread thinly across many types of curative and preventive services, resulting in poor quality. The public sector emphasizes curative hospital care, rather than complementing the private sector by narrowly targeting its limited resources to priority areas of primary and preventive care and services for the poor. And since hospitals are located in urban areas and the poor reside primarily in rural areas, the benefits of public expenditure accrue mostly to the nonpoor.

Second, the private sector is unregulated in an area where consumer information is extremely weak. Lack of regulation in the pharmaceutical market is a particular concern since patients often spend tremendous sums of money for unnecessary (and sometimes fake) medication. Because the

Figure 8.4 Health Facilities and Personnel in Rural Communes in Vietnam, 1993

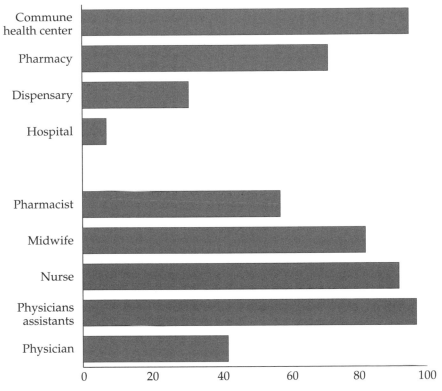

Percentage of people living in commune with resource

Source: 1993 Vietnam Living Standards Survey.

quality of public health care is so poor and medicines are available directly from drug shops, patients often bypass medical consultation and proceed directly to treatment.

These problems, along with the rapid changes in the health sector, suggest that it is appropriate for Vietnam to reconsider government's role in the sector, to see how both the public and the private sectors can become more effective in performing their unique functions. There are two main justifications for public intervention in the health sector. The first is to promote efficiency, such as through subsidies to raise the consumption of health services with positive externalities to a socially desirable level. Thus the government should focus its limited funds on health services that are pure public goods (mosquito vector control) and subsidize health services with significant externalities (immunizations, infectious disease control). Again to promote efficiency, government has a unique role to play in providing information to consumers on the value of preventive health care and in regulating the quality of health providers and pharmaceutical supplies—both areas in which consumers are poorly informed.

The other main justification for government intervention in the health sector is to enhance equity, which seems to be an important objective of Vietnam's leaders. Spending more of Vietnam's public resources on services used disproportionately by the poor (such as commune health centers) can enhance equity, as can providing subsidies targeted to the poor for other health services that are sometimes necessary but may be prohibitively expensive (such as hospitals). The successful mobilization of private resources in Vietnam has allowed a much higher level of access to health care—especially to drugs—than would be possible with public resources alone, given budget constraints. But the provision of public health measures may be suffering, and much of the private care purchased—especially by the poor—is in the form of self-prescribed drug purchases, which are at best not cost-effective and at worst detrimental to health. The advent of the private health sector represents a significant opportunity to mobilize additional resources and distribute quality health services to a broader range of people. However, unless the role of the public sector is carefully designed to complement that of the private sector, important opportunities to improve health may be forgone. Public support for preventive health measures, public information campaigns about the value of preventive health, and government regulation of the pharmaceutical sector are all areas to focus government efforts under the new market system.

Targeting Public Expenditure to the Poor

The complementarity of the public and private sectors can be enhanced by better targeting of public subsidies to the poor. Targeting can be improved by increasing the quality of the facilities the poor are most likely to use— that is, services for which demand is most income inelastic. Since most of the poor are in rural areas and already have good access to commune health centers, the government could target public expenditure to the poor by spending more to improve the quality of commune health centers (for example, improving personnel, equipment, and the availability of drugs). In particular, since drugs seem to be the component of health care for which demand is strongest, ensuring a better drug supply in commune health centers would draw more people in. The people who would most likely be attracted to the improved facilities are those who live closest—the poor.

The more inelastic the demand for commune health center care, the more effective the targeting of the poor by improving that care. The income elasticity of demand can be investigated using the VNLSS data.

The theory of the demand for medical care has been widely discussed in the literature (see, for example, Grossman 1970; Manning and others 1987; Behrman and Deolalikar 1988; Gertler and van der Gaag 1990).

Demand is a function of income, money prices, time prices, qualities, individual characteristics that affect health status, and such preferences as education, ethnic group, and religion. In the empirical model used here the community variables are proxied by village-level fixed effects. Income is measured by the value of per capita household consumption. Controls are included for age, gender, ethnicity, and religion.

An important issue in measuring the demand for medical care is that the decision to seek care is different from the decision on how much care to purchase. The reason is that diagnostic information and a recommendation on treatment, which affect future demand, are obtained at the first visit. Therefore, the two-part model that has become common in the literature is adopted here (see, for example, Manning and others 1987). In this model the expected number of visits can be decomposed into the product of the probability of seeking care times the expected expenditures conditional on seeking care:

$$E(\text{Exp} \mid X) = \text{Probability}(\text{Exp} > 0 \mid X) \times E(\text{Exp} \mid \text{Exp} > 0, X),$$

where X is a set of exogenous explanatory variables.

The two parts of the model were estimated separately for hospital care, commune health center care, private provider care, and drug expenditures. The resulting coefficients and standard errors are consistent even if the error terms between the two equations are correlated (Duan 1983, 1994; Heckman 1990). Since a fixed effects estimator does not exist for probit models, the first part was estimated using linear probability models. But it was confirmed that the probit results matched the linear probability results for the non–fixed effects specification. Separate models were also estimated for adults and children. The estimated coefficients and White heteroskedastistic consistent t-statistics are reported in appendix tables 8A.1–8A.4. Estimates are reported for models with and without commune fixed effects.

For all types of care the combined income elasticity is positive and significant in all the non–fixed effects models. But once the commune in which the person lives is controlled for, the income elasticities for adults in both the hospital and the commune health center models and for children in the commune health center model become small and insignificant. The estimated income elasticities using the coefficients from the fixed effects models are reported in table 8.5. Clearly, the income elasticity for commune health center care is the lowest for both adults and children. This, combined with the fact that the poor use commune health centers more than other providers, suggests that targeting quality improvements to commune health centers will benefit the poor the most.

Reforming Drug Policy

Improving access to medically appropriate drug supplies for people who are ill is a critical part of improving the quality of care at commune health

Table 8.5 Estimated Income Elasticities of the Demand for Medical Care

Provider	Adults	Children
Public hospital	0.056	0.266[a]
Public clinic	−0.037	−0.053
Private provider	0.111[a]	0.045[a]
Private pharmacy	0.345[a]	0.208[a]

a. Significantly different from zero at the 0.01 level.
Source: Authors' calculations.

centers. *Doi moi* has opened the door to many more sources for drugs. Yet effective use of drugs in many cases requires professional diagnosis and prescription. The effectiveness of current drug policy in regulating how drugs are dispensed in both the private and the public sectors clearly needs to be reevaluated. While reforming laws on access to drugs through professional prescription may be a good first step, it is unlikely to drastically change current use patterns, given the weak capacity for regulating compliance. New laws would probably be ignored by much of the population and may even raise the price of drugs. Instead, people need to be given incentives to seek professional diagnosis and treatment for serious illnesses.

To induce people to obtain professional medical advice along with drugs, the quality-adjusted price of medical care can be lowered by increasing quality or reducing prices. Quality of care is an important determinant of demand for health care. Unfortunately, assessing the exact impact of quality is extremely difficult using cross-sectional data and is impossible with the VNLSS. Studies using experimental designs have documented that people are willing to pay more at public health facilities when the quality of care improves: indeed, utilization rises when quality improves. Preferences revealed in a field experiment in Cameroon indicate that the quality-adjusted price of care drops when a reliable supply of generic drugs becomes available and is sold at public health centers (Litvack and Bodart 1993). In Vietnam raising quality from its currently poor level should increase the use of providers and the reliance on professional diagnosis, and thus improve the efficacy of treatment.

The first issue is where to improve quality. When households were asked about their perception of the quality of care at different providers in the 1996 Vietnam Social Sector Financing Study, most respondents rated the quality of commune health centers as very poor (Vietnam Government Statistics Office and Asian Development Bank 1996). Indeed, respondents ranked self-treatment (most often involving a private pharmacy or drug vendor) higher than commune health centers (Knowles and others 1997). Since commune health centers (and possibly district hospitals) are the most accessible providers for the majority of the population, especially for the poor, and the quality of care in the facilities is so low, it makes sense to start there. Increasing the quality of commune health centers not only would improve the use of drugs, it also would improve the targeting of public subsidies to the poor, since they use these facilities more than the nonpoor. And as the previous section showed, it is also a good method for targeting subsidies to the poor because of the low income elasticity for care at commune health centers.

Improving quality in the public sector will require across-the-board investments in human resources, diagnostic equipment, and facilities. But the main problem in commune health centers seems to be access to drugs and appropriate prescribing patterns, as evidenced by the huge expenditures on drugs in the private sector, even by the poor. The following analysis therefore focuses on improving access to professionally prescribed drugs as a way to lower the quality-adjusted price.

There are two possible ways to lower quality-adjusted prices. The first is to increase spending in commune health centers to improve quality—in particular, by enabling the public health system to provide essential drugs to its patients. Additional resources to offset the increased spending could be obtained by shifting public subsidies from hospitals to commune health centers. That would require hospitals to raise user fees in order to maintain their current level of spending. But since the poor use few hospital services, these fee increases would be incurred mostly by the rich. To protect the poor from the fee increases, poor patients who receive a referral from commune health centers could be given a fee waiver for subsequent hospital care. At the margin, shifting subsidies from hospitals to primary care should increase allocative efficiency.

A policy that involves providing all drugs free of charge would probably result in an excessive marginal public burden, given the current size and composition of public expenditures in Vietnam. But commune health centers could ask patients to share the cost of the drugs by paying a fee. As long as the fee for drugs is not so high as to deter use of the health centers, the improved supply of drugs will increase contacts. This policy could serve several purposes by increasing contact with the public health centers: it would improve access to proper diagnosis and a full course of therapy, and it would allow the delivery of important preventive services and public health messages. But improving the efficacy of public providers' prescribing patterns will also require a considerable effort (Chalker 1996).

Commune health centers may be able to offer drugs at less than private market prices by procuring low-priced generic drugs. That would increase competition with the private sector and could lead to lower prices in areas where profits are excessive. Studies have shown that the price of a drug has little to do with its manufacturing cost and far more to do with the competition in the market (Sarmiento 1995). The strong competition already characterizing the private drug market suggests that low-priced, high-quality drugs in the public sector might crowd out the lower end of the private pharmaceutical market.[2] That would have both good and bad repercussions. On the positive side, increased competition from the public sector would make reputation (rather than simply maintaining a stock of medicines) more important in the success of private pharmacies and so could serve as a self-regulating device. Only the pharmacies that offer good advice and provide efficacious medicines would stay in business. On the negative side, the private sector has proved to be a reliable supplier of drugs, while the public sector has not. If logistical glitches arise in the public pharmaceutical supply system and private pharmacies are driven out of business, people could be left without access to medicines. It is critical to consider and plan all aspects of public supply logistics to ensure a reliable supply of medicines (Quick and Lainge 1997).

If public health facilities do maintain their own supply of drugs, the critical question is how to finance the supply without greatly increasing government subsidies. For many curative drugs, public health facilities can sell cost-effective generics to patients at prices that nearly recover costs and yet are still below market prices. This is true at commune health centers, which are easily accessible for more than 95 percent of the population. The drug pricing policy could include some cross-subsidization to protect the needy. Vital life-saving medicines could be sold at a discount, while nonessential drugs at high demand could be sold at a profit. Wealthy people could be charged more than the poor. And drugs whose consumption involves public health externalities could be further subsidized. Such a pricing strategy is often used at religious health facilities. A model for estimating prices based on such cross-subsidization has been elaborated by Litvack, Shepard, and Quick (1989).

A second way to lower quality-adjusted prices is by reducing out-of-pocket costs for patients. This would involve providing a discount voucher for private sector drug purchases to those who first go to commune health centers. The profit motive would induce private pharmacies to locate close to commune health centers, so that people could purchase drugs at the same time that they seek diagnosis and prescription. But there would need to be strict regulations against price discrimination based on vouchers. Without such regulations, private providers could capture the subsidy by charging higher prices for those with vouchers, greatly reducing the benefit to the patient (Gertler and Solon 1995). There would also need to be additional incentive for private pharmacies to procure generic drugs; otherwise, they would continue to sell expensive brand-name drugs for which the profit margin is higher.

One solution considered by some countries is to encourage private pharmacies to charge the same absolute markup for the generics as they would for the brand-name drugs. Say the wholesale price of a brand-name drug for a full course of therapy is $10, while the generic form of the same medicine sells for $2 wholesale. If the retail markup for both is $4, the consumer would pay $6 for the generic rather than spend $14 for the brand-name medicine, and the pharmacy would retain the same profit. As demand increases and the volume of sales rises, the absolute markups could be lowered while still maintaining the same overall profits. Just as private pharmaceutical companies engage in major marketing efforts aimed at retailers and consumers, the government would need to undertake a major effort to promote generic drugs to private pharmacies and consumers.

Summary and Conclusion

Before *doi moi* Vietnam financed and delivered medical care entirely through the public sector. A series of factors have led to deterioration in the quality of care, especially in rural communes, where most of the poor live. This chapter examined how the reforms changed the role of the public sector in ensuring adequate access. In particular, it examined how well the private sector was able to fill the gaps left by the public sector and identified areas where changes in government policy could improve access to and benefits from medical care.

The results show that the private sector has become dominant in both the delivery and the financing of care during the transition period. Less than a third of all provider contacts are in the public sector, and more than 80 percent of expenditures are out of pocket. But much of the private market activity takes the form of self-diagnosis and drug purchases from private pharmacies or dispensaries. Indeed, more than two-thirds of illnesses are treated this way. An important concern with treatment without the advice of a medical professional is the accuracy of diagnosis and the efficacy of treatment.

Another finding is that the pattern of public spending benefits the poor the least. Government spending is concentrated on hospital care, which is used more by the well-off than by the poor. The benefits of spending for hospitals also accrue to the better-off because they live in and around urban areas, where hospitals are located, while the poor live primarily in rural areas, where public care is provided by commune health centers.

Is the private sector filling the gaps created by changes in the delivery of public health care? To some extent it is—though less so for the poor. *Doi moi* has mobilized private resources to ensure a level of access to care that would not have been possible with public resources alone, given budget constraints. But the emergence of the private sector is creating another gap. It is facilitating access for the nonpoor to private providers, and access for the poor to private pharmacies and drug dispensaries, which are supplying medicines where they would not otherwise be available. But the private drug sales are creating a gap by diverting people away from professional diagnosis and prescription toward self-diagnosis and self-prescription, a practice that leads to unhealthful drug consumption patterns in both choice of drugs and dosage. Self-medication for some illnesses not only is not cost-effective and possibly harmful to patients, it also contributes to public health hazards by leading to the development of antibiotic-resistant strains of bacteria.

An obvious policy to improve the use of drugs as well as the targeting of public subsidies to the poor is to increase the allocation of public resources to the health programs that the poor already use and for which demand is income inelastic. Since most of the poor already have access to commune health centers, public expenditures could be targeted to the poor by spending more to improve the quality of those facilities. The multivariate analysis provides some evidence that this policy should increase the use of commune health centers and reduce self-medication by the poor. Thus the policy would provide benefits to those who would not otherwise have sought consultation.

One way to generate the resources to improve health center care would be to reallocate public subsidies away from hospitals. The hospitals would have to raise user fees in order to maintain their current levels of spending. But since the poor use few hospital services, the fee increases would affect mostly the rich. To protect poor patients from the fee increases, those who receive a referral from a commune health center could be given a fee waiver for subsequent hospital care.

As part of the quality improvement program, the government needs to focus attention on drug policy, to better regulate how drugs are dispensed in both the private and the public sectors. An essential drugs policy that permits the public health system to procure cost-effective generic drugs and offer them to patients in the commune health centers would be beneficial. Improving the drug supply at these centers would increase their use and thus improve access to proper diagnoses, full courses of therapy, and important preventive services and public health messages during curative visits.

Improving the quality of commune health centers requires a financing strategy that ensures a steady supply of drugs. For many curative drugs, public health facilities could sell cost-effective generics to patients at prices that recover costs and are still below market prices. Since the poor already spend large amounts of money for drugs, they should be willing to pay lower prices while getting professional diagnosis and therapy prescription for free. The drug pricing policy could include some cross-subsidization to protect the needy. Other efforts could help improve the quality of commune health centers (such as renovations and new equipment), but they would not address the main problem—access to drugs.

The government has already started efforts to improve access to drugs. In 1993 anecdotal evidence from field trips by the authors and from reports of nongovernmental organizations indicated that most public health centers had very limited drug supplies (Oxfam 1996). But since then many community health centers have developed revolving drug funds whereby they purchase medicines from district or provincial sources (public or private) and sell them to patients. A recent social sector financing study indicated that the supply of essential medicines at community health centers was much stronger, in early 1996; 93 percent of the community health centers surveyed had penicillin in stock that they were selling to patients (Vietnam Government Statistics Office and Asian Development Bank 1996).

The analysis suggests that Vietnam's transition to the market in the health sector must be handled carefully. Wholesale transfer of functions to the private sector can lead to inefficient and ineffective forms of care. The private sector has the potential to complement the public sector, but today's situation of an unregulated private sector combined with an underfunded public sector is a dangerous one. Evidence suggests that the private sector could provide services and drugs to the nonpoor with proper regulatory oversight. But several important roles remain for the government. It needs to provide effective regulation of quality standards in both the public and the private sectors, especially with respect to drugs, as long as consumers lack sufficient knowledge to judge for themselves. To the extent that the government is concerned with equity, it needs to spend resources to ensure access of the poor to minimum quality care, especially in rural areas. Finally, it needs to fulfill the traditional role of providing key public goods, such as the control and treatment of infectious diseases.

Appendix

Table 8A.1 Two-Part Models of the Demand for Public Hospital Care

	Adults				Children			
	Probable expenditure > 0		Ln (expenditure)		Probable expenditure > 0		Ln (expenditure)	
Independent variable	1	2	1	2	1	2	1	2
Ln (household per capita consumption)	0.022 (2.10)	0.007 (0.66)	0.146 (0.92)	-0.41 (0.21)	0.038 (2.62)	0.026 (1.64)	0.375 (1.93)	0.853 (3.98)
Years of schooling	0.006 (4.36)	0.007 (4.28)	-0.23 (1.06)	0.002 (0.05)	— —	— —	— —	— —
Mother's years of schooling	— —	— —	— —	— —	-0.003 (0.51)	0.003 (1.20)	-0.071 (1.33)	-0.063 (1.23)
Father's years of schooling	— —	— —	— —	— —	0.007 (3.28)	0.004 (1.81)	-0.131 (3.19)	-0.101 (2.76)
Village fixed effects	No	Yes	No	Yes	No	Yes	No	Yes
R²	0.03	0.09	0.19	0.40	0.05	0.21	0.09	0.49
Sample size	4,136	4,136	408	408	1,865	1,865	134	134

Note: The models include dummy variable controls for age, gender, ethnicity and religion. For the sake of brevity, the coefficients are not reported.
Source: Authors' calculations.

Table 8A.2 Two-Part Models of the Demand for Commune Health Center Care

	Adults				Children			
	Probable expenditure > 0		Ln (expenditure)		Probable expenditure > 0		Ln (expenditure)	
Independent variable	1	2	1	2	1	2	1	2
Ln (household per capita consumption)	-0.017 (2.18)	-0.008 (0.95)	0.724 (3.98)	0.374 (1.27)	-0.019 (1.27)	-0.011 (0.64)	0.588 (7.54)	0.385 (0.95)
Years of schooling	0.002 (1.45)	0.002 (1.60)	-0.047 (1.79)	-0.041 (1.38)	— —	— —	— —	— —
Mother's years of schooling	— —	— —	— —	— —	-0.001 (0.34)	-0.002 (0.92)	0.056 (0.69)	0.115 (1.77)
Father's years of schooling	— —	— —	— —	— —	0.002 (0.71)	0.002 (1.03)	-0.041 (1.01)	-0.050 (1.30)
Village fixed effects	No	Yes	No	Yes	No	Yes	No	Yes
R²	0.02	0.10	0.33	0.61	0.05	0.16	0.29	0.41
Sample size	4,136	4,136	210	210	1,865	1,865	157	157

Note: The models include dummy variable controls for age, gender, ethnicity and religion. For the sake of brevity, the coefficients are not reported.
Source: Authors' calculations.

Table 8A.3 Two-Part Models of the Demand for Private Provider Care

	Adults				Children			
	Probable expenditure > 0		Ln (expenditure)		Probable expenditure > 0		Ln (expenditure)	
Independent variable	1	2	1	2	1	2	1	2
Ln (household per capita consumption)	0.049 (3.64)	0.062 (4.20)	0.724 (3.98)	1.080 (3.47)	0.068 (3.05)	0.049 (1.97)	0.370 (2.86)	0.114 (1.01)
Years of schooling	0.001 (0.46)	0.001 (0.47)	–0.047 (1.79)	–0.043 (1.38)	— —	— —	— —	— —
Mother's years of schooling	— —	— —	— —	— —	0.004 (1.19)	0.003 (0.94)	0.036 (1.54)	0.027 (1.29)
Father's years of schooling	— —	— —	— —	— —	–0.005 (1.43)	–0.002 (0.67)	–0.041 (1.78)	–0.032 (1.67)
Village fixed effects	No	Yes	No	Yes	No	Yes	No	Yes
R^2	0.04	0.13	0.33	0.63	0.05	0.22	0.35	0.61
Sample size	4,136	4,136	210	210	1,865	1,865	379	379

Note: The models include dummy variable controls for age, gender, ethnicity, and religion. For the sake of brevity, the coefficients are not reported.
Source: Authors' calculations.

Table 8A.4 Two-Part Models of the Demand for Private Drugs

	Adults				Children			
	Probable expenditure > 0		Ln (expenditure)		Probable expenditure > 0		Ln (expenditure)	
Independent variable	1	2	1	2	1	2	1	2
Ln (household per capita consumption)	0.018 (3.19)	0.028 (4.53)	0.390 (8.11)	0.314 (5.85)	–0.005 (0.50)	0.014 (1.36)	0.515 (7.54)	0.358 (4.74)
Years of schooling	–0.000 (0.69)	0.000 (0.14)	0.000 (0.00)	0.007 (0.99)	— —	— —	— —	— —
Mother's years of schooling	— —	— —	— —	— —	–0.002 (1.26)	0.004 (1.28)	0.006 (0.54)	0.010 (0.87)
Father's years of schooling	— —	— —	— —	— —	0.001 (1.05)	–0.002 (1.01)	–0.041 (4.36)	–0.029 (3.16)
Village fixed effects	No	Yes	No	Yes	No	Yes	No	Yes
R^2	0.06	0.14	0.11	0.19	0.10	0.23	0.17	0.31
Sample size	4,136	4,136	3,736	3,736	1,865	1,865	1,733	1,733

Note: The models include dummy variable controls for age, gender, ethnicity, and religion. For the sake of brevity, the coefficients are not reported.
Source: Authors' calculations.

Notes

1. This chapter defines private providers as providers who collect payments outside the public health center. It is difficult to draw the line between public and private in this area because public providers collect private payments for services they deliver in the health center and sometimes at their own home or the home of the patient. In addition, public providers write prescriptions for drugs that are purchased at private drug shops adjacent to public health centers.

2. As in all countries, some wealthy people are likely to continue to prefer brand-name medicines available in attractive pharmacies.

References

Behrman, Jere, and Anil B. Deolalikar. 1988. "Health and Nutrition." In Hollis Chenery and T. N. Srinivasin, eds., *Handbook of Development Economics.* Amsterdam: North-Holland.

Chalker, John. 1996. "Quantitative Evaluation of the Hai Phong Health Financing for Primary Health Care Project: Has Practice Changed at Commune Health Stations?" Save the Children U.K., United Kingdom.

Duan, N. 1983. "A Comparison of Alternative Models for the Demand for Medical Care." *Journal of Economic and Business Statistics* (April): 115–26.

————. 1994. "Choosing between the Sample Selection Models and the Multi-Part Model." *Journal of Business and Economics Statistics* (July): 283–89.

Gertler, Paul, and Orville Solon. 1995. "Who Benefits from Social Insurance in Low-Income Countries?" Paper presented at the annual meetings of the American Economic Association, San Francisco.

Gertler, Paul, and Jacques van der Gaag. 1990. *The Willingness to Pay for Medical Care: Evidence from Two Developing Countries.* Baltimore, Md.: Johns Hopkins University Press.

Grossman, M. 1970. "Health Capital." *Journal of Political Economy.*

Heckman, James. 1990. "Varieties of Selection Bias." *American Economic Review* 80(2): 313–18.

Knowles, James, Jere Behrman, Benjamin Diokno, and Keith McInnes. 1997. "Key Issues in the Financing of Vietnam's Social Services." Abt Associates, Bethesda, Md.

Litvack, Jennie, and Claude Bodart. 1993. "User Fees Plus Quality Equals Improved Access to Health Care: Results of a Field Experiment in Cameroon." *Social Science and Medicine* 37(3): 369–83.

Litvack, Jennie, Donald Shepard, and Jonathan Quick. 1989."Setting the Price of Essential Drugs: Necessity and Affordability." *Lancet* 8659: 376.

Manning, W., J. Newhouse, N. Duan, and others. 1987. "Health Insurance and the Demand for Medical Care." *American Economic Review.*

Oxfam U.K.-Ireland. 1996. "Report on the Financing and Delivery of Basic Services at the Commune Level in Ky Anh, Ha Tinh, Vietnam."

Quick, Jonathan, and Richard Lainge, eds. 1997. *Managing Drug Supply: The Selection, Procurement, Distribution, and Use of Pharmaceuticals.* Vol. 2. West Hartford, Conn.: Kumarian Press.

Sarmiento, Alvaro Zerdo. 1995. "Alternative Drug Pricing Policies in the Americas." Health Economics and Drugs DAP Series 1. World Health Organization, Geneva.

Vietnam Government Statistics Office and Asian Development Bank. 1996. "Social Sector Financing Study." Hanoi.

World Bank. 1993. *World Development Report 1993: Investing in Health.* New York: Oxford University Press.

————. 1995. "Vietnam: Poverty Assessment and Strategy." Report 13442-VN. East Asia and Pacific Region, Country Department I, Washington, D.C.

9

Will Vietnam Grow Out of Malnutrition?

Ninez Ponce, Paul Gertler, and Paul Glewwe

Vietnam's transition to a market economy has been very successful, as chapter 1 explained. Yet its transition may have created inequalities in income, health, and education. Moreover, Vietnam remains one of the world's poorest countries. Chapter 2 showed that nearly 55 percent of its 70 million people still lived in poverty in 1993, and 50 percent of children age five and under were stunted (had low height for age). Indeed, Vietnamese children are among the most malnourished in the developing world—though the rate of malnutrition is no worse, and in some cases better, than rates in countries with similarly low income levels. The previous chapter considered health care in general in Vietnam; this chapter looks at child health. In particular, it focuses on child nutritional status as measured by child height.

The nutritional status of a country's children is an important barometer of the well-being of its population. Good nutrition has been positively associated with both cognitive development in early childhood and eventual school performance. Benefits during adulthood include higher labor productivity and longer life expectancy. These long-run benefits suggest that improved child nutrition is not only an important objective in its own right but also can be regarded as an investment good, because it promotes the subsequent acquisition of human capital and, consequently, future economic growth.

Given these benefits of good nutrition, what guidelines should governments follow in formulating appropriate policies to promote it? In particular, when should governments take an active role, and what policies are most effective? From the perspective of economic theory, externalities in the form of social benefits are not necessarily the main reason for government intervention in child nutrition, since poor nutrition is not a contagious disease. A stronger reason is informational problems. Many households, espe-cially those in rural areas, have at best only partial information on child health and nutrition. This puts them at a disadvantage when trying to eval-uate advice and treatments given by private health care providers. This dis-advantage suggests that the government should take a major role in providing both information on and treatment for child nutritional prob-lems. In addition, concerns for equity also support a government role in improving nutritional outcomes. Governments that take a more active role soon face the question of how much to rely on economic growth to reduce malnutrition. This question is the main focus of the chapter.

Economic growth tends to improve nutritional status, but the effect varies considerably across countries. Growth may even fail to improve children's nutritional status: India's nutritional situation worsened during a period of growth. Yet the prevalence of underweight children typically falls substantially in countries where annual GDP growth rates exceed 5 percent. In Vietnam, where the growth rate has been 6 percent in recent years, malnutrition, as measured by weight for age, has fallen by more than 3 percent annually.[1]

Will high rates of economic growth in future years continue to improve children's nutritional status in Vietnam? To gain some insight into this question, the chapter examines the relationship between children's height and household income as measured by household per capita con-sumption expenditures. While cross-sectional analysis must be used with care when predicting the effect of growth on nutrition, understanding the income-height relationship will shed light on this issue. The question posed in the chapter is an important one not only for Vietnam but for many other developing countries. Yet few studies have looked at the effect of income on child height.[2]

The chapter begins by examining recent institutional changes associat-ed with the transition to the market that are likely to have affected child height. Next, drawing on data from the 1992–93 Vietnam Living Standards Survey (VNLSS), it examines the relationship between income and height, first using simple bivariate comparisons and then using multivariate analy-sis to control for other factors that confound the observed relationship.

Institutional Changes in Vietnam

Vietnam's transition to a market economy has led to tangible consumer and producer benefits. While one of the most important consequences has been higher incomes, there were several changes that had a more direct effect on children's nutritional status. Two of the most important were decollectivization of communal farms, which vastly improved the supply of food, and reduction of the government's role in the health sector.

The parceling of communal agricultural land to households and the establishment of their right to sell their products for profit marked a fundamental change in rural areas (see chapter 3). Before this reform, villages supported Communist Party cadres that monitored production on large communal farms. The reforms gave farm households a direct incentive to maximize their plot yields and relieved them of the burden of supporting nonproductive government cadres. Decollectivization is credited with productivity gains so large that Vietnam recently emerged as a major rice exporter.

Decollectivization improved the incomes and food security of farm households, with consequent benefits for their nutritional status (Jamison, Hung, and Rambo 1992). While agricultural households (which constitute about 80 percent of the population) benefited, nonagricultural households faced higher food prices. But many nonagricultural households benefited from growth in the industrial sector, so that increased income typically outpaced increases in food prices.

Vietnam's health sector faced new challenges after reunification in 1975, when the vast public health care network in the north was extended throughout the south. That expansion, coupled with weak and sometimes negative economic growth in the 1980s, strained the government's ability to finance both its extensive hospital and clinic network and its preventive outreach programs. The collapse of the Soviet Union in 1991 led to the loss of Vietnam's drug supply system, compounding the health sector's financial crisis.

In 1989 the government opened the door to private financing and delivery of health care in the hope of improving health services. In addition, public hospitals and, to a much smaller degree, public health centers began charging patients for consultations and drugs in order to raise funds for the public health sector. Doctors and nurses opened private practices, often in parallel with their public practice, and private pharmacies and drug vendors sprang up throughout the country. The private health sector expanded very quickly, with minimal government regulation to ensure quality, especially in pharmaceuticals and dispensing practices.

As chapter 8 discussed in detail, the shrinking government role in the health sector affected access, utilization, and quality of health care. Lower use of prenatal services, health education, growth monitoring, and immunizations may have compromised children's nutritional status. Because households were now required to pay all pharmaceutical expenses, poor households became less likely to purchase expensive prescriptions for illnesses and infections that can slow child growth. Thus privatization of the health sector may have offset some or all of the gains in nutritional status due to increased food supply.

The government's child nutrition policies are coordinated by the National Institute of Nutrition. The institute's role is to set and evaluate goals on nutritional status, but in recent years it has had almost no operating budget to achieve these objectives. In 1992 it set a series of goals to improve nutritional status by 2000. Although the institute considers stunting (low height-for-age) to be Vietnam's most important child nutrition problem, it has never set explicit numerical targets for reducing its incidence (World Bank 1993, 36). However, it has set an objective to reduce the prevalence of underweight children under five from more than 50 percent in 1989 to 25–30 percent by 2000. And the government has set a tacit goal of cutting the prevalence of underweight and stunted children by half over the next 10 years. But with no budget allocations for program interventions, it is unclear how these targets will be met other than indirectly through economic growth.

Nutritional Status in Vietnam

This section assesses child nutritional status in Vietnam using the height and weight data collected in the 1992–93 VNLSS. It begins by explaining how height and weight data can be used to assess nutritional status, and then examines the data from Vietnam.

Measuring Nutritional Status

Before turning to the data from the 1992–93 VNLSS, it is useful to discuss how nutritional status can be measured using data on children's height and weight, which are commonly referred to as anthropometric data. There are three commonly used indicators of the nutritional status of children based on anthropometric measures: height-for-age, weight-for-height, and weight-for-age (see Healy 1986). The basic intuition behind all of them is that children suffering from inadequate nutrition—whether because of insufficient food intake or a disease that interferes with the body's ability to convert food into energy—either grow more slowly or stop growing altogether. Malnourished children may also experience reductions in weight.

Consider a child's height, conditional on his or her age. Each time the child experiences inadequate nutrition, he or she will stop growing or grow more slowly. When the child's nutritional status improves, normal growth resumes, but the child is unlikely to catch up to the height that would have been attained if the incidence of poor nutrition had not occurred. Each time a child experiences poor nutrition, he or she falls further behind in height relative to a child with no such experiences. Thus height-for-age measures a child's cumulative nutritional status since birth. Because it primarily reflects events in the past, it is not a good indicator of current nutritional status.

Weight-for-height measures a child's current nutritional status. In the short run a child with inadequate nutritional intake has not had much time to fall (further) behind in height, but his or her weight could drop relatively quickly. Weight-for-height reveals nothing about past episodes of malnutrition, however, because the weight of children who are currently receiving adequate nutrition but have suffered from several periods of poor nutrition in the past will have adjusted to their current height. That is, because they are currently receiving adequate nutrition, their weight is in the normal range for a child of their height.

Weight-for-age reflects both stunting (low height-for-age) and wasting (low weight-for-height). A child who is stunted will have low weight compared with a healthy child of the same age because the stunted child's weight has adjusted to his or her shorter stature. A child currently experiencing malnutrition would also have lower weight-for-age. In general, therefore, weight-for-age is less useful than height-for-age and weight-for-height because it does not distinguish between short-term and long-term malnutrition.

All three measures of nutritional status—height-for-age, weight-for-height, and weight-for-age—can be expressed in terms of Z-scores. This measure indicates, in terms of standard deviations, how far a child's height-for-age (or weight-for-height or weight-for-age) is from that of an average healthy child of the same age (or same height). Height-for-age Z-scores, which are used most often in this chapter, are computed as follows (see Gibson 1990 for more details):

$$Z\text{-score} = \frac{H_c - H_r}{SD_r}$$

where H_c is the height of a child, H_r is the median height of a healthy child of the same age (reference child), and SD_r is the standard deviation of the distribution of heights for a reference population of healthy children of that age. A Z-score of –2 or below signals malnutrition; in a population of healthy children only 2–3 percent would have such a low Z-score. A Z-score of –3 or below indicates severe malnutrition, since less than 0.5 percent of children in a healthy population would have such a low Z-score.

This chapter follows the standard practice of using the U.S. National Center for Health Statistics (NCHS) reference population, in accordance with the World Health Organization's recommendations for measuring nutritional status (WHO 1983).[3] The empirical analysis is restricted to children under age 10 because there is relatively limited genetic variation in this prepubescent age group (Martorell, Mendoza, and Castillo 1988).

Malnutrition in Vietnam, 1992–93

Figure 9.1 uses the VNLSS data to show that patterns of wasting and stunting in Vietnam are similar to those found in other developing countries. Stunting increases rapidly from birth to age two, after which it levels off at a high rate of incidence. Wasting peaks in the second year of life, then declines. Both stunting and wasting patterns indicate that poor nutrition is most common during the first two years of life, especially from 6

Figure 9.1 Incidence of Child Malnutrition in Vietnam, Based on Three Indicators, 1992–93

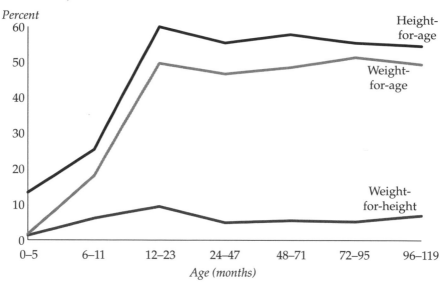

Source: 1992–93 Vietnam Living Standards Survey.

months to 24 months, the time that children are usually weaned and thus exposed to infectious diseases through liquid and solid foods. After two years of age stunting is much more common than wasting because children usually cannot catch up in height, but children who have low weight-for-height can regain a "normal" profile when their growth in height slows to allow their weight to catch up.

Another way to assess child malnutrition in Vietnam is to plot the median heights of children in the survey and compare them to NCHS standards. This is done in figure 9.2. The heights of Vietnamese children fall below the NCHS reference median after the age of 6 months. Vietnamese children fall further behind until about 24 months, after which they do not catch up to NCHS standards. Boys and girls fall behind at approximately the same pace.

How do Vietnamese children compare with children in other countries with similarly low incomes? International comparisons of child malnutrition typically focus on the prevalence of low weight-for-age among preschool children. In a comparison based on this indicator with other countries in its income group (annual GNP per capita between $200 and $300), Vietnam outperforms two of its Asian neighbors, Bangladesh and India, but has a higher proportion of underweight children than do Madagascar, Malawi, and Kenya (figure 9.3). While some countries with higher per capita incomes than Vietnam's have lower malnutrition rates,

Figure 9.2 Median Child Height in the U.S. National Center for Health Statistics and Vietnam Living Standards Survey Samples

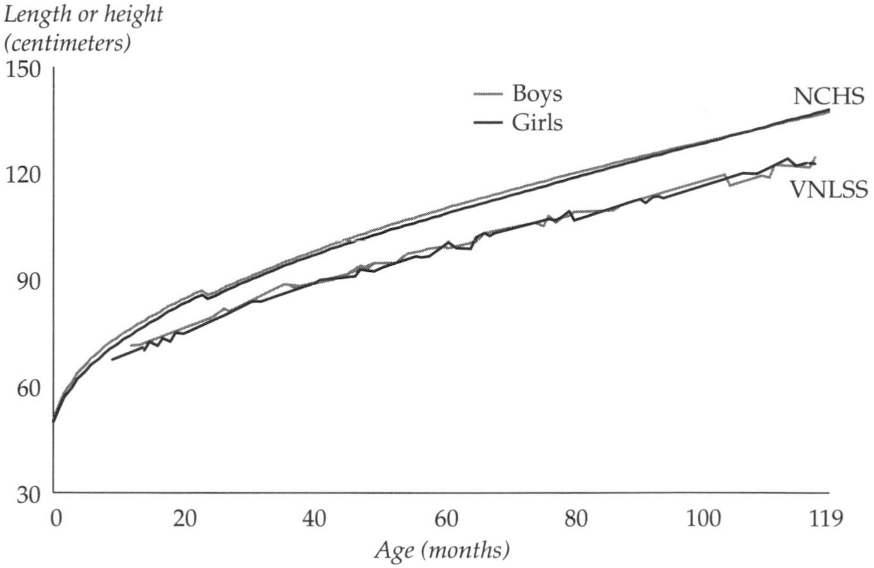

Length or height (centimeters)

Note: The kink at 24 months for the NCHS sample is due to the change in how height is measured. Children under 24 months are measured lying down (length), and children 24 months and older are measured standing up.
Source: 1992–93 Vietnam Living Standards Survey; U.S. National Center of Health Statistics data.

such as China and Egypt, others with higher incomes do not have substantially lower rates of child malnutrition, such as Senegal and the Philippines.

Figure 9.3 demonstrates that income is generally associated with lower child malnutrition, but deviations from this trend suggest the importance of other factors. One possible explanation for the deviations is the extent of public spending on health and nutrition, which is also shown in figure 9.3. For example, while China has a lower GNP per capita than the Philippines and Senegal, its malnutrition rate is also lower. This could be attributed to China's relatively high investment in health: while the Philippines spends 4 percent of its government budget on health, and Senegal spends 5 percent, China spends 10 percent. Factors outside the health sector may also play a role. Consider Egypt, which spends only 3 percent of its budget on health yet has the lowest prevalence of child malnutrition among the countries in figure 9.3. Many other economic and demographic factors—such as agricultural subsidies, women's literacy, and fertility policies—may affect a country's nutritional situation.

Figure 9.3 Income, Child Malnutrition, and Public Health Investments in 12 Developing Countries, 1989–92

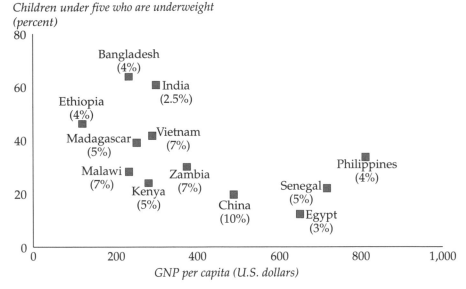

Note: Figures in parentheses are the share of public spending on health and nutrition.
Source: For Vietnam, 1992–93 Vietnam Living Standards Survey; for all other countries, United Nations 1994.

The Relationship between Income and Nutritional Status in Vietnam

This section investigates the relationship between income and nutritional status in Vietnam using data from the 1992–93 VNLSS and other sources. It begins with descriptive analysis, examining the correlation between income and nutritional status, then turns to multivariate regression analysis to assess the causal impact of income on nutritional status.

Descriptive Analysis

There are several ways to investigate the relationship between income and malnutrition in Vietnam. One is to examine income and nutritional status at different points in time. This is shown in figure 9.4, which shows a negative relationship between income and malnutrition in Vietnam over time. During 1982–85 Vietnam's economic growth stagnated, hampered by ineffective policies and by economic sanctions imposed by China, the Association of South-East Asian Nations, and the United States and other Western countries. In these years about 60 percent of Vietnamese children under age five were malnourished. During 1987–89 Vietnam introduced economic reforms, and many countries removed their trade sanctions. Per capita income increased, and the rate of malnutrition among young children dropped to 56 percent. By 1992–93 Vietnam's economy was growing rapidly and the malnutrition rate had dropped to about 50 percent.

Regional differences in Vietnam also shed light on the relationship between income and malnutrition. Figure 9.5 shows that four of the country's seven regions have malnutrition rates higher than the national average (53 percent): Red River Delta (56 percent), Central Highlands (59 percent), Northern Uplands (63 percent), and North-Central Coast (64 percent). North-Central Coast has the greatest proportion of children living in poverty and the greatest proportion of malnourished children. The Southeast, the richest region, has by far the lowest proportion of children who are malnourished (34 percent).

A third way to investigate the relationship between income and malnutrition in Vietnam is to look at changes in income and malnutrition across regions. Vietnam's transition from a socialist command economy to a socialist market economy has had differential benefits across regions. Urban areas, coastal areas, and the south have benefited the most, in part because of a longer tradition of entrepreneurship, better infrastructure, and more fertile soil. Figure 9.6 plots the resulting differences in economic growth against changes in malnutrition rates.

In three regions—Mekong Delta, Northern Uplands, and Central Highlands—the prevalence of underweight children increased, despite

Figure 9.4 GDP per Capita and Child Malnutrition in Vietnam, 1982–93

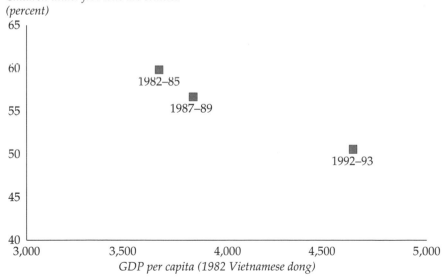

Source: For 1982–85 and 1987–89, National Institute for Nutrition data; for 1992–93, 1992–93 Vietnam Living Standards Survey.

Figure 9.5 Mean per Capita Household Expenditure and Child Malnutrition in Vietnam, by Region, 1992–93

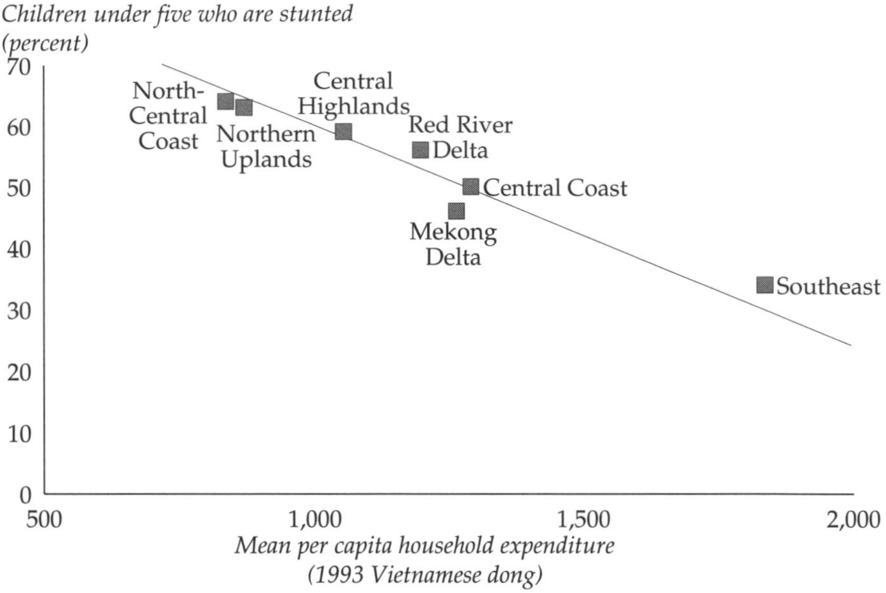

Children under five who are stunted
(percent)

Mean per capita household expenditure
(1993 Vietnamese dong)

Note: The line is the minimum least-squares distance to the points.
Source: 1992–93 Vietnam Living Standards Survey.

positive economic growth rates. The Mekong Delta had both the largest increase in malnutrition and the slowest GDP growth. In contrast, the Southeast enjoyed the highest economic growth and the largest decline in malnutrition. The remaining five regions were in between in terms of economic growth and changes in malnutrition.

To summarize, evidence from international comparisons, national comparisons over time, regional differences, and regional changes over time all suggest that increased economic growth is associated with reduced malnutrition in Vietnam. But the data examined so far do not control for other factors that may affect nutritional status. One such factor is the rapid change in the provision of public health services in Vietnam in the past few years. The following section will use data from the 1992–93 VNLSS to try to isolate and quantify the effect of income, as measured by per capita household consumption, on child height in Vietnam.

Multivariate Analysis

This section estimates the effect of household income on children's nutritional status, as measured by height-for-age, using data from the 1992–93 VNLSS. Since income may be an endogenous variable (as discussed further below), the econometric relationship of interest is a conditional demand function. The equation to be estimated is:

$$HAZ_i = \beta_0 + \beta_Y Y_i + \beta_C X_i^C + \beta_H X_i^H + \beta_L X_i^L + e_i,$$

where HAZ_i is the height-for-age Z-score of child i, Y_i is the per capita income of household I, X_i^C is a vector of characteristics of child i, X_i^H is a vector of characteristics (other than income) of the household in which child i lives, X_i^L is a vector of the characteristics of the local community in which child i lives, and e_i is an error term that measures unobserved characteristics of the child, and of his or her household or local community, that may affect height-for-age.

Several characteristics of the child may affect his or her height. First, there may be systematic differences by sex, which suggests that a variable indicating the sex of the child should be used. Second, the child's birth order may make a difference. For example, children born first may have an advantage in the first years of life before other children are born, because household resources are shared among fewer family members. Third, the child's age may matter. As seen in figure 9.2, in the first few months of life Vietnamese children have heights close to the NCHS standards, but afterward they fall behind. Thus age should be introduced in some form in the

Figure 9.6 Change in Prevalence of Child Malnutrition and Economic Growth in Vietnam, by Region

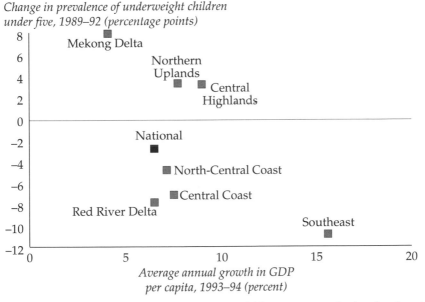

Change in prevalence of underweight children under five, 1989–92 (percentage points)

Average annual growth in GDP per capita, 1993–94 (percent)

Source: The change in prevalence of underweight children is computed using data from two cross-sectional samples: 1987–89 National Institute of Nutrition statistics and 1992–93 Vietnam Living Standards Survey. Regional growth rates are World Bank staff estimates.

regression equation. Finally, the age of the mother when the child was born may affect child health. Children born to relatively young mothers are more likely to be underweight and to suffer from other health problems than are children born to older mothers.

Several household characteristics other than income can affect child health, as measured by height. First, parents' education may have a strong effect, since well-educated parents can better diagnose and treat their children's health problems than can less-educated parents. The effect of parental education may not be the same for both parents, so it is best to have separate variables for mother's and father's education. Second, parents' height can affect child height in two ways: taller parents tend to have taller children, due to genetic variation in height that is independent of health status; and taller parents may be tall because they are inherently healthy, and their children may inherit this predisposition toward good health and thus also be taller. As with education, the effect of parents' height should be measured using separate variables for the mother and the father. Finally, the religious and ethnic group of the family may affect child health through associated cultural practices.

Characteristics of the local community that may affect child health include the local health environment (the prevalence of specific diseases and the presence and quality of sanitation, such as waste disposal and sources of drinking water), the health services available in the community, and the distances to the nearest health institutions outside the community. Although the 1992–93 VNLSS data contain some information on local health conditions and health services, much that may matter is simply not in the data. Rather than use the few variables that are available, which will almost certainly suffer from omitted variable bias (and possibly other econometric problems), the analysis gets around these problems by estimating community fixed effects regressions. That is, it assigns a dummy variable to each community that accounts for all community factors, observed and unobserved, that may affect child health. This implies that the estimates of the effect of child and household characteristics are identified from variation within each community. Since the variable of primary interest is household income, which varies substantially within each community, its effect on child health can be estimated even though the effect of community variables on child health cannot be identified.

Although most of the child and household variables described above can reasonably be assumed to be exogenous, that is not necessarily so for household income. The measure of income may be correlated with the error term. An obvious source of endogeneity is the household's labor force participation decision, which may depend on child health. Households may put healthier, taller children to work; thus these children would contribute to household income. Households may spend more for a smaller child to help the child catch up in growth. And the mother of a sickly child may decide not to work in order to care for the child at home.

In all cases the income variable is positively correlated with the error term and thus would tend to overestimate the effect of household income on children's nutritional status.

Ideally, the analysis would use instrumental variables that are correlated with household income but not with any of the unobserved household and child characteristics that determine child nutritional status and thus form the error term in the estimated equation. The analysis uses per capita land availability as the main identifying variable. There are conceptual problems with using land if it is bought and sold, since families may buy or sell land in response to their children's health status. But these problems may be less relevant in Vietnam, where agricultural land was until recently owned by communes. As part of decollectivization, the land was redistributed to commune members for their private use, according to simple rules that had nothing to do with child health. After this distribution, farmland still could not be bought and sold on the open market.

Table 9.1 reports the estimated coefficients and t-statistics for both the urban and rural samples. The estimation methods include ordinary least squares, commune fixed effects, and, for the rural sample only, instrumental variable fixed effects, with land as the identifying instrument for per capita household expenditure. The standard errors have been corrected to account for the fact that the sample was stratified by commune.

Table 9.2 provides descriptive statistics on all the variables used in the regressions. Both mothers and fathers are relatively well educated; the vast majority have finished primary school and a third to a half have finished lower secondary school. More than four-fifths of Vietnamese belong to the Kinh (ethnic Vietnamese) ethnic group; no other ethnic group accounts for more than 2 percent of the population. Most Vietnamese claim no religious affiliation, 26 percent are Buddhist, and about 9 percent are Christian. About 30 percent of the children in the sample are the eldest child in the family, which reflects relatively small family sizes for such a poor country.

Turn first to the control variables. Mother's and father's heights are positive and highly significant, as one would expect. More surprising is that parents' education is often not significant, which is at variance with results found in other countries (see Strauss and Thomas 1995). This result may reflect the fact that most mothers and fathers have at least a primary education. Another explanation may be that parental height captures many background characteristics that parental education tends to capture in studies that do not include parental height as an explanatory variable. Religion, but not ethnicity, is a significant determinant of child's height. The coefficient for age of mother at childbirth is small, but positive and usually significant, which supports the hypothesis that children born to relatively young mothers suffer worse health problems, other things being equal. For any child, being the oldest presents the most favorable outlook for height-for-age in rural areas (but not in urban areas). Finally, age category variables indicate that children in the age group 19–24 months have the lowest

Table 9.1 Multivariate Regression Results

Independent variable	Urban (N = 853)	
	Ordinary least squares	Ordinary least squares with fixed effects
Log real per capita expenditure[a]	0.22 (2.64)	0.20 (2.30)
Mother's height	0.053 (7.50)	0.049 (7.18)
Father's height	0.041 (5.58)	0.045 (6.13)
Mother's age at childbirth	0.018 (2.14)	0.015 (1.70)
Oldest child	0.101 (1.18)	0.072 (0.84)
Dummy for father present	−6.58 (−5.47)	−7.16 (−6.03)
Constant	−12.41 (−9.45)	−11.63 (−9.30)
Mother's education	1.93[b] F(6, 805)	1.69 F(6, 781)
Father's education	0.48 F(6, 805)	0.29 F(6, 781)
Age group	2.85[d] F(8, 805)	2.69[d] F(8, 781)
Females by age group	1.07 F(9, 805)	1.11 F(9, 781)
Ethnicity	1.69 F(3, 805)	1.32 F(3, 781)
Religion	12.57[d] F(4, 805)	11.60[d] F(4, 781)
Adjusted R^2	0.227	0.234

Note: All models were run with Huber-White corrections for errors due to cluster sampling.
a. Instruments for per capita expenditure are areas of perennial and annual land owned. The first stage's F statistic is 52.2, and both identifying variables are significant.
b. Significant at $p < 10\%$.

	Rural (N = 4,661)	
Ordinary least squares	Ordinary least squares with fixed effects	Instrumental variables with fixed effects[a]
0.28 (6.30)	0.25 (5.06)	0.24 (1.66)
0.043 (12.20)	0.040 (11.41)	0.040 (10.78)
0.033 (9.32)	0.031 (8.83)	0.031 (7.83)
0.013 (3.65)	0.014 (3.93)	0.014 (3.67)
0.096 (2.21)	0.100 (2.33)	0.100 (2.20)
−5.32 (−9.23)	−4.957 (−8.70)	−4.98 (−7.79)
−11.08 (−17.40)	−10.69 (−16.40)	0.009 (0.57)
2.34[c] F(6, 4477)	1.78[b] F(6, 4495)	1.37 F(6, 4447)
2.215[b] F(6, 4477)	2.82[d] F(6, 4495)	2.36[c] F(6, 4447)
19.2[d] F(8, 4477)	19.94[d] F(8, 4495)	17.25[d] F(8, 4447)
4.29[d] F(9, 4477)	4.94[d] F(9, 4495)	4.85[d] F(9, 4447)
3.34[d] F(7, 4477)	1.04 F(7, 4495)	1.00 F(7, 4447)
2.67[c] F(4, 4477)	3.62[d] F(4, 4495)	3.55[d] F(4, 4447)
0.212	0.227	—

c. Significant at $p < 5\%$.
d. Significant at $p < 1\%$.
Source: Authors' calculations.

Table 9.2 Description of Variables

Variable	Category, unit of measure	Type	Mean	Standard deviation
Family characteristics				
Mother's education	No schooling	Categorical	0.09	—
	Some primary	(5)	0.16	—
	Finished primary		0.36	—
	Finished lower secondary		0.30	—
	Finished upper secondary		0.09	—
Father's education	No schooling	Categorical	0.05	—
	Some primary	(5)	0.11	—
	Finished primary		0.36	—
	Finished lower secondary		0.35	—
	Finished upper secondary		0.13	—
Mother's height	Centimeters	Continuous	151.80	4.96
Father's height	Centimeters	Continuous	161.80	5.50
Mother's age at childbirth	Years	Continuous	27.40	6.03
Ethnicity	Kinh	Categorical	0.83	—
	Tay	(8)	0.02	—
	Thai		0.01	—
	Chinese		0.02	—
	Khome		0.02	—
	Moung		0.02	—
	Nung		0.02	—
	Other		0.05	—
Religion	Buddhist	Categorical	0.26	—
	Christian	(5)	0.09	—
	Animist/traditional		0.01	—
	Other		0.02	—
	None		0.63	—
Child characteristics				
Age group	0–6 months	Categorical	0.06	—
	7–12 months	(9)	0.05	—
	13–18 months		0.04	—
	19–24 months		0.05	—
	25–36 months		0.10	—
	37–48 months		0.10	—
	49–72 months		0.20	—
	73–96 months		0.20	—
	97–119 months		0.20	—
Female	1 = female			
	0 = male	Binary	0.51	—
Oldest child	1 = oldest			
	0 = otherwise	Binary	0.30	—

Source: Authors' calculations.

height-for-age Z-score, as would be expected given the data in figure 9.1.

Turn now to the effect of income. The effect is fairly consistent across all the models, with a coefficient ranging from 0.20 to 0.28. It is statistically significant for all specifications at standard levels, though the effect in the instrumental variable fixed effects model for rural areas is significant only at the 10 percent level. The following section uses these estimates to project the likely effect of future economic growth on child nutritional status in Vietnam.

Economic Growth and Child Growth: Future Prospects

Vietnamese children are among the most malnourished in Asia—indeed, in the entire developing world—in large part because Vietnam is one of the world's poorest countries. About 53 percent of Vietnamese children age five and under are stunted. But institutional changes during the recent transition to the market have improved food production and accelerated economic growth. As Vietnam pulls itself out of poverty, children's nutritional status will improve. The question is how fast the nutritional benefits will accrue.

The analysis in the previous section shows that children in higher-income families are less likely to be stunted, suggesting that the prevalence of stunting will decline as economic growth continues in Vietnam. The regression estimates for the coefficient on income can be used to predict the prevalence of malnutrition from 1994 to 2013 for different economic growth scenarios. The proportion of children stunted in 1994, the first year after the base year of 1993, can be computed as follows. Recall that children who are deemed stunted are more than 2 standard deviations below the reference median and thus have a height-for-age Z-score of less than –2. If a 6 percent per capita growth rate is assumed, the effect of growth on nutritional status is calculated by multiplying 6 percent by 0.24, the income coefficient from the instrumental variable estimates for rural areas (where 80 percent of the population resides), and adding the product to each child's height-for-age Z-score. This scalar increase moves up the Z-score for the entire sample, pulling some children out of malnutrition. The malnutrition rate is then calculated as the percentage of children who have Z-scores of less than –2. This can be continued for 20 years by sequentially adding the scalar increase to the previous year's Z-score and calculating the malnutrition rate for each year.

Using this method, projections were made for three different per capita growth rates: 3 percent, a growth rate considered low to modest; 6 percent, the government's target growth rate; and 9 percent, a rate reflecting a very optimistic scenario (figure 9.7). These projections are based on several assumptions. First, there are assumed to be no cohort effects or secular changes in height as the economy prospers. Second, all households across the income distribution are assumed to benefit equally from economic

Figure 9.7 Projected Child Malnutrition Rates in Vietnam Based on Three Economic Growth Rates, 1993–2013

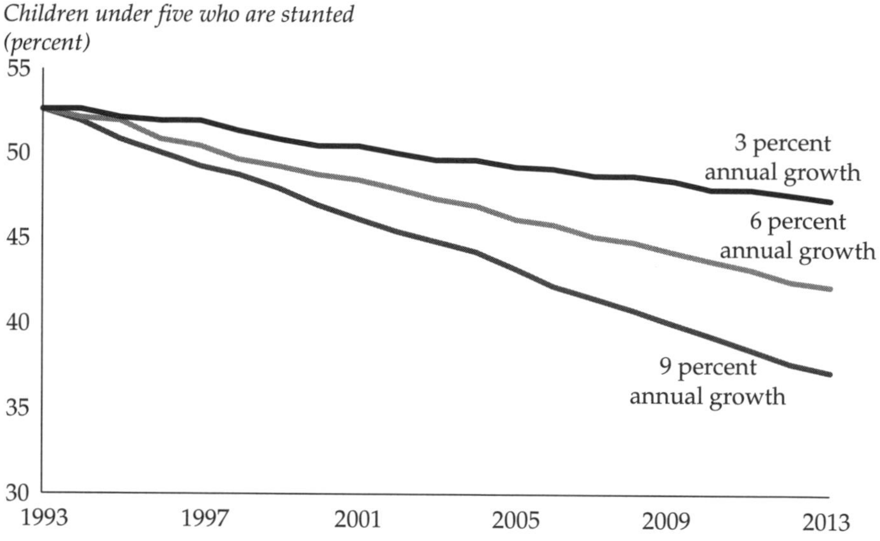

Children under five who are stunted
(percent)

Source: Authors' calculations.

growth. Third, other determinants of child nutritional status—particularly the local health environment and the availability, price, and quality of local health services—are assumed to remain unchanged.

The projections show that Vietnam will grow out of malnutrition, but rather slowly. If the country grows at its targeted rate of 6 percent a year, in 5 years the prevalence of malnutrition will be close to 50 percent, in 10 years it will be more than 45 percent, and in 20 years it will still exceed 40 percent. To reduce the prevalence of stunting by only 10 percentage points, Vietnam's economy would have to grow 9 percent a year for 15 years or 6 percent a year for 20 years.

Conclusion

This chapter began by asking how much the government can depend on economic growth to reduce malnutrition. The answer is very little. The analysis showed that economic growth has a relatively small effect on child nutrition. Even with very high rates of growth the incidence of stunting will still be nearly 40 percent in 2013. Greater progress will require policies explicitly aimed at improving child health and nutrition.

The Vietnamese government can act in several ways to improve child nutrition. It can implement public health interventions to reduce disease, meet the nutritional needs of growing children, and teach parents good health practices. It can also complement these interventions with social policies that improve health resources, knowledge, and information (for detailed recommendations see World Bank 1995). Failure by the government to take a more active role would dim the prospects for a better-nourished future generation even under the most optimistic scenarios for economic growth.

Notes

1. These examples and figures are from United Nations (1994). Although the authors of that report acknowledge that the figures may exaggerate Vietnam's improvement over time as a result of the uneven quality of data, they have no doubt that there has been a remarkable improvement (personal correspondence with John B. Mason, Technical Secretary, ACC/SCN, World Health Organization, Geneva, May 1996).

2. By contrast, there is a large literature on the effect of income on nutrient intake, particularly calorie intake (see Strauss and Thomas 1995 for a recent review of this literature). The general consensus is that increases in income do not lead to large increases in nutrient consumption, which suggests that increased income may also have only a modest effect on child nutritional status.

3. Use of U.S. NCHS standards raises the question of the appropriateness of American growth standards for non-American populations. While there is some evidence that the mean height of adults of East Asian origin is smaller than the mean heights of adults of European, African, and Indo-Mediterranean ancestry (Evelyth and Tanner 1976), most studies that have explored genetic and environmental interactions in the growth of children find that less than 10 percent of the worldwide height variation among children under 10 is due to genetics or race (Martorell and Habicht 1986). Other reasons for using the NCHS standards are practicality and consistency in undertaking normative analysis.

References

Evelyth, Phyllis B., and J. M. Tanner. 1976. *Worldwide Variation in Human Growth.* Cambridge: Cambridge University Press.

Falkner, Frank, and J. M. Tanner, eds. 1986. *Human Growth: A Comprehensive Treatise.* 2d ed. New York: Plenum Press.

Gibson, Rosalind. 1990. *Principles of Nutritional Assessment.* Oxford: Oxford University Press.

Healy, Michael J. 1986. "Statistics of Growth Standards." In Frank Falkner and J. M. Tanner, eds., *Human Growth: A Comprehensive Treatise.* 2d ed. New York: Plenum Press.

Jamison, Neil L., Nguyen Manh Hung, and A. Terry Rambo. 1992. "The Challenges of Vietnam's Reconstruction." George Mason University, Indochina Institute, Fairfax, Va.

Martorell, Reynaldo, and Jean-Pierre Habicht. 1986. "Growth in Early Childhood in Developing Countries." In Frank Falkner and J. M. Tanner, eds., *Human*

Growth: A Comprehensive Treatise. 2d ed. New York: Plenum Press.

Martorell, Reynaldo, Fernando Mendoza, and Ricardo Castillo. 1988. "Poverty and Stature in Children." In John C. Waterlow, ed., *Linear Growth Retardation in Less Developed Countries.* Nutrition Workshop Series 14. New York: Nestle Vevey/Raven Press.

Strauss, John, and Duncan Thomas. 1995. "Human Resources: Empirical Modeling of Household and Family Decisions." In Jere Behrman and T. N. Srinivasan, eds., *Handbook of Development Economics.* Vol. 3A. Amsterdam: North-Holland.

United Nations. 1994. *Update on the Nutrition Situation, 1994.* New York.

WHO (World Health Organization). 1983. *Measuring Change in Nutritional Status.* Geneva.

World Bank. 1993. "Vietnam: Population, Health, and Nutrition Sector Review." East Asia and Pacific Region, Washington, D.C.

———. 1995. "Vietnam: Poverty Assessment and Strategy." Report 13442-VN. East Asia and Pacific Region, Washington, D.C.

10

Poverty and Fertility in Vietnam

Jaikishan Desai

Do the poor have more children? If so, do they have more children because they are poor, or are they poor because they have more children? If they do have more children, is it because they want to or because factors associated with poverty prevent them from achieving their family size goals? And how feasible and justifiable is it to make welfare comparisons across individuals when they themselves choose the number of children they have and when these children yield satisfaction that cannot be completely captured in monetary terms? These are some of the questions that have been the focus of the debate over the past 30-odd years about the relationship between population growth and economic development.

In Vietnam concerns about population pressure on scarce land have long been at the top of the agenda, and the country has tried to cope with them through long-running family planning programs and attempts at redistributing population. But in recent times these concerns have taken on a new and different dimension as the country moves from a centrally planned economic system to one in which markets increasingly determine the allocation of resources. Coming on the heels of an era in which the state administered agricultural prices, allocated land, and provided education, health care, and family planning services at greatly subsidized prices, these changes naturally raise concerns about the future course of human capital formation and population growth.

Vietnam's population continues to grow rapidly. Yet the fertility rate has declined continuously, to probably less than three children per woman today, though substantial differences remain between rural and urban areas and among regions (see Jones 1982; Bannister 1985; and Allman and others 1991). Contraceptive knowledge is widespread, but prevalence rates for modern methods are comparatively low, at 52 percent. The low prevalence rate might be due to the excessive reliance on the intrauterine device (IUD), and the increased push to provide a wider mix of methods might well raise acceptance rates. Another factor, however, is that while family planning services have been virtually free, that can be expected to change as public sector cost recovery and private sector provision become important. Changes are already under way in the provision of more general health services and in education. Thus the cost-benefit environment of reproductive decisions has been undergoing a dramatic transformation for almost a decade, and this change is likely to accelerate in the coming years.

In this changing economic environment, whether the poor are able to meet their reproductive goals is of critical importance for government efforts aimed at accelerating growth while minimizing income inequality. Unfortunately, there is little research on fertility determinants in Vietnam. A Demographic and Health Survey was completed in 1988, but multivariate analysis of the resulting data has been limited. And information from this survey about the effects of poverty on fertility is likely to be scant because the survey collected no income or expenditure data. This chapter attempts to fill some of this gap by looking at the determinants of marital fertility.

The primary focus of the chapter is the effect of income on marital fertility, but it also looks at regional differences and at the effect of human and physical capital endowments, access to community infrastructure, migration, and such social factors as household structure and son preference. The mix of socioeconomic factors that influence family size decisions is particularly interesting in Vietnam. For a country that ranks among the poorest in the world, Vietnam has a remarkably literate population, with low infant mortality, widespread access to health care services, and a long standing family planning program. There are regional differences in these conditions, however: The northern part of the country is poorer but better educated than the south. Health care services, particularly family planning services, have been available longer in the north. More fundamental regional differences derive from the pattern of Vietnamese settlement, colonial administration, and postcolonial political and economic structures.

Social structures are also important for family formation patterns (see Dong 1991 and Huou 1991 for excellent discussions of family structures and relationships in Vietnam). A strong Confucian influence and hierarchical family structures that emphasize the importance of male progeny are reflected in a preference for sons. This preference has a tremendous bearing on fertility outcomes and might very well be the most important determinant of family sizes in the near future. For this reason the chapter separately examines the effect of son preference on fertility outcomes.

Data and Descriptive Information

The Vietnam Living Standards Survey (VNLSS) obtained data on fertility and contraception from women 15–49 years of age. In households with more than one woman in this age range, one woman was selected at random. All women selected were asked whether they had ever been pregnant and, if so, whether they had given birth. From women who had begun childbearing detailed fertility histories were obtained consisting of the dates, gender, survival status, and vaccination status of all live births. For the most recent birth, data were also obtained on prenatal care, place of delivery, assistance during delivery, birth weight, and duration of breastfeeding. All women who had been married at least once were asked their age at the time of marriage and then asked detailed questions on their knowledge and use of 13 traditional and modern methods of contraception. The survey did not obtain any information from women on their desired family size or fertility intentions.[1]

The sampling procedure (the selection of one woman at random from each household) tends to overrepresent women from households with fewer women aged 15–49.[2] This section discusses the bias resulting from this procedure and its implications for the selection of a sample for multivariate analyses. Next it presents some descriptive information on the fertility process, along with a comparison of fertility estimates with those from the Vietnam Demographic and Health Survey of 1988. Finally it describes the rationale underlying the sample selected for analysis of fertility determinants and discusses differences in the marital fertility of women aged 20–39 according to their schooling, their spouse's schooling, the land area in which their household has use rights, the region in which they live, the type of household in which they live, and their household's income.

Sample Bias

Selecting one woman at random in each randomly selected household yields a sample of women whose age distribution is distinctly different from that of all women aged 15–49. While the distribution of all women accurately reflects one side of the population pyramid of a high-fertility country, the sample of women selected for the fertility section of the survey includes fewer women younger than 25 and older than 39—and more women aged 25–39 (figure 10.1).

This undersampling of younger women is directly related to the sampling procedure, because the percentage of younger women who live in "multiwomen" households (those with more than one eligible woman) is much greater than the percentage of older women who do (table 10.1). For example, while 85 percent of women aged 15–19, and 58 percent of those aged 20–24, live in multiwomen households, fewer than 30 percent of women aged 25–39 do. At the same time, more than 50 percent of women over 39 live in households with at least one other eligible woman.

If there are no differences in age-specific fertility rates between sampled and nonsampled women, the estimated total fertility rate, calculated

Figure 10.1 Age Distribution of All Women Aged 15–49 in the Sampled Households and in the Fertility Sample

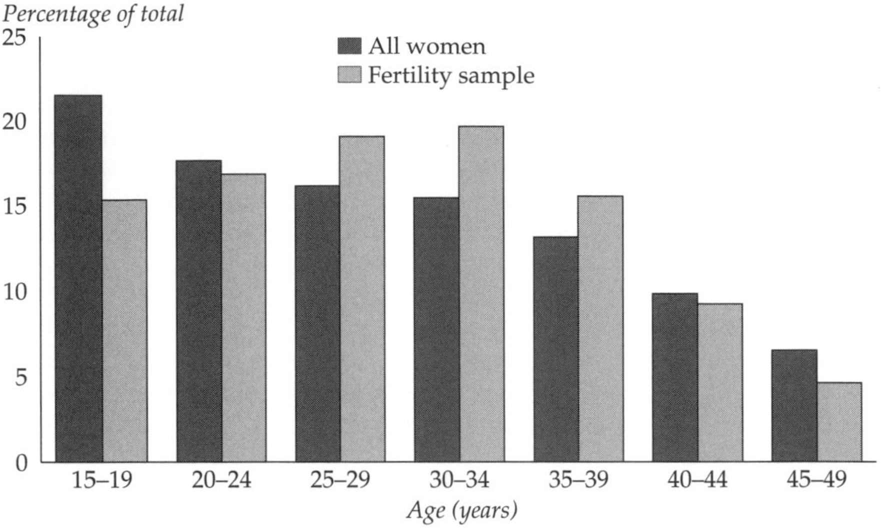

Percentage of total

Source: 1992–93 Vietnam Living Standards Survey.

by summing the age-specific fertility rates (and multiplying by the size of the age intervals), should be the same for both groups. The age composition difference should, therefore, have no bearing on the total fertility rate.[3] But that is not the case because marriage and household formation patterns are such that women selected for the fertility section are much more likely to have ever married than women not selected. Before marriage most women in Vietnam live with their parents, but after marriage most start new households with their spouses.[4] In these households they are

Table 10.1 Age Distribution of All Women Aged 15–49 in the Sampled Households and in the Fertility Sample

(percent)

	All women					Selected women			
Age cohort	Share of total	Share living in multiwomen households	Share ever married	Share selected	N	Share of total	Share living in multiwomen households	Share ever married	N
15–19	21.5	84.8	7.7	50.2	1,290	15.3	69.7	9.6	646
20–24	17.6	57.6	52.3	67.4	1,053	16.8	37.3	63.0	711
25–29	16.1	29.4	82.5	83.0	966	19.0	15.0	88.2	802
30–34	15.4	18.1	89.3	89.6	925	19.6	8.6	92.5	829
35–39	13.1	29.3	92.8	83.5	783	15.5	15.3	95.1	654
40–44	9.8	55.4	92.1	66.7	585	9.2	33.1	91.5	390
45–49	6.5	74.4	95.9	50.4	387	4.6	49.2	95.4	195
Total	100	50.0	65.3	70.6	5,989	100	29.1	74.5	4,227

Source: 1992–93 Vietnam Living Standards Survey.

likely to be the only woman between 15 and 49 years of age. While 65 percent of all women aged 15–49 have ever married, almost 75 percent of women in the sample have ever married. The importance of this difference lies in the fact that there is little childbearing outside formal marriage in Vietnam.

The sample's bias toward older women and married women implies that fertility rates calculated from the VNLSS data are bound to have an upward bias. As shown below, the difference can be as large as 30 percent, greatly obscuring the extent of the decline in fertility in recent years. One obvious solution to this problem is to use weights based on the probability of selection within a household. Weighting the selected woman's fertility experience by the number of women in her household would seemingly yield unbiased estimates. But this solution does not solve the problem because fertility experiences are fundamentally dependent on the age of the woman and because the age distribution of nonselected women is heavily weighted toward women younger than 25 and women older than 39 (see table 10.1), age groups in which fertility rates are typically low. By ignoring age differences between selected and nonselected women, the weighting procedure is likely to retain some of the upward bias.

Another implication of this bias is that multivariate analyses of fertility will suffer from selectivity bias unless attention is restricted to marital fertility. The reason is that marriage, which influences selection into the sample, is a conscious decision made by individuals. This selectivity bias is a particular problem for younger women, since those married at the time of the survey represent a selective sample of women who marry early and therefore have more years of exposure to the "risk" of childbearing. Correcting for this type of selectivity is all but impossible because cross-sectional data are unlikely to have variables that can be assumed to affect age at first marriage but simultaneously not affect subsequent fertility.

Fertility Patterns and Trends

The cross-sectional nature of the survey is reflected in the wide age range in the sample of 4,227 women selected for the fertility section (table 10.2).[5] Given the sequential nature of the childbearing process this wide range results in a sample of women at different stages of the process. For example, in the age cohort 20–24 only 63 percent of women have been married, but among women aged 30–34 fewer than 10 percent are unmarried. Similarly, while only 51 percent of the women aged 20–24 have had a first birth, almost 85 percent of those aged 25–29 have begun childbearing.

Information on the timing of first marriage shows that the fertility experiences of the two oldest cohorts of women in the sample—those aged 40 and above—are likely to have been directly influenced by the reunification struggle (see table 10.2). Most women under 40 began childbearing

Table 10.2 Demographic Characteristics of Women Selected for the Fertility Section of the 1992–93 Vietnam Living Standards Survey, by Age Cohort

Demographic characteristic	15–19	20–24	25–29
Sample size	646	711	802
Sample as a percentage of total	15.3	16.8	19.0
Marital status (percentage having status)			
Married, spouse in the household	7.6	57.8	80.8
Married, spouse away	1.6	3.7	3.2
Divorced	0.5	0.6	2.1
Separated	0.0	0.3	1.1
Widowed	0.0	0.7	0.9
Never married	90.4	37.0	11.9
Year of first marriage			
Interdecile range (end points)	1990–93	1987–92	1983–90
Interquartile range (end points)	1991–92	1989–91	1984–88
Fertility experiences (percentage experiencing event)			
First marriage	9.2	63.0	88.1
First birth	3.4	51.1	84.8
Second birth	0.2	18.9	62.8
Third birth	0.0	3.5	29.9
Fourth birth	0.0	0.6	9.7
Fifth birth	0.0	0.0	2.2
Sixth birth	0.0	0.0	0.6

Note: All percentages except those for first marriage are based on the entire sample. For first marriage, percentages are based on 4,217 women because information on age at marriage was missing for 10 women.

after reunification, with those under 30 beginning childbearing during the economic reform. The fertility experiences of women in their twenties and thirties should therefore provide an interesting set of data for assessing the role of economic factors in fertility decisions.

Table 10.3 presents more detailed statistics on the three parts of the childbearing process. Ages at first marriage and first birth yield information on when the childbearing process begins. Median live-birth intervals describe the spacing between births. And parity progression ratios indicate what proportion of women progress from one parity to another. The last two parts, often referred to as the *tempo* and the *quantum* of fertility, are critical for understanding the fertility process. The median live-birth intervals in table 10.3 are based on Kaplan-Meir estimates of the relevant survival function and they utilize the entire sample of women at risk of experiencing the relevant event. This is not possible with parity progression ratios because it is not possible to determine whether a woman who has not had a birth at the time of the survey is likely to have that birth sometime in the future or to terminate childbearing before the next birth. To determine the likelihood that a woman will have the higher parity birth, an artificial parity progression ratio is calculated, based on the sub-sample of women, at each parity, who had at least five years of exposure

30–34	35–39	40–44	45–49	Total
829	654	390	195	4,227
19.6	15.5	9.2	4.6	100
84.3	83.8	75.6	72.3	66.0
4.2	2.9	3.9	2.6	3.2
1.6	3.4	2.3	1.0	1.7
1.1	2.9	2.1	2.1	1.2
1.3	2.1	7.7	17.4	2.4
7.5	4.9	8.5	4.6	25.5
1978–86	1973–82	1968–79	1963–73	
1980–84	1975–80	1970–76	1965–70	
92.5	95.1	91.5	95.4	74.5
91.2	95.4	91.8	94.4	70.7
81.1	88.4	84.9	87.2	56.5
53.9	70.2	72.3	76.9	37.9
28.2	45.9	50.8	61.5	22.1
11.1	26.3	35.4	44.1	12.0
4.0	12.4	20.8	26.2	5.9

Source: 1992–93 Vietnam Living Standards Survey.

to the risk of having the next birth. This statistic is called the *quintum* of fertility.[6]

The statistics in table 10.3 show that about half of all women in the sample marry by age 21 and have a first birth within a year of marriage. Because of the bias discussed earlier, the median age at first marriage and first birth is likely to be higher. The effect of this bias can be gauged by comparing another summary statistic for marriage timing—the singulate mean age at marriage—for all eligible women in the sampled households with that for those selected for the fertility section. The singulate mean age at marriage, calculated using data on the percentage of women in different age cohorts who are single, is 22.2 for the selected women and 23.5 for all women in the surveyed households.

Median values for birth intervals show that the second birth follows within two and a half years of the first and that more than 90 percent of women have a second birth. Clearly, a two-child family is the minimum for most Vietnamese couples.[7] The third birth is spaced three years after the second, and the fourth, three years and three months after the third. Among women who have five or more years to advance to a higher parity, roughly 83 percent have a third birth and 73 percent a fourth. These sam-plewide averages are made up of the fertility experiences of women of dif-

Table 10.3 Statistics for the Fertility Process, by Age Cohort

Indicator	15–19	20–24	25–29
Age at first marriage (years)	—	21	21
	(643)	(708)	(801)
Age at first birth (years)	—	22	22
	(646)	(711)	(802)
Median live-birth interval (months)			
Second	—	33	30
	—	(363)	(504)
Third	—	39	37
	—	(134)	(240)
Fourth	—	30	45
	—	(25)	(78)
Fifth	—	—	45
	—	(4)	(18)
Quintum (percent)			
Second	—	91.4	92.7
	—	(35)	(396)
Third	—	50.0	80.8
	—	(3)	(182)
Fourth	—	—	60.0
	—	—	(50)
Fifth	—	—	50.0
	—	—	(2)
Mean number of children ever born			
1992–93 Vietnam Living Standards Survey	0.036	0.740	1.903
1992–93 Vietnam Living Standards Survey, weighted	0.022	0.545	1.701
1988 Vietnam Demographic and Health Survey	0.019	0.649	1.857

— The number of women experiencing the event is too small to obtain reliable estimates of the survival function and a median value.
Note: Numbers in parentheses are sample sizes—that is, the number of women at risk of experiencing the

ferent age cohorts, and it is differences in these experiences that contain the necessary information on a fertility transition.

Differences across the age cohorts reveal little change in the age at which women marry, but there is a statistically significant drop in the age at which women have their first child.[8] Because the sample bias toward married women is greater for younger cohorts, this apparent decline in age at first birth might be entirely due to sample composition. Differences in parity progression ratios (quintum values) and the length of the second birth interval reveal interesting information on changes in the childbearing process. There are no statistically significant differences in the estimated quintums for the second birth, suggesting that the fertility transition has little bearing on whether women have at least two children. But younger women do take longer to have a second birth, although this difference is still quite small—at most three months—and statistically significant only when comparing women aged 20–24 with those aged 25–29.

30–34	35–39	40–44	45–49	Total
21	21	22	21	21
(828)	(654)	(389)	(194)	(4,217)
23	23	24	23	23
(829)	(654)	(390)	(195)	(4,227)
29	30	31	35	30
(672)	(578)	(331)	(170)	(2,987)
38	34	33	34	36
(447)	(459)	(282)	(150)	(2,390)
45	36	36	36	39
(234)	(300)	(198)	(120)	(1,603)
45	45	37	37	46
(92)	(172)	(138)	(86)	(934)
94.1	94.4	93.2	92.9	93.7
(682)	(605)	(355)	(183)	(2,756)
77.8	84.3	85.7	88.8	82.6
(527)	(530)	(328)	(169)	(1,742)
71.1	72.0	73.5	81.6	72.9
(263)	(396)	(268)	(147)	(1,124)
64.1	67.6	73.1	74.1	69.9
(92)	(222)	(186)	(116)	(618)
2.701	3.503	3.790	4.277	2.110
2.563	3.604	4.018	4.552	1.872
2.978	3.890	4.749	5.756	2.132

relevant event. Weights are based on the number of women in a household and reflect the inverse of the probability of selection of one woman in a household.
Source: 1992–93 Vietnam Living Standards Survey and 1988 Vietnam Demographic and Health Survey.

The transitions to the third and fourth birth vary more across cohorts and provide better insight into the fertility transition under way in Vietnam. In younger cohorts third and fourth birth intervals are significantly longer, and somewhat smaller percentages of women "at risk" advance to the next parity. These patterns, explored in greater detail elsewhere (Desai 1995a), should be viewed with some caution because the relevant samples for these transitions are biased toward women who have the first two births sooner.[9] The bias is greater for younger women because a greater proportion of the childbearing experience of younger women is covered by the survey. Because these data show greater spacing and lower parity progression and at the same time are also biased toward higher-fertility women (those in younger cohorts), it is safe to conclude that the transition toward lower fertility is greater than that shown by these data.

The mean number of children born to a woman combines information on spacing and parity progression and is therefore a summary statistic that provides a quick look at fertility patterns. It is also the dependent variable for the multivariate analyses discussed in the following section. Values for the different cohorts indicate that each five-year span adds, on average, 0.8 birth, though after age 39 the addition for each five-year span is only 0.5 birth. Values from the 1988 Demographic and Health Survey lend further support to the earlier conclusion that fertility has been declining in recent years.

The age-specific fertility rates in table 10.4 are calculated using indirect methods of the Brass type (United Nations 1983). These rates, when compared with the age-specific rates from the 1988 Demographic and Health Survey, provide direct evidence of the fertility transition.[10]

The total fertility rate calculated from the fertility sample of the Living Standards Survey indicates a decline of 13 percent between 1988 and 1991–92, from 3.98 to 3.47. The decline is concentrated in the age groups 20–34 (figure 10.2). Since the surveys are roughly five years apart, a comparison of the age-specific fertility rates from the Demographic and Health Survey with those for adjacent (older) age groups from the Living Standards Survey, shows how cohort experience differs from what can be expected on the basis of a period rate such as the total fertility rate. For example, if women aged 20–24 in 1988 followed the fertility pattern of their immediate elders, they would have an age-specific fertility rate of 0.243. Instead, the age-specific fertility rate for women aged 25–29 in 1991–92 is 0.195, reflecting a 20 percent decline in fertility.

The decline in overall fertility, however, is likely to have been greater than 13 percent, because of the bias toward married women in the fertility sample from the Living Standards Survey. A rough estimate of this decline is obtained by calculating age-specific rates and a total fertility rate for all women aged 15–49. These rates were calculated by counting as births in

Table 10.4 Age-specific Fertility Rates and Total Fertility Rate

	1992–93 Vietnam Living Standards Survey			
	Fertility sample		*All women (weighted rates)*	
Age cohort	*Unadjusted age-specific fertility rate*	*Adjusted age-specific fertility rate*	*Unadjusted age-specific fertility rate*	*Adjusted age-specific fertility rate*
15–19	0.026	0.039	0.016	0.026
20–24	0.214	0.229	0.167	0.189
25–29	0.201	0.195	0.185	0.192
30–34	0.110	0.107	0.117	0.120
35–39	0.084	0.081	0.084	0.083
40–44	0.033	0.031	0.027	0.027
45–49	0.015	0.012	0.012	0.010
Total fertility rate	3.417	3.466	3.045	3.235

Note: Adjusted and unadjusted age-specific fertility rates are based on the calculations for Brass-type indirect estimation methods (see United Nations 1983). Weighted rates reflect all women aged 15–49 in the household.

the year before the survey—to women aged 15–49—all children 12 months and younger in the household and then inflating this figure for infant mortality.[11] While these calculations are admittedly crude, they incorporate assumptions that, if anything, should yield higher estimates than true ones. These calculations suggest that the total fertility rate for 1991–92 is on the order of 2.69, reflecting a decline of 33 percent from the 1987 estimate (see table 10.4).

Sample Selection and Socioeconomic Differences in Marital Fertility

The sample used for the multivariate analyses of the determinants of fertility consists of ever-married women between the ages of 25 and 39.[12] Attention is restricted to marital fertility because of the sampling bias discussed earlier. Those under 25 are excluded from the analyses because the bias is greater among younger women; and women over 39 are excluded because most of them began childbearing before reunification in 1975, so their childbearing experiences are directly influenced by the war (a large share of women over 39 are widowed; see table 10.2). It is also advisable to exclude older women because the relevance of survey-date conditions for explaining past fertility experiences is open to question when there is a long gap between the survey and the relevant fertility events.

Restricting the analyses to ever-married women implies that the results can only be used to infer about marital fertility. While this approach is limiting in some ways, it is more appropriate when one of the main issues of interest is the effect of poverty on fertility. The reason is that marriage represents a significant change in the locus of decisionmaking so that

1992–93 Vietnam Living Standards Survey				1988 Vietnam Demographic and Health Survey
All women (births in past year = infants who are household members)		All women (births in past year = infants who are household members x 1.10)		
Unadjusted age-specific fertility rate	Adjusted age-specific fertility rate	Unadjusted age-specific fertility rate	Adjusted age-specific fertility rate	Age-specific fertility rate
0.020	0.028	0.022	0.039	0.020
0.144	0.156	0.159	0.172	0.235
0.167	0.165	0.183	0.181	0.243
0.098	0.096	0.108	0.105	0.151
0.070	0.067	0.077	0.073	0.085
0.022	0.021	0.024	0.023	0.051
0.008	0.006	0.009	0.007	0.011
2.649	2.687	2.914	2.997	3.982

Source: Primary calculations from 1992–93 Vietnam Living Standards Survey data, and table 3.1 of National Committee for Population and Family Planning 1990.

Figure 10.2 Age-specific Fertility Rates of Women Aged 15–49, 1986–87 and 1991–92

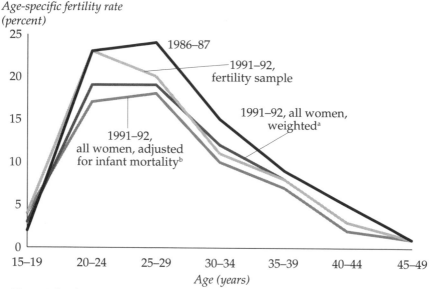

Age-specific fertility rate (percent)

a. The weighted age-specific fertility rates were calculated by weighing those obtained from the fertility sample by the number of women in the household.
b. The infant mortality rate was assumed to be 100. See text for further explanation.
Source: 1988 Vietnam Demographic and Health Survey, and 1992–93 Vietnam Living Standards Survey.

the economic conditions of married women are not comparable with those of unmarried women.[13] Measures of permanent income or potential income obtained from income or expenditure data in the survey year are not comparable for married and unmarried women. For married women they can be interpreted in terms of the resource constraints that couples face in making family size and child investment decisions. But for unmarried women they represent resource constraints in their parents' household. While these income measures too are probably relevant for the family size decisions that men and women make,[14] their interpretation in terms of the resource constraints that decisionmakers face is quite different.

Finally, the analyses pay greater attention to differences in rural fertility than in urban. This is partly dictated by the fact that commune-level data are only available for rural areas, and these variables are critical for identifying access to public infrastructure and the larger economy. But the focus on rural fertility is also driven by the small sample size available for urban fertility. This is not such a terrible limitation, because the data indicate that the total fertility rate in urban areas is close to replacement levels. Pooling the data is not feasible because F-tests for structural differences in coefficients (for children ever born) indicate significant differences in the effects of different variables in the two samples.

Before turning to the regression analysis, it is useful to briefly examine differences in cumulative marital fertility for the sample of rural women according to the socioeconomic characteristics of the women and their households (table 10.5). Women's schooling has a large effect on marital fertility, with the number of children ever born falling with each additional level of schooling. These differences are less striking for the youngest cohort of women, reflecting the short and almost universal transition from marriage to first birth. The pattern for spouse's schooling is almost identical. Since the simple correlation between women's schooling years and spouse's schooling years is 0.6, it will be interesting to see what effect spouse's schooling has once women's schooling is taken into account.

The amount of land to which a household has use rights also has a strong bearing on marital fertility. On the whole women in households with more land have more children, though those who have no land have higher fertility than those who have some. Women from nuclear households (those with only a household head, his wife, and their own children) have more children. This may reflect the higher income of nuclear households.

There are distinct regional differences in marital fertility, with women in the Central Highlands consistently having more children. Marital fertility is also high in the rural areas of the Mekong Delta and the Northern Uplands. Households in these regions have larger parcels of land and lower schooling levels, so these fertility differences may simply reflect the effect of those factors. The regression results presented in the following section help to determine whether there are any residual regional differences after these factors are taken into account. Also interesting are the substantial differences among the three northern regions. Women in the Red River Delta have the lowest fertility rate, followed by the North-Central Coast and the Northern Uplands. Thus some care needs to be exercised when making comparisons between the north and the south.

Per capita expenditure, often used as a measure of the standard of living, exhibits a clear inverse relationship with children ever born. This is to be expected because fertility has a direct (inverse) effect on per capita expenditure, which is calculated by dividing household expenditure by the number of people in a household. But this inverse relationship should not be interpreted in causal terms as implying that the poor have more children. As discussed below, when examining the effects of poverty on fertility, poverty needs to be defined in terms of the potential income of individuals.

Expenditure per adult is an appropriate measure of the potential income of couples. On the whole those with lower income have fewer chil-

Table 10.5 Mean Number of Children Ever Born to Married Women Aged 20–39 in Rural Vietnam, by Women's Age Cohort and Socioeconomic Characteristics

Characteristic	20–24	25–29	30–34	35–39	25–39
Level of schooling completed by woman					
No schooling	1.35	2.81	4.07	5.04	3.57
Primary incomplete	1.27	2.65	3.55	4.53	3.24
Lower secondary incomplete	1.28	2.27	3.13	3.79	2.72
Upper secondary incomplete	1.25	2.14	2.87	3.48	2.43
Upper secondary completed	0.94	1.78	2.48	2.86	1.90
Level of schooling completed by spouse					
No schooling	1.32	2.66	4.02	5.04	3.46
Primary incomplete	1.27	2.71	3.60	4.66	3.30
Lower secondary incomplete	1.29	2.28	3.13	3.86	2.73
Upper secondary incomplete	1.24	2.14	2.88	3.38	2.43
Upper secondary completed	0.97	1.78	2.44	2.79	1.90
Land area with use rights (square miles)					
No land	1.20	2.37	3.10	3.58	2.70
0–2,000	1.15	1.87	2.56	3.06	2.07
2,001–3,000	1.20	2.21	2.82	3.37	2.40
3,001–5,000	1.16	2.21	3.18	3.92	2.79
5,001–10,000	1.36	2.52	3.51	4.60	3.16
More than 10,000	1.36	2.62	3.62	4.75	3.18
Region					
Northern Uplands	1.35	2.35	3.41	4.17	2.78
Red River Delta	1.23	2.04	2.70	3.41	2.36
North-Central Coast	1.16	2.29	3.26	3.83	2.68
Central Coast	1.27	2.02	3.17	4.21	2.85
Central Highlands	1.20	3.17	3.79	4.67	3.34
Southeast	1.14	2.24	3.22	4.09	2.85
Mekong Delta	1.15	2.44	3.29	4.12	2.92
Household structure					
Nuclear	1.36	2.38	3.21	3.95	2.90
Vertical	1.07	1.99	2.91	3.76	2.20
Other	1.06	1.62	3.06	4.27	2.08
Real expenditure per adult quintile					
Poorest 20 percent	1.16	1.84	2.67	3.07	1.83
2	1.23	2.16	3.12	3.70	2.39
3	1.33	2.43	3.01	3.72	2.72
4	1.18	2.59	3.51	4.07	3.22
Richest 20 percent	1.36	2.49	3.16	4.19	3.33
Real expenditure per capita quintile					
Poorest 20 percent	1.38	2.56	3.62	4.60	3.12
2	1.42	3.33	3.23	4.07	2.79
3	1.26	2.29	2.98	3.90	2.67
4	1.00	1.91	2.81	3.69	2.42
Richest 20 percent	0.76	1.79	2.56	2.90	2.11
Sample size	394	584	589	477	2,044
Total	1.23	2.27	3.15	3.92	2.71

Source: 1992–93 Vietnam Living Standards Survey.

dren, though the relationship appears to be quite weak, particularly for the youngest cohort of women. Among women aged 25–39 the real differences appear to be between women from the poorest quintile and those who are better off. Since income is associated with human and physical capital and varies dramatically across regions of Vietnam, it remains to be seen whether it has any bearing on marital fertility once these other factors are taken into account.

Do the Poor Have More Children?

The number of children a woman has is the result of a complex interaction of psychological, social, economic, and biological factors. Individuals make decisions about sexual interaction, family size, composition, and rate of acquisition of children, but then must also balance these decisions with the biological reality of the reproductive process. The decisionmaking part of the reproductive process is often referred to as the demand for children, and the biological aspect as the supply of children. Balancing family size desires with the biological reality of the reproductive process is necessary because sexual interaction, quite independent of its being an essential input into the child production process, is welfare-enhancing. Thus the psychological, social, and economic costs of contraception, both modern and traditional, are the third component that determines fertility.

Theoretical Background

Decisions on childbearing are driven by three sets of factors. The first set consists of preferences for the number and spacing of children, expected expenditures on children, parents' lifestyle, type of contraception, and the like. The second reflects the relative prices—implicit and explicit—of various consumption activities, and the third relates to the income parents can expect to generate over their remaining years. This potential income depends on the value of the parents' labor time, the nonlabor inputs they use in production, and the prices of outputs they produce. Other things equal, those with greater endowments of human and physical capital are likely to have higher potential incomes, as are those who can obtain inputs at lower cost and sell output at higher prices.

Since the decision on family size has a life-cycle perspective, so should the assessment of who is poor and who is not. For examining whether the poor have more children or not, the appropriate concept of poverty is thus one based on potential income. A consumption-based measure is plausible if it is possible to distinguish between the consumption of the decision-maker and that of the children within a household. If so, poverty could be defined in terms of the consumption of the decisionmakers and the consumption of the children and an examination of the tradeoff between the number of children couples decide to have and their own lifestyles—similar to explorations of the child quantity-quality tradeoff—would be possible. But this would not be an examination of the effects of poverty on fertility, because in a life-cycle framework both are simultaneously decided on by the decisionmakers.

In assessing whether the poor have more children, it is therefore necessary to consider how potential income influences fertility through each of the three sets of factors outlined above: the demand for children, reproductive capacity, and contraception. On the demand side, other things equal, we should expect those who have more income to want more children. A positive income effect is to be expected since children are normal goods. But could there could be reasons to expect those who have less income to want more children, as casual empiricism indicates?

If parents trade off child quality for quantity and the income elasticity of demand for quality is substantially greater than that for quantity, parents could be expected to want fewer but higher-quality children as their incomes increase. Alternatively, if there are substantial differences in the net economic returns parents expect to receive from their children in future years and these are related to the incomes of parents—in the absence of children's contributions—poorer parents can be expected to want more children. For example, in a land-scarce environment with fragmented capital markets, additional family labor may be one of the few avenues for economic advancement. Expected support in old age would be important when income-generating capacity is negligible and capital markets have not allowed an accumulation of savings. But both arguments relate to the shadow price of children, which might be lower for poorer parents. To the extent that the shadow price of children is controlled for, a regression of a fertility variable on a measure of potential income should yield a positive coefficient.

The effects of potential income on the ability to produce children, or the supply of children, are easier to specify. Higher incomes often imply better nutrition, which can, at least in theory, have a positive effect on fecundity. Conversely, those with lower incomes might have lower fecundity. But research findings suggest that this effect is meaningful only in extreme circumstances bordering on famine conditions. Higher incomes also are usually associated with greater access to and use of health care facilities, particularly prenatal and postnatal care, and since these influence the survival chances of the newborn, higher incomes can be expected to be associated with better reproductive performance.

Contraceptive use, because of the associated time and out-of-pocket expenses of modern contraception, can be expected to be greater among those with higher incomes, who therefore are likely to be better equipped to attain their reproductive goals. This brief discussion suggests that if proper statistical controls are introduced for the "price" of children, the costs of contraception and health services, the rental costs of capital, and the like, we should expect to see a positive relationship between income and fertility.

What is the likely relationship between poverty and fertility in rural Vietnam? Several factors should be borne in mind when considering this relationship. The sample chosen for analysis consists of ever-married women who began childbearing after reunification in 1975. Because schooling, health care, and family planning services were extended to the southern part of the country after 1975, differences in access to these services are likely to be less relevant for regional differences in fertility. Differences in knowledge of health and family planning practices and in quality of health care might still be important.

Regional differences are relevant not just because the southern part of the country is considerably better off than the northern part, but also because the north has higher levels of human capital and a longer history of family planning programs. Moreover, there are substantial differences in social structure between the north and the south, deriving partly from historical and partly from political and economic factors. The south has always been more of a frontier area, with higher land-per-capita ratios. Differences in the way the French administered the north and the south, and then stark differences between communist North Vietnam and capitalist South Vietnam, contributed to differences in patterns of economic activity and village organization (Jamieson 1993). The social structure is likely to be more open (less hierarchical) in the south, and the scope for individual decisionmaking therefore greater.

Probably more important to the analysis of fertility differences in Vietnam is the effect of state provision of schooling, health care, and family planning on the cost-benefit calculus of childbearing. The lack of private sector choices implies that quality-related price differences were probably unimportant for much of the period examined. There have been changes in the past 10 years, but whether these have touched rural areas is open to question. Against this background, a positive relationship can be expected between income and fertility even without much control for price differences.

Selection of Variables

The measure of potential income used in this chapter is the log of household expenditure per adult. The household expenditure variable is calculated for the 12 months preceding the survey and was deflated by regional price indices to eliminate the effect of spatial variation in prices (see chapter 2 for details on how this was calculated).[15] Total household expenditure (equal to income less changes in savings and assets) is another possible measure for potential income. But total household expenditure is likely to suffer from greater heterogeneity over the life cycle, a factor that is relevant because the dependent variable measures cumulative fertility experiences. From figure 10.3, which plots mean values of different measures of potential income against the age of the household head, it can be seen that

Figure 10.3 Life-cycle Variation in Different Household Expenditure Measures

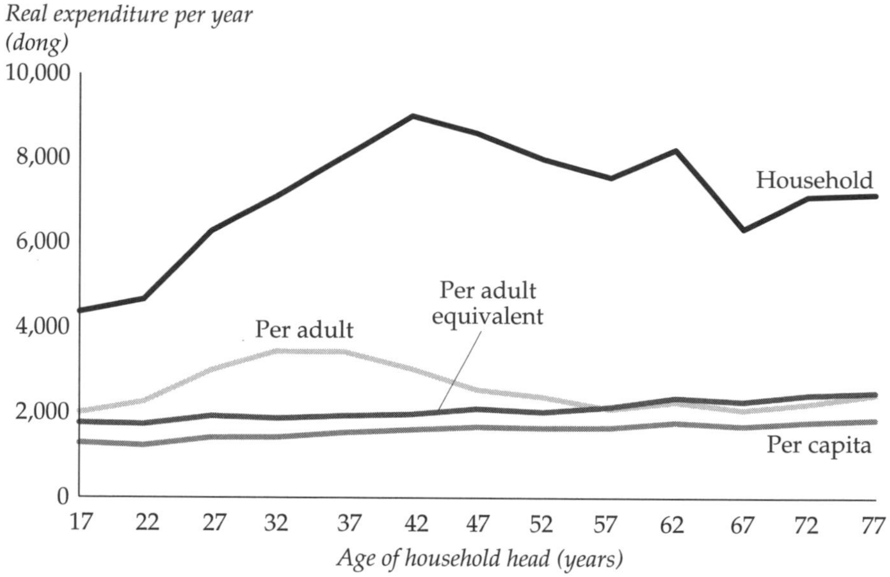

Real expenditure per year (dong)

10,000

8,000

Household

6,000

Per adult
equivalent

4,000

Per adult

2,000

Per capita

0

17   22   27   32   37   42   47   52   57   62   67   72   77

Age of household head (years)

Note: Data Cover the 12 months before the survey.
Source: 1992–93 Vietnam Living Standards Survey.

expenditure per adult more closely approximates the life-cycle variation in permanent income suggested by theory.

The possibility that household expenditure per adult is endogenous cannot be discounted, however. One reason relates to the contributions children make to household income. When children contribute to household income, causation would certainly also work in the reverse direction, with higher fertility causing higher incomes. Unlike Benefo and Schultz (1994), Montgomery and Kuoame (1993), and Ainsworth (1989), who use the entire sample of women aged 15–49, this chapter restricts the sample to women aged 25–39. While that greatly reduces the problem of potential endogeneity, children's high labor force participation rates after age 11 or 12 indicate that their economic contributions remain an important factor, particularly for women 35 and older. Even if the labor contributions of young children are discounted, expenditure per adult is likely to be endogenous because of changes in the time allocation of household members for childcare.

Ignoring the potential endogeneity of consumption expenditure can lead to biased estimates of all coefficients, so the standard approach to this problem is to use instrumental variables techniques. Household expenditure per adult is regressed on a set of exogenous instruments, and then predicted values of the variable are used in the fertility regression. The set of instruments used must include some variables that do not appear in the fertility regression, it should make an important contribution to the first-stage regression, and the predictive ability of the first-stage regression should be reasonably good. Finally, a Hausman test of exogeneity can be used to test the endogeneity of the consumption variable.

The appendix contains the results of first-stage regressions for a rural sample, an urban sample, and an alternative commune fixed effects specification used below. The set of potentially identifying variables includes dummy variables for the main occupation of the household head's father, the main occupation of the household head's mother, and dummy variables for whether the household cultivates crops and receives agricultural extension services. Occupation of the household head's parents can be reasonably expected to have little direct bearing on the fertility of the selected woman, particularly since most of the selected women are the spouse of the household head. At the commune level, identifying variables include dummy variables for whether there is a daily or periodic market in the commune, and commune prices of paddy, urea, and phosphate.[16] While these factors influence the earnings of the household, they are unlikely to have a direct effect on the fertility of the selected women.

The instrumenting regressions are reasonably well identified. The coefficients for the dummy variables for the main occupation of the household head's mother and the dummy for periodic markets in the commune are significant at the 1 percent level. The coefficient for the real price of phosphatic fertilizer is also significant, though only at the 10 percent level. The results indicate strong life-cycle and household human capital effects, along with significant differences between male-headed and female-headed households of different types. Significant regional differences are also evident, as is the importance of commune-level factors. The model does reasonably well explaining 32 percent (44 percent for the fixed effects specification) of the variation in household expenditure per adult. While one can't be certain that the variable has been purged of all endogeneity, the first-stage regressions appear to be adequate. Hausman tests of exogeneity were also conducted, and the results are reported in the discussion that follows: it should be borne in mind that the validity of these procedures depends on the appropriateness of the zero restrictions imposed on the instrumenting regressions.

The other variables selected for the fertility regressions and their hypothesized effects are as follows. Age of the woman is included to control for the duration of exposure to childbearing. The survey covers more of the fertility experience of older women, so age should be expected to have a positive effect on fertility. Age also represents cohort effects, and in a regime of declining fertility at least part of the lower observed fertility of younger women can be expected to translate to lower completed fertility at some point in time.

Schooling variables are included for both the selected woman and her spouse. For the spouse the variable is specified in terms of number of years of schooling, while for the selected woman dummy variables are included for some (but incomplete) primary schooling, some (but incomplete) lower secondary schooling, some (but incomplete) upper secondary schooling, and more than upper secondary schooling. These dummy variables were constructed on the basis of grades completed at the time of the survey, even though they are specified in terms of number of years of schooling. A dummy variable specification for women's schooling allows more flexible specification of schooling effects than a linear or quadratic form.

The effects of women's schooling are widely recognized in the literature on fertility and investment in children's human capital. The effects operate through differences in preferences for the number and quality of children, through higher opportunity cost of time spent in childcare, and through higher incomes. These factors influence both the number of children women want to have and their willingness to use contraception to control their fertility. Education effects can also be expected to operate through the biological process (the supply of children) through better use of prenatal care, choice of health facilities for delivery, postnatal care, and health care investments in infants.[17] It is reasonable to hypothesize that the net effect of women's schooling is negative—that is, that women with more schooling have lower fertility.

The effects of husband's schooling (and occupation) are often interpreted as income effects, because men typically are less involved in child rearing and the opportunity cost of their time thus has a smaller effect on the shadow price of children. But men's schooling can be expected to have a substantial impact on the adoption and effective use of modern contraception, even though the dominant contraceptive in use in Vietnam, the IUD, is a female contraceptive. The total effect of husband's schooling can therefore be positive or negative depending on whether the income effect is stronger or whether other effects operating through shadow price and the adoption and effective use of contraceptives are dominant.

Land area variables are included to assess the effect of physical capital resources on fertility decisions.[18] As a productive resource, land endowments have income effects similar to those from adult human capital, as well as price effects deriving from the employment opportunities they can provide for family labor.[19] The shadow price effect depends on labor market conditions, the type of crops cultivated, and the use of mechanized equipment. In Vietnam labor hiring varies considerably across the country; half of farmers in the Southeast and Mekong Delta hire labor, but fewer than a fifth of farmers in the northern regions do so. On the whole, land area can be expected to have a fertility-enhancing effect, though its strength is likely to vary across the country.[20]

The other variables included in the model attempt to control for social and economic influences on childbearing either through a modification of individual preferences or through an alteration in the effects of price and income factors. No a priori hypotheses are proposed for most of these dummy variables, though in some cases clearer effects are definable.

Dummy variables are included for women from vertical and other nonnuclear households. The base group consists of nuclear households (70 percent). Vertical households are defined as those with nuclear members and at least one of the following relatives of the household head: parents, parents-in-law, daughters, sons-in-law, or grandchildren. *Other households* is a residual category consisting of households in which some relationships are other than nuclear or vertical. Social pressures may be greater in nonnuclear households, especially since they are more likely to contain either the eldest or the youngest son of the household head. But it is also possible that the presence in the household of more than one woman of childbearing age represents a positive support mechanism and a greater pool of childcare knowledge and resources.

Dummy variables are also included for women who were widowed and women who were separated or divorced at the time of the survey. Here the interpretations are clearer. These marital statuses represent interruptions in the exposure to childbearing risk and should have a negative effect on fertility. While the dummy variable for widowed women is unambiguously exogenous, that for separated or divorced women should, at least theoretically, be viewed as endogenous. But it is treated as exogenous for two reasons. First, even though women's status in Vietnam has improved substantially in the past three to four decades, social life is male-dominated. Family and social relationships, under the strong influence of Confucian philosophy, emphasize a subordinate role for women. So for women a large share of separations and divorces may represent nonvoluntary marital states.[21] Second, a more practical reason, treating this dummy variable as endogenous requires developing an instrument for it, and it is all but impossible to find suitable identifying variables for this purpose. Excluding the variable is not an option because correlation with household expenditure would result in a clear omitted-variable bias.

A dummy variable is included for ethnic minorities, which include all non-Kinh and non-Chinese ethnic groups in Vietnam. Ethnic minorities have significantly higher fertility rates than the Chinese and the majority Kinh and have been less touched by the economic and social changes of the past 50 years. These groups also have significantly lower education, and they are concentrated in certain parts of the country—the Northern Uplands, the Central Highlands, and the Mekong Delta. The dummy variable attempts to assess whether differences remain after controlling for education, land area, age, and income. Dummy variables are also included for Buddhists and for Catholics. Almost two-thirds of Vietnamese state no religious affiliation, and a fourth report that they are Buddhists. No particular effects are hypothesized for these variables.

Finally, to assess whether there are residual regional differences in fertility outcomes, a set of six dummy variables are used for six of the seven regions of the country; the Red River Delta forms the base group. Variables reflecting commune characteristics are also introduced in some models to determine the role of access to and quality of infrastructure in fertility outcomes. Survey cluster-level differences are particularly important in Vietnam because cross-regional movement of goods and resources was limited before economic reforms. Means and standard deviations for the dependent variable and all independent variables are presented in table 10.6.

Regression Results

Table 10.7 presents the results of three regressions for children ever born to ever-married women aged 25–39 in rural Vietnam. The first two columns show ordinary least squares regression results for a model that does not include a measure of potential income.[22] The next two columns contain the results of an ordinary least squares regression model that includes a variable for the log of real expenditure per adult in the household in which the woman resides. The third set of results are for an instrumental variables regression using the predicted value of log of real expenditure per adult.[23] All models correct for heteroskedasticity, and the t-ratios are based on White-corrected standard errors; the Breusch-Pagan chi-square statistics are significant at 1 percent.

The regression results show that women's schooling has a strong and significant fertility-depressing effect. Differences between women who have a few years of primary schooling and those who have no schooling (the base group) appear only when a measure of potential income is added to the model; when income is treated as endogenous, the difference disappears.[24] The coefficient for the schooling of a woman's spouse is also negative and significant in all models. Coefficients for both spouses' schooling increase when income is added to the model, demonstrating the positive effect schooling has through increases in potential income.[25]

Land area has a positive and significant effect that declines as land area increases. Interestingly, adding a measure of potential income to the model does not cause substantial changes in the coefficients. Interacting land area with the age of the woman yields a positive coefficient, indicating that the land effect is smaller for younger women. This may reflect cohort differences, with greater crop specialization and labor hiring diluting the labor demand effect that would be stronger in an agricultural system geared toward paddy cultivation and household food security.

Women in vertical households have fewer children, as do those who are widowed, separated, or divorced. A similar model estimated for currently married women yielded almost identical results. Neither of the religion variables is significant, nor is the dummy variable for the ethnic minorities. The dummy variable for migration is significant when income is treated as exogenous, but not when income is instrumented. In models that control for commune-level factors the coefficient is very significant,

Table 10.6 Means and Standard Deviations of Dependent and Independent Variables for Fertility Regression Models for Married Women Aged 25–39 in Rural Vietnam

Variable	Mean	Standard deviation
Children ever born	3.062	1.54
Age in years	31.687	4.11
Schooling: 1–4 years	0.201	0.401
Schooling: 5–8 years	0.297	0.457
Schooling: 9–11 years	0.332	0.471
Schooling: 12+ years	0.090	0.286
Vertical household	0.194	0.396
Other household	0.030	0.170
Widow	0.015	0.122
Separated or divorced	0.034	0.181
Land area cultivated (square miles)	5.675	7.724
Land area squared	91.832	587.373
Spouse's years of schooling	7.267	3.641
Log household expenditure per adult (real)	7.736	0.517
Predicted log household expenditure per adult (real)	7.736	0.294
Ethnic minority	0.157	0.364
Buddhist	0.243	0.429
Christian	0.072	0.259
Northern Uplands	0.180	0.384
North-Central Coast	0.145	0.352
Central Coast	0.090	0.287
Central Highlands	0.039	0.193
Southeast	0.086	0.281
Mekong Delta	0.189	0.392
Moved from place of birth	0.307	0.461
Child delivery important health problem in commune	0.296	0.457
Maternal and child health program in commune in past five years	0.956	0.206
Distance to nearest health center (kilometers)	9.440	6.679
Wage work available for children	0.409	0.492
Peak season women's wages (real)	8.182	3.814
Road passes through commune	0.862	0.344
Road impassable at times	1.821	0.384
Percentage of land in commune of good quality	23.891	27.938
Percentage of land in commune of medium quality	49.847	27.543
Industrial enterprise in commune	0.453	0.498
Lower secondary school in commune	0.882	0.322
Upper secondary school in commune	0.105	0.306
Lower secondary school fees (real)	61.092	79.033

Source: 1992–93 Vietnam Living Standards Survey.

Table 10.7 Regression Results for Children Ever Born to Ever-married Women Aged 25–39 in Rural Vietnam

Variable	Ordinary least squares (basic)	
	Coefficient	t-statistic
Intercept	−1.745	5.83
Age in years	0.170	21.23
Schooling: 1–4 years	−0.218	1.33
Schooling: 5–8 years	−0.579	3.60
Schooling: 9–11 years	−0.728	4.39
Schooling: 12+ years	−1.125	6.23
Vertical household	−0.231	2.90
Other household	−0.428	1.87
Widow	−1.164	3.85
Separated or divorced	−1.563	10.51
Land area cultivated (square miles)	0.039	4.30
Land area squared	−0.000	2.95
Spouse's years of schooling	−0.035	3.37
Log household expenditure per adult (real)	—	—
Ethnic minority	−0.003	0.03
Buddhist	−0.022	0.28
Christian	0.144	1.05
Northern Uplands	0.400	4.34
North-Central Coast	0.439	4.95
Central Coast	0.163	1.33
Central Highlands	0.669	2.72
Southeast	0.111	0.83
Mekong Delta	0.112	1.03
Moved from place of birth	−0.104	−1.50
Sample size	1,650	
R^2	0.37	
Breusch-Pagan test for heteroskedasticity (chi-square statistic, df = 22 or 23)	256.21	
Hausman exogeneity test: chi-square statistic		

— Variable not included in regression.
Source: 1992–93 Vietnam Living Standards Survey.

indicating that those who migrated from their place of birth have lower fertility.

After education, income, and other social characteristics are controlled for, the results show that women in the Northern Uplands, North-Central Coast, and the Central Highlands have significantly higher fertility than women in other parts of the country. The coefficient for the Central Highlands is smaller and less significant when potential income is added to the model. These results are interesting for two main reasons. First, they show that discussions of fertility in Vietnam should not be cast simply in terms of north-south differences. Even though the Northern Uplands, the North-Central Coast, and the Red River Delta have similar political pasts, the economic conditions in the Northern Uplands and North-Central

Ordinary least squares		Instrumental variables	
Coefficient	t-statistic	Coefficient	t-statisic
−5.141	9.19	−3.669	2.94
0.154	18.66	0.166	19.74
−0.354	2.19	−0.229	1.40
−0.726	4.56	−0.595	3.70
−0.882	5.36	−0.742	4.48
−1.311	7.34	−1.147	6.34
−0.087	1.07	−0.197	2.35
−0.332	1.52	−0.401	1.81
−1.183	4.31	−1.148	3.83
−1.492	9.90	−1.555	10.61
0.034	3.86	0.036	3.90
−0.000	3.15	−0.000	2.82
−0.050	4.94	−0.043	3.70
0.542	7.12	0.275	1.57
0.067	0.60	0.055	0.47
0.017	0.22	−0.016	0.21
0.121	0.88	0.136	0.99
0.424	4.62	0.416	4.48
0.539	6.07	0.491	5.02
0.082	0.67	0.129	1.04
0.512	2.23	0.599	2.41
−0.055	0.42	0.035	0.25
−0.020	0.19	0.060	0.51
−0.130	1.93	−0.108	1.57
	1,650		1,650
	0.39		0.37
	266.52		286.07
			51.10

region are quite different from those in the Red River Delta. Second, these results indicate that the higher fertility observed in the Mekong Delta, as discussed above, is related to larger land area and lower education. Once these factors are controlled for, there are no differences between the Red River Delta and the Mekong Delta.

Let us turn now to the main issue of interest, the relationship between poverty and fertility. The results of the ordinary least squares regression show that in rural areas potential income has a significant positive effect on fertility—that is, the poor have fewer children. The income elasticity at the mean is 0.177, suggesting that a doubling of incomes would raise cumulative fertility by 17 percent. When income is treated as endogenous and the expenditure-based income variable is instrumented, the coefficient is smaller but, more important, no longer significant. The chi-square statistic for the Hausman exogeneity test is significant at the 1 percent level, suggesting that income is not exogenous. But as the following discussion shows, commune-level characteristics are important determinants of fertility in rural Vietnam, and when these are included in the model the conclusion based on ordinary least squares is valid.

Table 10.8 contains the results of three specifications; two use data on commune infrastructure, and the other controls for unobserved commune effects through a fixed effects specification. The first two columns of the table contain results of an ordinary least squares regression that includes commune characteristics and the log of expenditure per adult. The next two columns show the results of a similar model with expenditure instrumented, and the last two the results of the fixed effects specification. These specifications are significantly better than the basic models in table 10.7. For the commune variables model this better fit can be assessed by the significant (joint) F-test for the commune variables, and for the fixed effects model, by the significant F-test for the commune-specific dummy variables.[26]

The coefficient for expenditure per adult is positive and significant in all three models. Including commune-level factors increases the income coefficient over that in corresponding models that do not control for commune-level differences. The fixed effects specification that provides the best fit has an R^2 of 0.44 and the largest value for the income coefficient, with an associated income elasticity of 0.205 at the mean. In other words, a doubling of income increases fertility by 20 percent. These results show quite clearly that in rural Vietnam the poor have fewer children than the better-off.

Controlling for unobserved commune characteristics with a fixed effects specification also increases the coefficients of the schooling variables, and the dummy variable for less than primary schooling is now significant at 5 percent. The coefficient for land area is smaller and weaker, however, though still significant at the 5 percent level. The regional differences noted earlier are stronger, and those who migrated from the province of their birth appear to have fewer children.

On the whole, commune-level indicators of access to and quality of infrastructure perform poorly. Women in communes that had a maternal and child health program in the five years preceding the survey have lower fertility, as do women closer to primary health care centers. Controls for land quality suggest that women in communes with a larger percentage of good-quality land have higher fertility. In communes with a lower secondary school women have higher fertility, a result somewhat contrary to expectations, since easier access to schools would be expected to imply lower costs of child quality and therefore greater substitution away from quantity to quality. Communes that have a road passing through have lower fertility, a result that might reflect the effects of greater trade with the national economy, greater migration to urban areas, and associated disruption in exposure to the risk of childbearing or more effective family planning information activities.[27]

To assess the effect of son preference on cumulative fertility, without using a measure of son preference that is itself affected by cumulative fertility, the analysis restricts the sample to women who have had at least one live birth.[28] This selection criterion does not introduce a selectivity bias because son preference, by definition, implies a choice to have at least one child. Moreover, in societies in which childbearing is almost synonymous with marriage and a family, childlessness is not an option that couples actively choose.[29]

If the first birth can be taken to be a nondecision once the decision on marriage has been made and the sample is restricted to women who have begun childbearing, a measure based on the gender of the first birth can be treated as exogenous.[30] This analysis uses the number of first-born sons who survive at least one year as an indicator of son preference. If son preference has a strong bearing on fertility, those who have at least one son from the first pregnancy would be expected to have fewer children thereafter. Of course this measure does not address the possibility that parents' son preference might be formalized as a target number of sons rather than at least one son. While in theory such a choice is plausible, at present fertility rates in rural Vietnam it might not be an issue for most childbearing couples.

Table 10.9 shows the results of a fixed effects regression for children ever born to ever-married rural women aged 25–39 who have begun childbearing. The coefficient for the son preference variable is negative and significant at the 1 percent level. This result implies that after age, education, income, household structure, land resources, and religious affiliation are controlled for, those who have at least one surviving son from their first pregnancy have fewer children. Son preference is therefore an important part of the decisionmaking calculus of parents in rural Vietnam. Interactions of this variable with parents' schooling, land area, income, and region, explored in Desai (1995a), suggest that the effect is smaller for those who have more land—that is, those who have more land and a surviving son have fewer additional children. Thus sons and land area are substitutes. Son preference is stronger in the Central Coast and the Mekong Delta, where those who have a son from the first pregnancy are likely to have more children.

As a final step, regressions were also estimated for an urban sample of ever-married women aged 25–39. Only the results from the instrumental variables model and the fixed effects specification are shown in table 10.10; the first-stage regressions for expenditure per adult are shown in the appendix. The urban results differ in some important ways from the rural results. In urban areas income has no significant effect on marital fertility, regardless of whether income is treated as endogenous or exogenous and regardless of whether commune-level factors are controlled for or not. A

Table 10.8 Regression Results for Children Ever Born to Ever-married Women Aged 25–39 in Rural Vietnam, Taking into Account Effects of Commune Characteristics

	Ordinary least squares	
Variable	Coefficient	t-statistic
Intercept	−4.852	7.65
Age in years	0.154	18.97
Schooling: 1–4 years	−0.442	2.72
Schooling: 5–8 years	−0.792	4.94
Schooling: 9–11 years	−0.961	5.81
Schooling: 12+ years	−1.349	7.60
Vertical household	−0.058	0.72
Other household	−0.244	1.10
Widow	−1.212	4.29
Separated or divorced	−1.537	10.36
Land area cultivated (square miles)	0.026	3.12
Land area squared	−0.000	2.99
Spouse's years of schooling	−0.052	5.12
Log household expenditure per adult (real)	0.581	7.64
Ethnic minority	0.121	1.06
Buddhist	−0.054	0.69
Christian	0.072	0.49
Northern Uplands	0.441	3.94
North-Central Coast	0.613	5.32
Central Coast	0.155	1.14
Central Highlands	0.714	3.06
Southeast	0.105	0.69
Mekong Delta	−0.049	0.34
Moved from place of birth	−0.134	2.01
Child delivery important health problem in commune	−0.128	1.53
Maternal and child health program in commune in past five years	−0.384	2.69
Distance to nearest health center (kilometers)	0.015	2.69
Wage work available for children	−0.100	1.23
Peak season women's wages (real)	0.006	0.49
Road passes through commune	−0.368	2.84
Road impassable at times	−0.137	1.50
Percentage of land in commune of good quality	0.003	1.67
Percentage of land in commune of medium quality	0.002	1.24
Industrial enterprise in commune	−0.080	1.10
Lower secondary school in commune	0.220	2.03
Upper secondary school in commune	0.112	1.03
Lower secondary school fees (real)	−0.000	0.77
Sample size	1,650	
R^2	0.41	
F-statistic (df = 34,1615 or 136,1513)	27.7	
Breusch-Pagan test for heteroskedasticity (df = 36)	281.64	
Joint F-test for commune variables: $F_{(13, 1616)}$	2.61	
F-test for fixed effects specification: $F_{(119, 1513)}$		
Hausman exogeneity test: chi-square statistic		

Source: 1992–93 Vietnam Living Standards Survey.

Instrumental variables		Fixed effects	
Coefficient	t-statistic	Coefficient	t-statistic
−4.576	3.39	−5.904	3.76
0.165	19.67	0.168	20.30
−0.319	1.94	−0.369	2.42
−0.667	4.14	−0.737	4.63
−0.820	4.95	−0.848	5.04
−1.190	6.63	−1.148	5.79
−0.161	1.89	−0.132	1.50
−0.310	1.39	−0.283	1.52
−1.161	3.79	−1.219	4.76
−1.595	11.11	−1.600	9.09
0.027	3.00	0.018	2.11
−0.000	2.55	−0.000	2.21
−0.050	4.17	−0.057	4.51
0.464	2.37	0.628	2.90
0.141	1.17	0.135	0.84
−0.088	1.10	−0.104	0.98
0.070	0.46	0.005	0.03
0.445	3.95		
0.598	5.06		
0.193	1.39		
0.728	2.91		
0.130	0.80		
−0.000	0.02		
−0.113	1.67	−0.159	2.12
−0.088	1.05		
−0.324	2.25		
0.015	2.54		
−0.097	1.18		
0.011	0.91		
−0.375	2.86		
−0.122	1.26		
0.003	1.43		
0.002	1.13		
−0.092	1.22		
0.248	2.25		
0.175	1.57		
−0.000	0.76		
	1,650		1,650
	0.40		0.44
	24.9		8.63
	293.59		
	2.38		
			1.80
	16.50		

Table 10.9 Regression Results for Children Ever Born to Ever-married Women Aged 25–39 Who Have Begun Childbearing in Rural Vietnam: Commune Fixed Effects Specification

Variable	Instrumental variables		Fixed effects	
	Coefficient	t-statistic	Coefficient	t-statistic
Intercept	−3.191	2.93	−5.060	3.32
Age in years	0.162	19.88	0.163	20.72
Schooling: 1–4 years	−0.283	1.76	−0.378	2.58
Schooling: 5–8 years	−0.617	3.90	−0.705	4.62
Schooling: 9–11 years	−0.710	4.40	−0.728	4.51
Schooling: 12+ years	−1.100	6.30	−1.057	5.54
Vertical household	−0.132	1.62	−0.113	1.33
Other household	−0.085	0.40	−0.059	0.32
Widow	−1.226	4.09	−1.291	5.31
Separated or divorced	−1.654	11.72	−1.653	9.89
Land area cultivated (square miles)	0.029	3.20	0.019	2.34
Land area squared	−0.000	2.66	−0.000	2.55
Spouse's years of schooling	−0.056	4.90	−0.060	4.91
Log household expenditure per adult (real)	0.402	2.07	0.550	2.62
Ethnic minority	0.170	1.48	0.213	1.37
Buddhist	−0.052	0.69	−0.047	0.46
Christian	0.184	1.33	0.170	1.04
Northern Uplands	0.469	4.43		
North-Central Coast	0.569	4.95		
Central Coast	0.205	1.54		
Central Highlands	0.745	3.03		
Southeast	0.157	1.00		
Mekong Delta	0.037	0.26		
Moved from place of birth	−0.108	1.65	−0.170	2.36
Number of surviving sons from first birth	−0.294	5.11	−0.284	4.78
Child delivery important health problem in commune	−0.140	1.75		
Maternal and child health program in commune in past five years	−0.295	2.10		
Distance to nearest health center (kilometers)	0.017	3.10		
Wage work available for children	−0.108	1.35		
Peak season women's wages (real)	0.007	0.65		
Road passes through commune	−0.322	2.48		
Road impassable at times	−0.121	1.29		
Percentage of land in commune of good quality	0.003	1.67		
Percentage of land in commune of medium quality	0.001	0.88		
Industrial enterprise in commune	−0.071	0.98		
Lower secondary school in commune	0.239	2.23		
Upper secondary school in commune	0.217	2.04		
Lower secondary school fees (real)	−0.000	−0.63		
Sample size	1,616		1,616	
R^2	0.41		0.46	
F-statistic (137, 1478)			9.20	
Breusch-Pagan test for heteroskedasticity (df = 33)	273.23		288.71	
F-test for fixed effects specification: F(119, 1478)			1.91	

Source: 1992–93 Vietnam Living Standards Survey.

Table 10.10 Regression Results for Children Ever Born to Married Women Aged 25–39 in Urban Vietnam

Variable	Instrumental variables		Fixed effects	
	Coefficient	t-statistic	Coefficient	t-statistic
Intercept	0.279	0.15	–0.065	0.03
Age in years	0.126	7.57	0.128	9.06
Years of schooling	–0.115	5.66	–0.087	4.32
Vertical household	–0.343	2.75	–0.250	1.71
Other household	0.011	0.06	–0.012	0.06
Widow	–0.279	1.06	–0.180	0.39
Separated or divorced	–0.453	1.97	–0.504	2.09
Land area cultivated (square miles)	–0.001	0.15	–0.008	0.53
Spouse's years of schooling	–0.004	0.20	–0.002	0.10
Log of household expenditure per adult (real)	–0.135	0.58	–0.103	0.33
Chinese	–0.057	0.27	–0.210	0.77
Ethnic minority	0.192	0.21	–0.144	0.27
Buddhist	0.156	1.14	0.236	1.54
Christian	0.803	2.47	0.036	0.13
Northern Uplands	0.246	1.17		
North-Central Coast	0.198	0.82		
Central Coast	0.551	3.55		
Southeast	0.097	0.59		
Mekong Delta	0.102	0.59		
Moved from place of birth	–0.130	1.16	–0.178	1.60
Sample size	426		426	
R²	0.35		0.44	
F-statistic (19, 406)			7.09	
Breusch-Pagan test for heteroskedasticity (chi-square statistic, df = 24)	244.1			
F-test for fixed effects (df = 29,382)			2.75	

Source: 1992–93 Vietnam Living Standards Survey.

woman's schooling still has a strong fertility-reducing effect, but her spouse's schooling has no significant effect on fertility. Understandably, land area has no effect on marital fertility in urban areas. Women in urban areas in the Central Coast have higher fertility, as do urban women who are Catholic. But as in rural areas, women in vertical households have lower fertility, a pattern possibly related to the stronger parental influence in crowded urban dwellings. These religious and household structure differences are largely localized, because in the commune fixed effects specification they are no longer significant.

Conclusion and Policy Directions

Population growth has been a major concern for the Vietnamese leadership for many years, and the country has had a long and effective family planning program that has managed to reduce fertility considerably.

Along with the increases in primary enrollment and in access to primary health care, this reduction in fertility has undoubtedly improved the population's well-being and is a direct consequence of the socialist emphasis on public provision of social services. So it is not surprising that there is much concern among policymakers and grassroots workers about what forces will be unleashed by the market economy. Of particular concern is the condition of the poor, because their ability to acquire education, health, and family planning services is likely to be constrained in an economy in which purchasing power dictates access.

In this context the relationship between poverty and the number of children couples have is of great importance because couples who have more children usually trade off quantity for quality, investing less in each child. Even in a transition economy education differences are critical in determining the earnings, productivity, and economic welfare of households, but these differences are likely to be even more important in a market economy. The fertility process can therefore lead to an intergenerational carryover of poverty, an issue of concern in a country that emphasizes equality.

But the regressions for cumulative fertility in this chapter show that in rural areas the poor have fewer children than the better-off. This positive relationship between income and fertility is to be expected, since children should be normal goods. This relationship conflicts with commonplace expectations that the poor have more children because the typical definition of who is poor and who is not is based on a per person measure of well-being that is inappropriate for looking at the effects of poverty on fertility. An appropriate measure of poverty needs to be based on the adequacy or inadequacy of resources over the life cycle—a measure of potential or permanent income. While this measure is likely to be closely associated with a per person measure, the relationship is by no means perfect.

The regressions also show that women with more schooling have fewer children, as do women whose spouse has more schooling. In rural areas the results indicate strong positive effects of land area cultivated and significant regional differences, with higher fertility in the Northern Uplands, the North-Central Coast, and the Central Highlands. Poor access to infrastructure also raises fertility, suggesting that isolation from information and health and education services might allow women less control over childbearing.

Son preference remains an important aspect of childbearing decisions in Vietnam. While this chapter has not been aimed at determining the extent to which economic factors are responsible for the preference for sons, results of other chapters in this book and an in-depth study of gender in Vietnam (Desai 1995b) suggest that economic factors are likely to be important. For example, there are substantial differences in earnings between men and women even though women work almost as many hours as men, and differences in school enrollment between girls and boys have reappeared after being eliminated just a few years ago.

What do these results say about the future course of fertility decline in Vietnam? The fertility rates calculated in this chapter, though based on a sample biased toward married women, indicate that fertility fell by about 13 percent between 1987 and 1992. If the bias is taken into account, the drop in fertility is likely to be as high as 30 percent, with the total fertility rate somewhat less than 3. This decline is encouraging, but substantial rural-urban and regional differences remain: the total fertility rate in rural areas is 3.7, compared with around replacement level in urban areas, and the Northern Uplands, the Central Highlands, and the Mekong Delta have significantly higher fertility rates than other regions. So while a fertility transition is clearly under way, its future course is uncertain because the cost-benefit environment for childbearing decisions is undergoing tremendous change.

The prereform environment effectively subsidized child rearing through state provision of education, health, and family planning services. The evolving environment shifts more of the costs of child rearing to parents. In addition, agricultural liberalization is likely to cause greater differentiation in land and labor markets. The new land law gives effective control over land for longer periods and allows transfer of title to other households, and the emergence of an agricultural labor market is likely to enhance the cost implications of child rearing. These changes in the economic system reward differences in the human capital parents have and the resources they have access to, producing greater differences in household incomes. This should also contribute to greater differences in childbearing patterns.

The finding that the poor have fewer children raises some concern that as the economy grows, an income effect might lead to higher fertility, slowing the fertility transition. This income effect might be quite weak, however, because at the same time that incomes are rising, schooling and health care costs and consumption opportunities are also increasing. Moreover, fertility has never been as drastically suppressed in Vietnam as it has been in China, so economic growth need not be associated with increased possibilities to meet unfulfilled family size goals. On balance, these factors should lead to a continuation of the fertility transition because fewer couples will find larger families economically beneficial than will find smaller families beneficial.

There are other reasons to think that the transition to lower fertility rates will continue. The strong beneficial impact of women's schooling is encouraging and suggests that the success of the family planning program in lowering fertility owes much to the increase in women's schooling over the years. But there are signs of a significant decline in girls' enrollment. Although this drop in enrollment is likely to increase fertility in the coming years, the effect might be quite small. The expansion in women's education since reunification and in their role in the economy is bound to have changed the way women perceive their personal and social roles. And the changes in their perceived roles have likely affected their decisions about marriage and the pace of childbearing and their choice of contraception. Further, the social acceptability of conscious family limitation—a prerequisite for a fertility transition—has probably taken firm hold in Vietnamese society, and these attitudinal changes are unlikely to be reversed.

Yet son preference remains strongly entrenched in the Vietnamese psyche and is likely to make large reductions in fertility difficult to achieve. What can be hoped for is that the technological transformation of agriculture and the transition to a market economy, with its rewards to human capital, will reduce the economic rationale for gender preference. Public policy has an important part to play here, as it does in broader population and reproductive health issues.

Markets allocate resources most efficiently when consumers and producers act in their best interests. This efficiency is predicated on several conditions, at least one of which—that consumers have complete information—is easily violated in the case of contraceptives. Consumers are unlikely to have complete information about modern contraceptives—how they work, where they can be obtained, what their possible side effects are—in many developing countries, particularly in rural areas. A shortage of information is not the only barrier to the functioning of markets for contraceptives. There is the additional issue of potential conflicts in the preferences and objectives of sexual partners. When the benefits of using contraceptives are disproportionately derived by women and women's bargaining position in household resource allocation decisions is lower than men's, use of contraception can be lower than optimal if women's fertility preferences differ from men's. On the supply side the potential profits from contraceptive provision might not be large enough—because of small markets—to induce private providers to enter the market (Desai 1997). In these instances, even without distortions induced by government intervention, market outcomes might not be efficient.

Even when efficient, market outcomes might not be acceptable on grounds of equity—in terms of ability to pay, gender, or geographic location. And market outcomes might not be socially optimal if private actions have associated externalities that lead to consumption and production at less than socially optimal levels. For contraception, externalities are typically viewed as those resulting from population growth, though today prevention of sexually transmitted diseases and HIV is equally important. Such externalities support public policy and government intervention in this area of human behavior, though not necessarily public provision of contraceptives. Governments can intervene in markets by informing, regulating, mandating, financing, and providing commodities (Musgrove 1996), and a judicious mix is required that aims at promoting efficiency while ensuring a certain degree of equity.

In Vietnam these issues have a distinct flavor. That Vietnamese policymakers consider slower population growth critical to development is beyond doubt. The impetus for a strong family planning program and population redistribution comes from decades-long concerns about population pressure on scarce land. The concern about high population growth rates not only indicates widespread belief in the negative externalities associated with population growth in Vietnam, it also derives at least in part from the financing requirements of the universal provision of social services under socialism. Until recently there was no private provision of information or services, so thinking about policy directions needs to encompass introducing and enlarging the role of the private sector and refining the role of the public sector.

A greater role for the private and nongovernmental sector in delivery of services in urban areas is certainly called for; market conditions can sustain private providers, and the entry of the private sector would free up much-needed public resources for improving service delivery in rural areas (Desai 1997). That fertility is already near replacement levels in urban areas indicates a strong demand for contraception there, so the transition to private provision should cause no large decline in contraceptive use. Densely populated rural areas, such as in the Red River Delta, could also sustain private providers, though here the government might need to finance the delivery of services by the private sector. In other rural areas the public sector will need to continue providing family planning services, with an increased effort to broaden the choice of contraceptive methods.

Sustained government effort is required in disseminating information. The Living Standards Survey shows that more than 90 percent of women in Vietnam are aware of modern contraception, particularly IUDs. But awareness is not the same as adequate information, and the survey also shows that women aware of contraceptives do not always use them, for a wide variety of reasons—perceived side effects, inadequate information, disapproval of husbands. Provision of information is a complex issue because contraceptives involve a deeply personal aspect of daily life; influence fertility preferences, which might have strong social and religious implications; and, most important, directly impinge on the interaction between men and women. Although much contraceptive information is geared toward women, use of contraception in marriage also depends on the preferences of men, and so more effort needs to go to informing and influencing men.

As is evident from the results of this chapter, a particularly important issue for policy is son preference. What are the policy options for influencing son preference? Even more important, should policy attempt to influence fertility preferences? If externality concerns are important and it can be reasonably argued that national goals might be inconsistent with individual preferences, there is justification for influencing fertility preferences. In Vietnam high population density, extensive poverty, and limited government resources might provide sufficient grounds for believing that externalities associated with high population growth rates are largely negative. Other grounds for public intervention to influence fertility preferences derive from the viewpoint that individual decisions are myopic and based on limited information about the future. In the environment of rapid change associated with the transition to a market economy this viewpoint is reasonable, at least for rural areas. Moreover, public policy aimed at influencing preferences is far less intrusive in individuals' decisionmaking than are public interventions that distort the functioning of markets or impose quantitative restrictions, as the one-child policy of China does.

Son preference is a challenging area for public policy. To the extent that son preference is based on perceived differences in the net economic benefits derived from girls and boys, several policy options are available. Education policies that encourage parents to invest in the schooling of their daughters may be the least distortionary intervention and can go a long way toward narrowing the substantial male-female differences in earnings in Vietnam (Desai 1995b). Much progress has been made since reunification in closing the gender gap in education, but there is evidence that the gap, only recently bridged, is starting to reappear (Desai 1995b). Employment policies that prohibit wage discrimination and provide women with greater occupational choice are more intrusive, require greater monitoring and enforcement, and influence only the wage sector of the economy, but are nevertheless important in altering the perceived economic benefits of boys and girls.

Eliminating the economic rationale for gender preference should have a fairly large effect, but by itself is unlikely to end son preference because of the strong cultural underpinnings of this preference. Tackling these cultural aspects is more difficult because it requires altering the preferences of parents in very specific ways. That is not to say that it is impossible: some argue that preference changes—over generations—are much more important in explaining the Western European fertility transition than price and income factors (Cleland and Wilson 1987). One option is to leave the change to modernization, urbanization, and economic development, but governments, political leaders, and social institutions routinely influence the viewpoints of individuals and so are in a position to address the cultural underpinnings of son preference. In Vietnam the efforts of the much-revered Ho Chi Minh in attacking centuries-old discrimination against women are a prime example of the effect national leaders can have on society.

Appendix

Table 10A.1 Instrumenting Regressions for Log of Real Household Expenditure per Adult in Rural Areas

Variable	Instrumental variables		Fixed effects	
	Coefficient	t-statistic	Coefficient	t-statistic
Intercept	6.481	28.56	6.817	44.11
Age of household head	0.046	7.08	0.042	6.75
Age of household head squared	−0.000	6.86	−0.000	6.64
Years of schooling of household head	0.063	6.00	0.052	4.88
Years of schooling of household head squared	−0.002	2.50	−0.001	1.85
Female head, spouse in household	0.086	1.82	0.047	1.02
Female head, spouse not in household	0.381	5.48	0.409	6.05
Female head, separated or divorced	−0.402	4.23	−0.415	4.49
Female head, widowed	−0.339	3.94	−0.353	4.24
Female head, never married	0.404	0.89	0.345	0.78
Number of adults with no schooling	−0.527	5.07	−0.457	4.55
Number of adults with primary schooling	−0.036	1.21	−0.079	2.68
Number of adults with less than 9 years of schooling	−0.052	1.75	−0.091	3.03
Number of adults with less than 12 years of schooling	−0.060	1.90	−0.038	1.19
Number of adults with 12 or more years of schooling	−0.029	0.76	−0.054	1.39
Land area cultivated (thousands of square meters)	0.019	6.99	0.019	6.81
Land area squared	−0.000	2.43	−0.000	2.81
Ethnic group of head, Chinese	0.166	0.84	0.110	0.55
Ethnic group of head, minority	−0.210	5.51	−0.118	2.28
Northern Uplands	0.060	1.51		
North-Central Coast	−0.076	1.87		
Central Coast	0.183	3.89		
Central Highlands	0.210	3.19		
Southeast	0.182	3.26		
Mekong Delta	−0.010	0.18		
Head's father's main occupation, agriculture or fishing	−0.013	0.41	−0.017	0.55
Head's mother's main occupation, agriculture or fishing	−0.103	2.37	−0.106	2.44
Agricultural household	−0.276	5.45	−0.233	4.43
Agricultural extension worker visited	0.035	1.34	0.031	1.04
Road passes through commune	−0.070	1.64		
Commune road impassable at times	−0.156	5.24		
Industrial enterprise in commune	0.046	1.88		
Daily market in commune	0.031	1.11		
Periodic market in commune	−0.087	2.31		
Percentage of land in commune of good quality	0.000	0.09		

(Table continues on next page.)

**Table 10A.1 Instrumenting Regressions for Log of Real Household
Expenditure per Adult in Rural Areas (continued)**

Variable	Instrumental variables		Fixed effects	
	Coefficient	t-statistic	Coefficient	t-statistic
Percentage of land in commune				
of medium quality	0.002	2.95		
Male peak agricultural wage (real)	0.014	3.59		
Price of paddy per kilogram in commune	0.041	0.57		
Price of urea per kilogram in commune	−0.048	0.98		
Price of phosphate per kilogram in commune	0.110	1.93		
Sample size	1650		1650	
R²	0.32		0.44	
F(39, 1610) or F(141, 1508)	19.83		8.53	
F-statistic for Joint F-test for				
commune variables F(11, 1610)			8.47	
F-statistic for fixed-effects model specification:				
F(119, 1508)			3.61	

Source: 1992–93 Vietnam Living Standards Survey.

Table 10A.2 Instrumenting Regressions for Log of Real Household Expenditure per Adult in Urban Areas

Variable	Instrumental variables		Fixed effects	
	Coefficient	t-statistic	Coefficient	t-statistic
Road passes through commune	−0.070	1.64		
Intercept	7.695	21.81	7.999	51.10
Age of household head	0.013	0.89	−0.001	0.22
Age of household head squared	−0.000	0.77	0.039	5.19
Years of schooling of household head	0.057	2.45	0.037	0.57
Years of schooling of household head squared	−0.001	0.48	0.569	3.81
Female head spouse in household	0.079	1.21	−0.479	2.72
Female head spouse not in household	0.659	4.30	−0.428	2.40
Female head separated or divorced	−0.560	3.02	−0.422	0.81
Female head widowed	−0.484	2.65	−0.686	1.94
Female head never married	−0.350	0.66	−0.422	0.81
Number of adults with no schooling	−0.476	1.31	−0.686	1.94
Number of adults with primary schooling	−0.178	3.05	−0.168	2.97
Number of adults with less than 9 years of schooling	0.100	2.08	−0.076	1.62
Number of adults with less than 12 years of schooling	−0.084	1.87	−0.100	2.30
Number of adults with 12 or more years of schooling	−0.000	0.01	0.010	0.56
Land area cultivated (thousands of square meters)	0.003	0.55	−0.024	0.64
Ethnic group of head, Chinese	0.361	3.07	0.265	2.09
Ethnic group of head, minority	−0.248	1.06	−0.479	1.96
Northern Uplands	−0.592	6.17		
North-Central Coast	−0.710	5.92		
Central Coast	−0.041	0.51		
Southeast	0.151	1.86		
Mekong Delta	−0.003	0.03		
Head's father's main occupation, agriculture or fishing	0.017	0.25	0.025	0.37
Head's mother's main occupation, agriculture or fishing	0.132	1.97	0.054	1.97
Agricultural household	−0.065	0.68	−0.028	0.25
Agricultural extension worker visited	−0.109	0.88	−0.037	0.29
Sample size	426		426	
R^2	0.39		0.48	
F(26, 399 or 49, 376)	9.79		7.21	
F-statistic for fixed-effects model specification: F(29, 376)			5.57	

Source: 1992–93 Vietnam Living Standards Survey.

Notes

The author gratefully acknowledges the comments and suggestions of David Dollar, Paul Glewwe, Jennie Litvack, and two anonymous referees, as well as the financial support of the Research Committee of the World Bank. The opinions expressed are, however, those of the author and should not be attributed to these individuals or the World Bank.

1. The selection of one woman for the fertility section was done in the first round of the survey, with the actual data collection for this section taking place in the second round. No specific attempt was made to use female interviewers for this section. While that may have biased the responses somewhat, it is more likely to have done so for the data on contraception and less so for the data on fertility used in this chapter.

2. The probability of selection at the last stage is inversely proportional to the number of women aged 15–49 in the household.

3. The estimated crude birthrate, however, would be affected by differences in age composition.

4. Women married to the eldest son in a household are likely to join the household of their spouse's parents, while others are more likely to set up new households with their spouses soon after marriage. See chapter 2 in Desai (1995b) for more details.

5. The bias toward married women discussed in the previous section should be borne in mind while interpreting all information in this section.

6. Restricting the sample of women in this way is based on an implicit assumption that if a woman intends to have another birth, she will do so within five years of the previous one.

7. A two-child family is also the size promoted by the family planning program of the Ministry of Health.

8. Log-rank and Wilcoxon tests for differences in survival functions for age at first birth for women aged 20–39 (five-year age cohorts) are significant at 5 percent. These tests also show that there are significant differences in age at first marriage, though this is not apparent from the median values reported in table 10.3. See Desai (1995a) for details.

9. This bias is unrelated to the sampling bias discussed earlier.

10. The fertility rates from the 1987 Demographic and Health Survey appear in table 3.1 of National C mmittee for Population and Family Planning (1990). It is not clear whether these are calculated using Brass-type methods or simply based on information on births (in the reference years) to women interviewed in the survey.

11. The infant mortality rate is assumed to be 100, a value considerably higher than what is widely believed to be the figure for Vietnam. Since it is not possible to obtain average parities for all women aged 15–49, adjustment factors (for adjusting fertility rates calculated on the basis of births in the year before the survey) from the fertility sample were used. See Desai (1995a) for details.

12. Similar analyses using a larger sample of women aged 20–39 yielded results largely similar to those reported here, even though the inclusion of younger women lends a selectivity bias toward early age at marriage.

13. This is particularly the case when, as in Vietnam, women (and men) reside with their parents before marriage, and with their spouse or spouse's parents after marriage. Before marriage women residing with their parents contribute to household income, but are unlikely to have as much bargaining power in household decisions as after marriage, when they are either the head of the household or the spouse of the household head.

14. One could argue that resource constraints in the parents' household have an important bearing on their children's fertility preferences and, because of private transfers between parents and children, could also be relevant for the resource constraints of the decisionmaking couple.

15. As Benefo and Schultz (1994) point out, using per capita expenditure or the per adult equivalent is not appropriate because the construction of these measures results in a "direct feedback effect" of fertility. A measure similar to that used here is also used in other recent analyses of fertility data from Living Standards Surveys (Montgomery and Kouame 1993; Ainsworth 1989).

16. A joint F-test for the commune variables is significant at the 1 percent level.

17. It could be argued that schooling also has a biological effect on fertility through improved nutrition for women, but the evidence on the relationship between nutrition and fertility is relatively weak and shows that except in cases of extreme nutritional stress, the nutritional effects are weak if not nonexistent.

18. The land variable refers to the land area to which that the household has use rights, which is not necessarily equal to the area that a household cultivated in the year before the survey.

19. The appropriate measure of land represents the land endowments to which couples have secure use rights at the time of the family size decision. Area cultivated at the time of the survey might be a poor proxy for endowments, and suffer from endogeneity problems if there is an active rental market in the region. This is a serious limitation of the labor demand hypothesis of Schutjer and Stokes (1984).

20. Schutjer and Stokes (1984) also hypothesize a separate negative effect deriving from the role of land as a source of income security in old age. This land security hypothesis is based on land ownership and the idea that land and children might be substitute assets for old age security. In the time span covered by this fertility sample the security role of land might have been unimportant in Vietnam, because the new land law had not gone into effect at the time of the survey and commune land allocations were still very important.

21. Another reason for making this assumption is that the sample is entirely rural, and in rural areas the economic options for women are considerably more limited than in urban areas. Some data exploration was conducted to ascertain whether fertility, in particular the inability to produce sons, could itself have been a reason for separation or divorce. None of the 56 women in the sample who were separated or divorced was childless, and the composition of children born to these women shows no striking imbalance in the sex ratio. So it is unlikely that childlessness or inability to produce sons was a reason for separation or divorce.

22. A Poisson regression model, a more appropriate specification since children arrive sequentially and should therefore be represented by a counting process, was also estimated and the results were found to be almost identical to the ordinary least squares results. Since use of instrumental variables in a Poisson regression context might not be appropriate, the more conventional approach of using a normal regression model is followed.

23. Results for the first-stage regression, discussed earlier, are shown in the appendix.

24. As will be clear from the following discussion, a more appropriate specification of the model—one that controls for commune-level unobservables—shows that even those who have a year or two of schooling have significantly lower fertility.

25. Interacting a woman's years of schooling with those of her spouse does not suggest complementarity or substitutability between the two forms of human capital.

26. A random effects specification was also tried but rejected in favor of the fixed effects specification.

27. The variables included in the final set of models are the result of substantial exploratory work that is not reported here.

28. See Haughton and Haughton (1994) for a more complete treatment of son preference in Vietnam.

29. The pattern of universal marriage in many developing countries suggests that while timing of marriage might be a choice, whether or not to marry might not be.

30. This of course depends on the assumption that before childbirth parents have no way of knowing the sex of the unborn child. At least for Vietnam it is reasonable to assume that modern fetus monitoring technology is not widely available for the purpose of determining the sex of the child.

References

Ainsworth, Martha. 1989. *Socioeconomic Determinants of Fertility in Côte d'Ivoire.* Living Standards Measurement Study Working Paper 53. Washington, D.C.: World Bank.

Allman, James, and others. 1991. "Fertility and Family Planning in Vietnam." *Studies in Family Planning* 22(5): 308–17.

Bannister, Judith. 1985. "The Population of Vietnam." International Population Reports. U.S. Department of Commerce, Bureau of the Census, Washington, D.C.

Benefo, Kofi Darkwa, and T. Paul Schultz. 1994. *Determinants of Fertility and Child Mortality in Côte d'Ivoire and Ghana.* Living Standards Measurement Study Working Paper 103. Washington, D.C.: World Bank.

Cleland, John, and Christopher Wilson. 1987. "Demand Theories of the Fertility Transition: An Iconoclastic View." *Population Studies* 41: 5–30.

Desai, Jaikishan. 1995a. "Fertility and Contraception in Vietnam." World Bank, Africa Region Country Department I, Washington, D.C.

————. 1995b. *Vietnam through the Lens of Gender: An Empirical Analysis Using Household Survey Data.* Hanoi: United Nations Development Programme.

————. 1997. "The Private Sector in Family Planning Services: Demand and Supply Issues." The POLICY Project. Futures Group International, Washington, D.C.

Dong, Do Thai. 1991. "Modifications of the Traditional Family in the South of Vietnam." In Rita Liljestrom and Tuong Lai, eds., *Sociological Studies on the Vietnamese Family*. Hanoi: Social Sciences Publishing House.

Haughton, Jonathon, and Dominique Haughton. 1994. "Measuring Son Preference in Vietnam: Methodology and Evidence." Northeastern University, Department of Economics, Boston, Mass.

Huou, Tran Dinh. 1991. "Traditional Families in Vietnam and the Influence of Confucianism." In Rita Liljestrom and Tuong Lai, eds., *Sociological Studies on the Vietnamese Family*. Hanoi: Social Sciences Publishing House.

Jamieson, Neil L. 1993. *Understanding Vietnam*. Berkeley: University of California Press.

Jones, Gavin W. 1982. "Population Trends and Policies in Vietnam." *Population and Development Review* 8(4): 783–810.

Montgomery, Mark R., and Aka Kouame. 1993. "Fertility and Schooling in Côte d'Ivoire: Is There a Tradeoff?" Technical Working Paper 11. World Bank, Africa Technical Department, Human Resources and Poverty Division, Washington, D.C.

Musgrove, Philip. 1996. *Public and Private Roles in Health: Theory and Financing Patterns*. World Bank Discussion Paper 339. Washington, D.C.

National Committee for Population and Family Planning. 1990. *Vietnam Demographic and Health Survey, 1988*. Hanoi.

Schutjer, Wayne A., and C. Shannon Stokes. 1984. "Access to Land and Fertility in Developing Countries." In Wayne A. Schutjer and C. Shannon Stokes, eds., *Rural Development and Human Fertility*. New York: Macmillan.

United Nations. 1983. *Manual X: Indirect Techniques for Demographic Estimation*. New York.

Appendix
Description of the Vietnam Living
Standards Survey (VNLSS)

The Vietnam Living Standards Survey (VNLSS) is a nationwide household survey that was conducted between October 1992 and October 1993. This appendix provides information on the content of the different questionnaires and the overall design of the survey.

Household Questionnaire

The VNLSS used three separate questionnaires: a household questionnaire, a community questionnaire for rural areas only, and a price questionnaire. Each questionnaire contains several modules (sections), each of which collects data on different topics. The household questionnaire collects data on household demographic structure, education, health, employment, migration, housing conditions, fertility, agricultural activities, household nonagricultural businesses, food expenditures, nonfood expenditures, remittances and other sources of nonlabor income, savings and loans, and anthropometric (height and weight) measurements. The questionnaire was completed in two interviews, two weeks apart. Sections 0–8 were conducted in the first interview, sections 9–14 were conducted in the second interview, and section 15 was administered in both interviews. The following paragraphs briefly describe each section.

Section 0. Survey Information

The date of the interview, the religion and ethnic group of the household head, the language used by the respondent, and other technical information related to the interview are noted in Section 0A. Section 0B summarizes the results of the survey visits—that is, whether a section was completed on the first or the second visit. Section 0C contains written observations and remarks by the interviewer and the supervisor; these were not included in the computer files.

Section 1. Household Membership

Section 1A lists the age, sex, marital status, and relation to household head of all people who spent the previous night in the household's dwelling and for household members who are temporarily away from home. Household members were defined to include "all the people who normally live and eat their meals together in this dwelling." Section 1B collects information on the parents of all household members, including their schooling, occupation, and whether they are alive. Section 1C collects information on children of household members who live elsewhere and are less than 30 years of age. Children who have died are not included. Information on the age, schooling, and current place of residence of each such child is recorded.

Section 2. Schooling

Data were collected on self-reported literacy and numeracy, school attendance and completion, and current enrollment for all household members of school age and older. For those who were enrolled in school at the time of the survey, information was also collected on school attendance, distance and travel time to the school, expenses, and scholarships.

Section 3. Health

In this section data on any illness or injury experienced in the four weeks preceding the date of the interview were obtained for all household members. For those who reported being ill in the past four weeks, information was obtained on the duration and type of illness, type of care sought, distance and travel time to the health care provider, and cost of both the medication and the consultation. All individuals, whether ill or not in the past four weeks, were asked if they had been ill in the 12 months before the survey and, if so, the total amount they had spent on health care during those months. Finally, several questions on smoking were asked of all individuals six years of age and older.

Section 4. Employment

All individuals age six and older were asked to respond to the economic activity questions in Section 4, beginning with questions on the nature of their work in the past seven days. For persons who did not work in the past seven days, data were collected on job search and the reason for not seeking employment. For those who worked in the past seven days, information was collected on hours worked, length of employment, type of employer, distance and travel time to place of work, money and in-kind compensation, and benefits. Similar questions were asked for any secondary job in the past seven days. Questions were asked on search for additional employment, including the kind of work sought. If the main work in the past 12 months was different from the main or secondary job during the past seven days, the same information was collected for that work as well. Type of work and years of experience were collected for any occupation held prior to employment in the main job in the past 12 months. Again, if there was a secondary job in the past 12 months different from the other jobs, data on work conditions and compensation were collected. Finally, days and hours spent doing household chores in the past seven days were collected for each respondent.

Section 5. Migration

All household members aged 15 and older responded to the questions on migration in Section 5. If not born in their current place of residence, respondents were asked their province of birth and whether their place of birth was a village, town, or city. The age at which individuals left their place of birth was recorded, as well as the main reason for leaving. In addition, individuals were asked the main reason for coming to their current place of residence, the province they had come from before moving to their current place of residence, and whether the previous place was a village, town, or city. Finally, respondents were asked how many different places they had lived for periods of more than three months in their life.

Section 6. Housing

This section contains information on the type of dwelling, housing characteristics, and housing expenses for all households interviewed. Information was collected on the number of rooms in the dwelling, ownership status, wall material, roof material, water source, toilet type, utility expenses, and square meters of living area. Respondents were also asked for the current resale value of the dwelling. The section also contains information on type of cooking fuel used and, for households whose primary or secondary cooking fuel was wood, the time and distance involved in collecting wood.

Section 7. Respondents Chosen for Second Interview

Here the principal respondent for round one was asked to identify the household member who knows the most about all the agricultural and livestock activities of the household, the household member who shops for food, and the household member who knows the most about the other household expenses, income, and savings of household members. The respondent was also asked to identify the three most important businesses and trades belonging to the household, and the household members who know most about them. Finally, a woman was selected at random from among the women in the household between the ages of 15 and 49 to respond to the fertility module.

Section 8. Fertility

In each household one woman aged 15–49, randomly selected in Section 7, responded to the questions in this section. If a household contained no woman in this age range, Section 8 was not completed. The selected woman is asked if she had ever been pregnant and, if so, whether she had ever given birth. Women who respond that they have are asked the birth-date and sex of all children they have given birth to, including children who died. If the child is no longer alive, the woman is asked how long the child survived. The woman is asked about the birth and breast-feeding of her last child, the age at which she was married, and the number of mis-carriages she has had. Section 8B gathers information on knowledge, use, source, and cost of six modern and six traditional methods of family planning.

Section 9. Agropastoral Activities

This section is by far the largest section of the household questionnaire, with many subsections that contain information on different aspects of agricultural production and related livestock activities—collectively referred to as agropastoral activities. Section 9A collects information on a household's control over land of different tenures. These include land allo-cated by the commune, auctioned land, privately held land, rented or sharecropped land, swidden land, cultivated water surface, and forest land. Section 9B contains detailed output information for all crops grown by the household. This information is obtained separately for each crop and includes (in most cases) information on quantity produced, value of output, quantity sold in the market, quantity given to the cooperative, quantity kept for seeds, quantity fed to livestock, and quantity given as gifts. Section 9C contains information on crop by-products. Section 9D obtains detailed crop-specific information on inputs (seeds, manure, fertil-izer, insecticides, and so on) and transportation costs. Information on other inputs, such as hired labor and packing and storage costs, are obtained at an aggregated level for each household. Section 9E contains information on food items produced by transforming home-grown crops, if they were subsequently sold. Section 9F collects information on livestock, poultry, and other animals owned by the household. Section 9G collects information on animal products, such as milk, eggs, silk, and manure, and section 9H collects similar information for water animals (fish, shrimp, and so on). Section 9I collects information on extension services for livestock, and section 9J contains information on livestock expenditures. Finally, sections 9K and 9L collect data on farm implements and machinery owned by the household, respectively.

Section 10. Nonfarm Self-employment

Section 10 gathers data on household businesses for the three most important enterprises operated by the household. The respondent for each enterprise is the household member most familiar with its operation (as identified in Section 7). Data are gathered on the ownership, number of employees, and type of employee compensation for each enterprise. For each business, expenditures over the past 12 months on wages, raw materials, and taxes are collected. The respondent is asked how much, in money and goods, was received from sales and how much of the enterprise's product was consumed by the household since the first interview. Information on ownership, sales, and purchases of assets—buildings, land, vehicles, tools, and other durable goods—in the past 12 months is also collected.

Section 11. Food Expenses and Home Production

Section 11A records the amounts spent on holidays, primarily Tet (new year) but also January 15, July 15, the Autumn Moon Festival, and Independence Day. The main reason for separating holiday expenses from normal expenses, a departure from the standard Living Standards Measurement Survey (LSMS) format, is to take into account the fact that in Vietnam Tet often results in significant departures from normal spending patterns. Section 11B collects detailed information on market purchases (including those obtained through barter) and consumption from home production for 45 food items. Information is obtained for expenses since the interviewer's first visit. For a longer recall period (12 months) data are obtained on the number of months (in the preceding 12 months) each food item was purchased, the number of times purchases were made during those months, the quantity purchased each time, and the value per purchase.

Section 12. Nonfood Expenditures and Inventory of Durable Goods

This section collects information on nonfood household expenditures from the household member identified in Section 7 as the one most able to answer nonfood expenditure questions. In Section 12A respondents were asked to recall the amount spent since the first interview (approximately two weeks) on daily expenses such as lottery tickets, cigarettes, soap, personal care products, cooking fuel, matches and candles, and gasoline. In Section 12B expenditure data, both in the past two weeks and the past 12 months, were collected for shoes, cloth, clothing, home repairs, public transport, paper supplies, kitchen equipment, medical services, domestic servants, jewelry, entertainment, and other goods. Purchase price, year of purchase, and resale value of durable goods owned were collected in Section 12C. Relation and location of the recipients of remittances sent out from the household are noted in Section 12D (remittances received by the household are recorded in Section 13A).

Section 13. Other Income

Section 13 collects data on money and goods that come into the household as remittances or from other sources unrelated to employment, such as employee welfare funds, dowries, sales of consumer durables, rental of buildings, and so on.

Section 14. Credit and Savings

Section 14 collects information on the amount of money owed by household members to people or institutions outside the household. If money or goods have been borrowed, or borrowed and repaid by any household member in the past 12 months, information is collected on those loans, including the source and amount of the loan, interest, side payments, collateral, repayment schedule, reason for borrowing, and number of loans from the same source. The household is asked to list different types of savings, if any, including bank deposits, bonds, cash (dong), U.S. dollars, gold, and value of paddy. The respondent is also asked the total value of all savings accounts.

Section 15. Anthropometrics

Anthropometric measurements are completed for each household member. Data were collected on weight, height, and arm circumference. It was also noted if female respondents were pregnant or breast-feeding. If a person was not measured the reason why is noted.

Community Questionnaire (Rural Areas Only)

A community questionnaire was administered by the team supervisor and completed with the help of local government officials, teachers, health care workers, and knowledgeable farmers. The questionnaire was administered only in rural areas. Section 1 (Demographic Information) includes the population of the community, a list of principal ethnic groups and religions, the age of the community, and whether it has grown in the past five years. Section 2 (Economy and Infrastructure) collects data on the community's principal economic activities and its access to a motorable road, electricity, pipe-borne water, restaurant or food stall, post office, daily market, and public transport. There are also questions on employment, migration for jobs, and the existence of community development projects.

In Section 3 (Education) the community questionnaire asks the distance to primary and middle schools. For up to three primary schools, and for the nearest lower- and upper-secondary schools, information is obtained on whether it is public or private, how many classes there are, and when it was built. Enrollment rates and reasons why children do not attend school are also collected. Section 4 (Health) collects data on distance and travel time to the nearest of each of several types of health workers (doctor, nurse, pharmacist, midwife, bonze, and traditional healer) and each of several types of health facilities (hospital, dispensary, pharmacy, and clinic). The questions in Section 5 (Agriculture) include the type of crops grown in the community, how often and when they are planted and harvested, and how the harvest is generally sold. This section also includes questions on land quality and type, the use of pesticides and irrigation, and the availability of extension services, agricultural cooperatives, and machinery. Data are also gathered on the local land market and agricultural and nonagricultural wages in the community.

Price Questionnaire

In rural areas (commune numbers 1 to 120) price data were collected by the team supervisor for 36 food items, 31 nonfood items, 9 medicines, 7 insecticides and fertilizers, and 5 types of services from local markets. A separate set of prices is available for urban areas (commune numbers 121 to 150). These were collected by the General Statistical Office as part of a separate effort to construct price indices in Vietnam, and their values are comparable to those of rural prices.

Sample

The remaining sections of this appendix discuss the design of the survey, particularly the sample, survey management, and organization of the field work. The sample covers 4,800 households from all areas of Vietnam. The sample design was self-weighted, so that each household in Vietnam had the same probability of being selected. The overall sampling frame was stratified into two groups, urban and rural, with sampling carried out separately in each group (strata). About 20 percent of Vietnamese households live in urban areas, so the sample stratification ensures that 20 percent of selected households come from urban areas. Two lists of all communes were drawn up (one of urban communes and another of rural communes), province by province, in "serpentine" order.[1] Within each list communes were selected to ensure that they were spread out evenly among all provinces in Vietnam.

The VNLSS sample design is the following. Within each province in Vietnam, rural areas can be broken down into districts, and districts can be divided into communes (*Xa*). Urban areas in all provinces consist of centers or towns, which are divided into quarters (*Quan*), and then divided further into communes (*Phuong*). The total number of communes in Vietnam, both urban and rural, is about 10,000, and the average population in each is about 6,500. Each survey team covers 32 households in four weeks, 16 households in one area and 16 in another area. For convenience all 32 households were selected from the same commune. This implied that 150 communes had to be randomly selected (32 × 150 = 4,800), 30 in urban areas and 120 in rural areas. Within urban areas communes can be further divided into clusters (*Cum*). Two clusters were selected from which to draw two "workloads" of 16 households (16 from each of the two clusters). The same was done in rural areas, where each commune is divided into several villages (*Thon*). The average size of urban clusters and rural villages is slightly less than 1,000 households.

The VNLSS sample was drawn in three stages. Because the General Statistical Office in Hanoi knows the current population of all 10,000 communes in Vietnam (but not of each cluster or village within each commune), 150 communes were selected from the 10,000 with a probability of selection proportional to population size. At the second stage information was gathered from the 150 selected communes on the population of each cluster (in urban areas) or village (in rural areas), and two clusters or villages were randomly drawn with a probability proportional to population size. Finally, the third stage involved randomly selecting 20 households (16 for the sample plus 4 "extras" to serve as replacements if any of the 16 "originals" could not be interviewed) within each cluster or village from a list of all households within each cluster or village. Note that the first stage of the sample is based on information from the 1989 Census, but the second and third stages use updated information available from the communes. The first and second stage samples were drawn in Hanoi, while the third stage was drawn in the field.

Survey Management

The VNLSS was jointly managed by the State Planning Committee (SPC) and the General Statistical Office (GSO) of Vietnam.[2] At the highest level of management was a steering committee consisting of four persons—one director and three vice directors. Immediately below this committee was a standing committee (also known as the "working group") of six persons, three from the SPC and three from the GSO. The standing committee did much of the detailed work, such as preparing questionnaires and manuals, organizing training courses, and managing day-to-day survey activities. Both the steering committee and the standing committee were based in Hanoi.

The survey itself was carried out by 15 teams, each composed of six members: one supervisor, two interviewers, one anthropometrist (anthropometrician), one data entry operator, and one driver. Eight teams were located in northern Vietnam (either based in Hanoi or in some other major city) and seven teams were based in the midlands or the south (two based in Da Nang, three in Ho Chi Minh City, and two in the Mekong Delta). As in other LSMS (World Bank) surveys, data entry was done in a decentralized manner (described below), which allowed for interviewers to return to households to check errors detected by the data entry program.

Organization of Field Work

When a team arrived in a village (rural areas) or cluster (urban areas), the supervisor met with local authorities to explain the purpose of the survey and distribute materials for publicity and letters to the households selected to be surveyed. The 20 households (16 original and 4 replacement) randomly drawn in each village or cluster were selected by the supervisor immediately after arriving in the village or cluster, following detailed instructions given in the supervisor's manual.[3] The supervisor also filled out the community and price questionnaires in collaboration with the anthropometrist.

The household questionnaire was completed by the interviewers in two separate interviews. The first visit (round 1) covered Sections 0–8, while the second visit covered Sections 9–14. Section 15 (anthropometric measurements) was completed by the anthropometrist during both visits. The typical interview time for completing half of the questionnaire (one round) was intended to be two to three hours; thus about four to six hours would be required over two separate visits for one completed household questionnaire. Each team completed 32 household interviews during each four-week period, 16 per team interviewer. Round 1 (Sections 0–8) was conducted in one cluster or village in the first week. The next week consisted of completing round 1 in the other cluster or village in the same commune. In the third week the team returned to the first cluster or village and completed the remainder of the questionnaire (Sections 9–14) for each household. The same was done in the second cluster or village in the fourth week.

The decentralized data entry was done as follows. After completing the first half of the household questionnaire (Sections 0–8) in the first cluster or village during the first week, all 16 half-completed questionnaires were given to the data entry operator located at the team's base, who then entered the data on a personal computer using a customized data entry program. The data entry program performed range and consistency checks on all data in the questionnaire and produced reports (lists) of all data for which problems arose. Upon returning to the first village in the third week to complete the questionnaire (and, similarly, upon returning to the second village in the fourth week) discrepancies detected by the data entry program could be corrected. After four weeks of work were completed in a given cluster or village, the teams either moved to the next commune or took a one-week break.

Duties of the supervisor also included observing some interviews and randomly revisiting some of the interviewed households to check the quality of the work done by the interviewer. A complete description of these and other supervisory tasks are found in the supervisor's manual.

The field work for the VNLSS began in October 1992 and ended in October 1993. Although the first two weeks were difficult, due to the complexity of the survey, work proceeded smoothly thereafter. In addition to supervisory visits by members of the steering and standing committees, two international consultants made supervisory visits to all teams in the early months of the survey.

Notes

1. Serpentine ordering ensures that provinces that are adjacent to each other geographically are adjacent on the list.

2. In 1995 the State Planning Committee was reorganized and is now called the Ministry of Planning and Investment.

3. There were also one or two communes in which the villages or clusters themselves needed to be chosen (because the necessary information had not been received in Hanoi in time). In these cases the supervisor also made the selection, again following detailed instructions in the supervisor's manual.